CALIFORNIA EDITION

HOUGHTON MIFFLIN

Math Steps

HOUGHTON MIFFLIN

Boston • Atlanta • Dallas • Denver • Geneva, Illinois • Palo Alto • Princeton

Grateful acknowledgment is given for the contributions of

Student Book

Rosemary Theresa Barry
Karen R. Boyle
Barbara Brozman
Gary S. Bush
John E. Cassidy
Dorothy Kirk
Sharon Ann Kovalcik
Bernice Kubek
Donna Marie Kvasnok
Ann Cherney Markunas
Joanne Marie Mascha
Kathleen Mary Ogrin
Judith Ostrowski
Jeanette Mishic Polomsky
Patricia Stenger
Annabelle L. Higgins Svete

Teacher Book Contributing Writers

Dr. Judy Curran Buck
Assistant Professor of Mathematics
Plymouth State College
Plymouth, New Hampshire

Dr. Richard Evans
Professor of Mathematics
Plymouth State College
Plymouth, New Hampshire

Dr. Mary K. Porter
Professor of Mathematics
St. Mary's College
Notre Dame, Indiana

Dr. Anne M. Raymond
Assistant Professor of Mathematics
Keene State College
Keene, New Hampshire

Stuart P. Robertson, Jr.
Education Consultant
Pelham, New Hampshire

Dr. David Rock
Associate Professor,
Mathematics Education
University of Mississippi
Oxford, Mississippi

Michelle Lynn Rock
Elementary Teacher
Oxford School District
Oxford, Mississippi

Dr. Jean M. Shaw
Professor of Elementary Education
University of Mississippi
Oxford, Mississippi

Printed in the U.S.A.

ISBN: 0-395-98007-0

11 12 13 14 15-B-05 04 03 02 01 00

Contents

UNIT 1 • TABLE OF CONTENTS

Geometry

We will be using this vocabulary:

corner point where sides meet
solid 3-dimensional figure
plane figure 2-dimensional figure
side lines on a 2-dimensional figure
symmetrical if a figure can be folded in half and the two parts match or the parts are mirror images

Dear Family,

During the next few weeks our math class will be learning about geometry – solid and plane figures.

You can expect to see homework that provides practice in identifying spheres, cylinders, cubes, rectangular prisms, cones, pyramids, triangles, circles, squares, and rectangles. You may wish to keep the following as a guide.

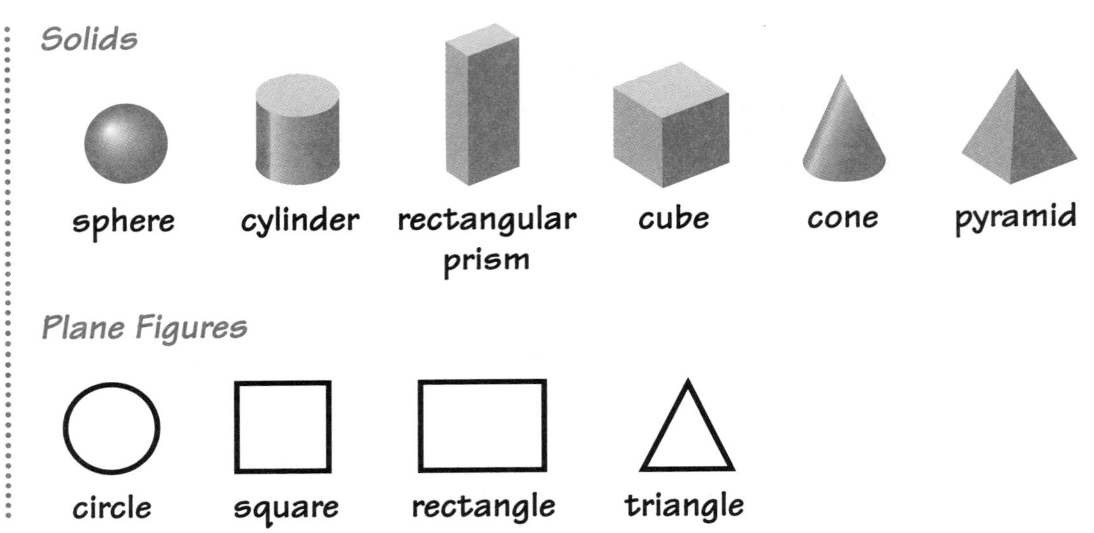

Recognizing shapes can help children solve spatial problems.

Sincerely,

Name ____________________

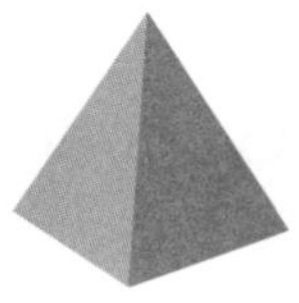
pyramid

sphere

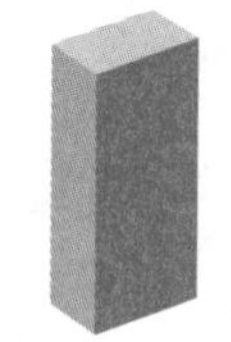
rectangular prism

cone

cube

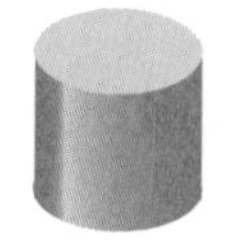
cylinder

Ring each object that has the same shape.

1.

2.

3.

4.

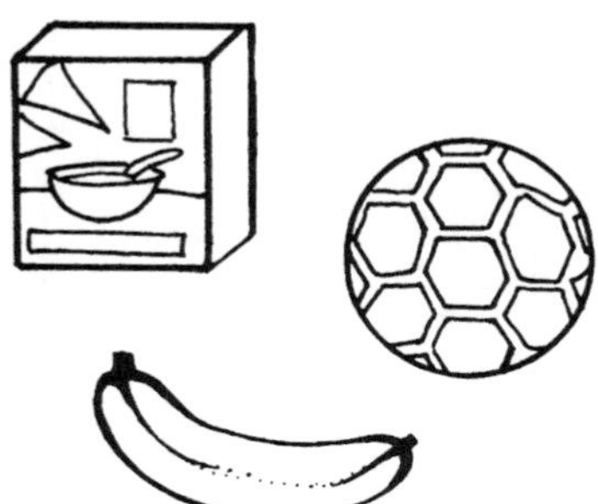

5.

6.

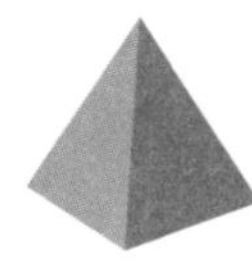

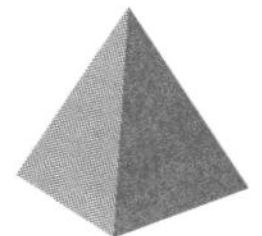

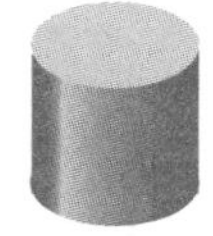

pyramid sphere rectangular prism cone cube cylinder

Problem Solving
Reasoning

Look at the solids.
How can you sort them into two groups?
Draw to show your sort.
Tell how you sorted the solids.

7.

★ Test Prep

Which item is the same shape as the baseball?
Mark the space under your answer.

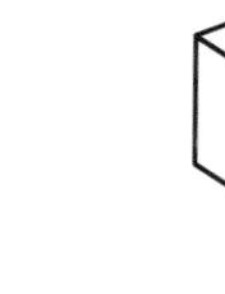
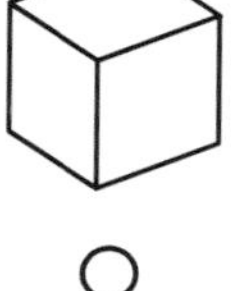

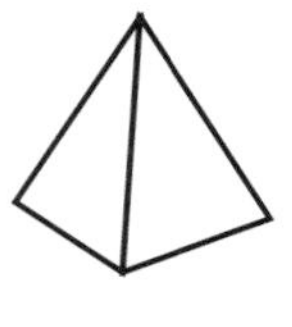

○ ○ ○

Name ______________________________

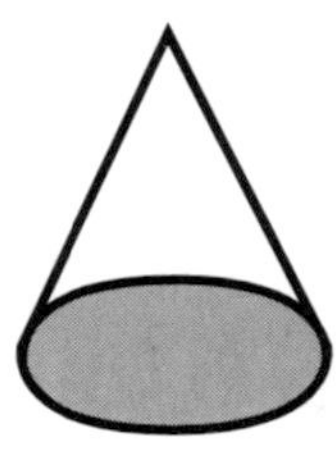

The **face** of this cone is a circle.

Look at the solid.
Ring the figure that matches the shaded face of each solid.

1.

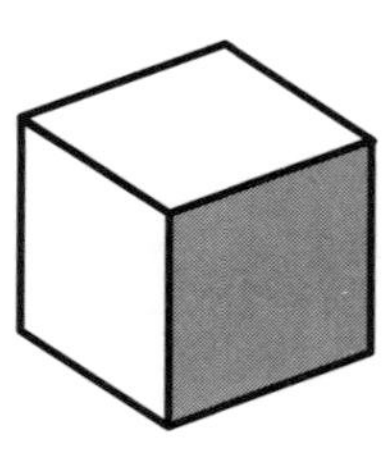  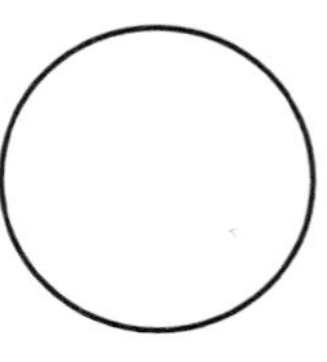  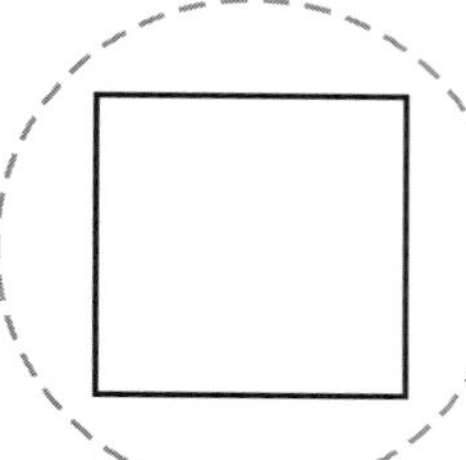

2.

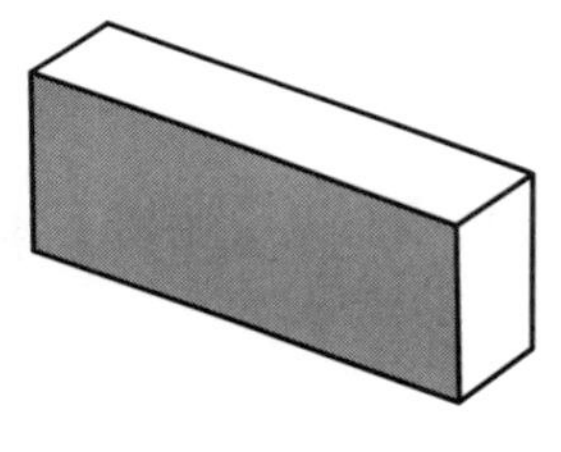 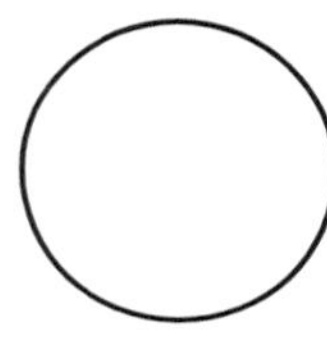 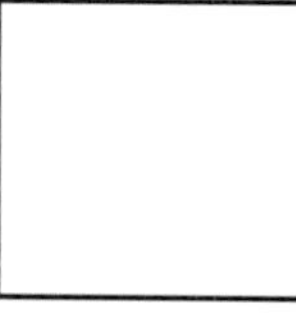 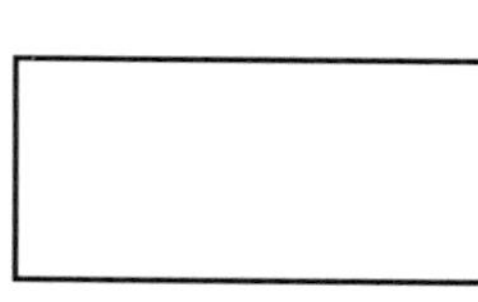 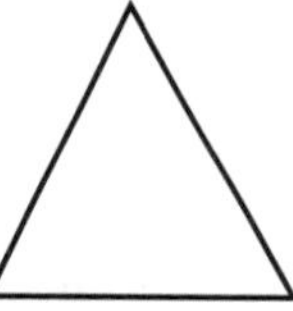

3.

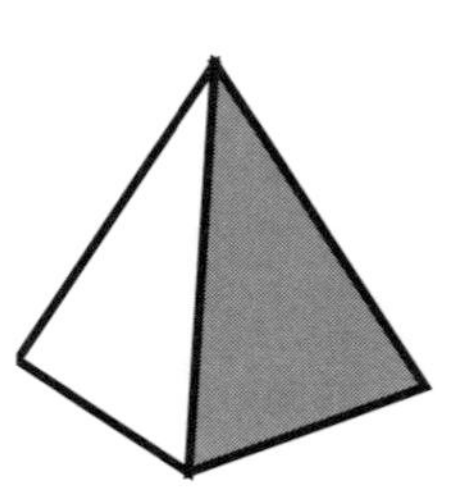  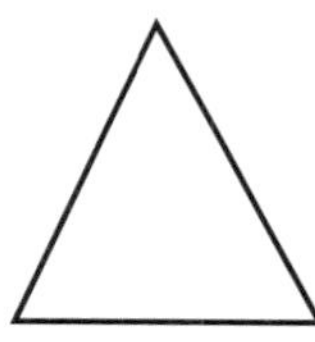 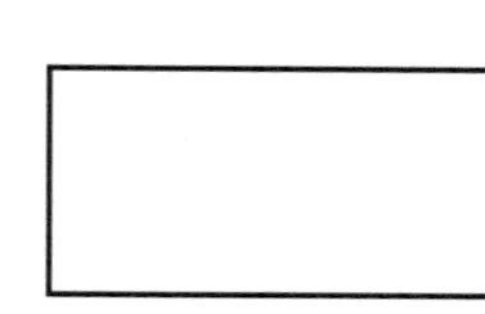 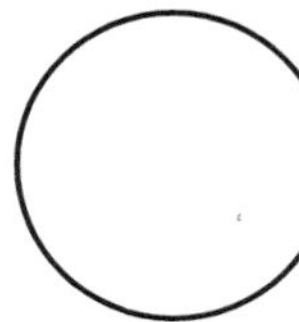

4.

  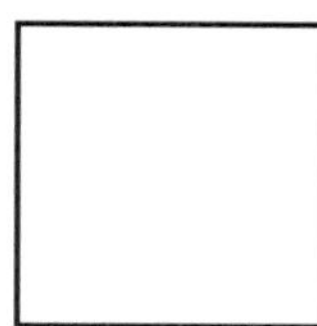 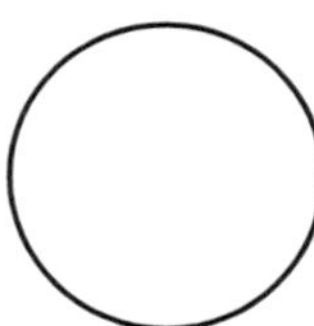 

Look at the object.
Ring the figure that matches the shaded face.

5.

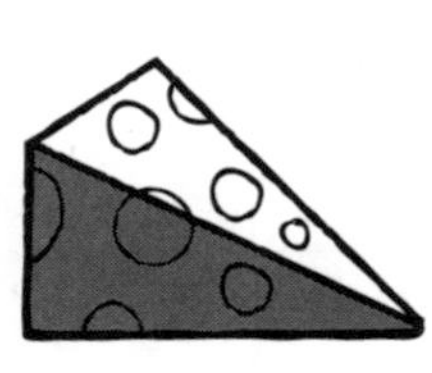 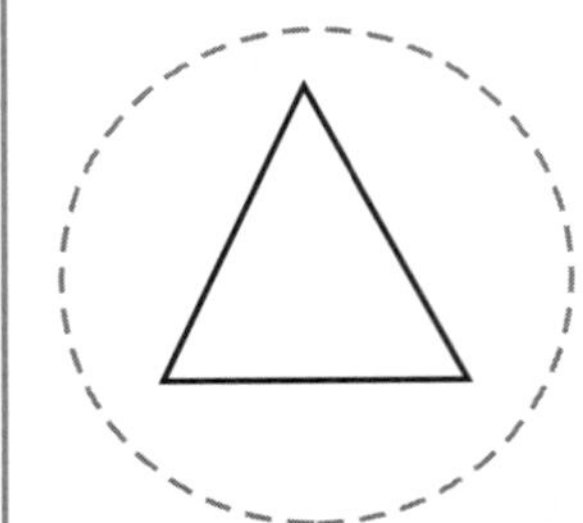 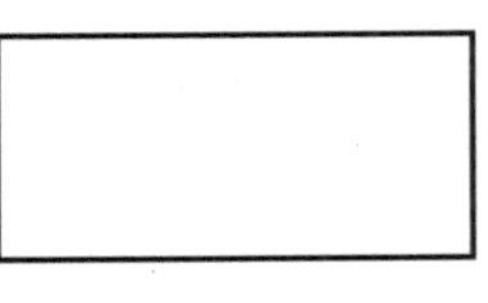 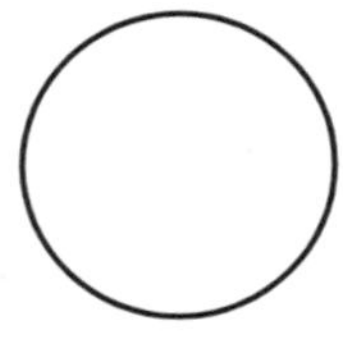 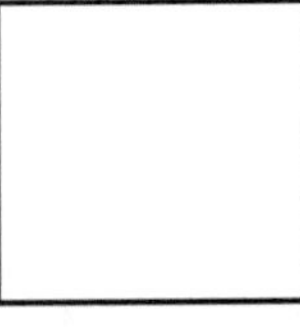

6.

   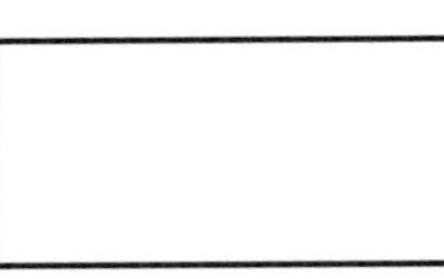 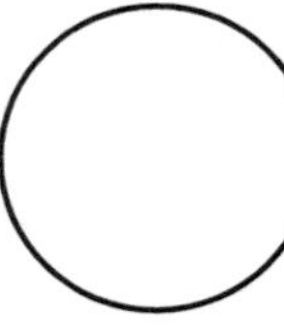

7.

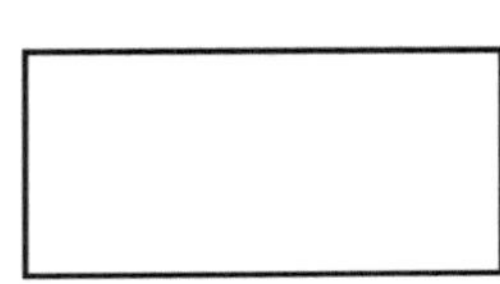 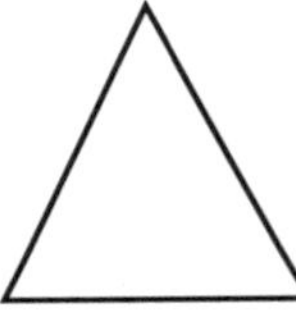 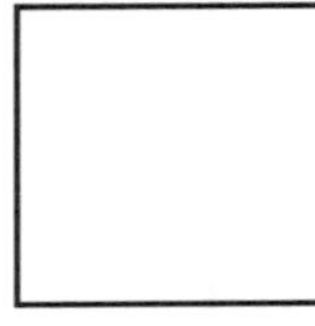 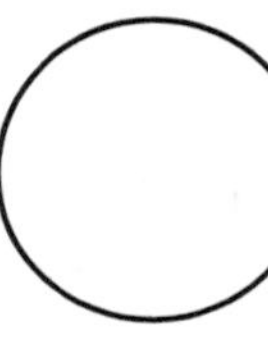

Problem Solving Reasoning Describe and compare the faces of the solids in items 5 and 6.

★ Test Prep

Which figure matches the shaded face?
Mark the space under your answer.

 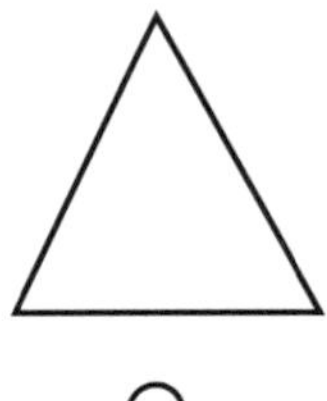 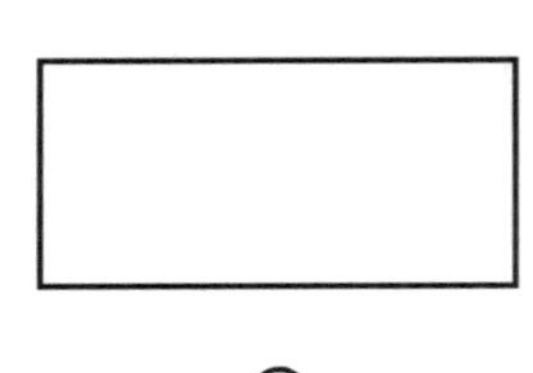 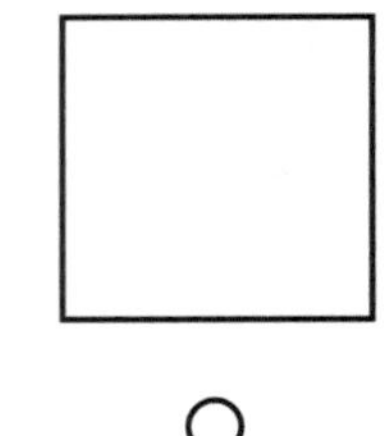

Name ______________________________

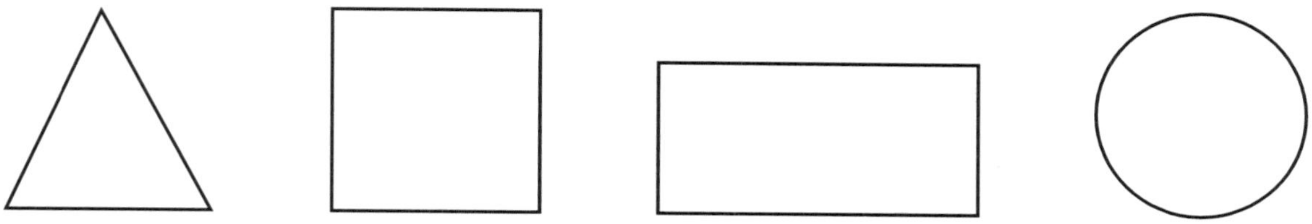

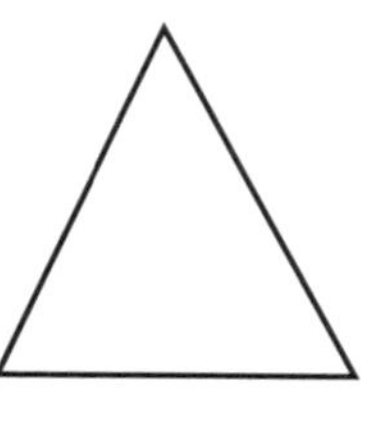
triangle

square

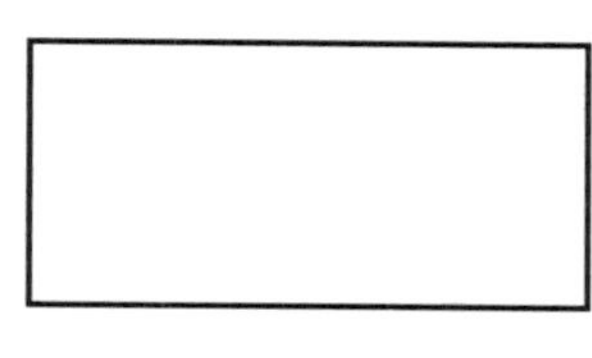
rectangle

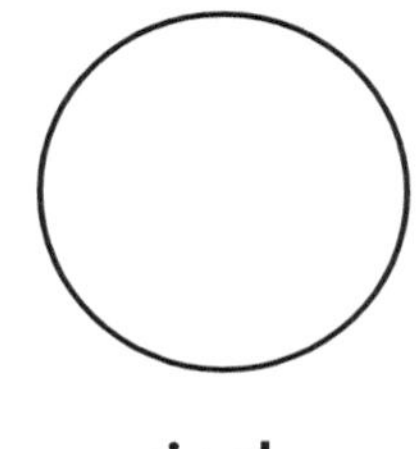
circle

Color the triangles blue.
Color the squares red.
Color the rectangles green.
Color the circles yellow.

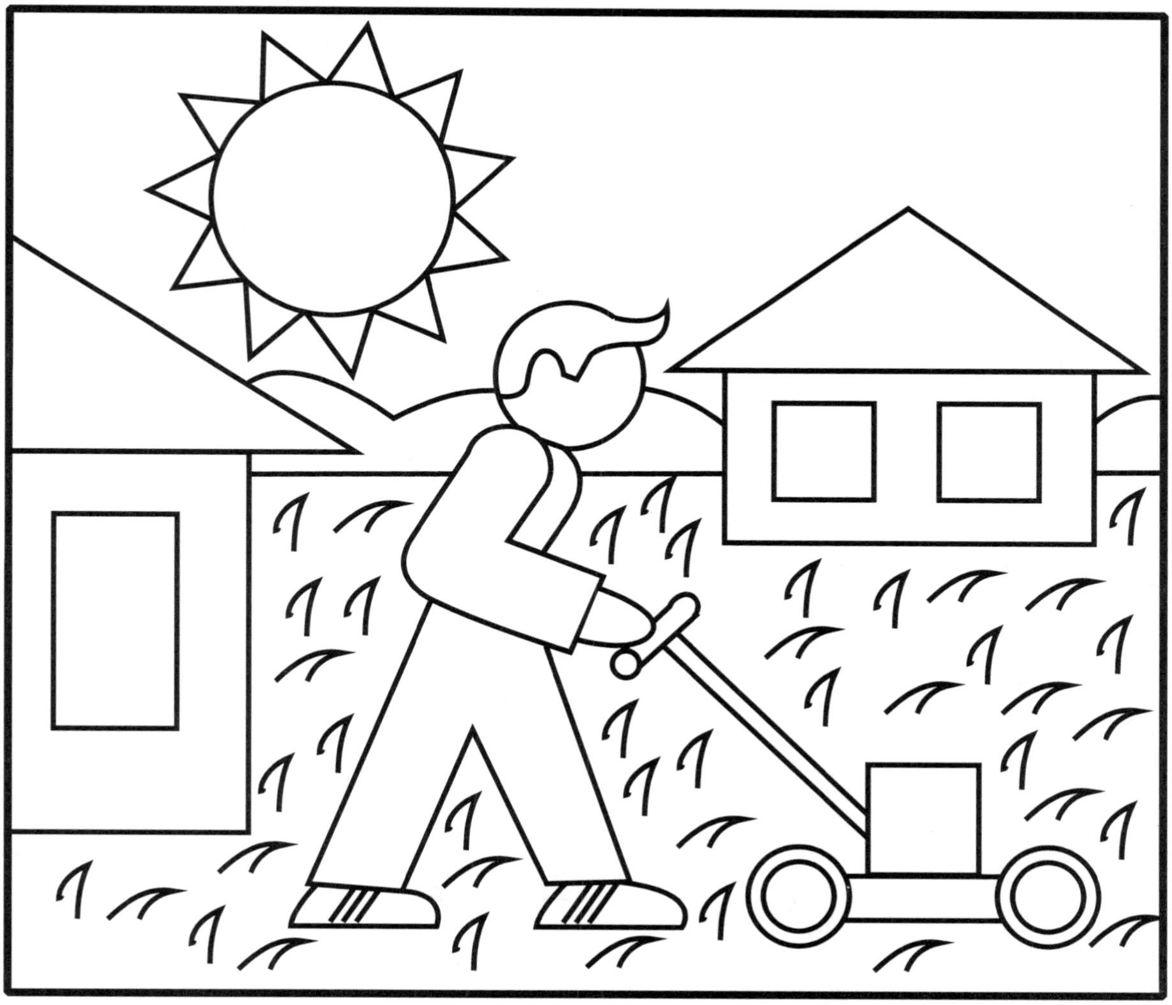

Ring the triangles.

1.

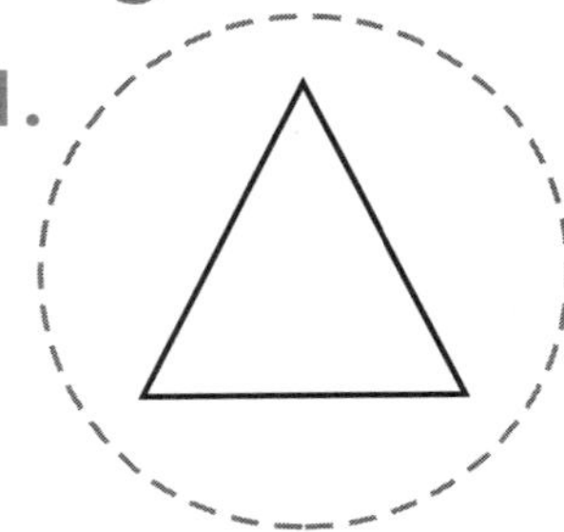
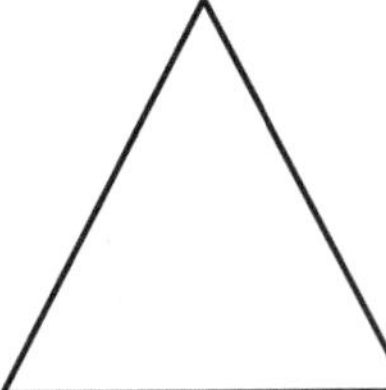

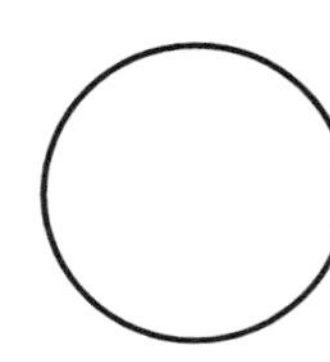
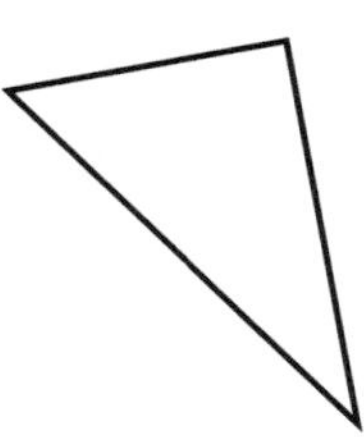

Ring the rectangles.

2.

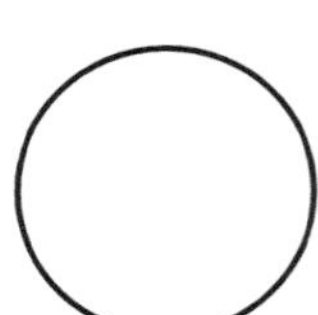
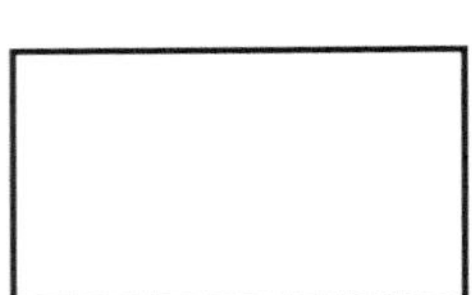
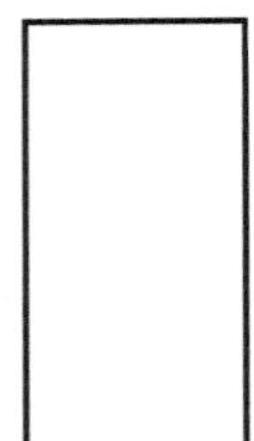
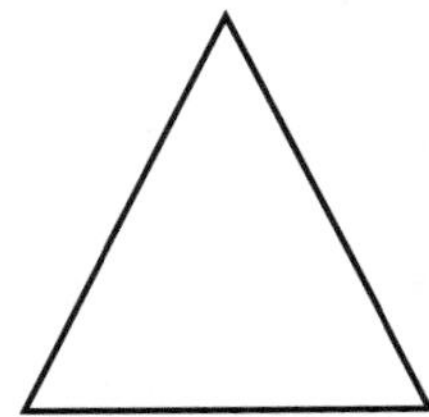

Problem Solving
Reasoning

Tell how the rectangles in exercise 2 are alike and different.

Quick Check

Ring the sphere.

1.

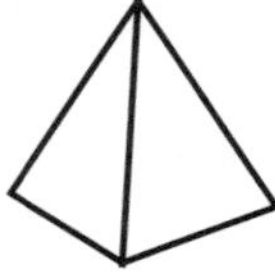

Ring the figure that matches the shaded face.

2.

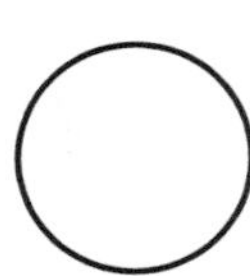

Ring the square.

3.

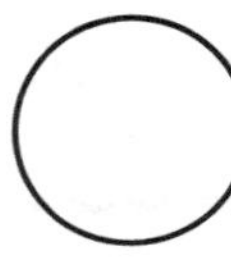

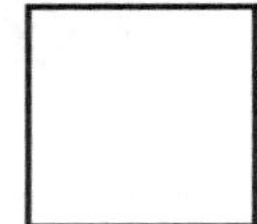

Name ______________________________

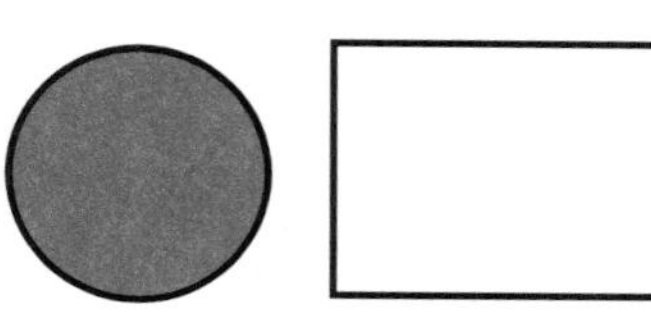

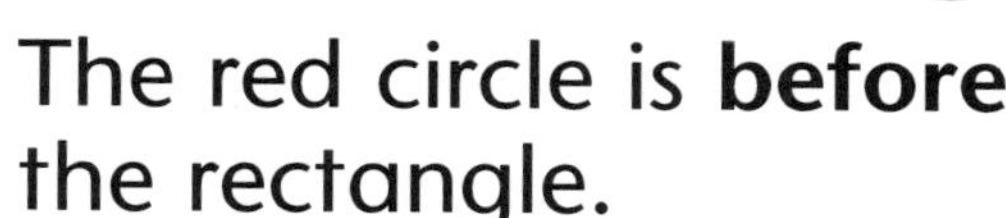

The red circle is **before** the rectangle.

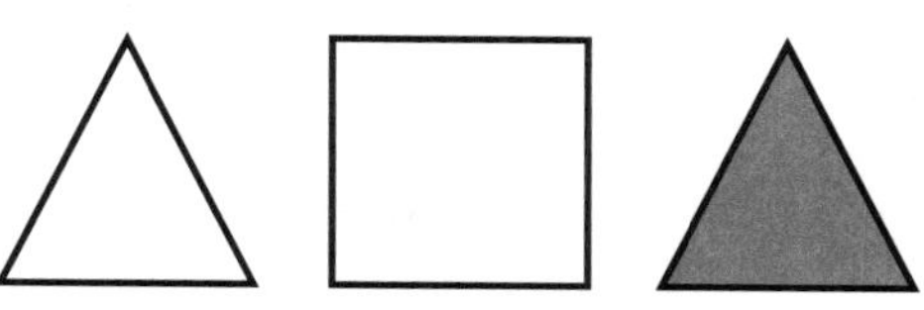

The red triangle is **after** the square.

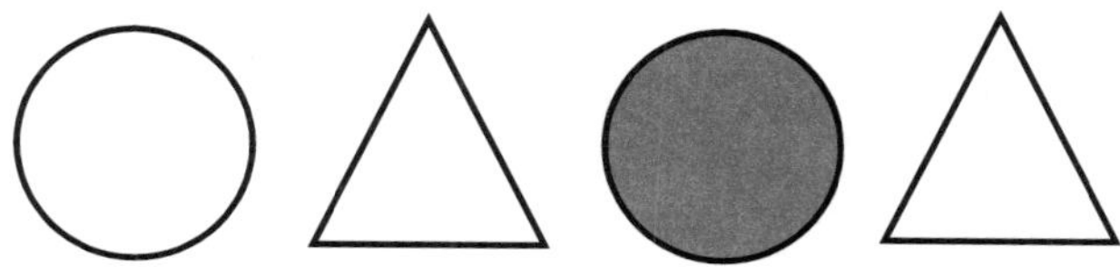

The red circle is **between** the triangles.

Color the circle that is before the rectangle.

1.

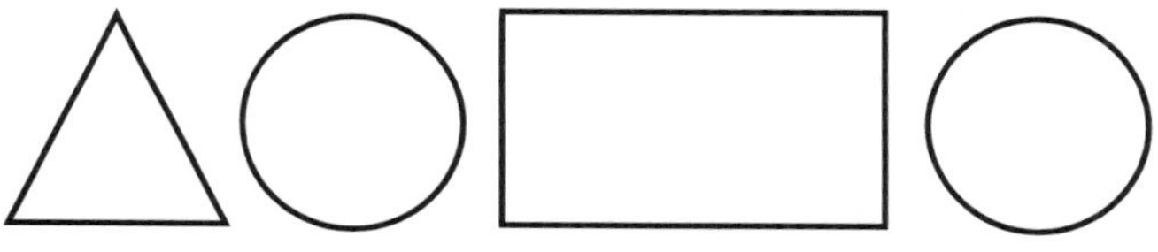

2.

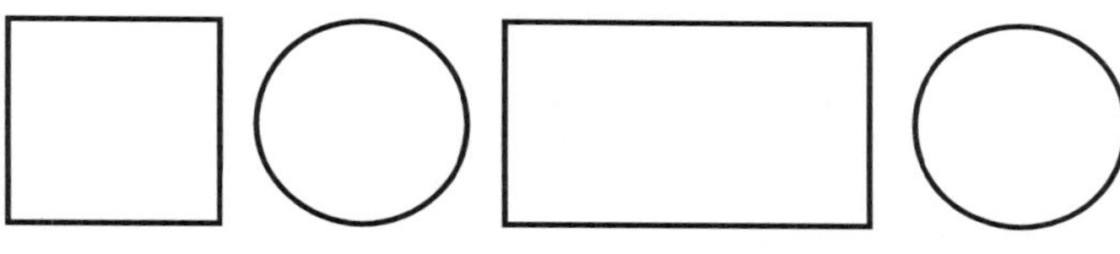

Color the triangle that is after the square.

3.

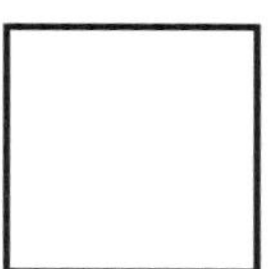

4.

Color the circle that is between the triangles.

5.

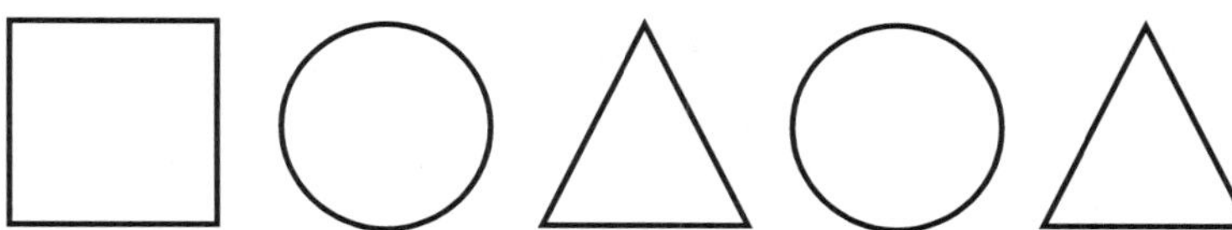

Color the triangle that is after the circle.

6.

Color the square that is between the two squares.

7.

Color the rectangle that is between two rectangles.

8.

Problem Solving Reasoning Tell how you know which rectangle to color in exercise 8.

★ Test Prep

Which item shows the colored circle after the rectangle? Mark the space under your answer.

9

○ ○ ○

Name ______________________

STANDARD

Trace each side. Write how many sides and corners.

1.  4 sides 4 corners 

2. 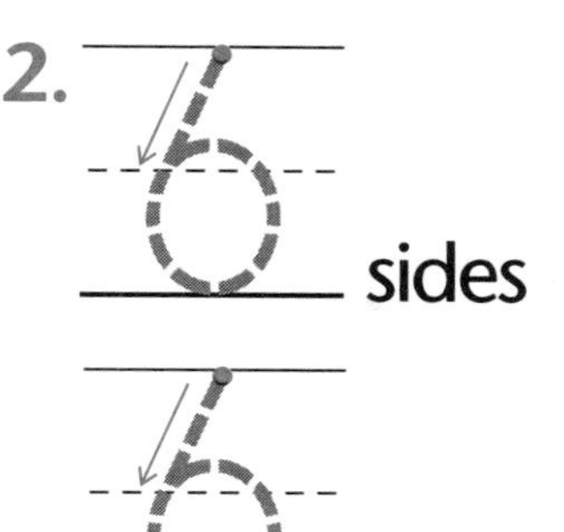 6 sides 6 corners 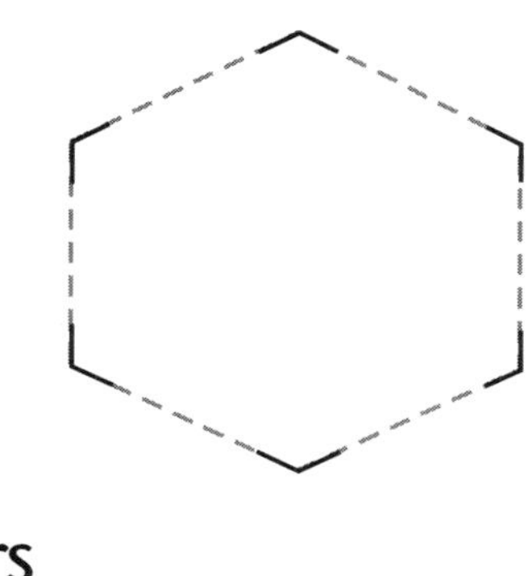

3. ______ sides ______ corners 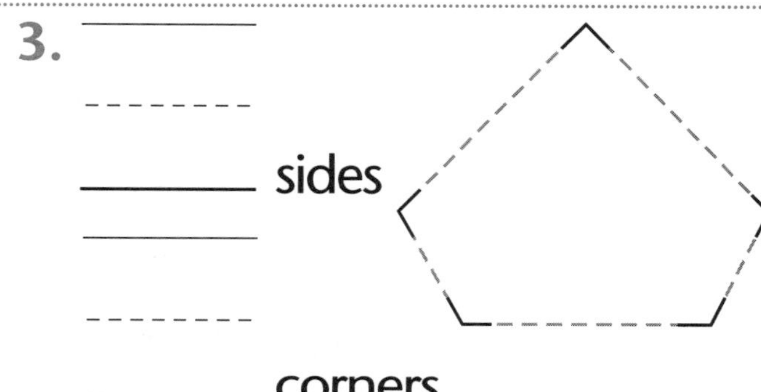

4. ______ sides ______ corners 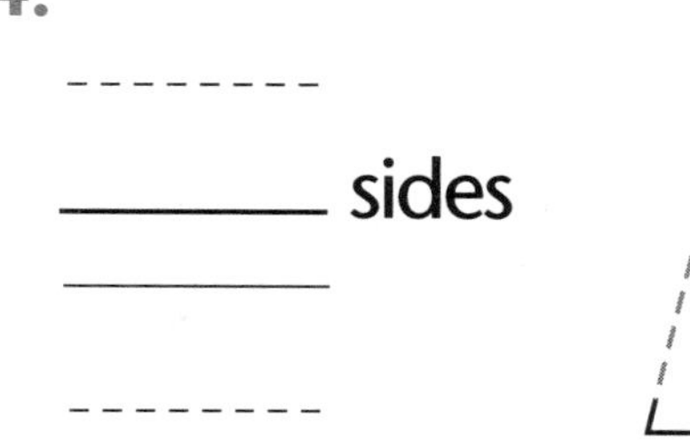 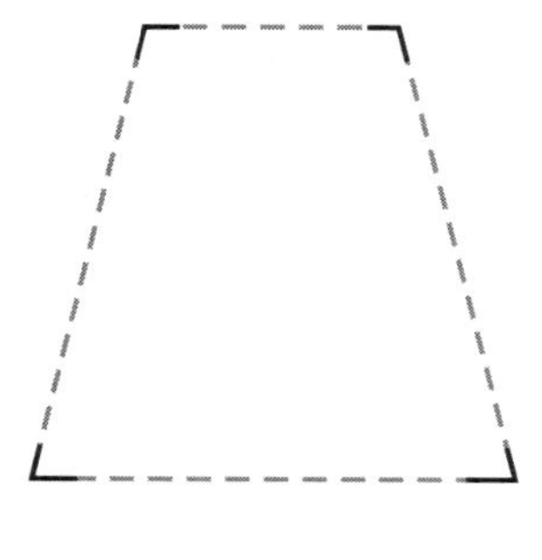

5. ______ sides ______ corners 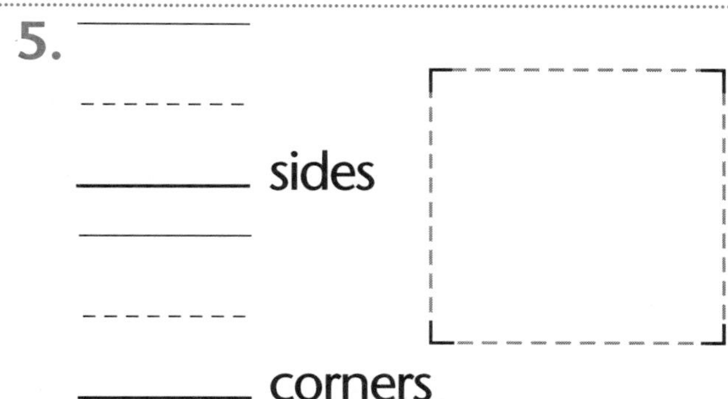

6. ______ sides ______ corners 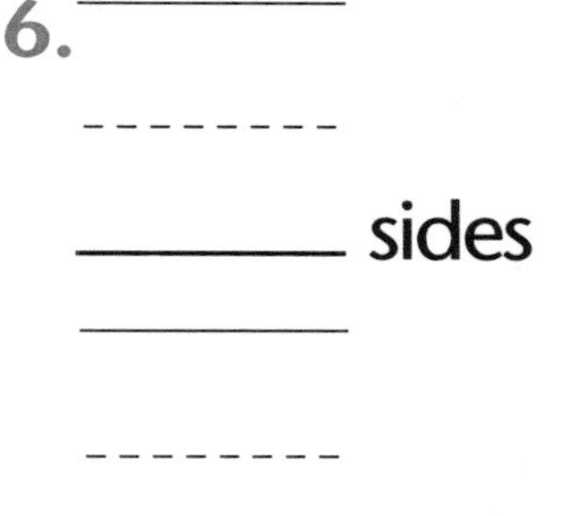 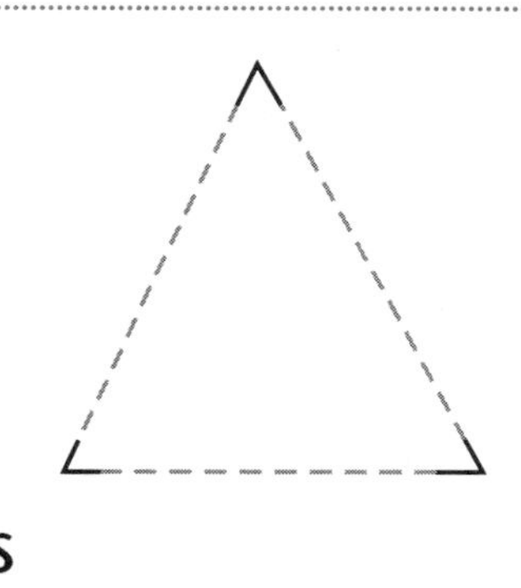

7. ______ sides ______ corners 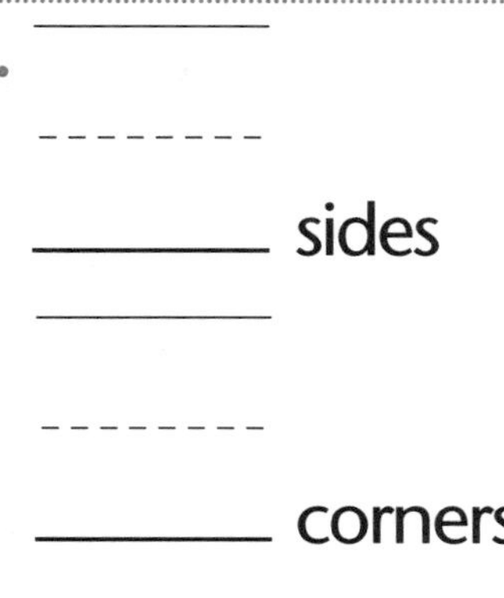 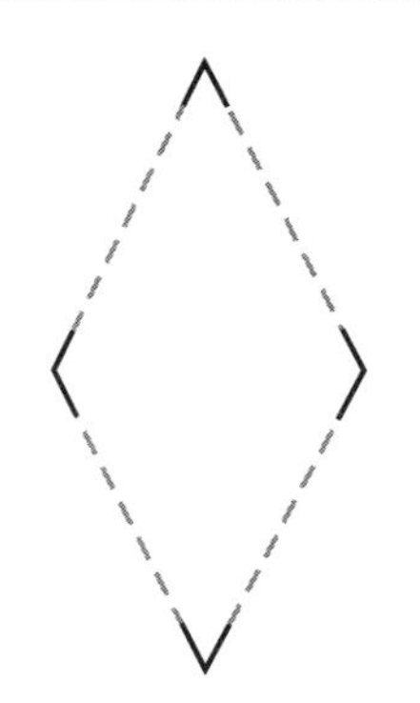

8. ______ sides ______ corners

Problem Solving
Reasoning

Look at the group of figures.
Think about sides and corners.
Draw a figure that belongs.
Draw a figure that does not belong.

9.

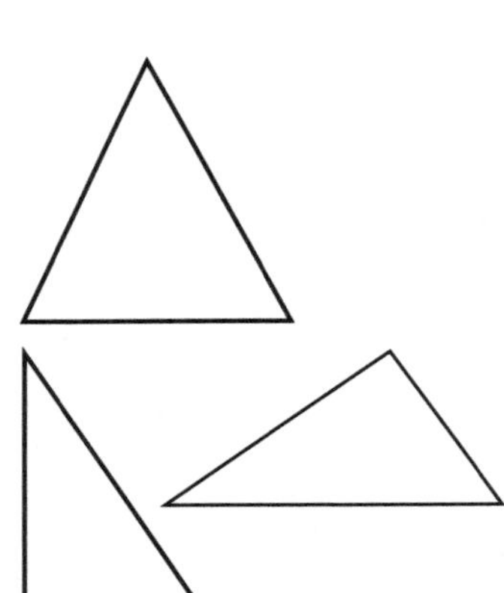

Belongs

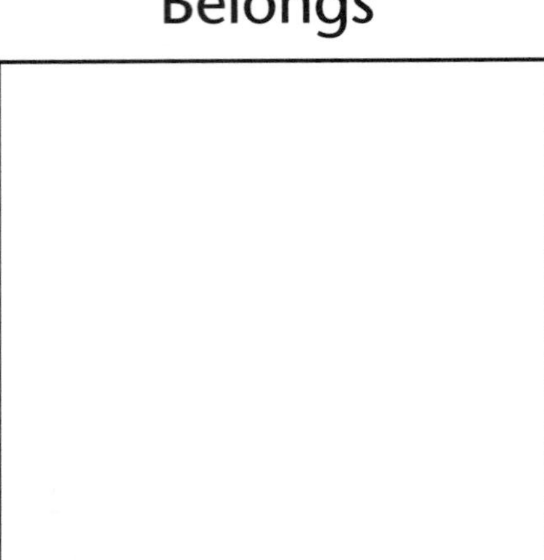

Does not belong

10.

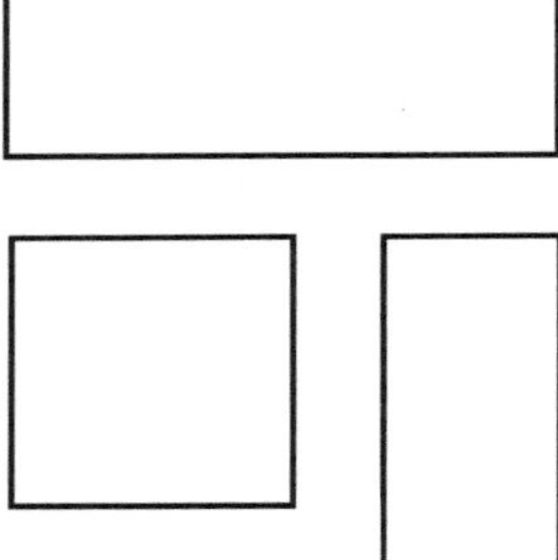

Belongs

Does not belong

★ Test Prep

Which figure has 4 sides and 4 corners?
Mark the space under your answer.

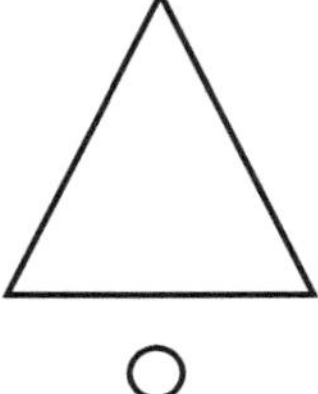

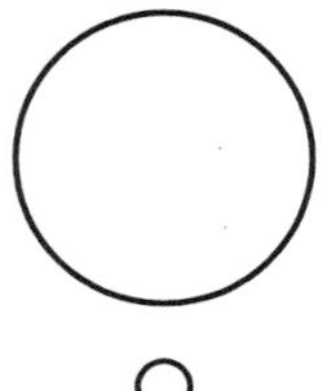

Name ______________________________

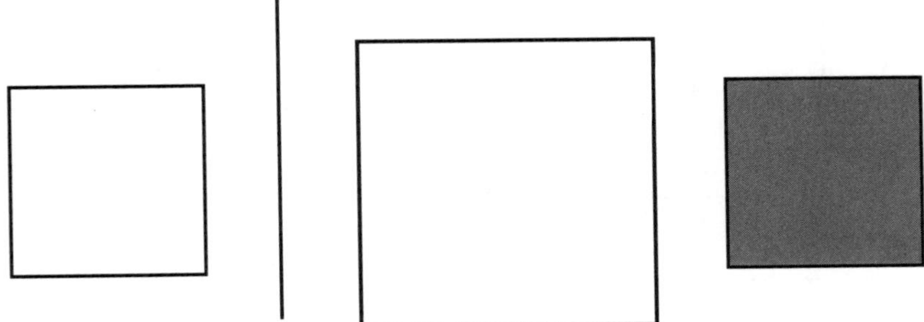

Color the figure that is the same size and same shape.

1.

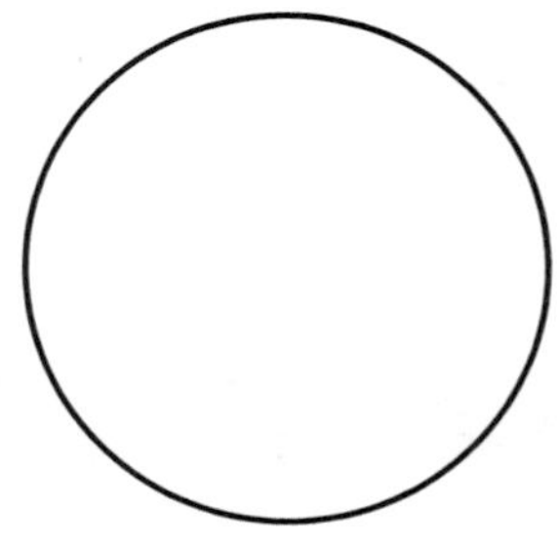

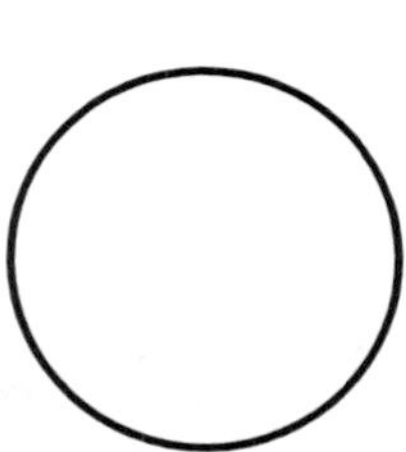

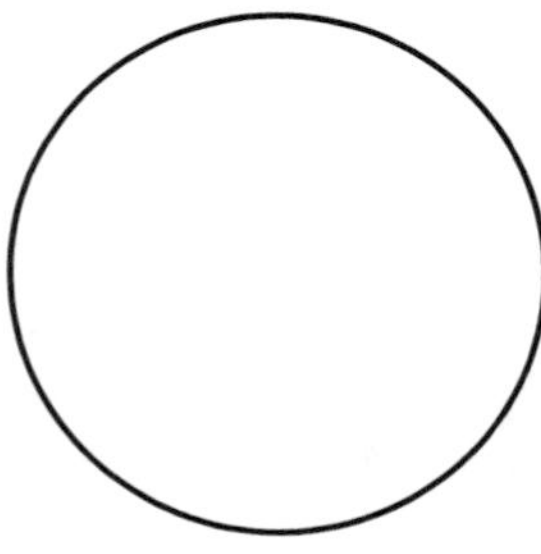

2.

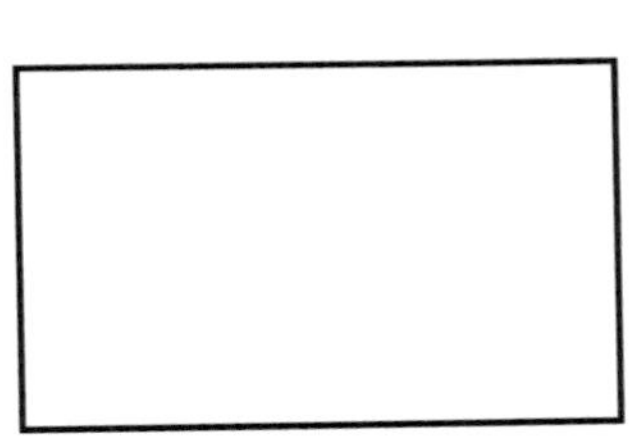

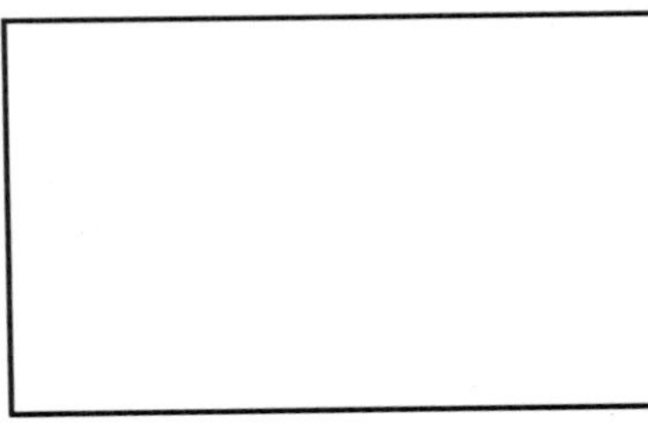

3.

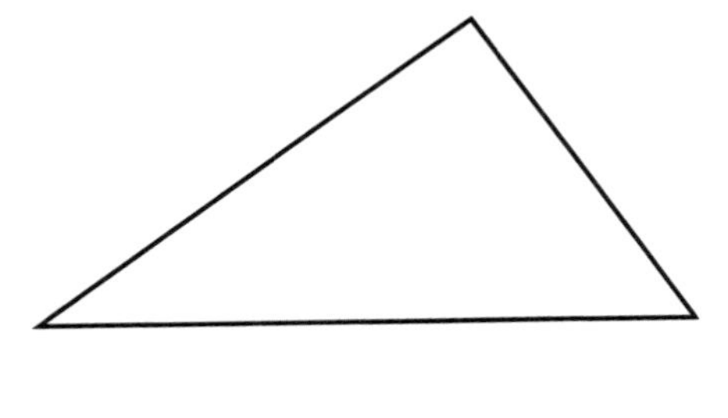

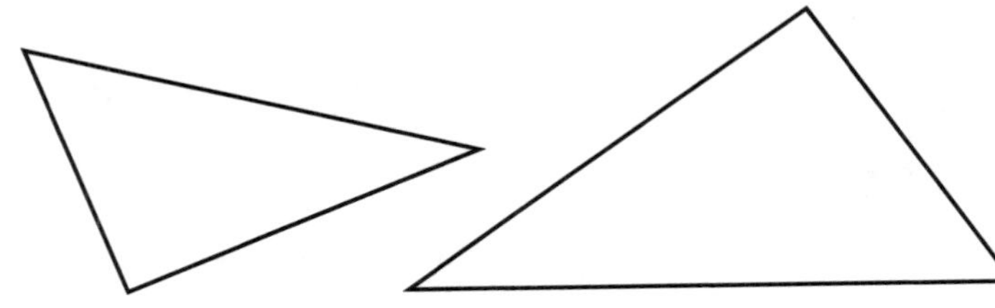

Color the figure that is the same size and shape.

4.

5.

Quick Check

Color the square that is after the circle.

1.

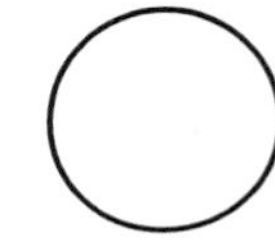

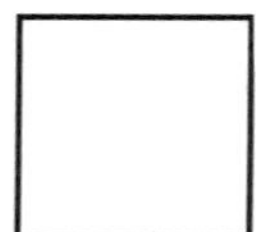

Write the number of corners.

2.

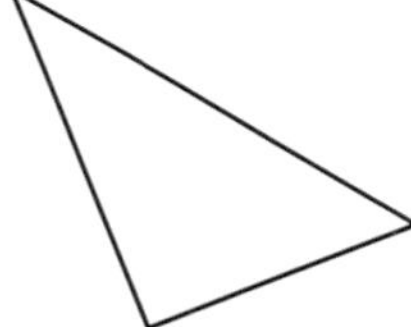

_______ corners

Color the figure that is the same size and shape.

3.

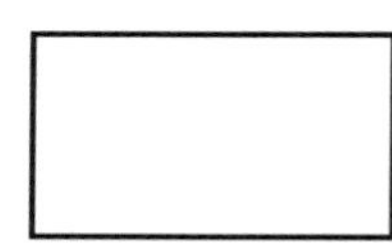

Name ______________________________

Problem

What figure most likely comes next?

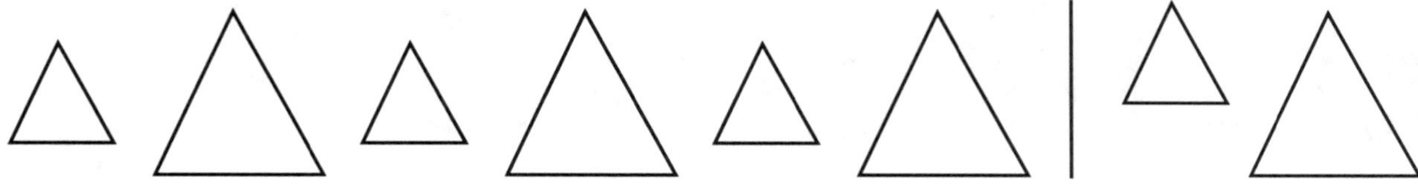

1 Understand

2 Decide

3 Solve

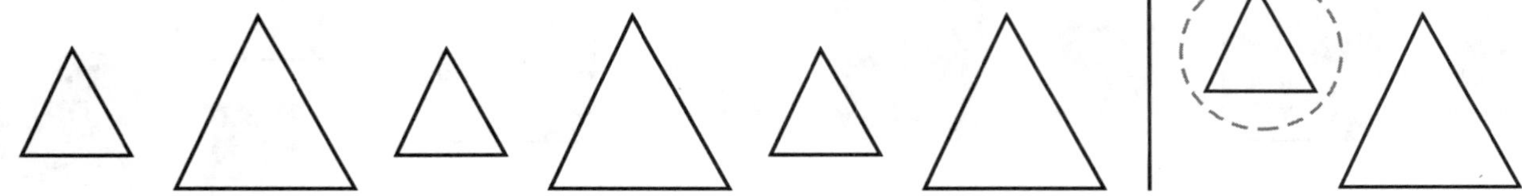

4 Look back

Ring the figure that most likely comes next.

Think about **size.**

I.

Ring the figure that most likely comes next.

Think about **color**.

2.

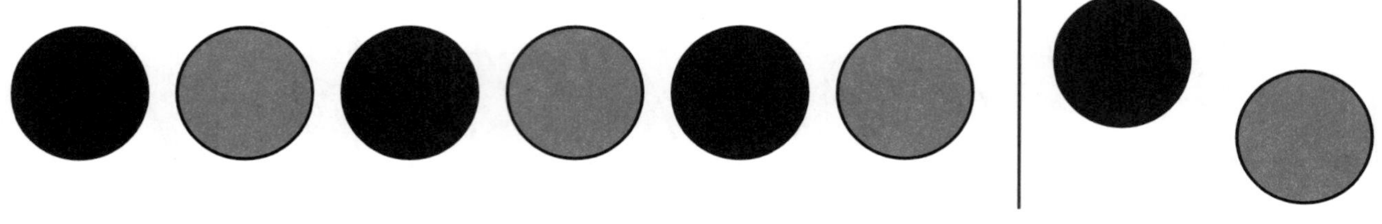

Think about **shape**.

3.

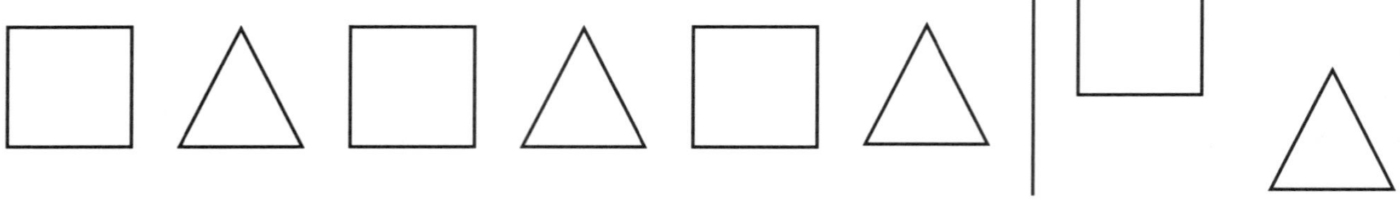

Think about **size** and **color**.

4.

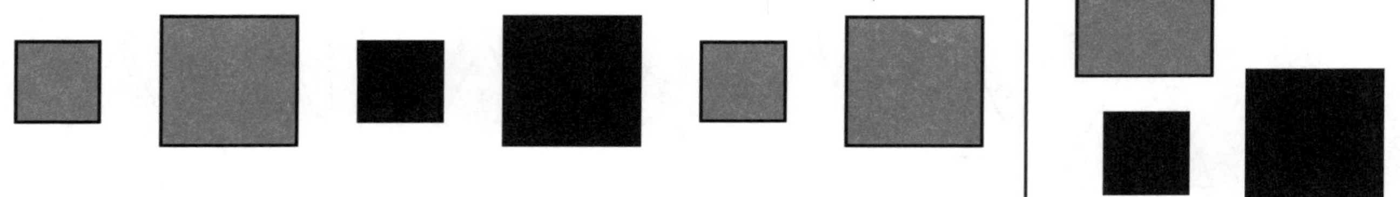

Think about **shape** and **size**.

5.

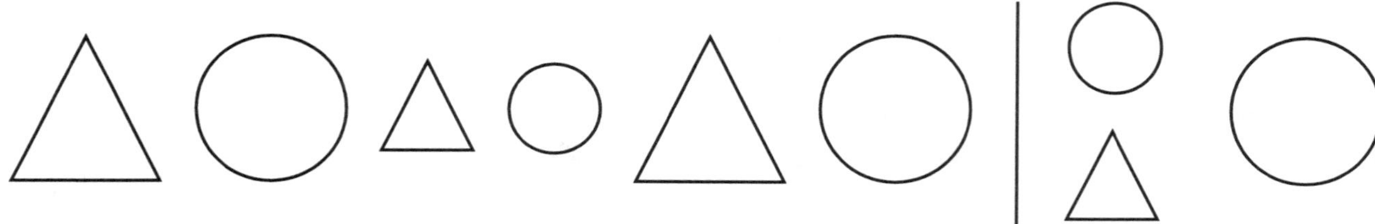

Think about **color** and **shape**.

6.

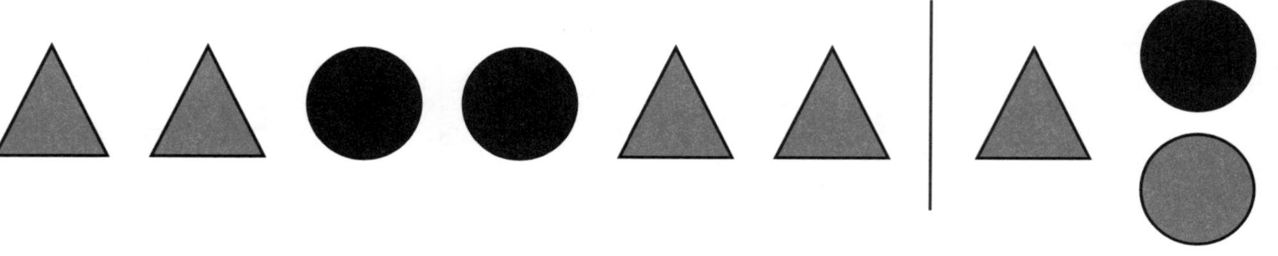

Name ____________________

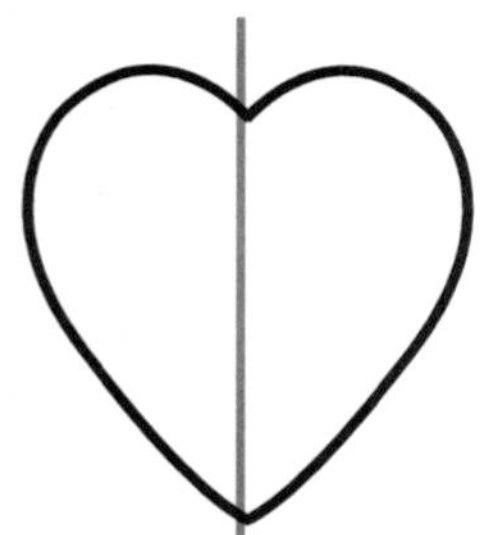

Both parts of this heart match.

Ring the objects with matching parts.

1.

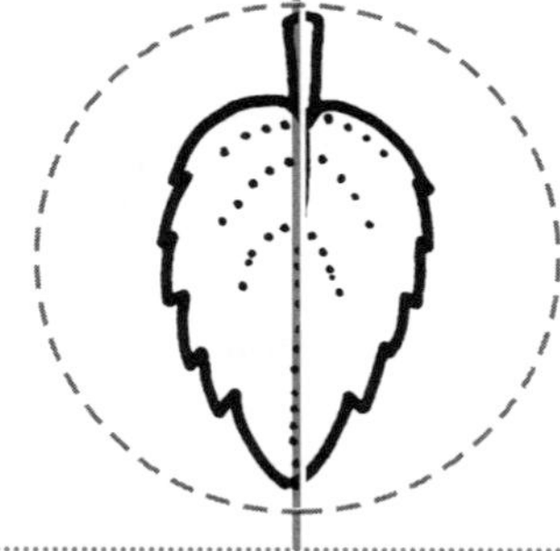

2.

3.

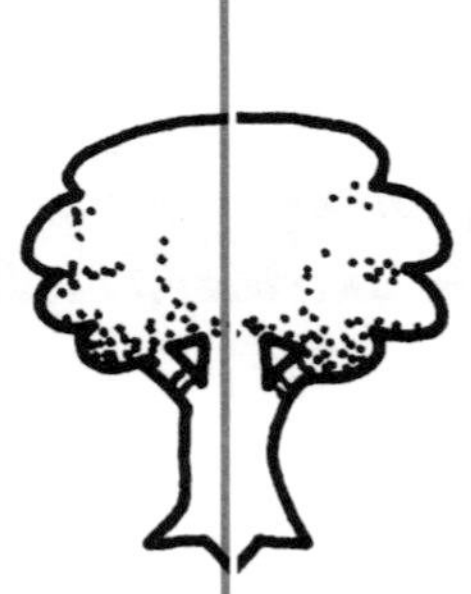

4.

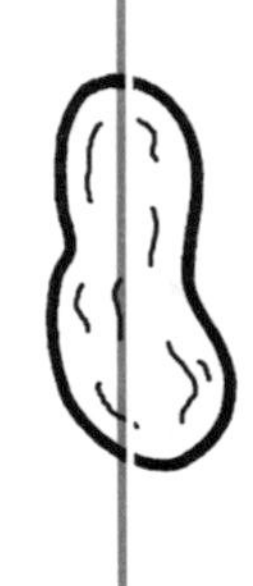

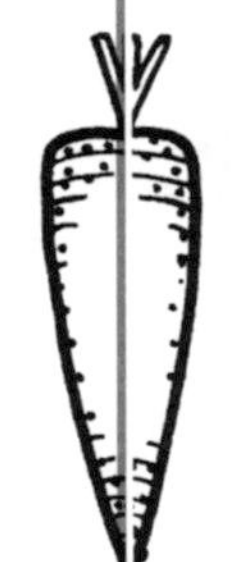

Draw a line to make two parts that match.

5. 

6. 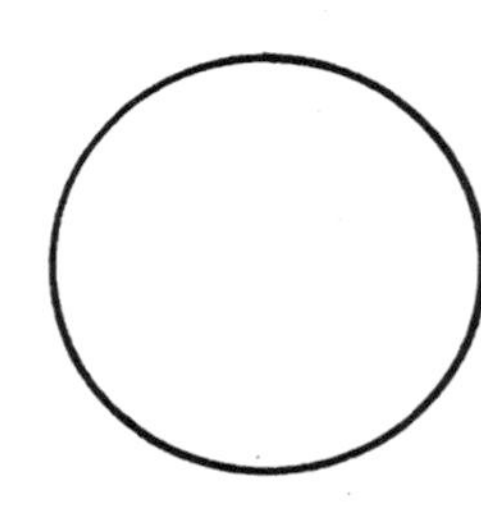

7. 

8. 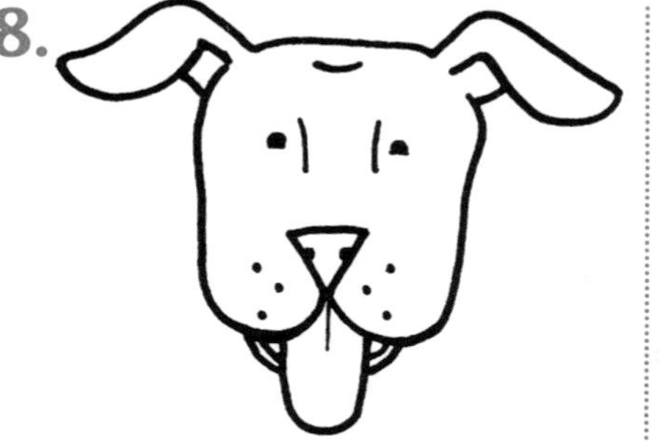

9. 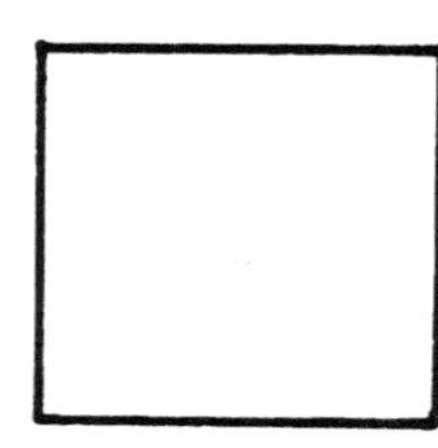

10. 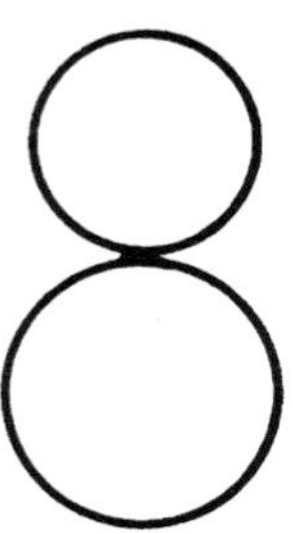

Problem Solving Reasoning

Use the circles. Draw lines to show different ways to make the two parts match.

11. 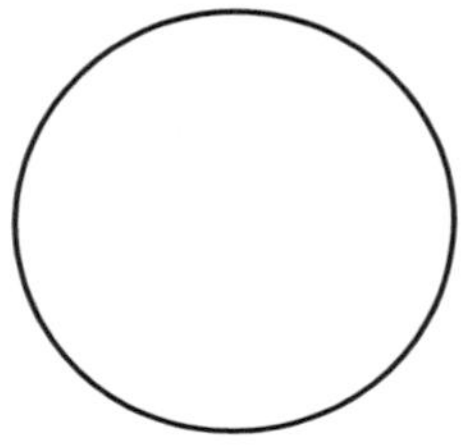 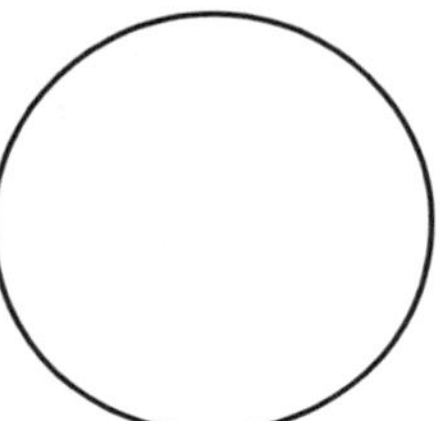 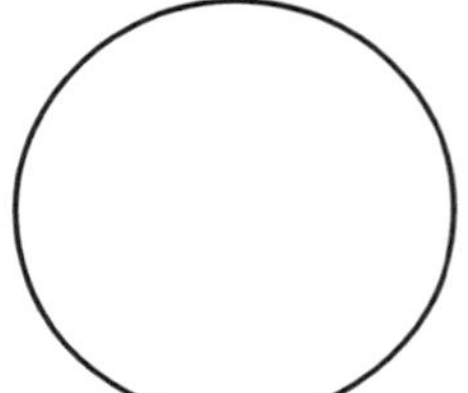 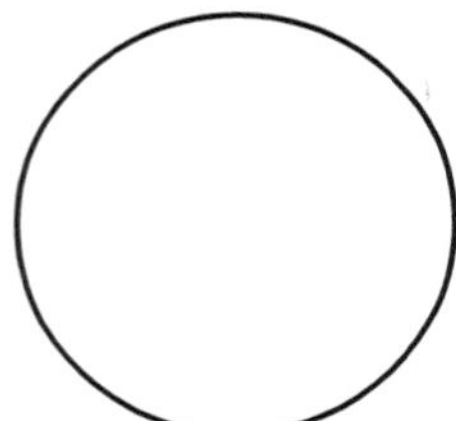

★ Test Prep

Which figure shows a line of symmetry?
Mark the space under your answer.

12 

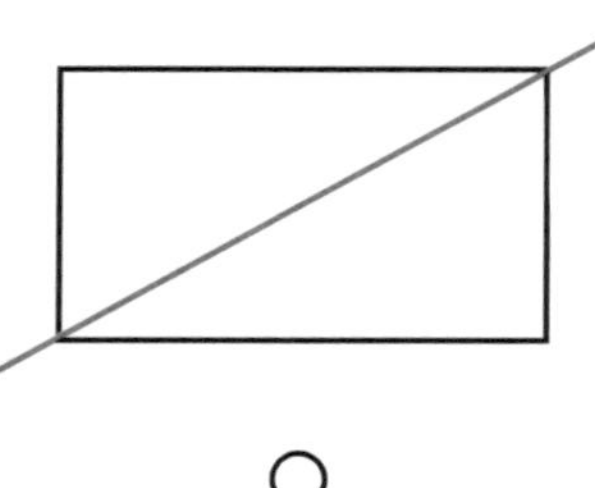
○

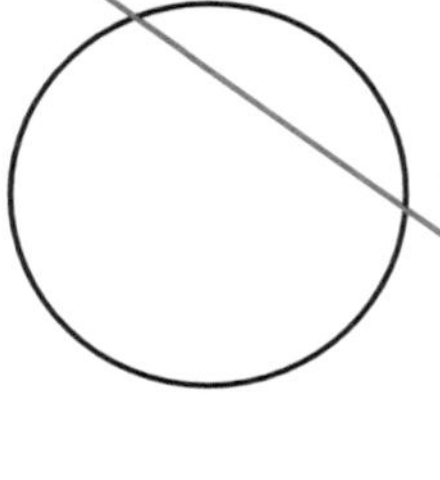
○

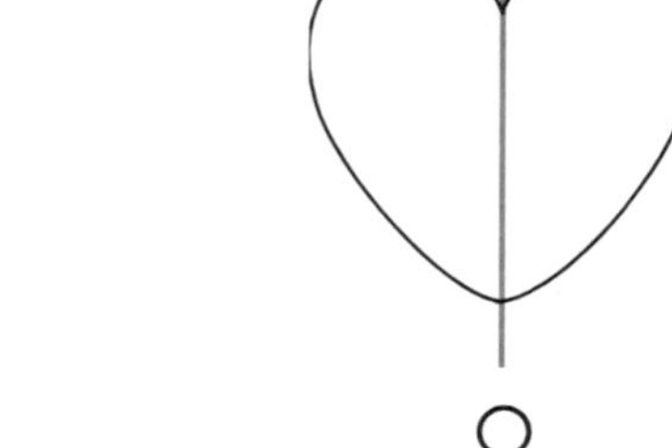
○

Name ______________________________

STANDARD

Problem Solving Plan
1. Understand 2. Decide 3. Solve 4. Look back

Draw to complete the picture.

1. Draw an X on the that is far from the

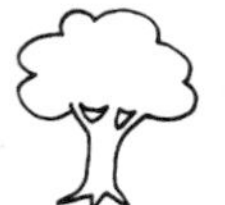

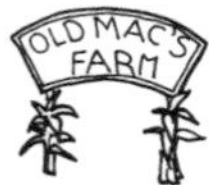

sign.

2. Draw a 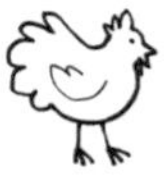 next to the .

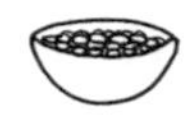

3. Draw a 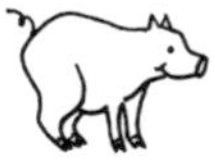 near the .

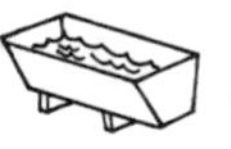

4. Draw a to the left of the .

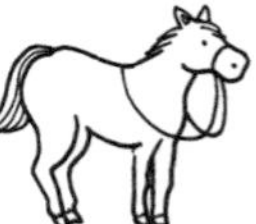

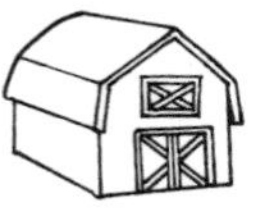

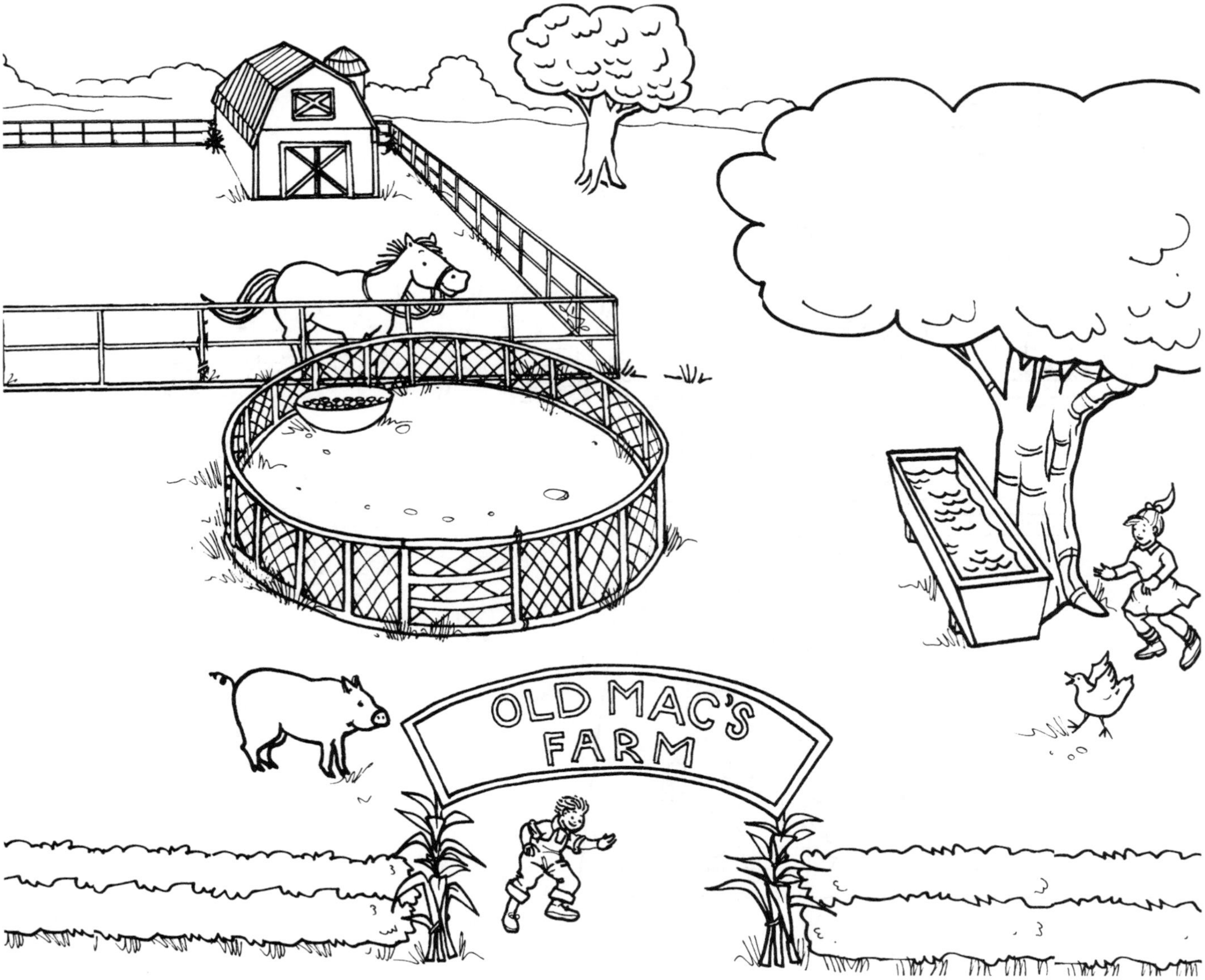

Draw to complete the picture.

5. Draw a  below the  .

6. Draw a  above the  .

7. Draw a  behind the 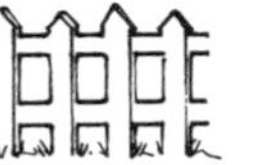 .

8. Draw a  next to the  .

9. Draw yourself to the right of the  .

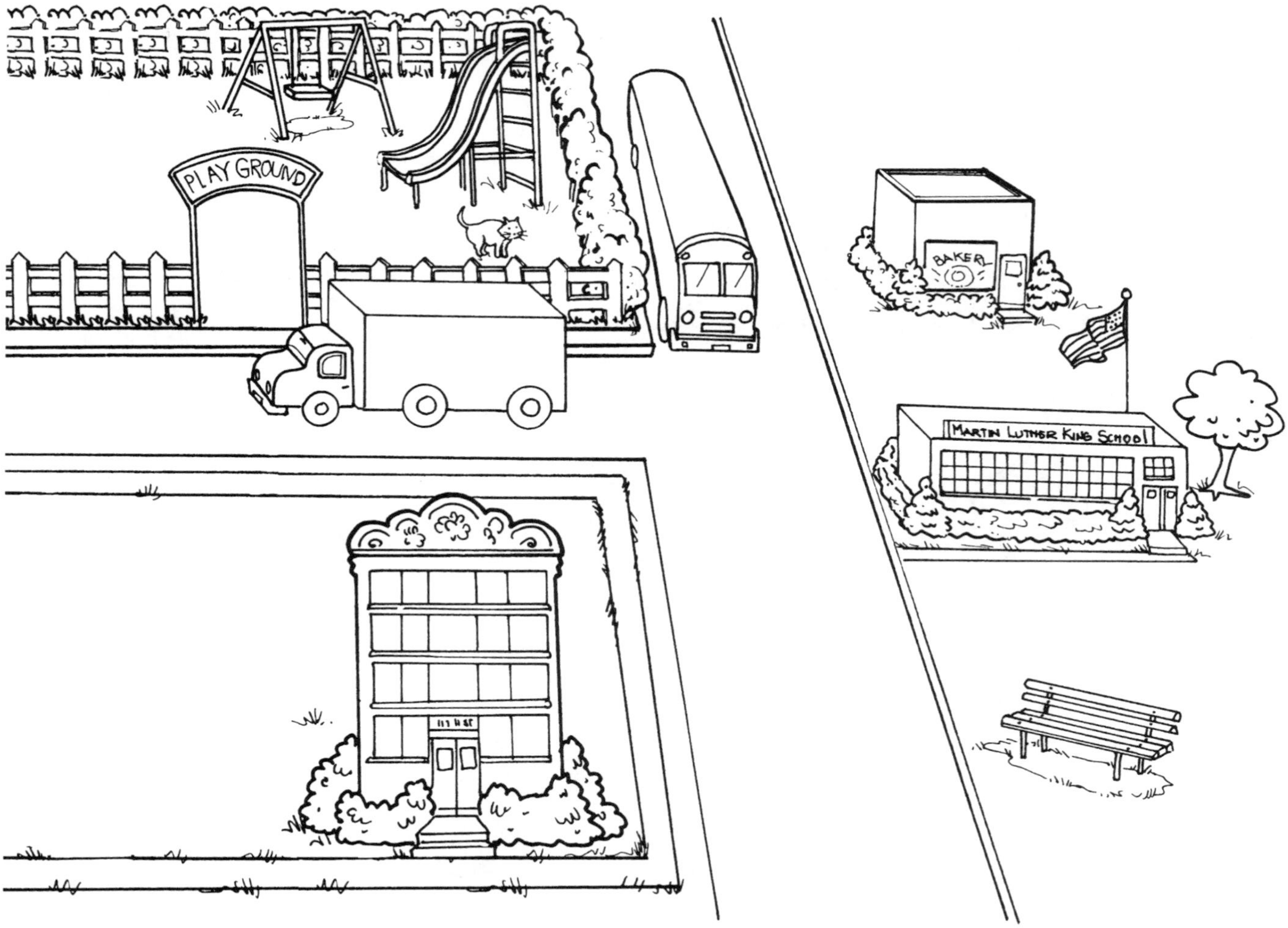

Name ______________________________

Start at 0.
Follow the directions.

1. Go **right** 3 spaces.
   Then go **up** 1 space.
   Draw a ☆.

2. Go **right** 2 spaces.
   Then go **up** 4 spaces.
   Draw a △.

3. Go **right** 1 space.
   Then go **up** 3 spaces.
   Draw a ⌂.

4. Go **right** 4 spaces.
   Then go **up** 3 spaces.
   Draw a ○.

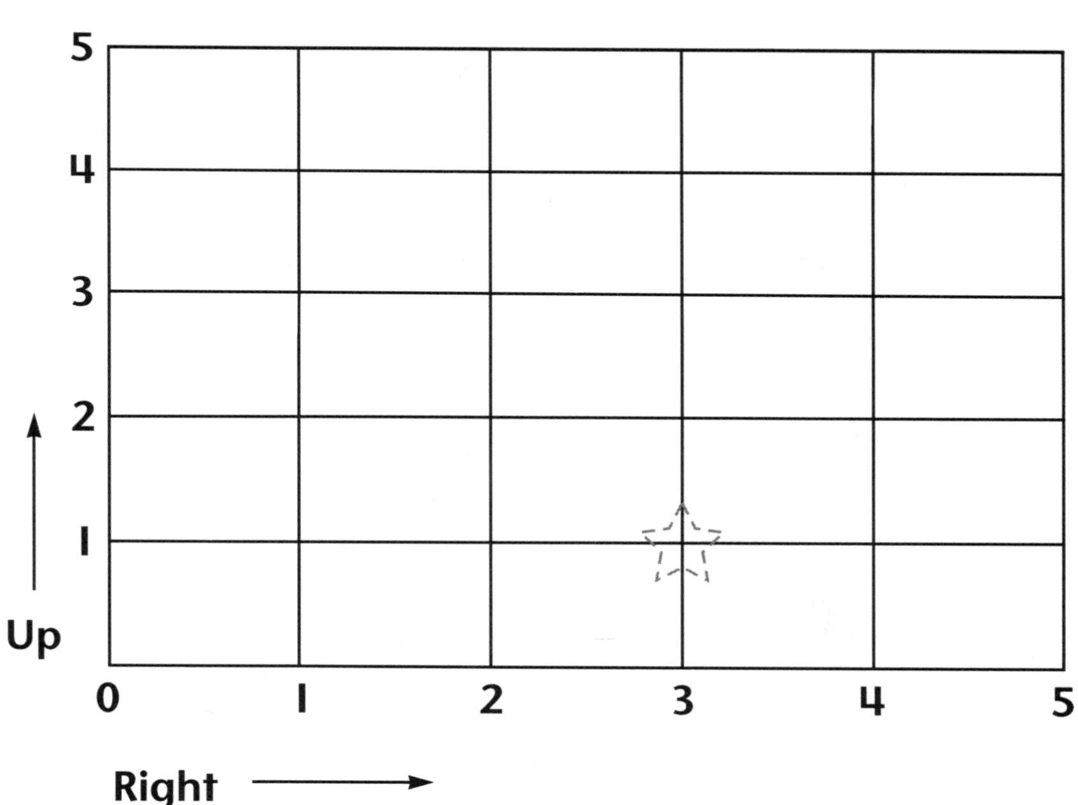

Help locate each figure on the grid.

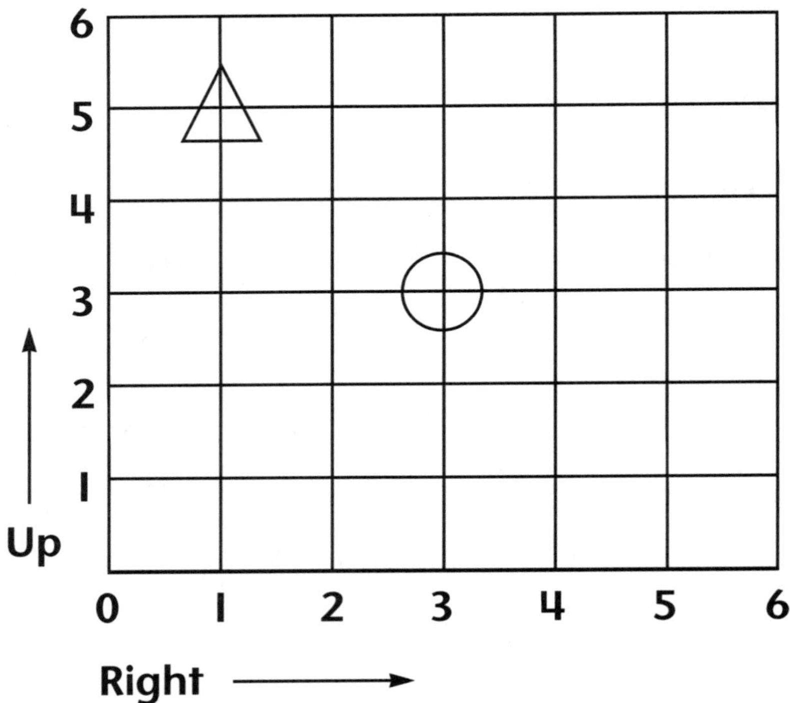

Look for the figure on the grid.
Write the numbers to complete the directions.

5. △ Go **right** 1, then **up** 5.

6. ○ Go **right** ______, then **up** ______.

★ Test Prep

Which picture shows the coat below the hat?
Mark the space under your answer.

7 

 ○

 ○

 ○

Name ____________________

Ring each object that has the same shape.

1.

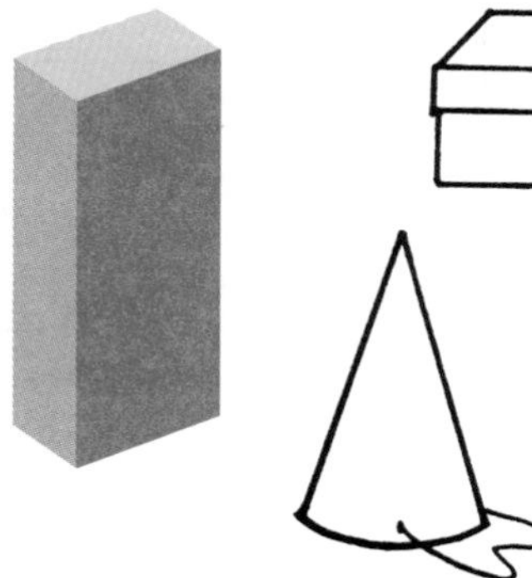

2.

Ring the figure that matches the shaded face of the solid.

3.

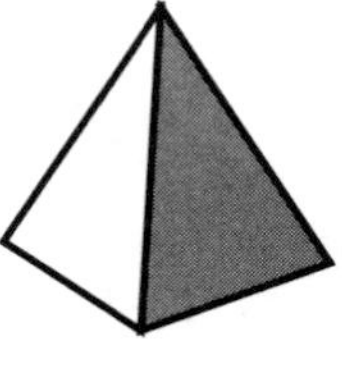
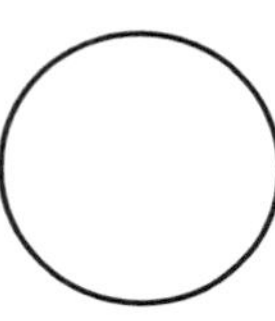

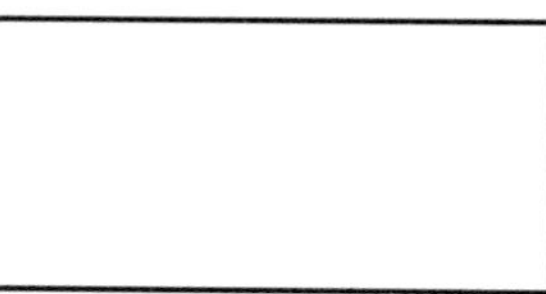

Ring the squares.

4.

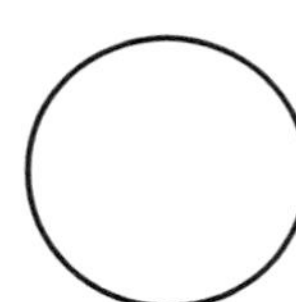
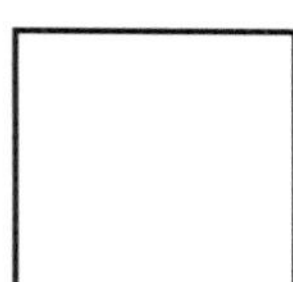

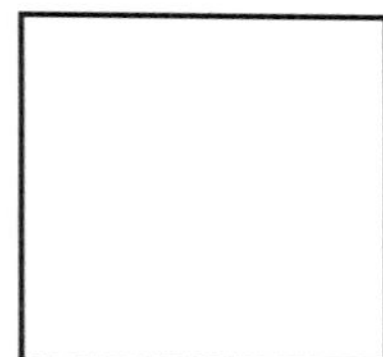

Ring the triangle that is after the square.

5.

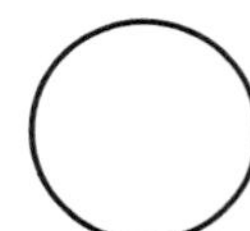

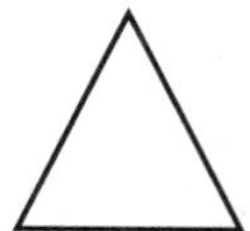

6.

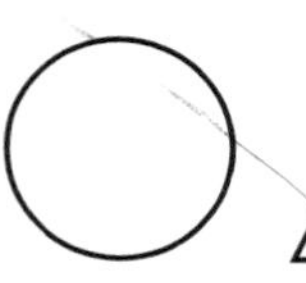

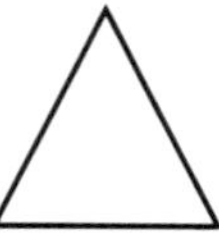

Write how many sides and corners.

7.

_____ sides

_____ corners

8.

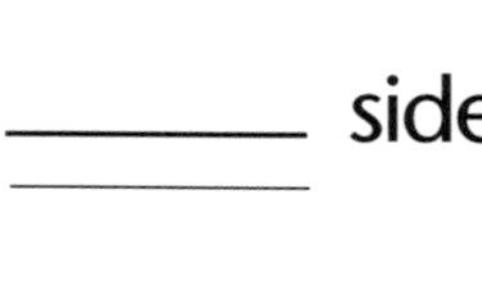

_____ sides

_____ corners

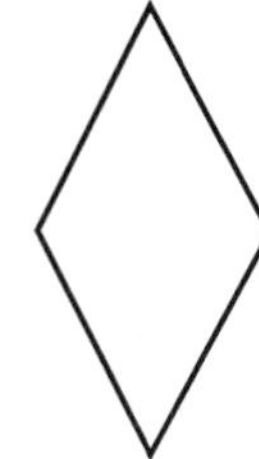

Ring the figure that is the same size and shape.

9.

Draw a line to make two parts that match.

10. 11. 12.

Problem Solving
Reasoning

Ring the figure that most likely comes next.

13.

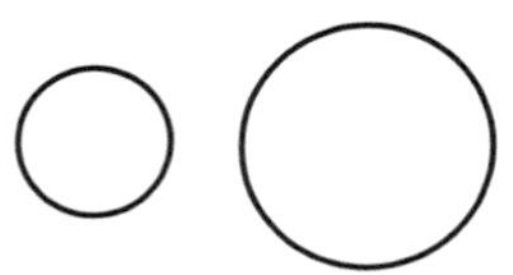
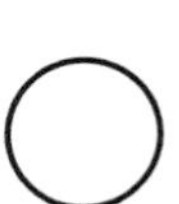
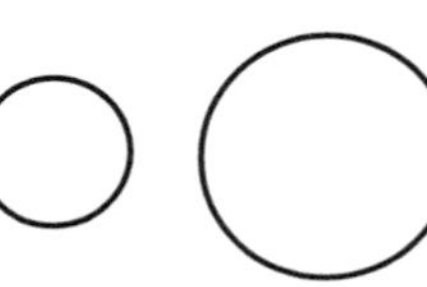
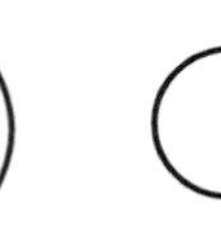
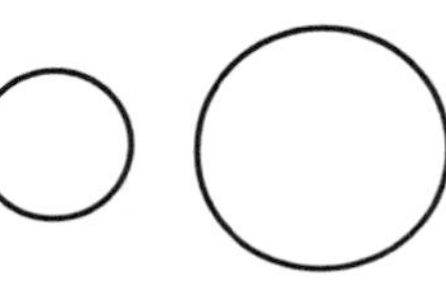
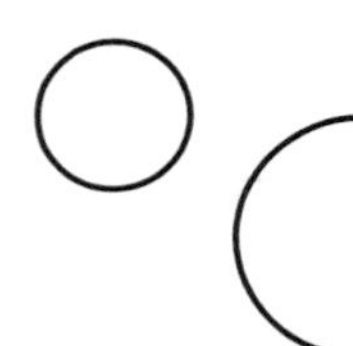

Ring the picture that shows the doll above the cat.

14.

Name ______________________________

1

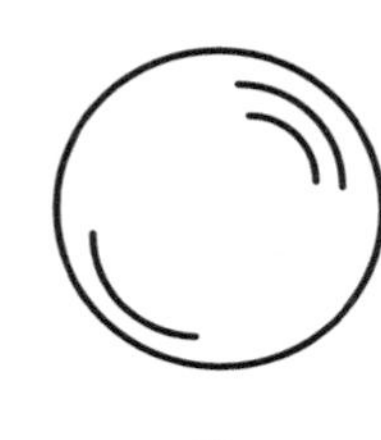
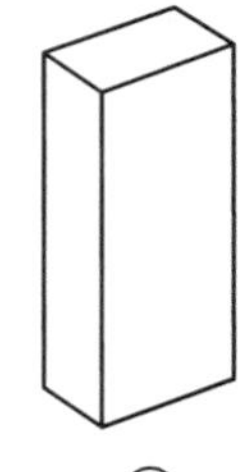
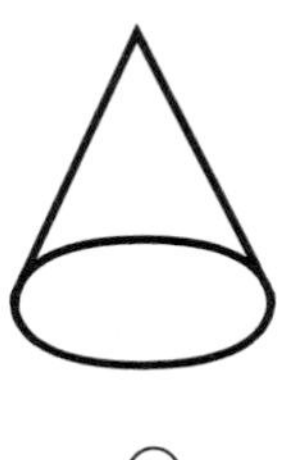

2

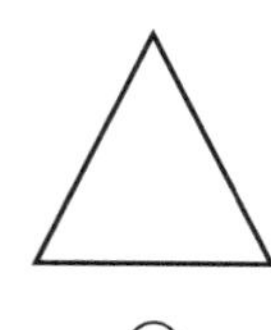
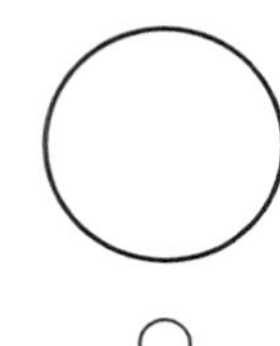
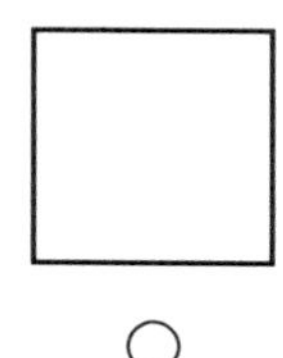

3

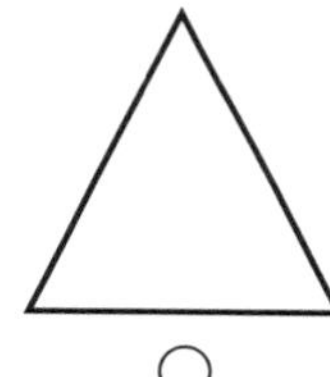
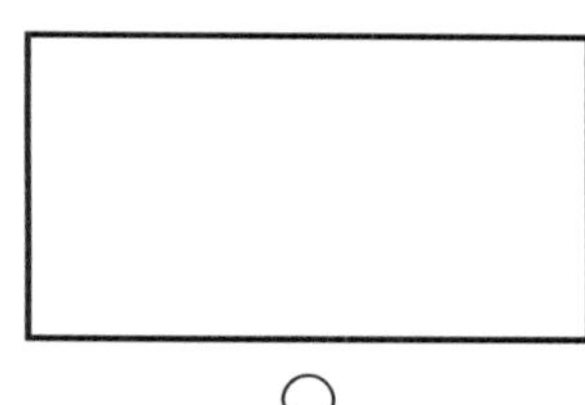
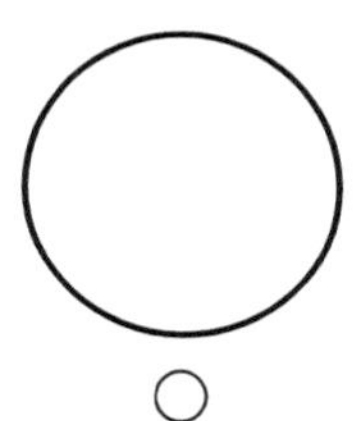

4

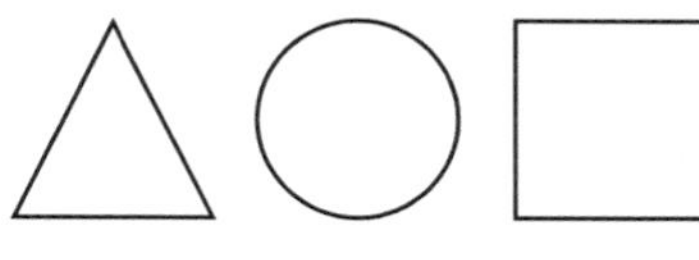
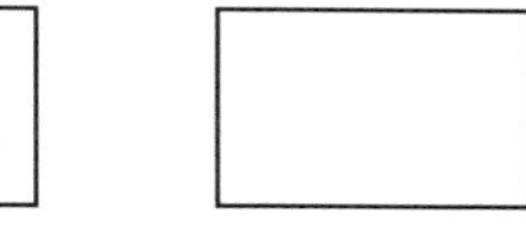

5

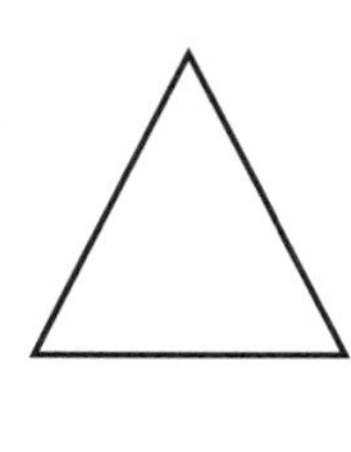
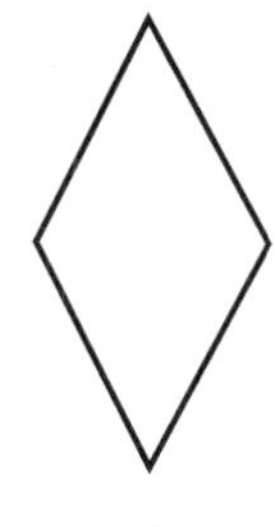
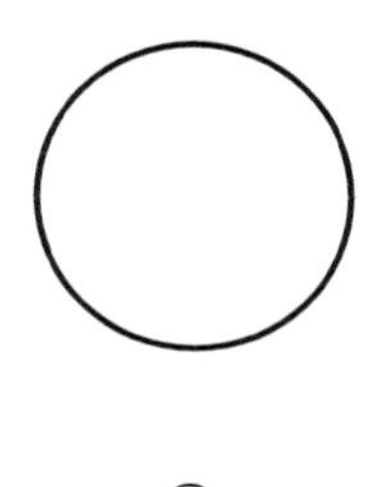

6

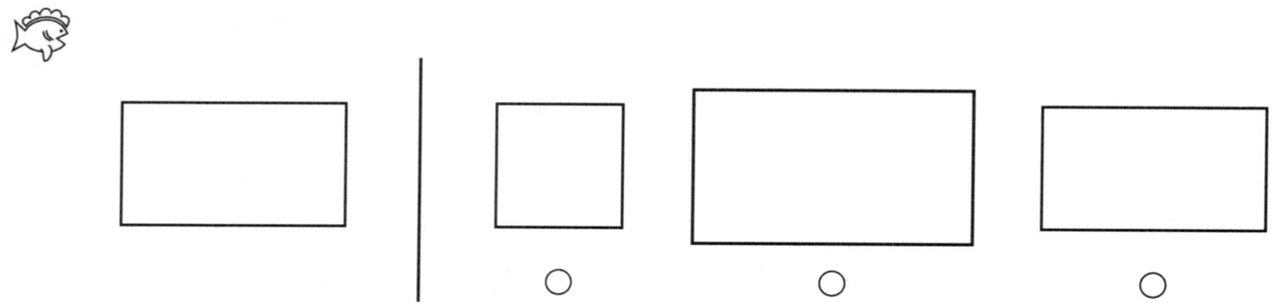

7

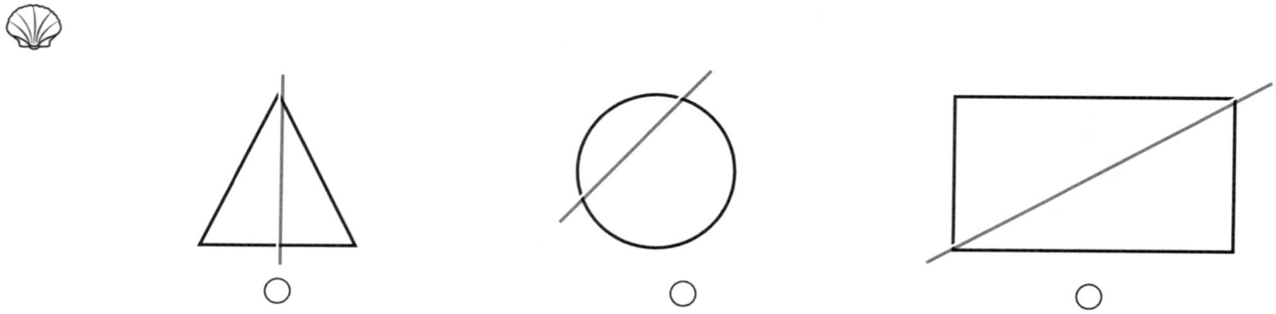

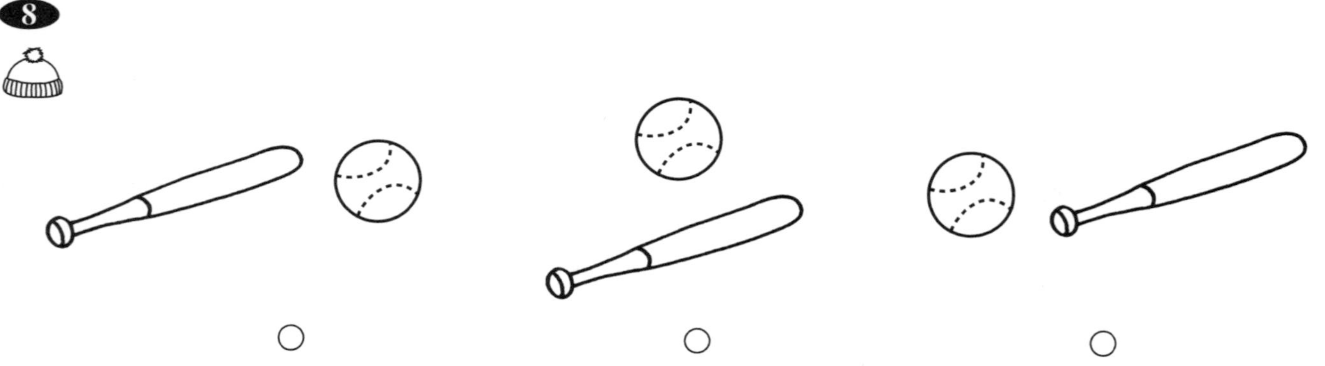

8

9

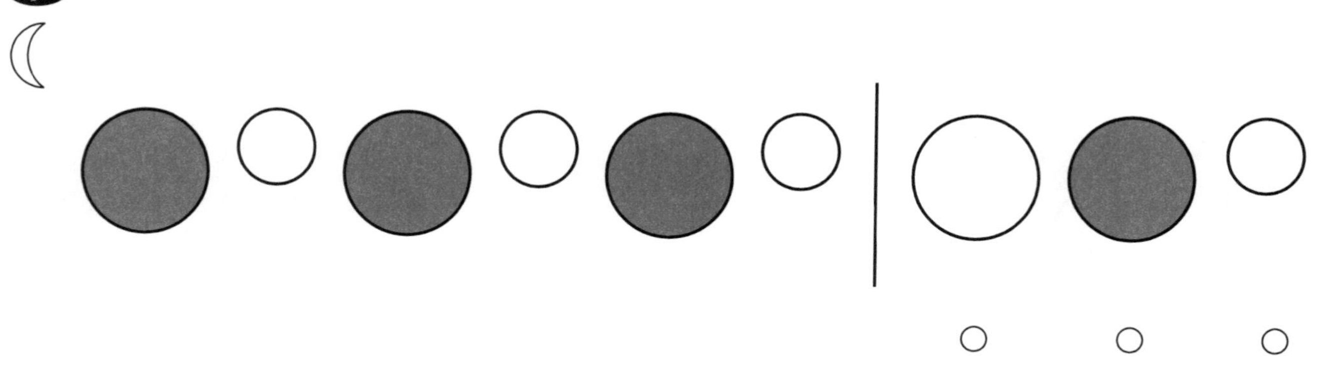

UNIT 2 • TABLE OF CONTENTS

Numbers through 10 and Data

We will be using this vocabulary:

more and fewer to compare two groups
greater to compare two numbers
greatest to compare three or more numbers
lesser to compare two numbers
least to compare three or more numbers

Dear Family,

During the next few weeks our math class will be counting groups and writing the numbers 0 through 10.

You can expect to see homework that provides practice in recognizing and comparing numbers.

As we learn to recognize and compare numbers using symbols, you may wish to keep the following as a guide.

Comparing Numbers using Symbols

6 is less than **7**

$6 < 7$

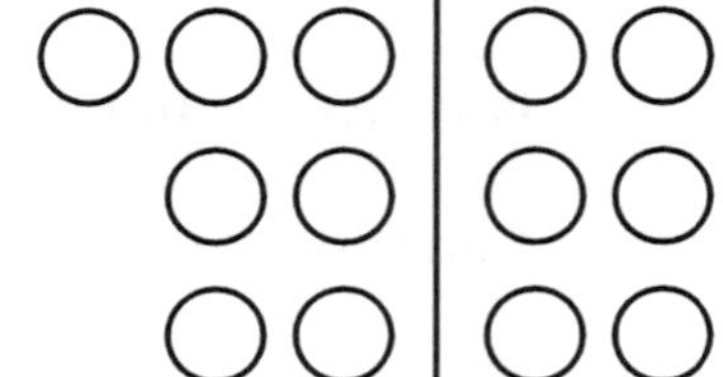

7 is greater than **6**

$7 > 6$

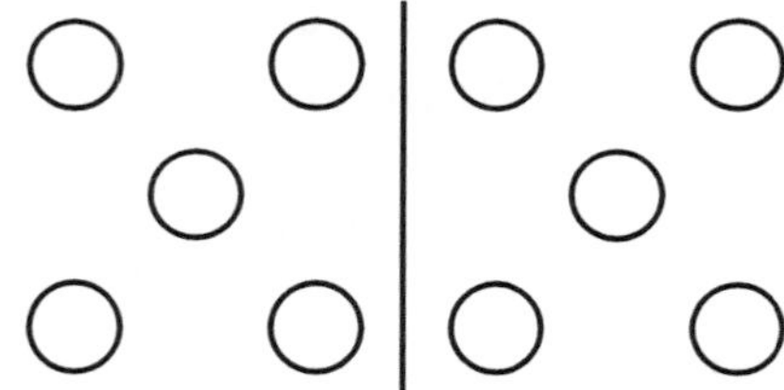

5 is equal to **5**

$5 = 5$

Using symbols correctly is important when comparing numbers.

Sincerely,

STANDARD

Name ____________________

Match the objects.
Ring the group that has more.

1.

2.

3.

4.

Match the objects.
Ring the group that has fewer.

5. 6.

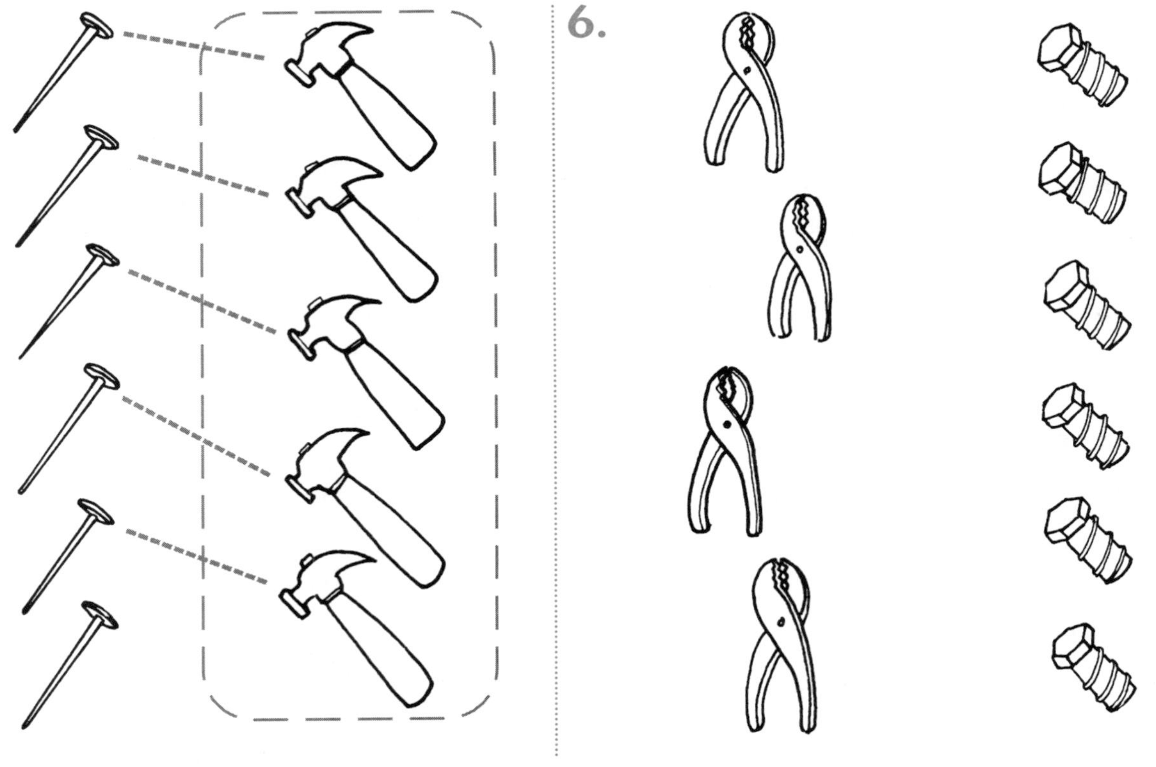

Problem Solving
Reasoning

Draw I fewer than □ □ □ □ .

7.

★ Test Prep

Which group shows more stars?
Mark the space under your answer.

8

Name ______________________________

Problem

Martina has more balloons than Alex.
How many balloons could Martina have?
How many balloons could Alex have?

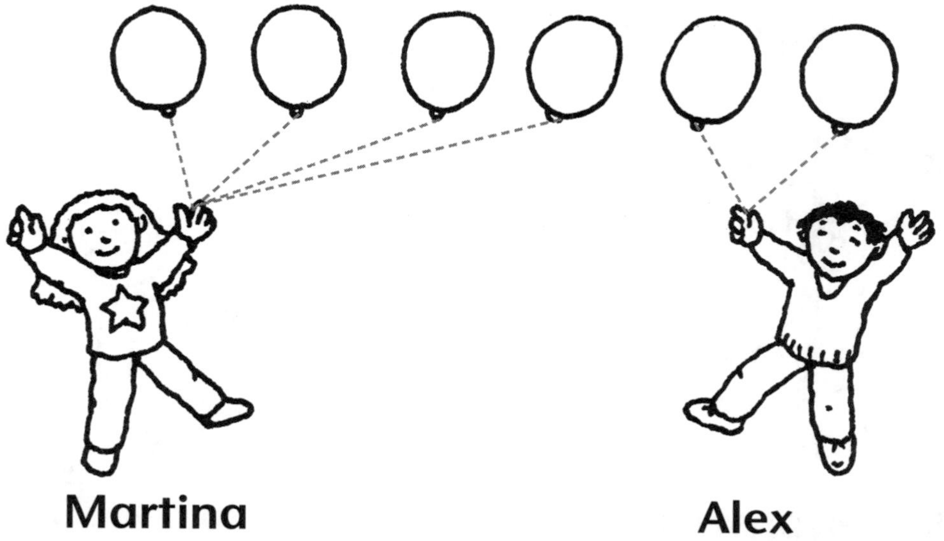

Martina **Alex**

1 Understand

2 Decide

3 Solve

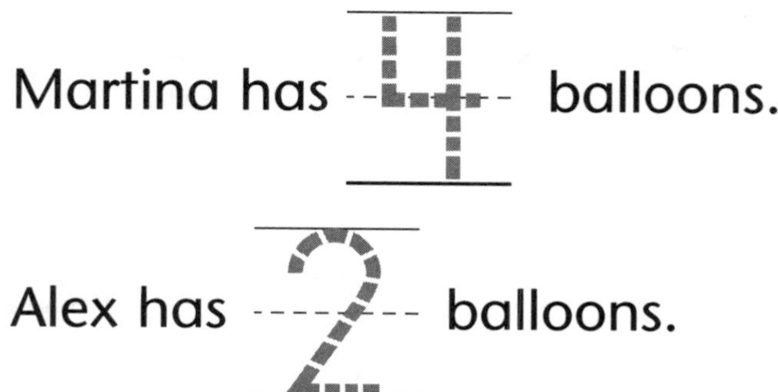

Martina has 4 balloons.

Alex has 2 balloons.

4 Look back

Draw to solve.

1. Rita has fewer balloons than Max.

   How many balloons could Rita have? ______

Is there another answer?
Try it again.

2. Rita has fewer balloons than Max.

   How many balloons could Rita have? ______

STANDARD

Name ______________________________

zero

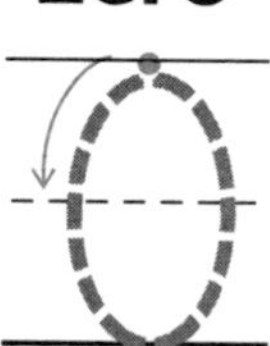

one

two

three

Write the number.

1. 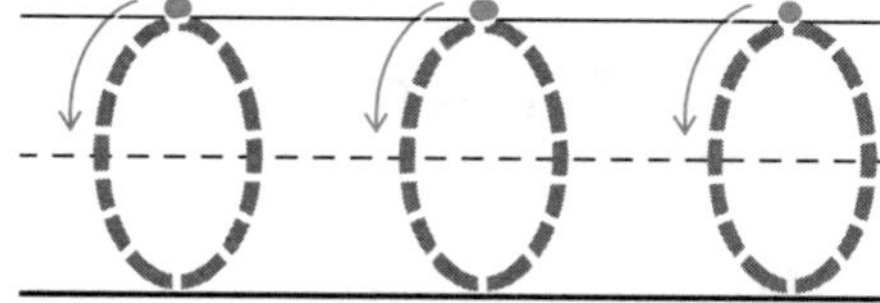

2. 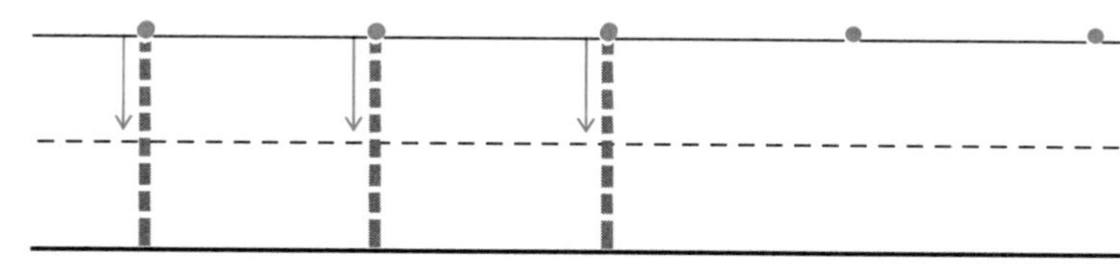

3. 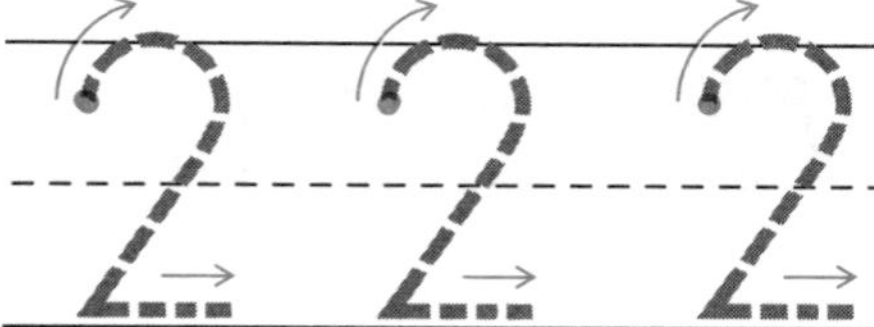

4. 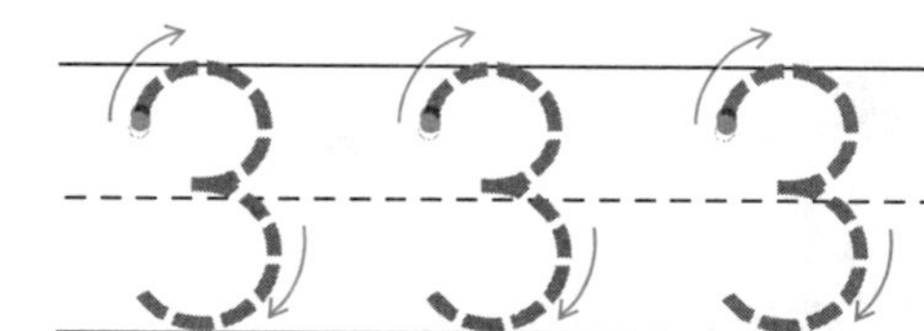

Write how many.

5.

2

6.

Draw the crayons.

7.

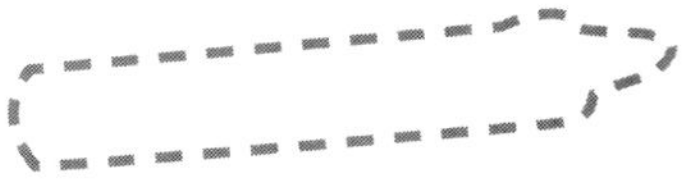

I one

8.

3 three

Problem Solving
Reasoning

Draw things that come in twos.

9.

★ Test Prep

Which group has this number of flags?
Mark the space under your answer.

10

3

○

○

○

STANDARD

Name ________________________________

four

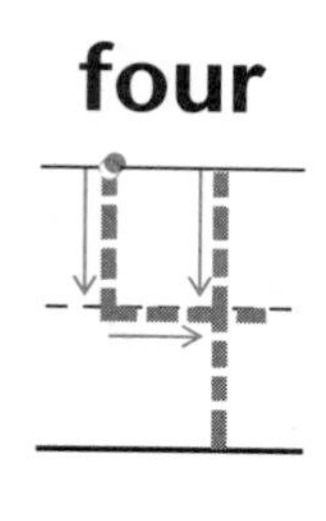

five

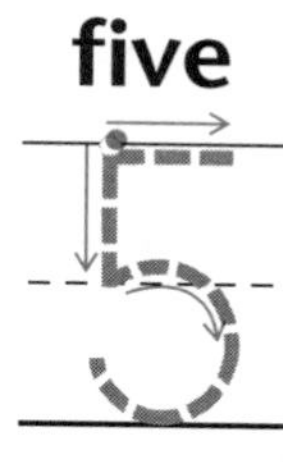

six

Write the number.

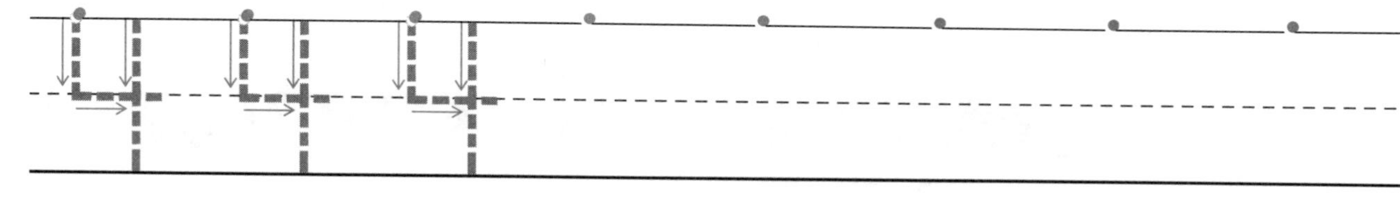

2.

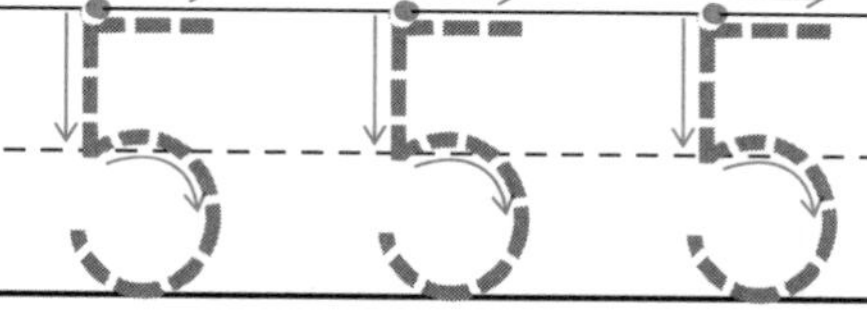

3.

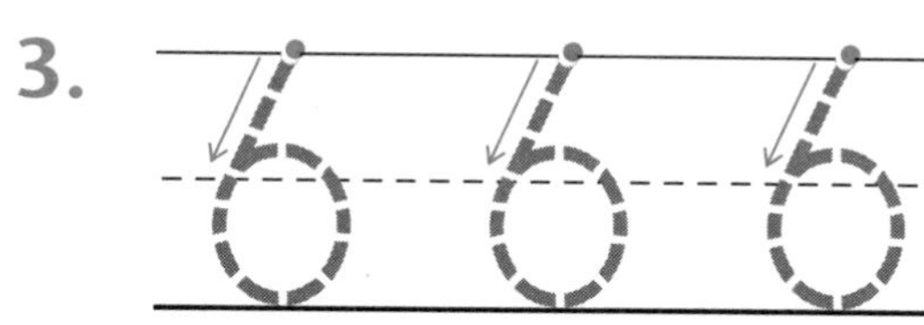

Write how many.

4.

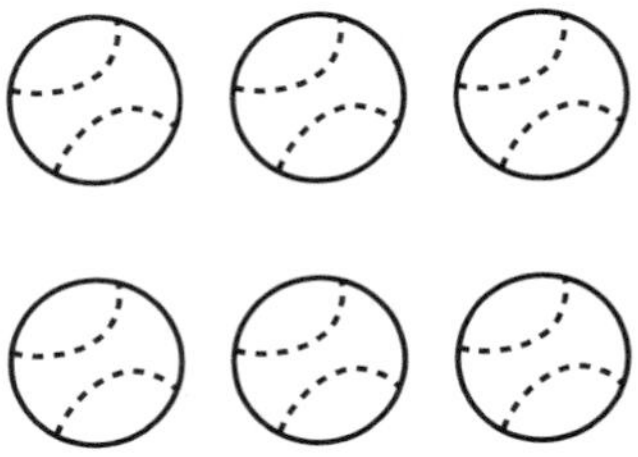

______

5.

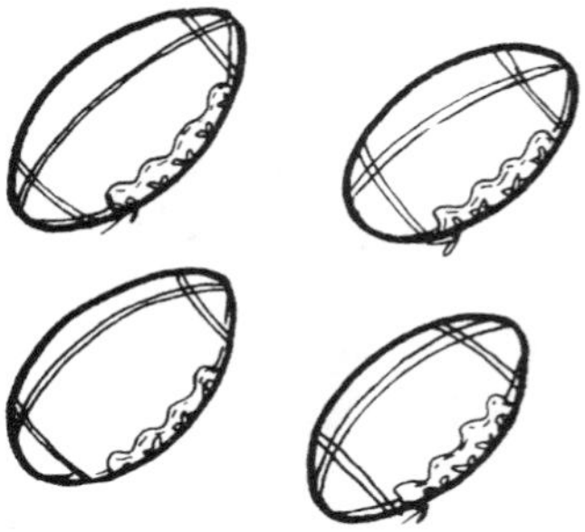

______

Problem Solving
Reasoning

Write the number. Draw that number of balls. Ring the group that has fewer.

6.

______ **five**

______ **four**

Quick Check

Ring 1 more than □ □ □.

1.

Write how many.

2.

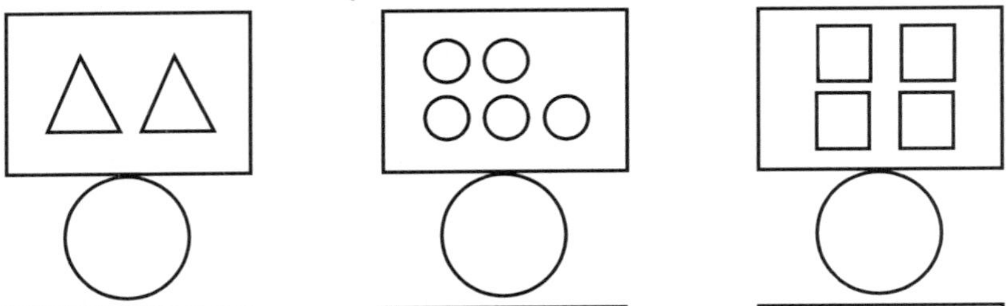

3.

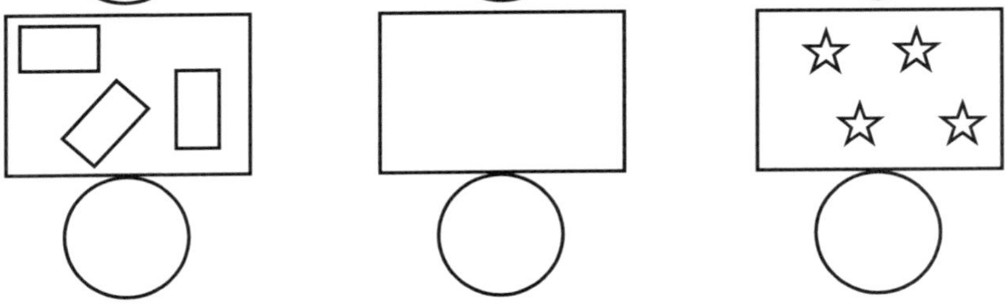

Name ____________________

seven

7

eight

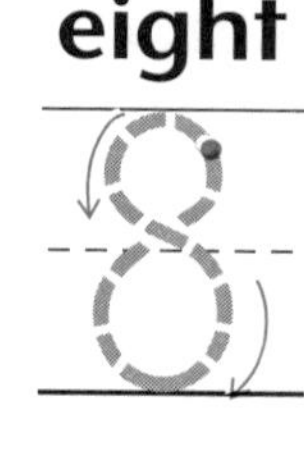

Write the number.

1. 7 7 7

2. 8 8 8

Write how many.

3.

4.

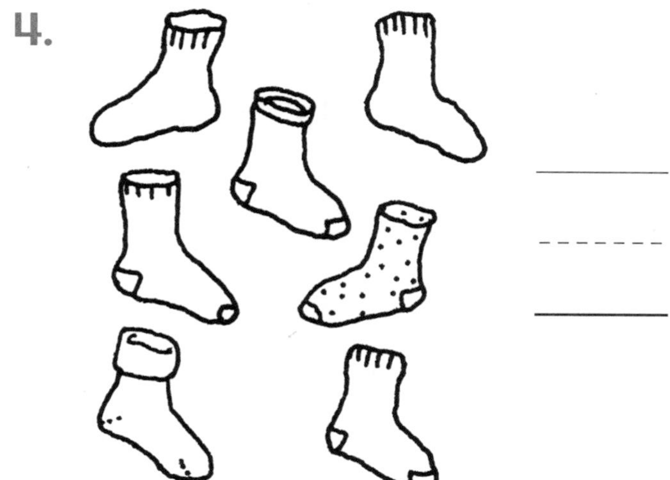

Write how many.

5.

6.

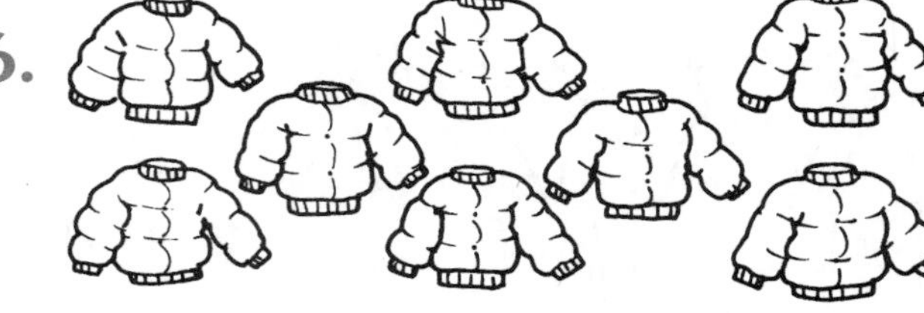

Problem Solving Reasoning

Write the number. Draw that number of hats. Ring the group that has more.

7.

seven	eight

★ Test Prep

Which group has this number of hats?
Mark the space under your answer.

8

7

STANDARD

Name ______________________________

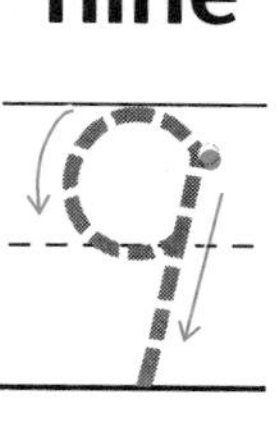

nine

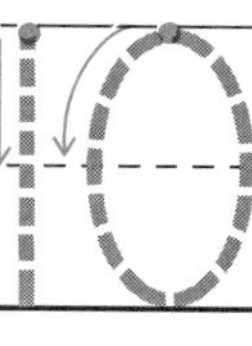

ten

Write the number.

1. 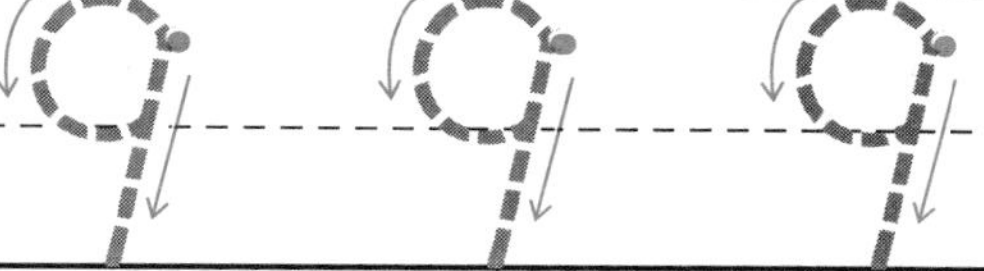

2. 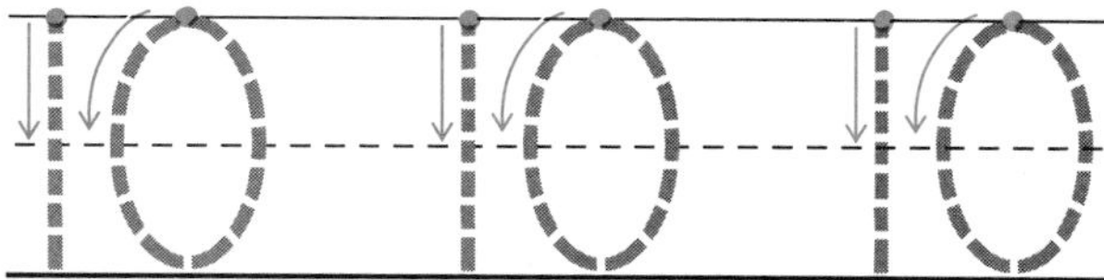

Write how many.

3. 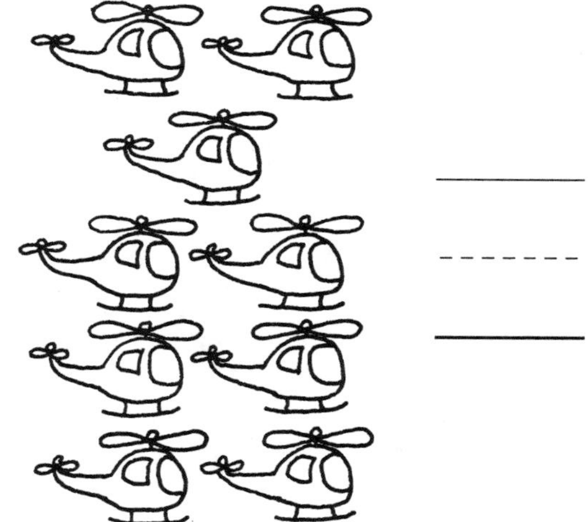

4. 

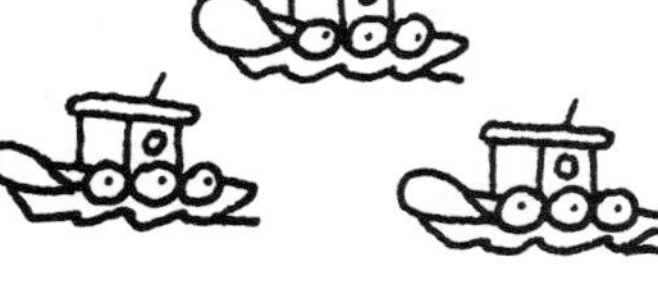

Write how many.

5.

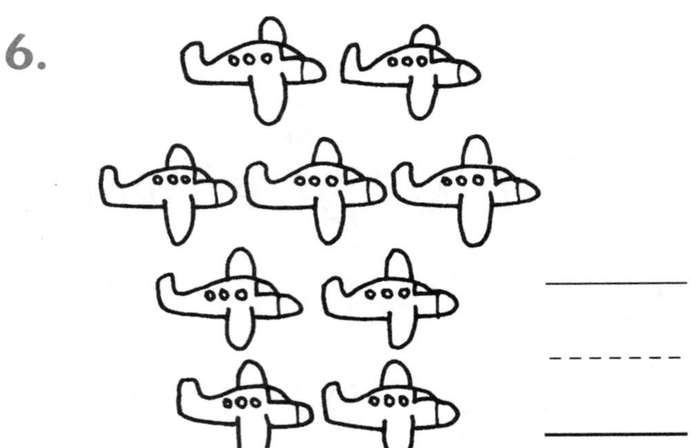

6.

Problem Solving
Reasoning

Write the number.
Draw that number of cars.

7.

nine

What number is one more than 9?

★ Test Prep

Which group has this number of boats?
Mark the space under your answer.

8

10

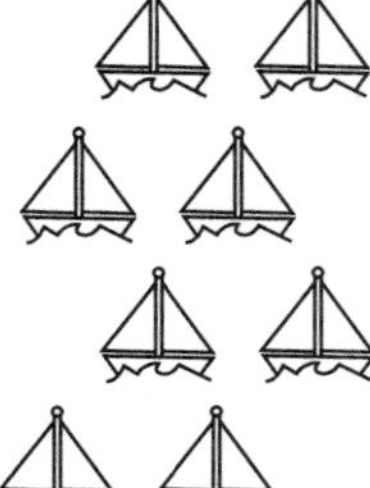

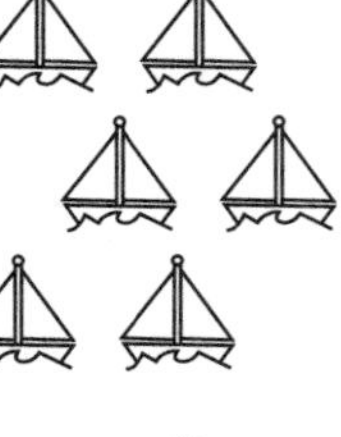

Name ______________________

Draw balls to match the number.

1. 5

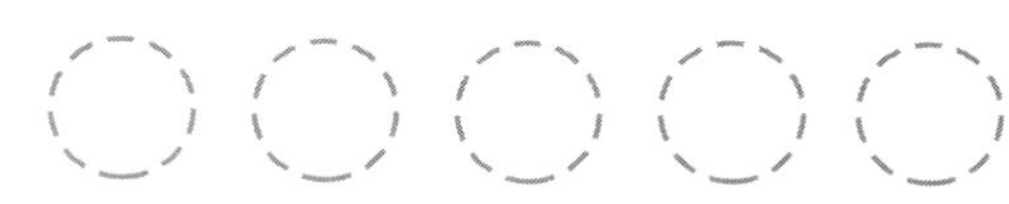

2. 8

3. 10

4. 7

5. 4

6. 9

7. 6

Draw and write what will most likely come next.

8. 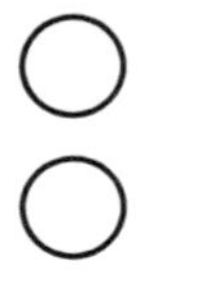 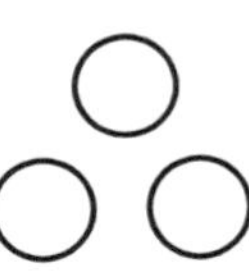  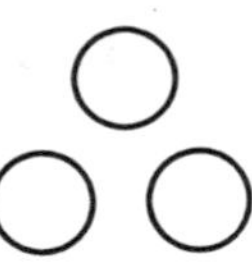  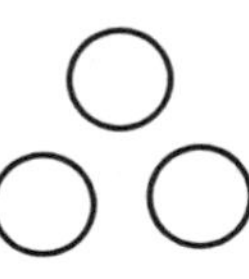

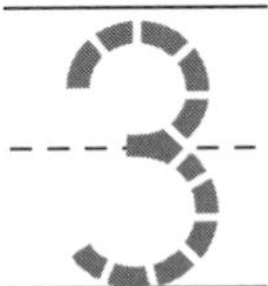  

2 3 2 3 2 3 ____

9. Show the pattern another way.

Problem Solving Reasoning Look at the picture.

10. How many ? ____

11. How many ? ____

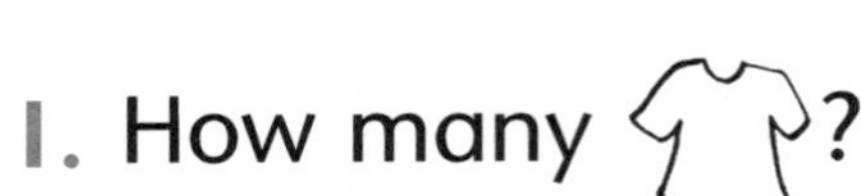

✓ Quick Check

Write how many.

1. 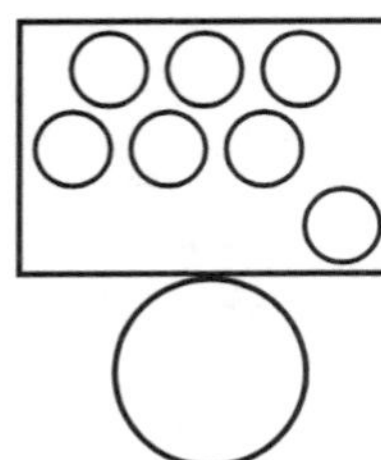 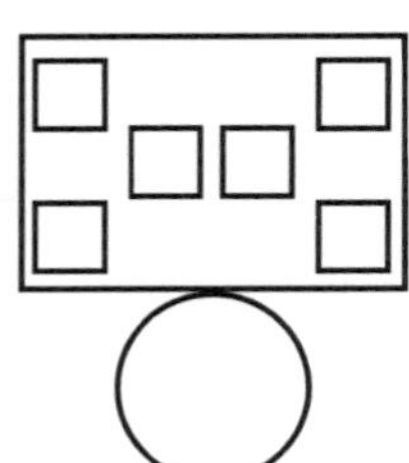 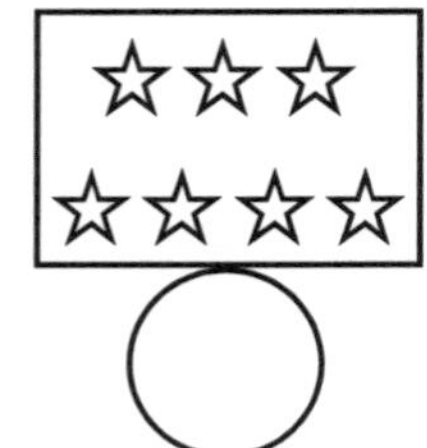

Name ______________________________

I penny

I cent

I¢

I penny

I cent

I¢

Ring the pennies you need.

I.

2.

3.

Write the amount.

4. 

4 ¢

5.     

____ ¢

Problem Solving Reasoning

Write the amount.
Ring the group that shows more.

6.  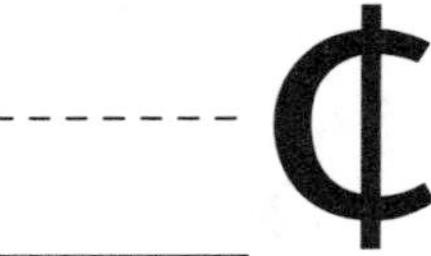

____ ¢

____ ¢

★ Test Prep

What is the amount?

Mark the space under your answer.

7     

3¢	5¢	4¢
○	○	○

Name ______________________________

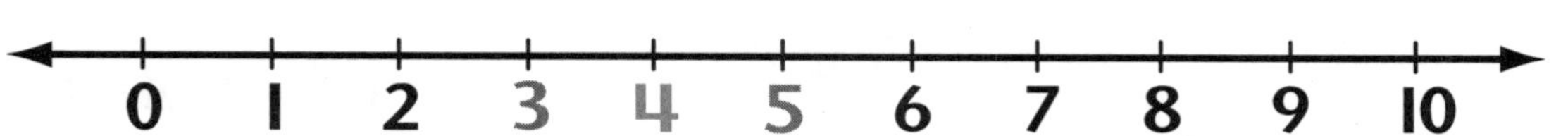

The number **4** is **just after 3**.

The number **4** is **just before 5**.

The number **4** is **between 3** and **5**.

Write the number.

1. Which number is between **4** and **6**? [5]

2. Which number is between **0** and **2**? [ ]

3. Which number comes just after **8**? [ ]

4. Which number comes just after **6**? [ ]

5. Which number comes just before **1**? [ ]

6. Which number comes just before **10**? [ ]

Write the missing numbers.

7. Between

0, [1], 2

4, [ ], 6

8. Just before

[1], 2, 3

[ ], 8, 9

9. Just before and just after

[2], 3, [4]

[ ], 9, [ ]

Write the missing numbers.

10.

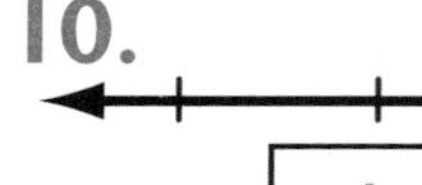

0 [1] 2 3 [4] [5]

11.

3 [ ] [ ] [ ] 7

12.

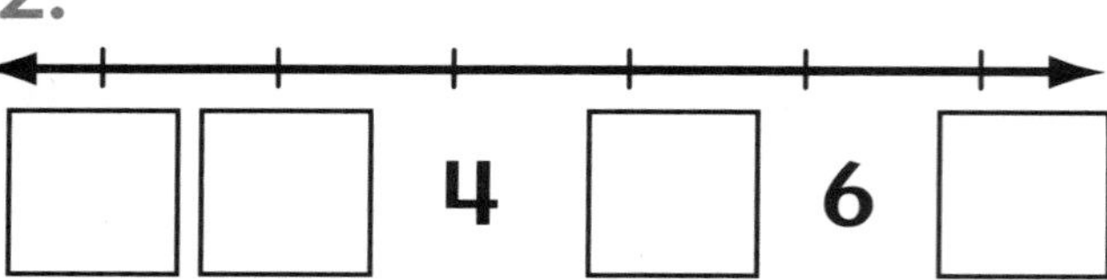

[ ] [ ] 4 [ ] 6 [ ]

13.

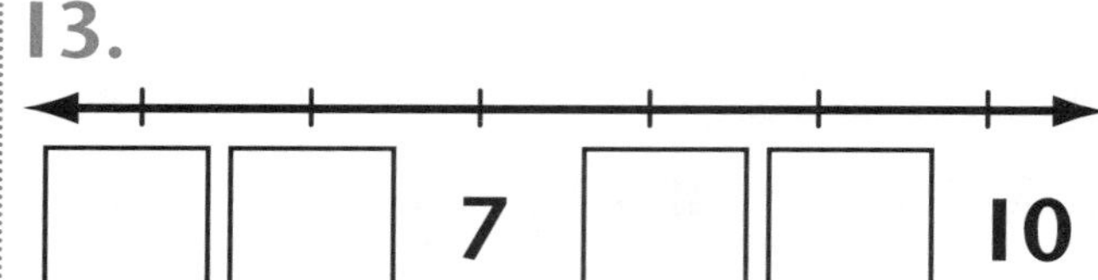

[ ] [ ] 7 [ ] [ ] 10

Problem Solving Reasoning

Write the missing numbers. Do you see a pattern? Explain.

14. 8, 7, 6, , [ ], , [ ]

★ Test Prep

Which number comes just after the number shown? Mark the space under your answer.

3

2	4	5
○	○	○

Name ______________________________

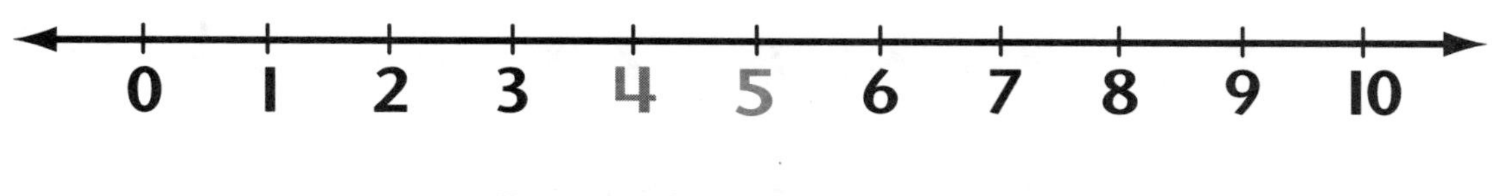

5 is greater than 4.

Ring the greater number.

1.	2	5	2.	3	1	3.	9	7
4.	2	3	5.	1	2	6.	8	10
7.	7	4	8.	2	0	9.	4	0
10.	6	1	11.	6	7	12.	4	2
13.	6	4	14.	3	6	15.	7	5
16.	8	9	17.	10	7	18.	3	5

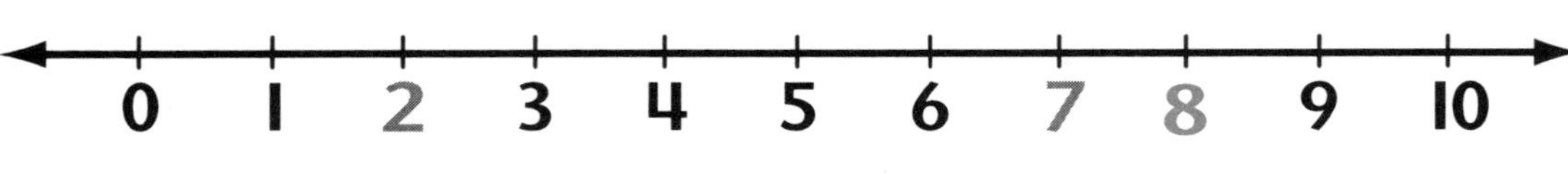

7 (8) 2

8 is the **greatest**.

Ring the greatest number.

19. 5 6 (9)

20. 8 7 2

21. 3 2 0

22. 4 6 3

Problem Solving Reasoning

Write 3 numbers that are greater than 4.

23. ☐, ☐, ☐

Quick Check

Write the value.

1.        ☐

Write the missing numbers.

2. 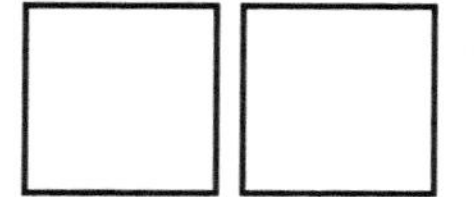  

☐ ☐ 3 ☐ 5 ☐

Ring the greatest number.

3. 5 2 4

Name ______________________________

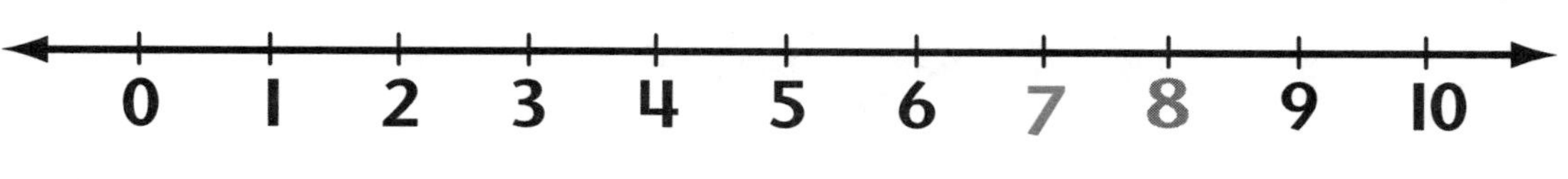

7 is less than 8.

Ring the number that is less.

1. 2 3	2. 0 5	3. 7 5
4. 9 10	5. 3 1	6. 6 8
7. 6 3	8. 10 8	9. 3 5
10. 6 7	11. 0 4	12. 6 4
13. 4 7	14. 8 7	15. 4 1
16. 9 7	17. 5 4	18. 1 2

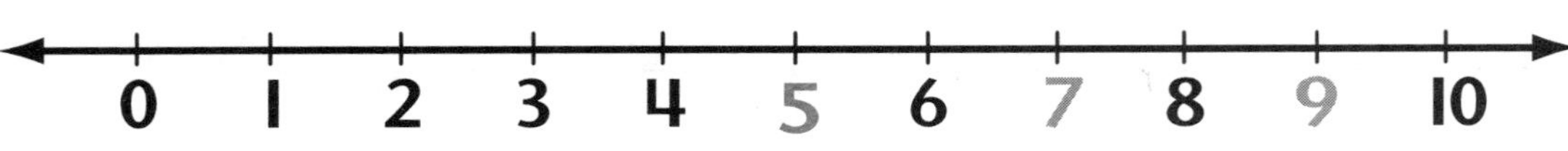

5 9 7

5 is the **least**.

Ring the number that is least.

19.  6 7 9

20. 0 3 1

21. 9 7 4

22. 6 3 10

23. 2 3 4

24. 6 1 5

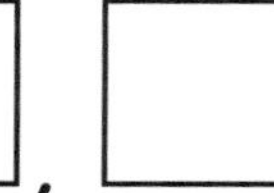

Write 3 numbers that are less than 7.

25. ☐, ☐, ☐

★ Test Prep

Which number is less than the number shown?
Mark the space under your answer.

8	9	8	7
	○	○	○

Name ______________________________

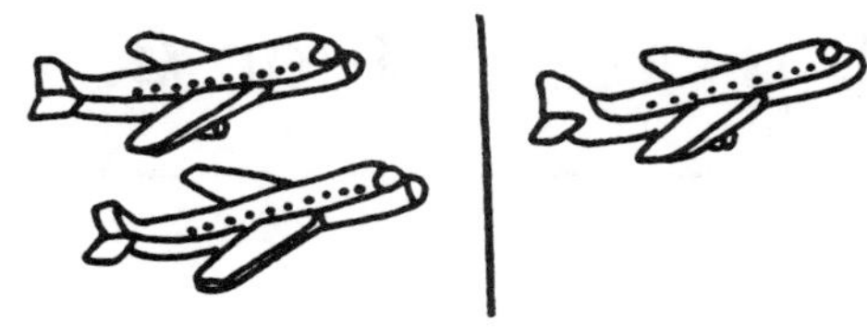

2 is greater than **1**.

2 > 1

4 is less than **5**.

4 < 5

Write < or > in the 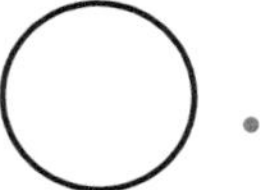 **.**

1.

3 (<) **4**

2.

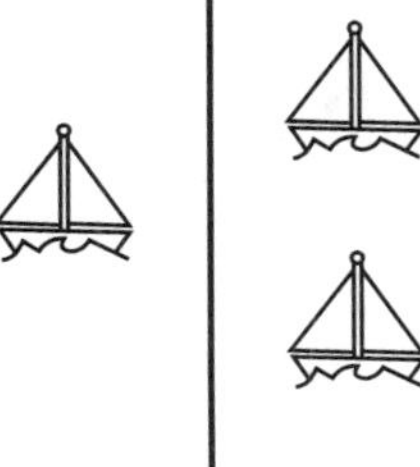

1 ( ) **2**

3.

5 ( ) **8**

4.

7 ( ) **1**

5.

4 ( ) **7**

6.

6 ( ) **7**

7.

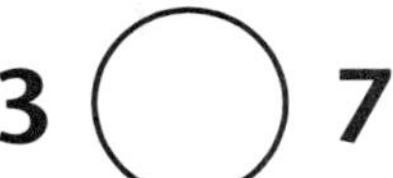

3 ( ) **7**

8.

2 ( ) **0**

9.

5 ( ) **6**

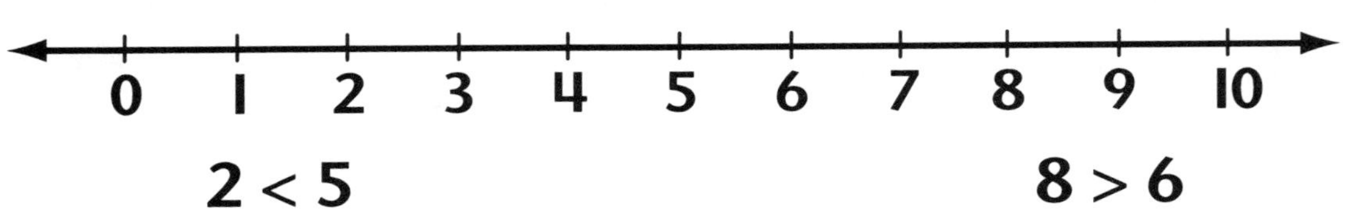

$2 < 5$

2 is less than **5**.

$8 > 6$

8 is greater than **6**.

Write $<$ or $>$ in the ◯ .

10.

11.

12.

13.

14.

15.

Problem Solving
Reasoning

16. How does the number line help you compare the numbers?

____

____

★ Test Prep

Which is true?

Mark the space under your answer.

$10 < 7$	$8 > 6$	$3 > 6$
○	○	○

STANDARD

Name ______________________________

$4 < 5$

4 is less than **5.**

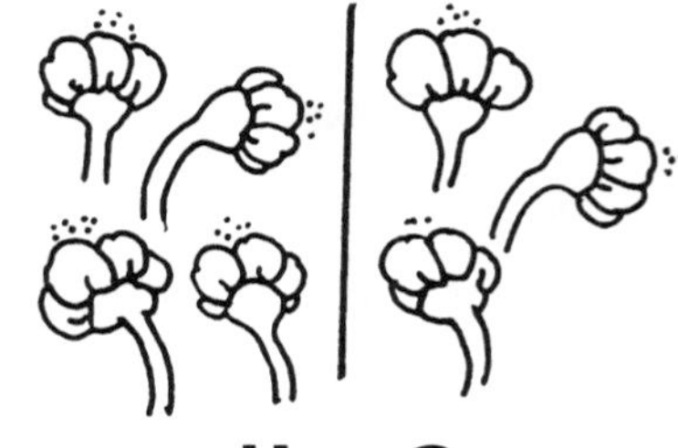

$4 > 3$

4 is greater than **3.**

$4 = 4$

4 is equal to **4.**

Write <, >, or = in the  .

1. 4  5	2. 2 ○ 3	3. 6 ○ 6
4. 5 ○ 2	5. 6 ○ 8	6. 8 ○ 3
7. 5 ○ 5	8. 1 ○ 2	9. 3 ○ 4
10. 6 ○ 4	11. 5 ○ 1	12. 8 ○ 8
13. 2 ○ 7	14. 3 ○ 2	15. 6 ○ 1

Write <, >, or = in the ◯ .

16. 9 (>) 8

17. 6 ◯ 6

18. 7 ◯ 9

19. 8 ◯ 8

20. 3 ◯ 4

21. 6 ◯ 10

Problem Solving
Reasoning

Write the number.

22. □ > 2

23. □ = 6

24. □ < 8

✔ Quick Check

Ring the number that is less.

1. **10** **8**

2. **6** **3**

Ring the number that is least.

3. **4** **2** **7**

Write <, >, or = in the ◯ .

4. 1 ◯ 1

5. 7 ◯ 6

6. 3 ◯ 9

7. 2 ◯ 4

Name ______________________________

Tally marks can help you count.

1	2	3	4	5
one	two	three	four	five
|	||	|||	||||	~~||||~~

6	7	8	9	10
six	seven	eight	nine	ten
~~||||~~ |	~~||||~~ ||	~~||||~~ |||	~~||||~~ ||||	~~||||~~ ~~||||~~

Toss a penny 10 times.
Use tally marks to show your results.
Write the totals.

1.

	Tally	Total
Heads		
Tails		

Sergio tosses a coin 10 times.
These are his results.

	Tally	Total
Heads		
Tails		

Problem Solving
Reasoning

Use the chart.

2. Complete the chart.

3. How many times did Sergio toss heads? ☐

4. How many times did Sergio toss tails? ☐

5. Did Sergio toss more heads or tails? ____________

★ Test Prep

Which set of tally marks means 4?
Mark the space under your answer.

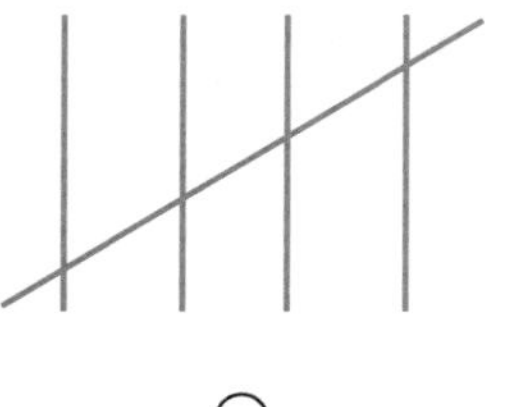

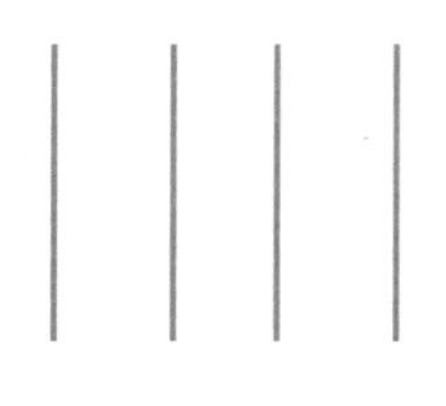

○ ○ ○

Name ______________________________

Spill 5 pennies out of a cup.
Sort them by heads and tails.
Place the pennies on the graph.
Trace to show heads and tails.

1.

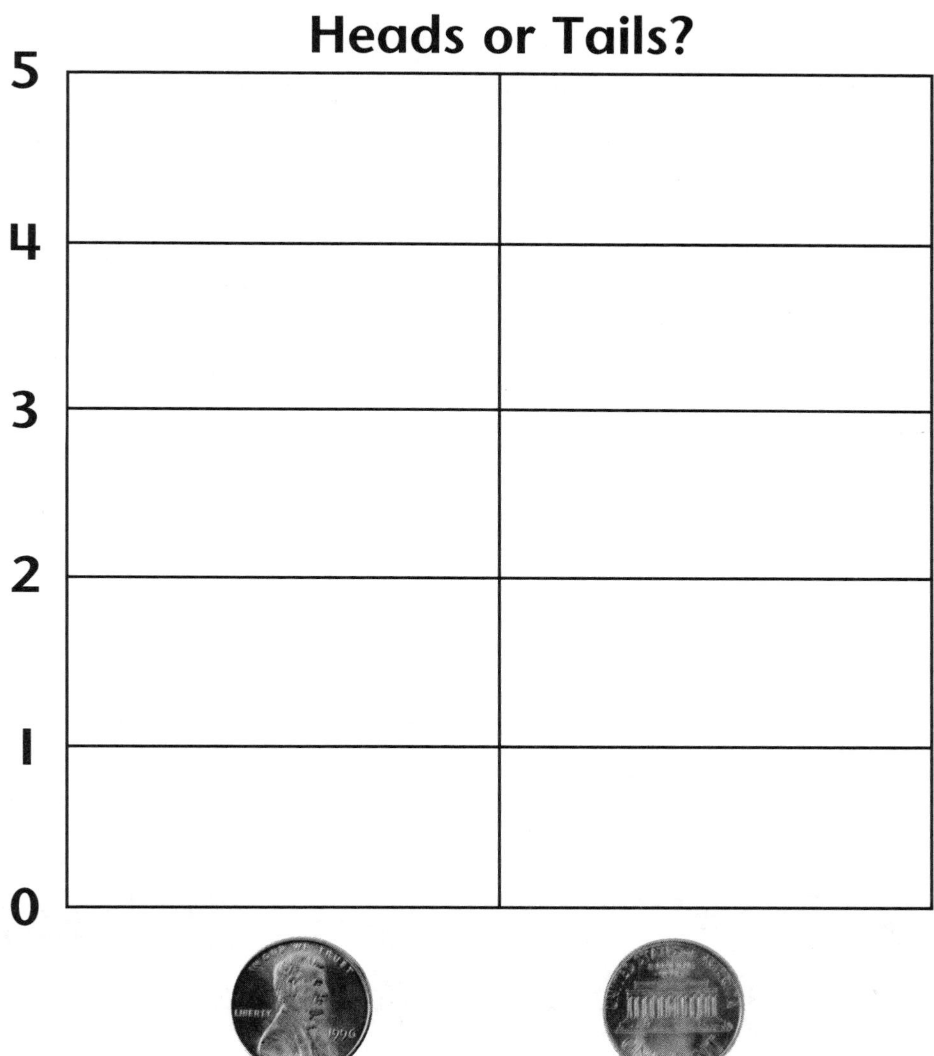

Problem Solving
Reasoning

2. Which did you get more often, heads or tails? ____________

Write the number.

3.

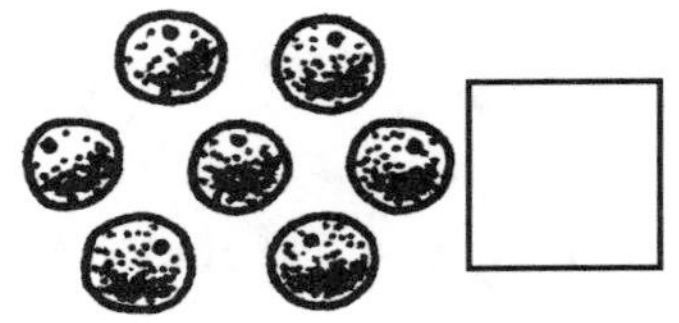

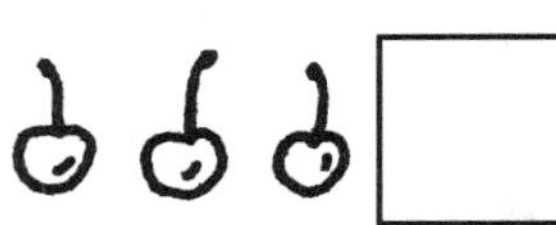

Fill in the graph.

4.

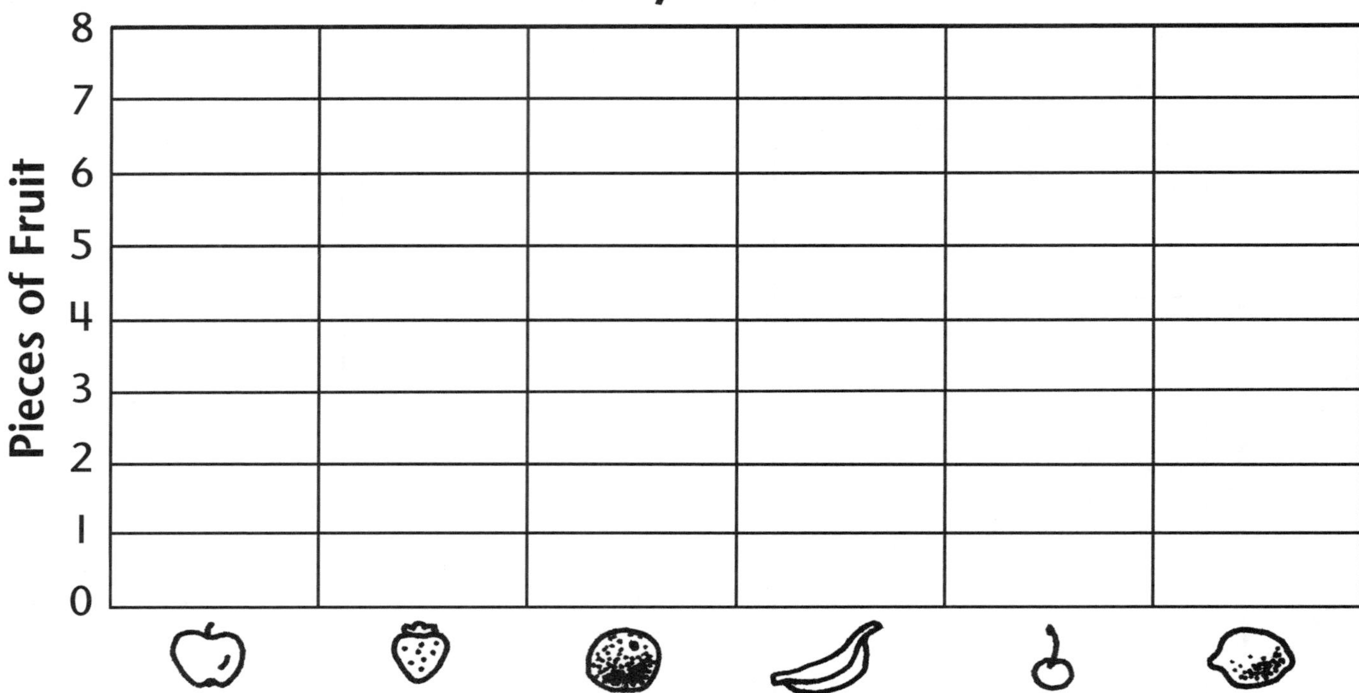

★ Test Prep

How many bananas? Mark the space under your answer.

How many?

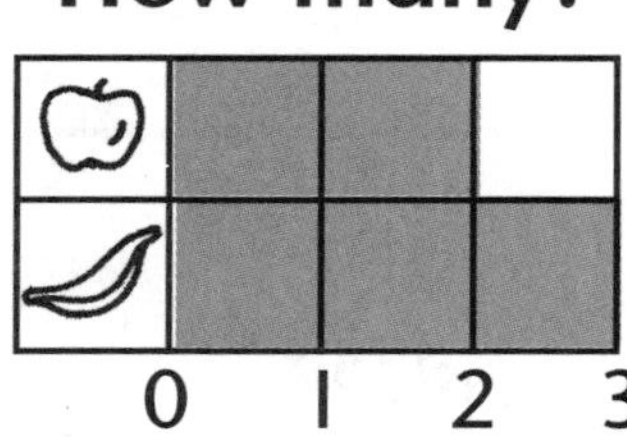

1	2	3
○	○	○

Name ______________________

Each child voted for an animal.

Problem Solving Plan			
1. Understand	2. Decide	3. Solve	4. Look back

(stick figure) = 1 vote

Favorite Class Animals

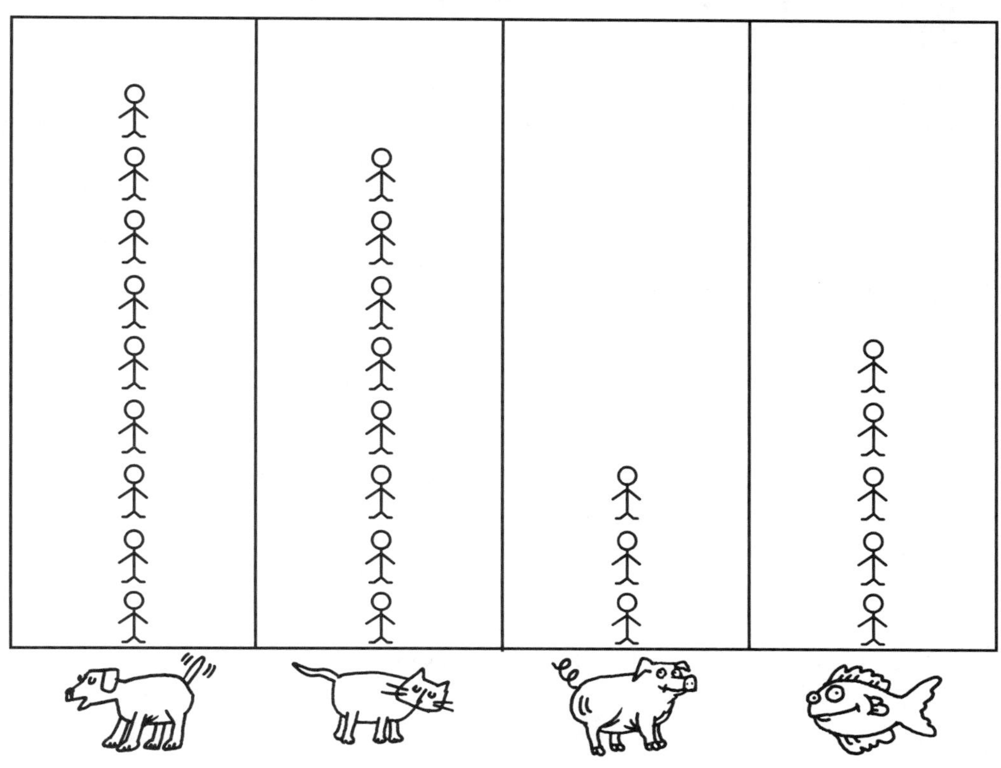

Use the graph to answer the questions.

Think How many (stick figure) do I see?

1. How many children voted for  ? 8

2. How many children voted for  ?

3. How many children voted for  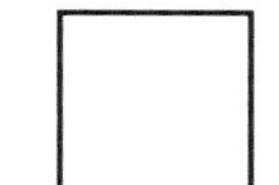 ?

Ring the animal that has the greatest number of votes.

4.    

Each child voted for a favorite sport.

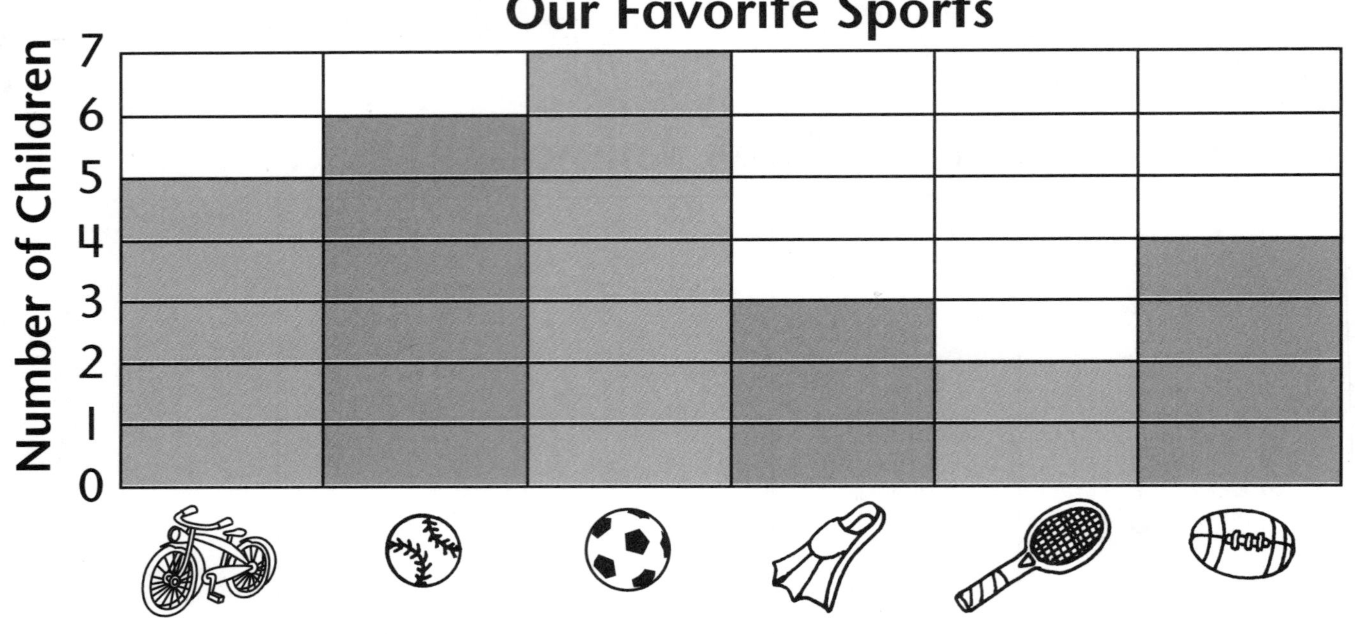

Use the graph to answer the questions.

Think Where is the object pictured?
At what number does the bar stop?

5. How many children like  ? 2

6. How many children like  ?

7. How many children like  ? 

Extend Your Thinking Ring your answer.

8. Do more children like  or ?  

9. Which sport got the least number of votes?

Name ______________________________

Match the objects.
Ring the group that has more.

1\.

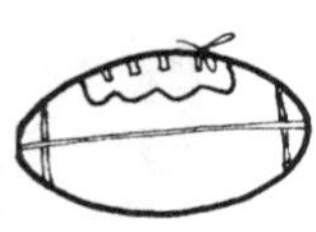

2\.

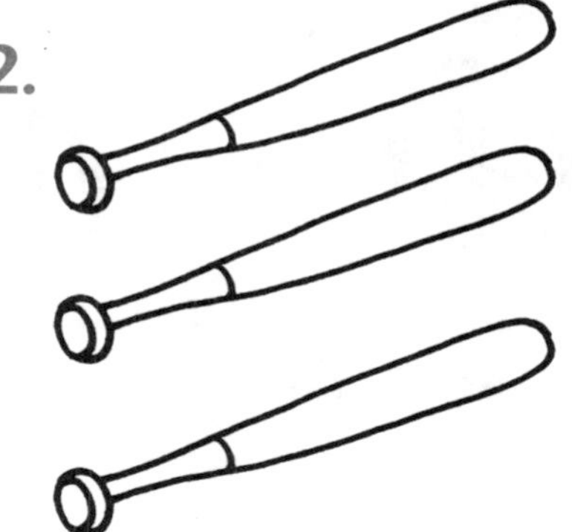

Match the objects.
Ring the group that has fewer.

3\.

4\.

Write how many.

5\.

______

6\.

______

Write the amount.

7.

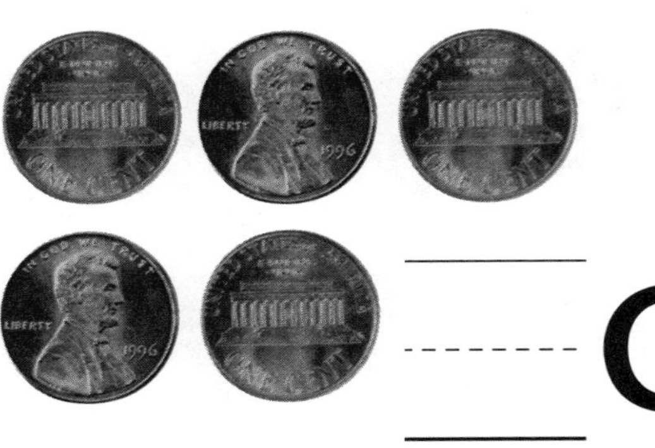

______ ¢

8.

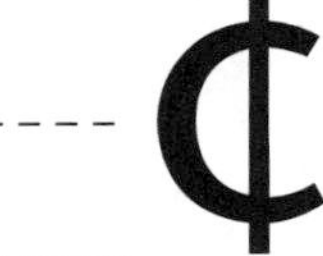

______ ¢

Write the missing numbers.

9.

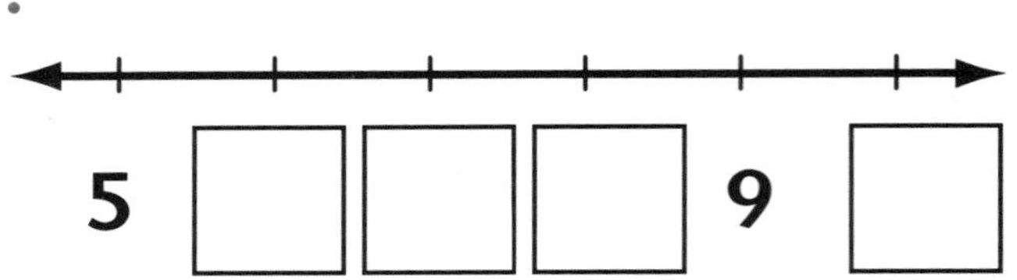

10.

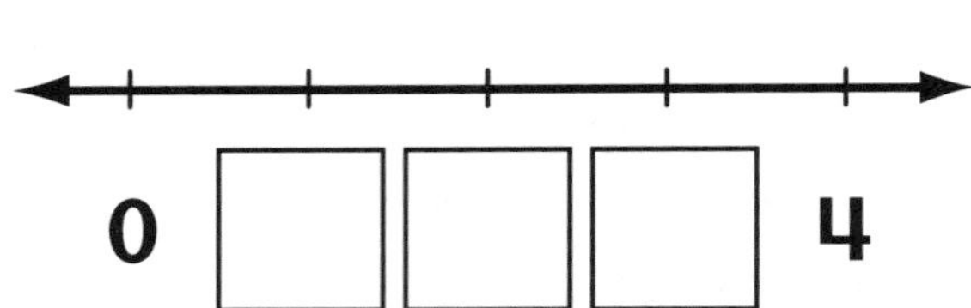

Write <, >, or = in the ◯.

11. 6  6

12. 9 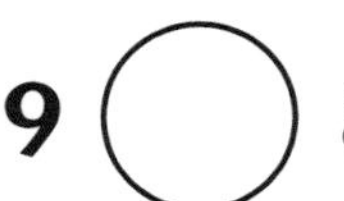 8

13. 5 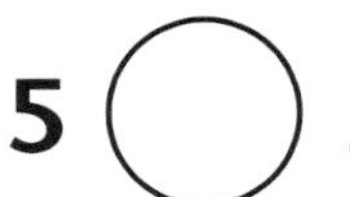 2

Problem Solving
Reasoning

Draw a picture to solve.

Maria and Patrick have **5** marbles all together.
Maria has more marbles than Patrick.
How many marbles could Maria have?

14.

Maria has ______ marbles.

Name ______________________________

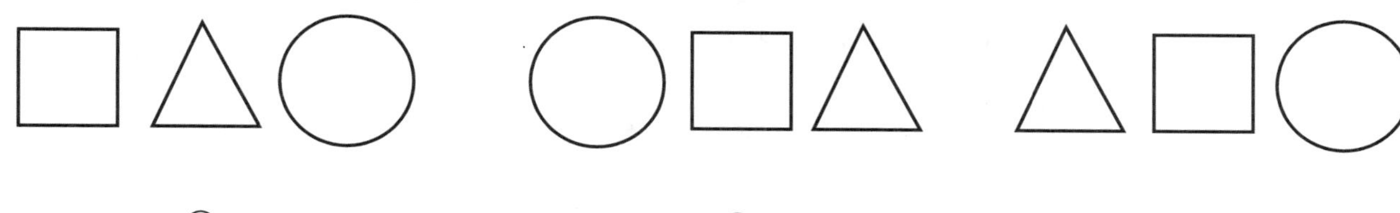

○ ○

○ ○

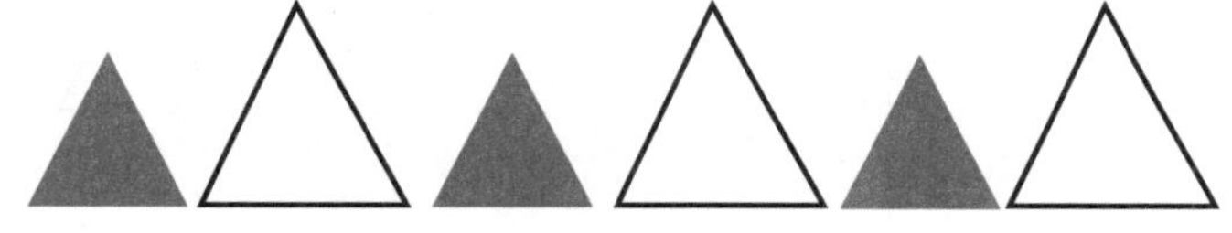

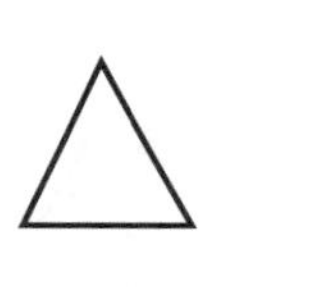

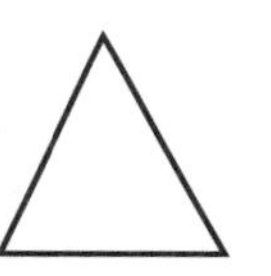

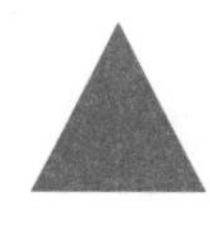

○ ○ ○

○ ○ ○

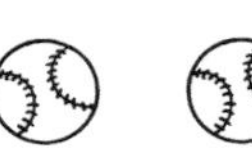

7

7 = 6 ○ 4 = 5 ○ 4 = 4 ○

UNIT 3 • TABLE OF CONTENTS

Addition Facts through 6

UNIT 3 • TABLE OF CONTENTS

We will be using this vocabulary:

addend one of the numbers added in an addition problem
sum result of an addition problem
number sentence an equation, such as $1 + 1 = 2$
order property Changing the order of the addends does not change the sum. $3 + 2 = 5$; $2 + 3 = 5$

Dear Family,

During the next few weeks our math class will be learning addition facts with sums through 6.

You can expect to see homework that provides practice with these addition facts. You may wish to keep the following sample as a guide.

Sums through 6

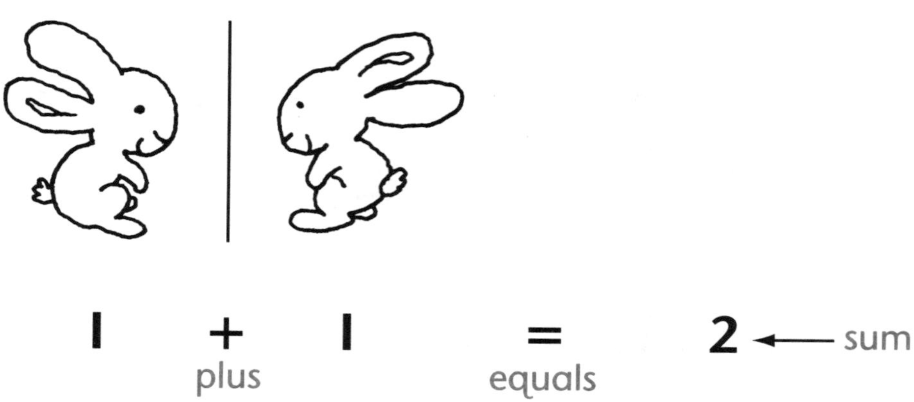

$1 + 1 = 2$ ← sum

plus equals

Knowing that addition is joining two or more groups to find the whole or the sum will help children identify addition situations in their lives.

Sincerely,

Name ______________________

Listen.
Use counters to act out the story.
Write how many.

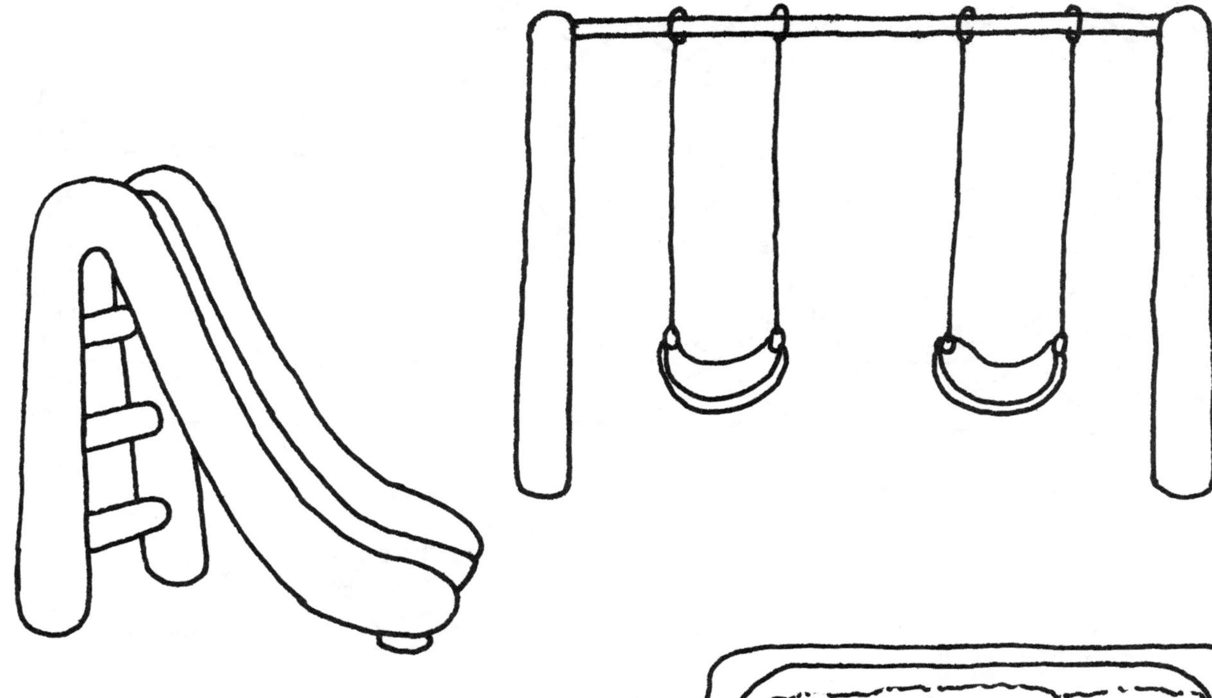

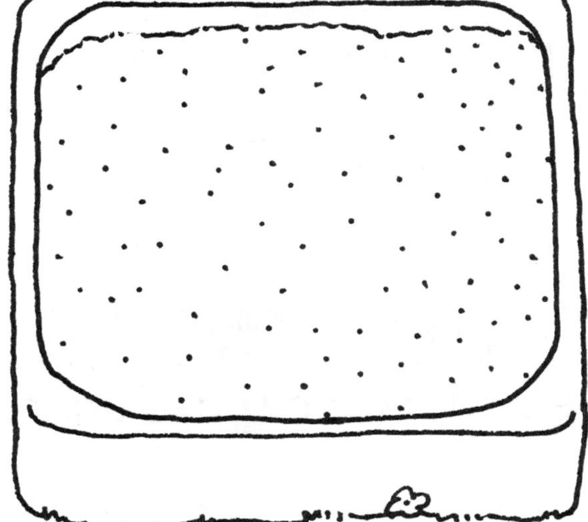

1. How many children? 4

2. How many children? ____

3. How many children? ____

Listen.
Use counters to act out the story.
Write how many.

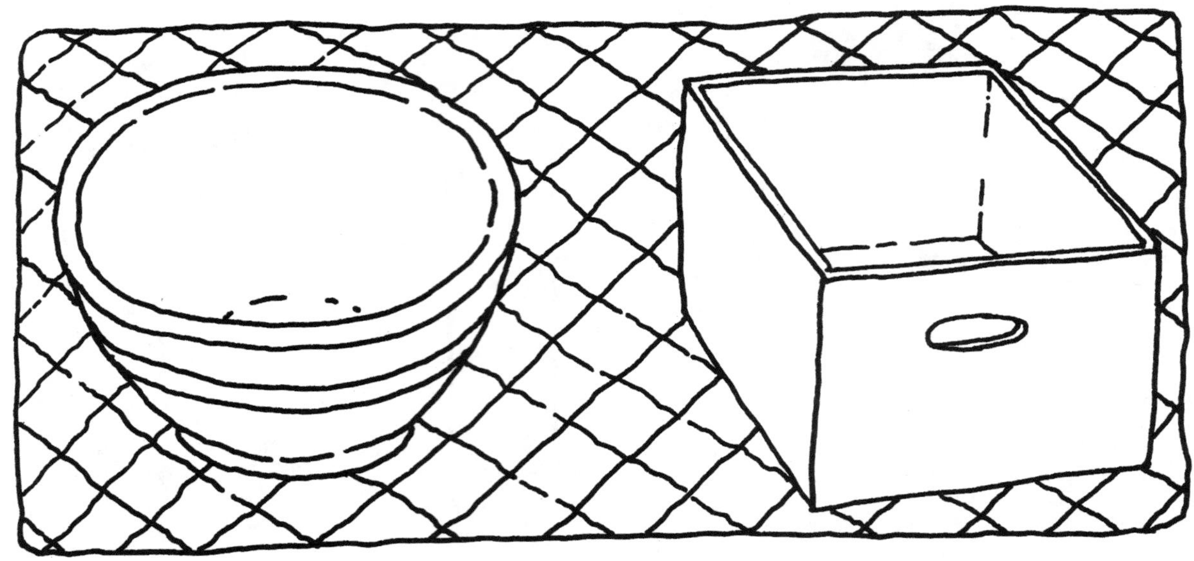

4. How many  ? _____

5. How many  ? _____

6. How many  ? _____

★ Test Prep

Listen. Mark the space under your answer.

3	5	6
○	○	○

Name ______________________________

number sentence: 1 + plus 1 = equals 2 ← sum

Complete the number sentence.

1.

1 + 1 = 2

2.

2 + 2 = ☐

3.

2 + 1 = ☐

4.

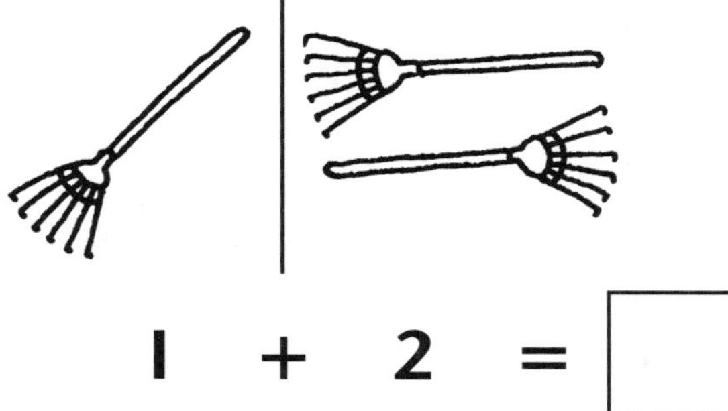

1 + 2 = ☐

5.

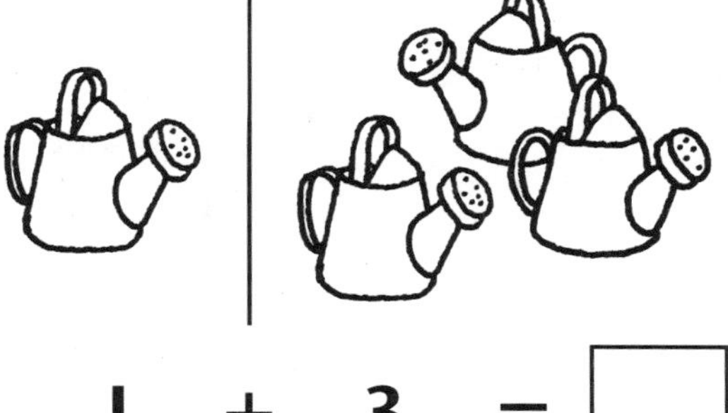

1 + 3 = ☐

6.

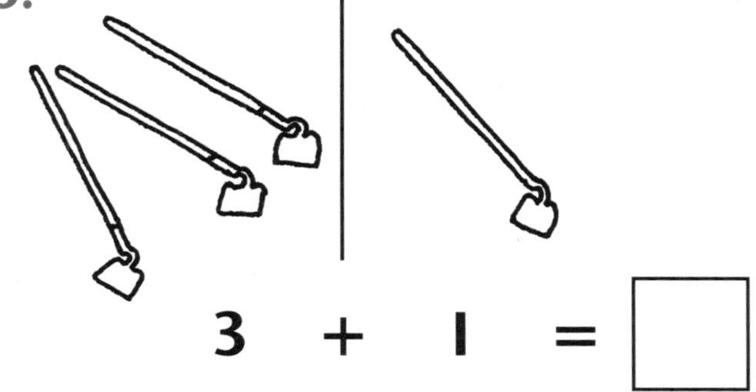

3 + 1 = ☐

Complete the number sentence.

7. 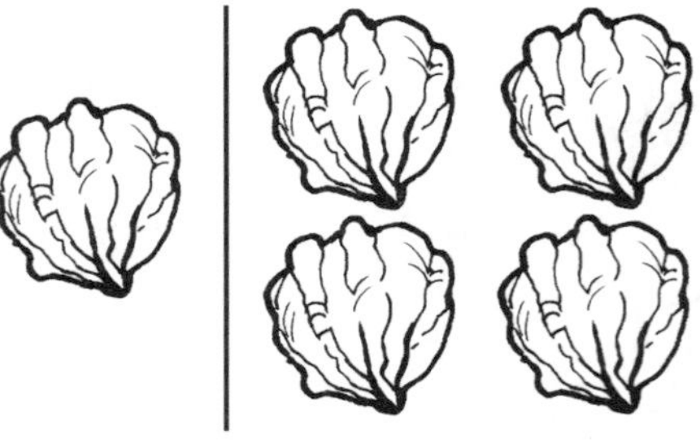

1 + 4 = 5

8. 

4 + 1 = ☐

9. 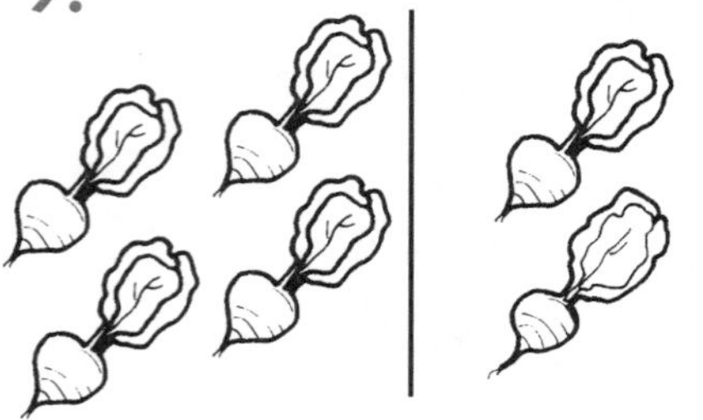

4 + 2 = ☐

10. 

2 + 4 = ☐

Problem Solving **Reasoning**

There are many ways to name 6. Show one.

11. ____ + ____ = ☐

★ Test Prep

Which number belongs in the box?

Mark the space under your answer.

12  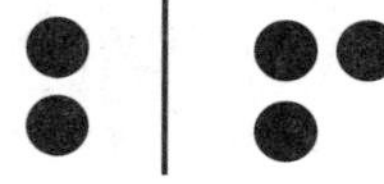

2 + 3 = ☐

5	6	7
○	○	○

STANDARD

Name ___________________________

Problem

1 Understand

2 Decide

3 Solve

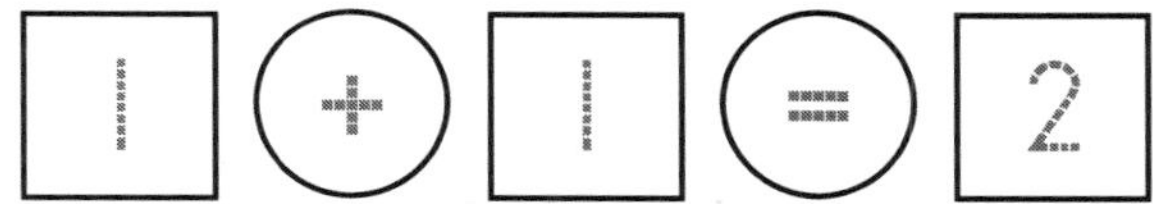

4 Look back

Write a number sentence for each picture.

1.

□ + □ = □

2.

Write a number sentence for each picture.

3.

□ ○ □ ○ □

4.

□ ○ □ ○ □

5.

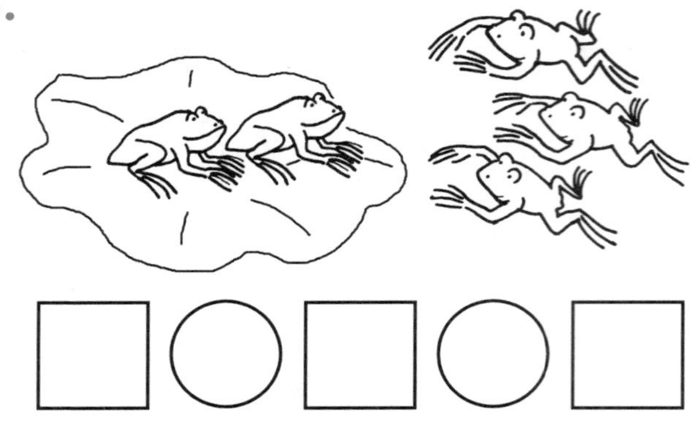

□ ○ □ ○ □

6.

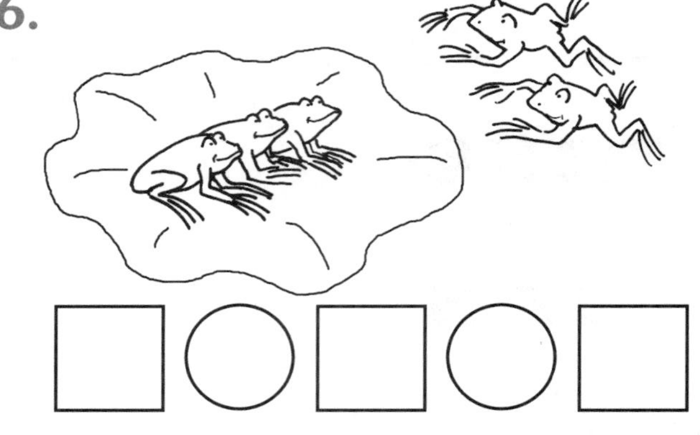

□ ○ □ ○ □

7.

□ ○ □ ○ □

8.

□ ○ □ ○ □

Draw a picture to match the number sentence.

9. **2 + 2 = 4**

Name ________________________________

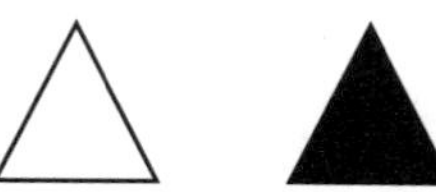

I and I more is [2]

I + I = [2]

Complete.

1.

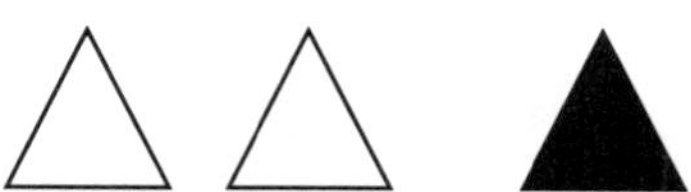

2 and I more is [ ]

[ ] + [ ] = [ ]

2.

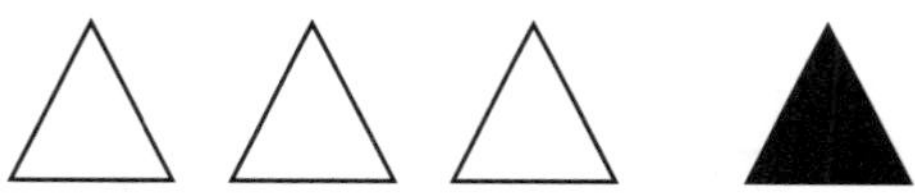

3 and I more is [ ]

[ ] + [ ] = [ ]

3.

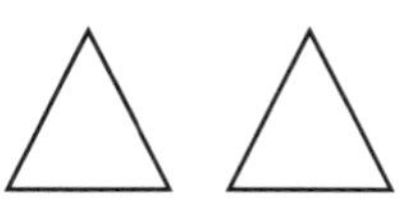

4 and I more is [ ]

[ ] + [ ] = [ ]

Complete.

4.

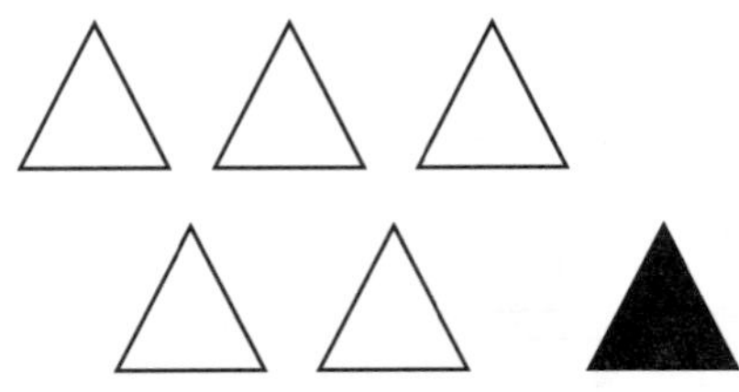

5 and 1 more is ☐

☐ + ☐ = ☐

Solve.

5. 1 + 1 = ☐

6. 2 + 1 = ☐

7. 3 + 1 = ☐

8. 4 + 1 = ☐

9. 5 + 1 = ☐

10. 0 + 1 = ☐

Problem Solving Reasoning How do you find 1 more of a number?

Quick Check

Complete.

1. 3 + 2 = ☐

2. 3 + 3 = ☐

3. 3 + 1 = ☐

4. 4 + 1 = ☐

Name ____________________

$2 + 1 = \boxed{3}$ sum

$$\begin{array}{r} 2 \\ +\ 1 \\ \hline \boxed{3} \end{array}$$
sum

Write the sum.

1.
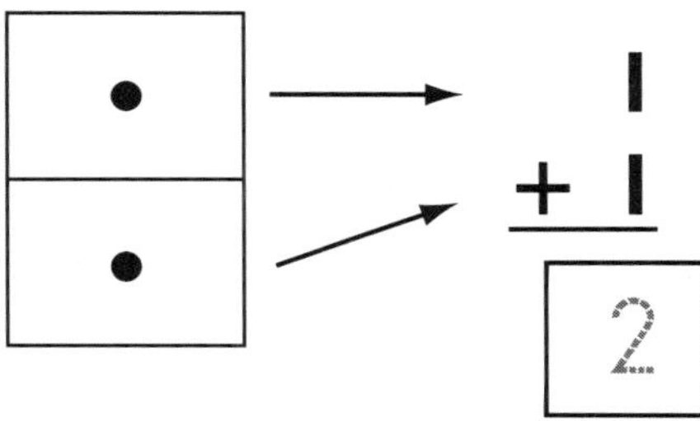

2.
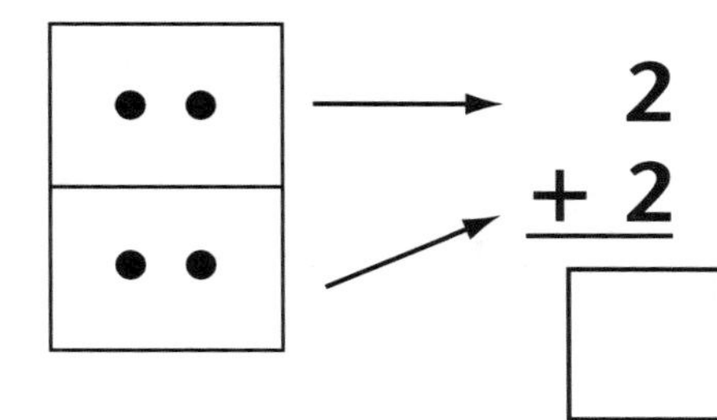

3.
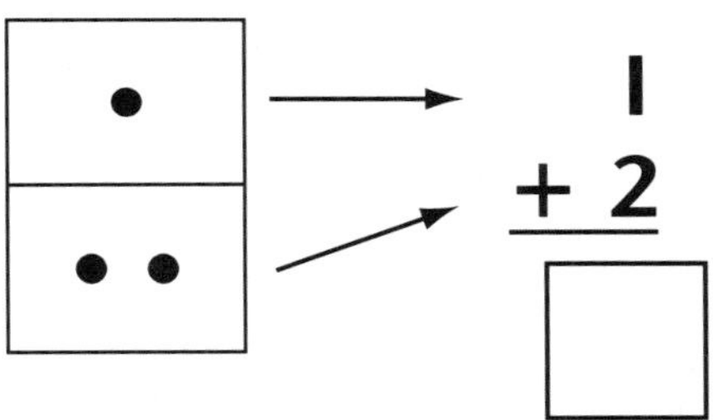

4.
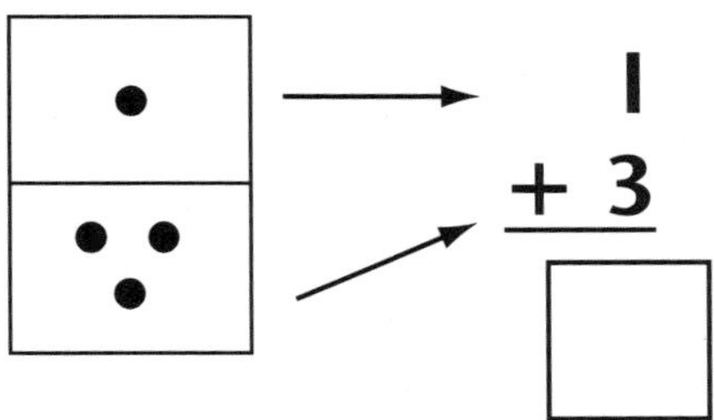

5.
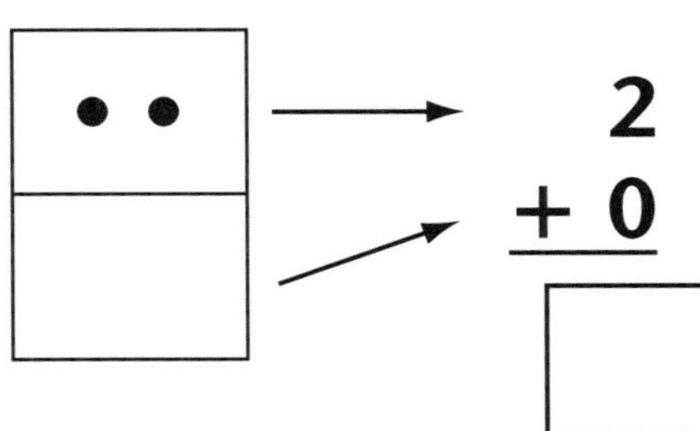

6.
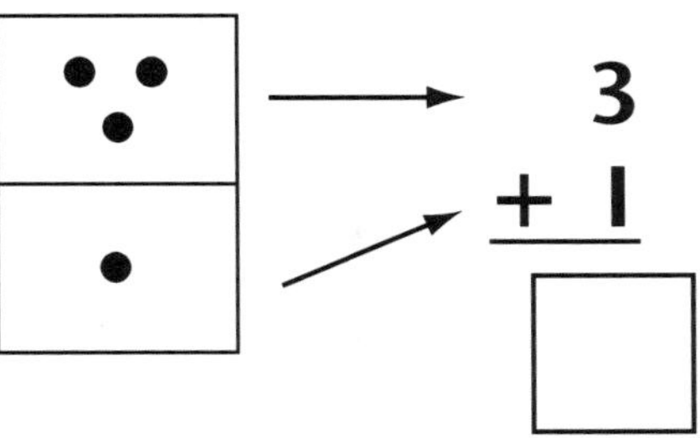

Write the sum.

7.

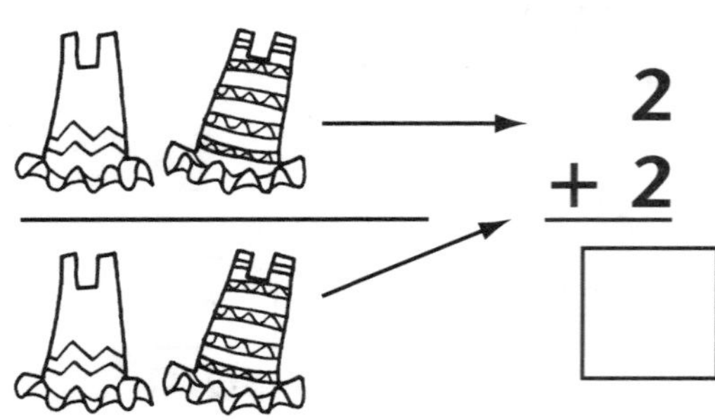

$$\begin{array}{r} 2 \\ +\ 2 \\ \hline \square \end{array}$$

8.

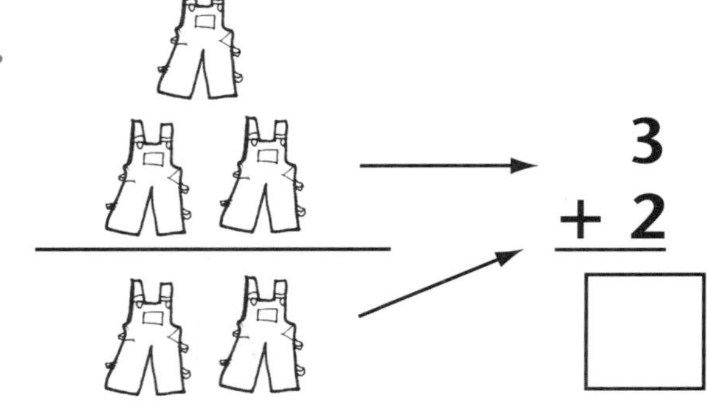

$$\begin{array}{r} 3 \\ +\ 2 \\ \hline \square \end{array}$$

9.

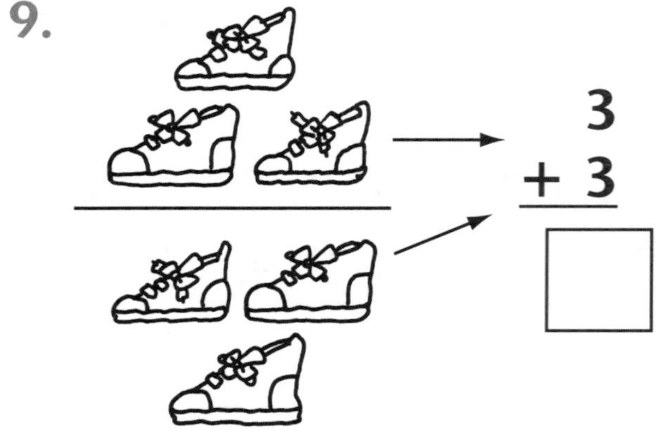

$$\begin{array}{r} 3 \\ +\ 3 \\ \hline \square \end{array}$$

10.

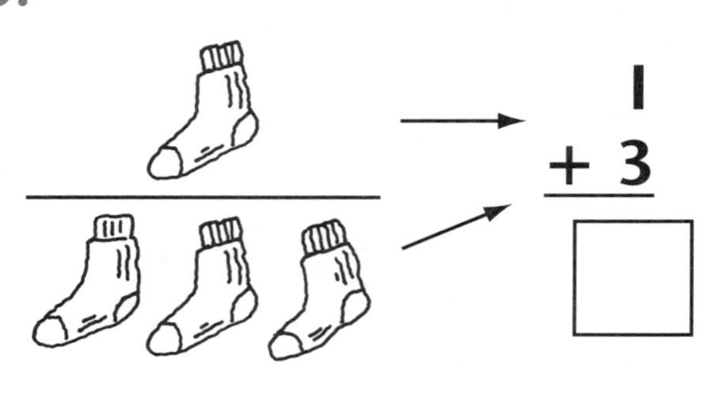

$$\begin{array}{r} 1 \\ +\ 3 \\ \hline \square \end{array}$$

Problem Solving
Reasoning

Does changing the way you write a number sentence change the sum of the numbers? Explain.

★ Test Prep

Which addition sentence shows the picture?
Mark the space under your answer.

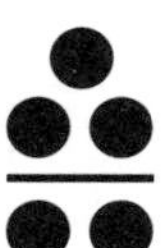

$\begin{array}{r} 3 \\ +\ 2 \\ \hline 5 \end{array}$	$\begin{array}{r} 3 \\ +\ 3 \\ \hline 6 \end{array}$	$\begin{array}{r} 2 \\ +\ 2 \\ \hline 4 \end{array}$
○	○	○

Name ______________________________

Add.

1.

2 + 0 = [2]

2.
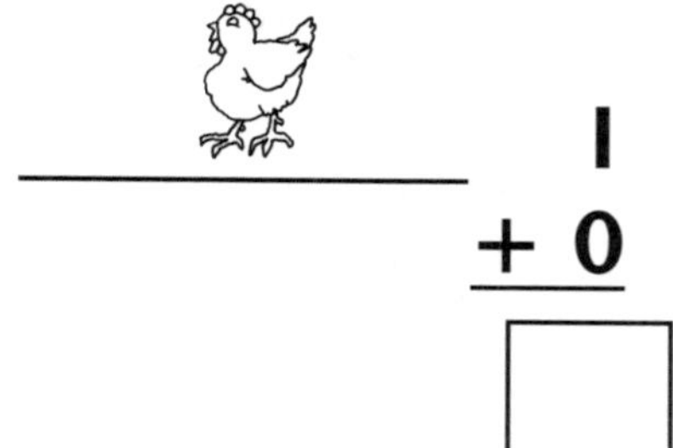

$$\begin{array}{r} 1 \\ +\ 0 \\ \hline \square \end{array}$$

3.
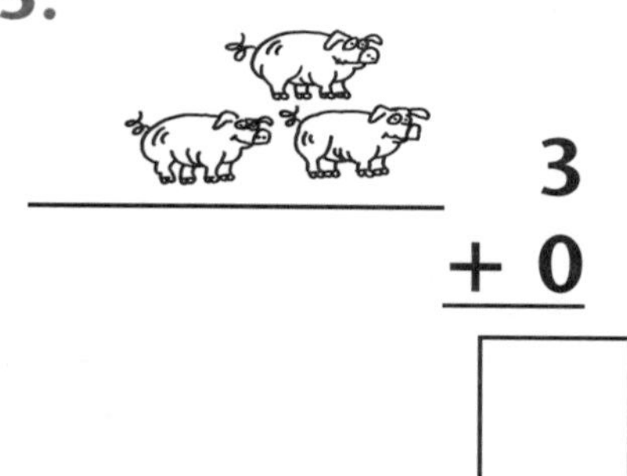

$$\begin{array}{r} 3 \\ +\ 0 \\ \hline \square \end{array}$$

4.

0 + 2 = □

5.

0 + 4 = □

6.

$$\begin{array}{r} 0 \\ +\ 3 \\ \hline \square \end{array}$$

Draw a picture. Complete.

7.
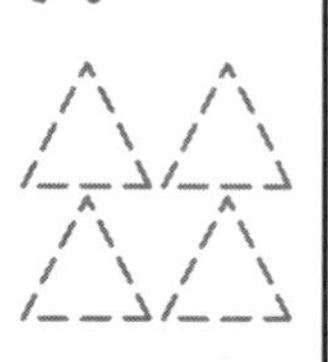

4 + 0 = [4]

8.
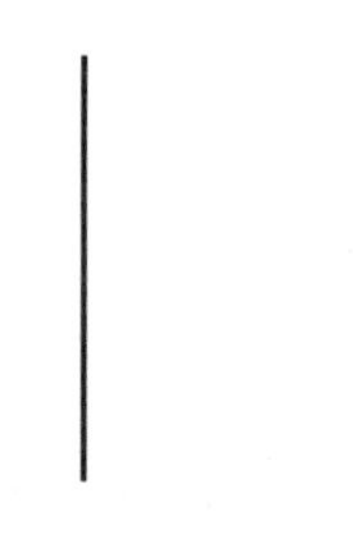

0 + 0 = □

9.

$$\begin{array}{r} 1 \\ +\ 0 \\ \hline \square \end{array}$$

10.

0 + 6 = □

11.

$$\begin{array}{r} 5 \\ +\ 0 \\ \hline \square \end{array}$$

12.

$$\begin{array}{r} 0 \\ +\ 2 \\ \hline \square \end{array}$$

Write the number sentence.

13.

4 + 0 = 4

14.

☐ + ☐ = ☐

15.

☐ + ☐ = ☐

Complete.

16.

$$\begin{array}{r} 2 \\ +\ 0 \\ \hline 2 \end{array}$$

17.

$$\begin{array}{r} \square \\ +\ \square \\ \hline \square \end{array}$$

18.

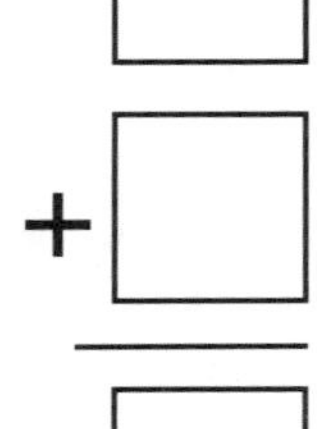

$$\begin{array}{r} \square \\ +\ \square \\ \hline \square \end{array}$$

Problem Solving Reasoning How many fingers would you hold up if you held up 0 on one hand and 0 on the other?

★ Test Prep

Which number correctly completes the number sentence? Mark the space under your answer.

19 

5 + 0 = ☐

0	5	6
○	○	○

Name ______________________________

2 + 3 = 5

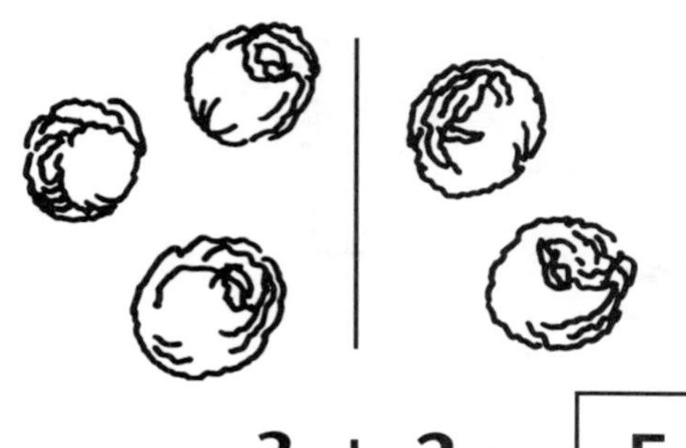

3 + 2 = 5

Write the sum.

1.

1 + 2 = ☐

2 + 1 = ☐

2.

0 + 3 = ☐

3 + 0 = ☐

3.

1 + 3 = ☐

3 + 1 = ☐

4.

2 + 3 = ☐

3 + 2 = ☐

5.

1 + 4 = ☐

4 + 1 = ☐

6.

2 + 4 = ☐

4 + 2 = ☐

$$\begin{array}{r} 2 \\ +\ 1 \\ \hline 3 \end{array} \qquad \begin{array}{r} 1 \\ +\ 2 \\ \hline 3 \end{array}$$

Add.

7.

$$\begin{array}{r} 4 \\ +\ 0 \\ \hline 4 \end{array} \qquad \begin{array}{r} 0 \\ +\ 4 \\ \hline 4 \end{array}$$

8.

$$\begin{array}{r} 5 \\ +\ 1 \\ \hline \end{array} \qquad \begin{array}{r} 1 \\ +\ 5 \\ \hline \end{array}$$

9.

$$\begin{array}{r} 3 \\ +\ 1 \\ \hline \end{array} \qquad \begin{array}{r} 1 \\ +\ 3 \\ \hline \end{array}$$

10.

$$\begin{array}{r} 3 \\ +\ 2 \\ \hline \end{array} \qquad \begin{array}{r} 2 \\ +\ 3 \\ \hline \end{array}$$

11.

$$\begin{array}{r} 6 \\ +\ 0 \\ \hline \end{array} \qquad \begin{array}{r} 0 \\ +\ 6 \\ \hline \end{array}$$

12.

$$\begin{array}{r} 4 \\ +\ 1 \\ \hline \end{array} \qquad \begin{array}{r} 1 \\ +\ 4 \\ \hline \end{array}$$

Problem Solving
Reasoning

13. If you already know that **4 + 2 = 6**, what other number sentence for **6** do you know?

____

Name ________________________________

Climb down the ladders.
Write the sums.

14.	1 + 5 = 6	→	5 + 1 =
15.	3 + 3 =	→	3 + 3 =
16.	5 + 0 =	→	0 + 5 =
17.	0 + 6 =	→	6 + 0 =
18.	2 + 4 =	→	4 + 2 =
19.	0 + 4 =	→	4 + 0 =
20.	2 + 0 =	→	0 + 2 =
21.	1 + 4 =	→	4 + 1 =
22.	3 + 2 =	→	2 + 3 =
23.	2 + 2 =	→	2 + 2 =
24.	3 + 0 =	→	0 + 3 =
25.	0 + 1 =	→	1 + 0 =
26.	1 + 3 =	→	3 + 1 =
27.	2 + 1 =	→	1 + 2 =
28.	0 + 0 =	→	0 + 0 =

2 + 4 = 6

4 + 2 = 6

Add. Match the partners.

29.	1 + 5 = 6		1 + 2 =
30.	2 + 1 =		3 + 2 =
31.	1 + 0 =		1 + 3 =
32.	2 + 3 =		0 + 1 =
33.	6 + 0 =		0 + 6 =
34.	3 + 1 =		5 + 1 = 6

Quick Check

Complete.

1. $\begin{array}{r} 3 \\ +\ 2 \\ \hline \square \end{array}$

2. 0 + 3 = ☐

3. 5 + 1 = 6
   1 + 5 = ☐

4. 3 + 1 = 4
   1 + 3 = ☐

I penny	I penny	I nickel	I nickel

I cent	I cent	5 cents	5 cents
I¢	I¢	5¢	5¢

How much money?

I.

2 ¢

2.

☐ ¢

3.

☐ ¢

4.

☐ ¢

5.

☐ ¢

6.

☐ ¢

7.

☐ ¢

8.

☐ ¢

How much for both?
Ring the coins needed.

9.
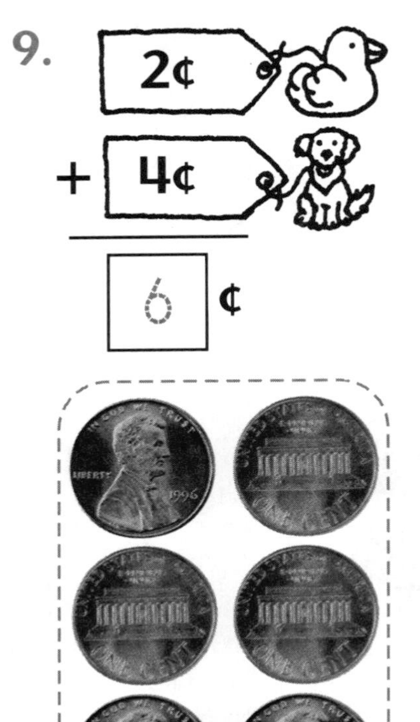

10.
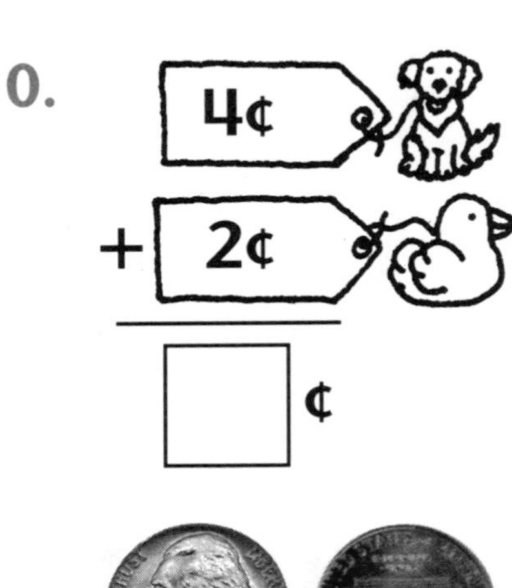

11.
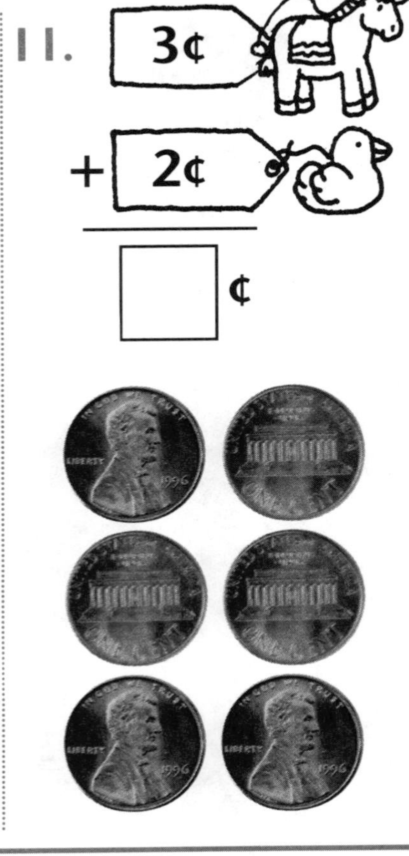

Problem Solving
Reasoning

12. You have a 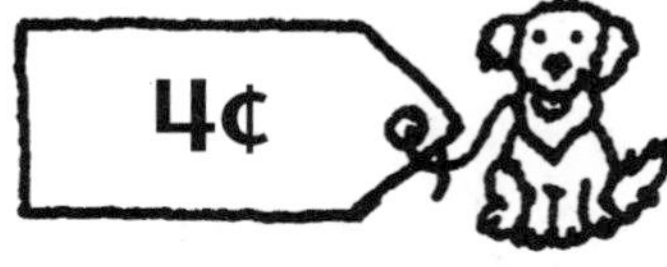 .
Do you have enough to buy a 4¢ ? Explain.

★ Test Prep

How much money? Mark the space under your answer.

2¢	5¢	6¢
○	○	○

Name ______________________________

Problem Solving Plan			
1. Understand	2. Decide	3. Solve	4. Look back

Can you tell a story for the picture?

$$\begin{array}{r} 4 \\ +\ 1 \\ \hline 5 \end{array}$$

Tell a story. Complete.

Think How do I use the pictures to tell a story?

1. 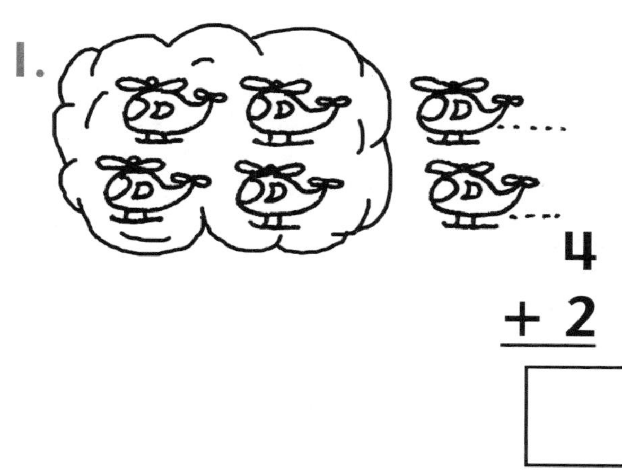

$$\begin{array}{r} 4 \\ +\ 2 \\ \hline \square \end{array}$$

2. 

$$\begin{array}{r} 5 \\ +\ 1 \\ \hline \square \end{array}$$

3. 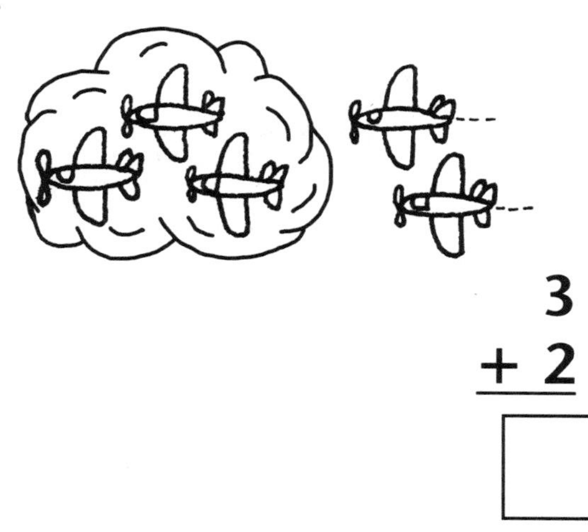

$$\begin{array}{r} 3 \\ +\ 2 \\ \hline \square \end{array}$$

4. 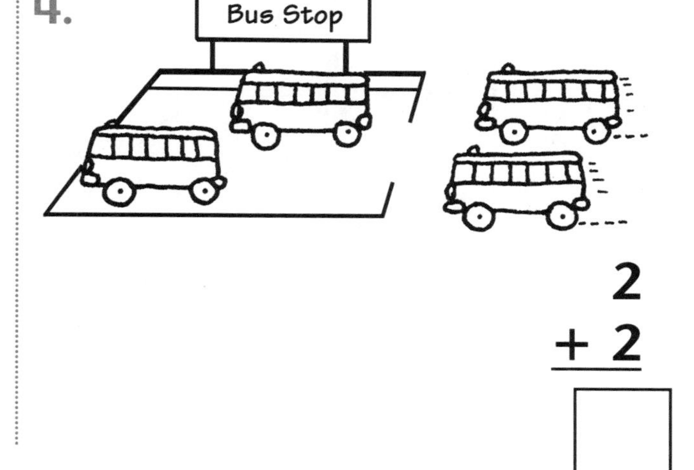

$$\begin{array}{r} 2 \\ +\ 2 \\ \hline \square \end{array}$$

Tell a story. Ring the matching fact.

5.

$$\begin{array}{r} 2 \\ +\ 2 \\ \hline 4 \end{array} \qquad \begin{array}{r} 3 \\ +\ 1 \\ \hline 4 \end{array}$$

6.

$$\begin{array}{r} 3 \\ +\ 3 \\ \hline 6 \end{array} \qquad \begin{array}{r} 2 \\ +\ 4 \\ \hline 6 \end{array}$$

Extend Your Thinking

Tell a story to match the fact. Draw a picture.

7. $\begin{array}{r} 1 \\ +\ 5 \\ \hline 6 \end{array}$

STANDARD

Name ______

Complete.

1.

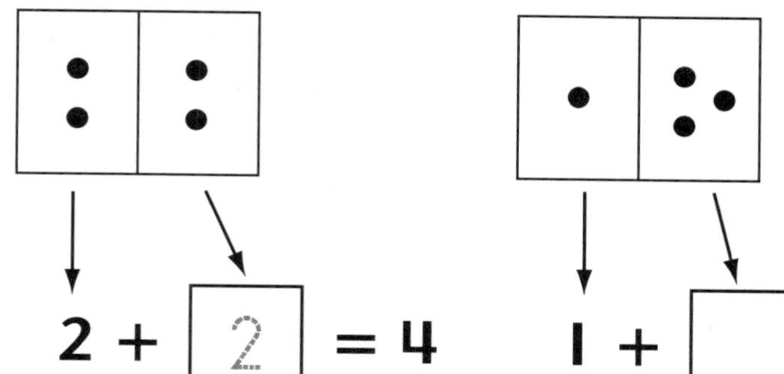

2 + [2] = 4

1 + [ ] = 4

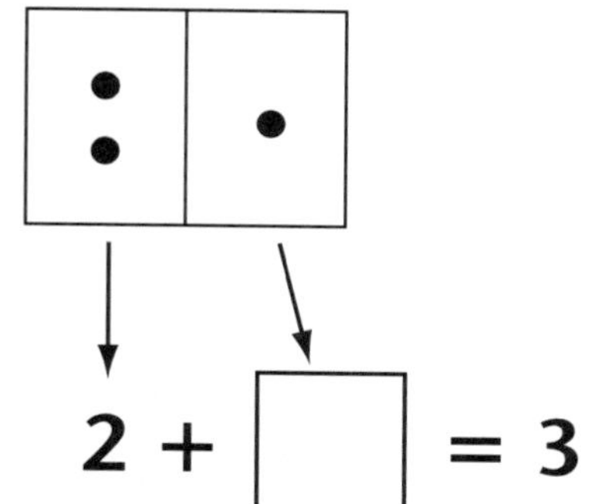

2 + [ ] = 3

2.

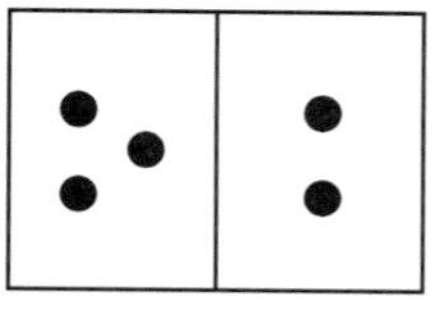

3 + [ ] = 5

2 + [ ] = 6

1 + [ ] = 5

3.

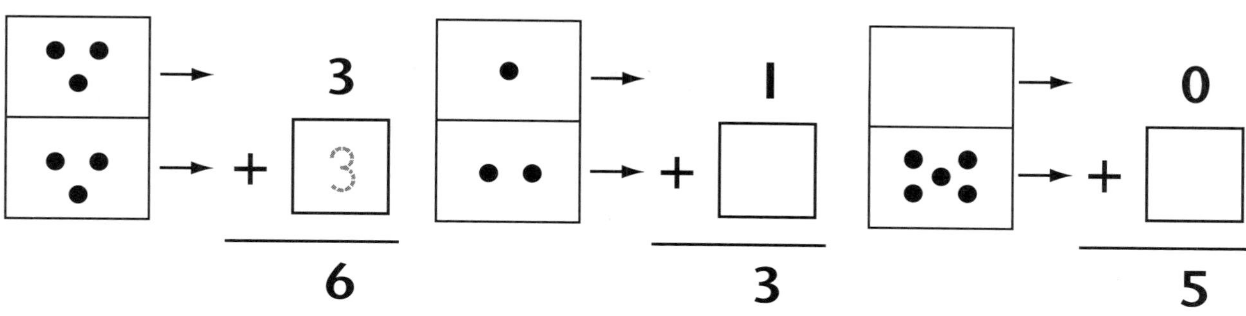

3 + [3] = 6

1 + [ ] = 3

0 + [ ] = 5

4.

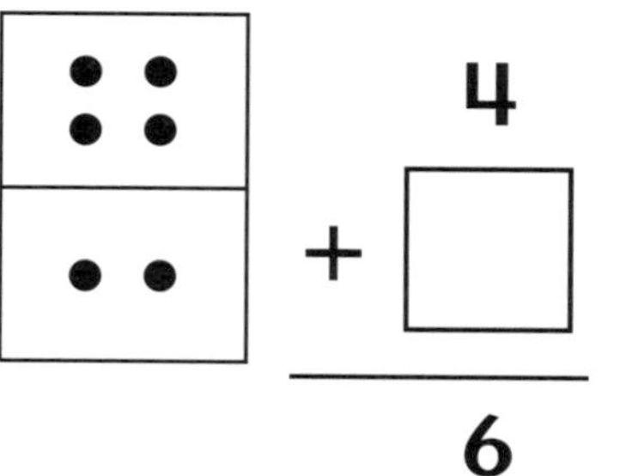

4 + [ ] = 6

3 + [ ] = 4

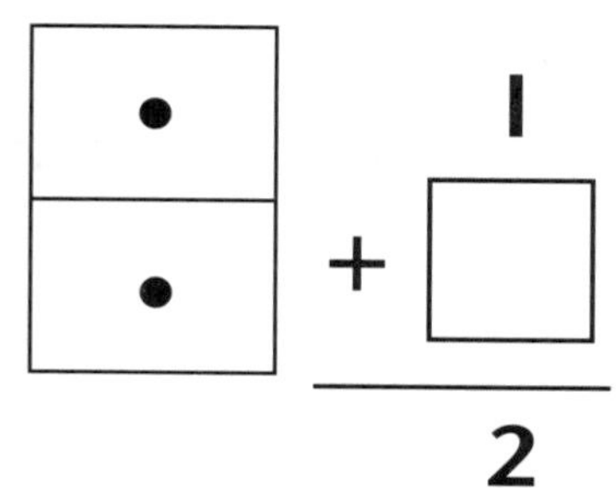

1 + [ ] = 2

Complete.

5. 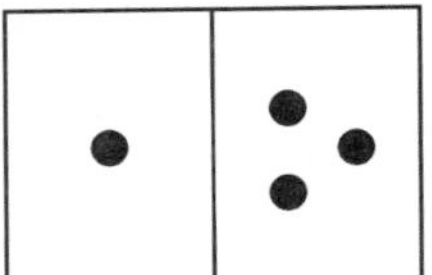 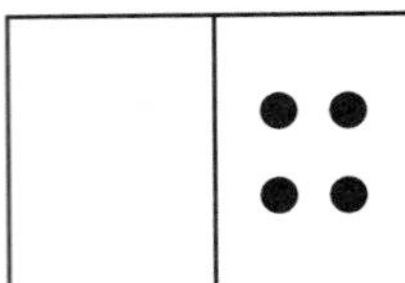 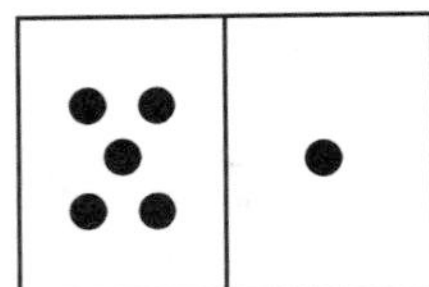

1 + ☐ = 4   0 + ☐ = 4   5 + ☐ = 6

6. 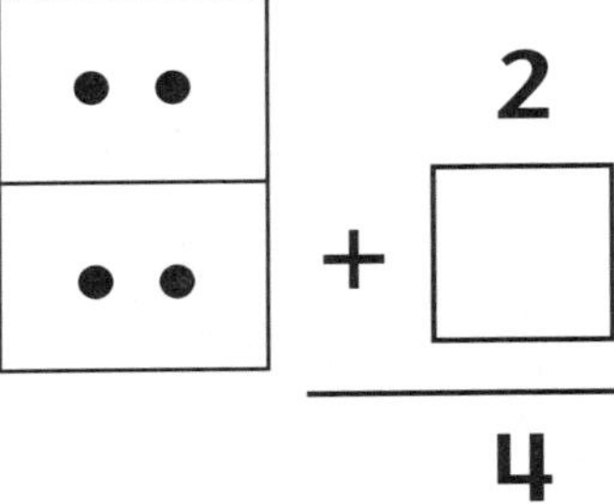

2	2	4
+ ☐	+ ☐	+ ☐
4	5	5

7. 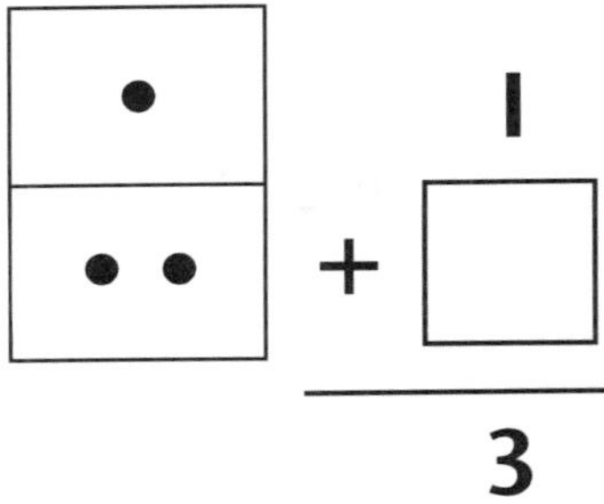

1	1	3
+ ☐	+ ☐	+ ☐
3	6	3

★ Test Prep

What number is missing in the number sentence?
Mark the space under your answer.

8

 3 + ☐ = 5

2	3	5
○	○	○

Name ______________________________

Add.

1. $\begin{array}{r} 2 \\ +\ 1 \\ \hline \end{array}$

2. $\begin{array}{r} 2 \\ +\ 3 \\ \hline \end{array}$

3. $\begin{array}{r} 5 \\ +\ 1 \\ \hline \end{array}$

4. $\begin{array}{r} 2 \\ +\ 4 \\ \hline \end{array}$

5. $\begin{array}{r} 4 \\ +\ 0 \\ \hline \end{array}$

6. $2 + 4 =$ ____

7. $6 + 0 =$ ____

8. $3 + 1 =$ ____

9. $1 + 2 =$ ____

How much money?

10.   ☐ ¢

11.   ☐ ¢

How much for both?

Ring the coins needed.

12. 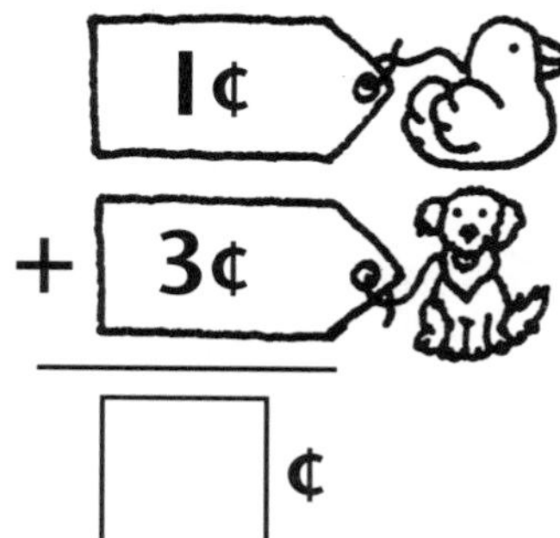

☐ ¢

13. 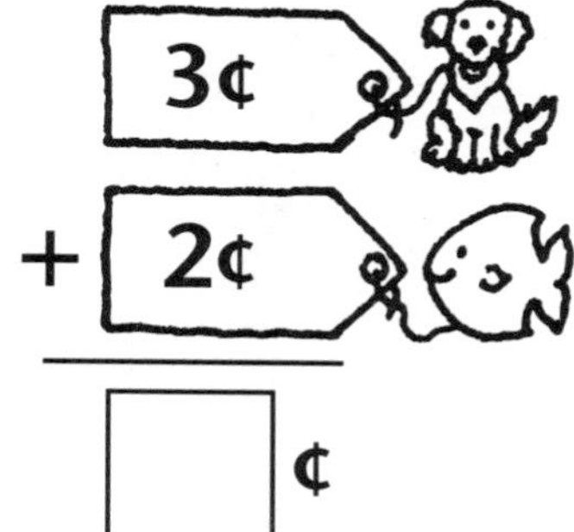

☐ ¢

Problem Solving
Reasoning

Write the number sentence.

14.

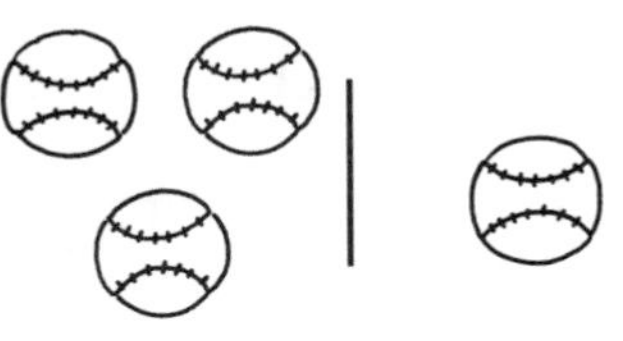

☐ + ☐ = ☐

15.

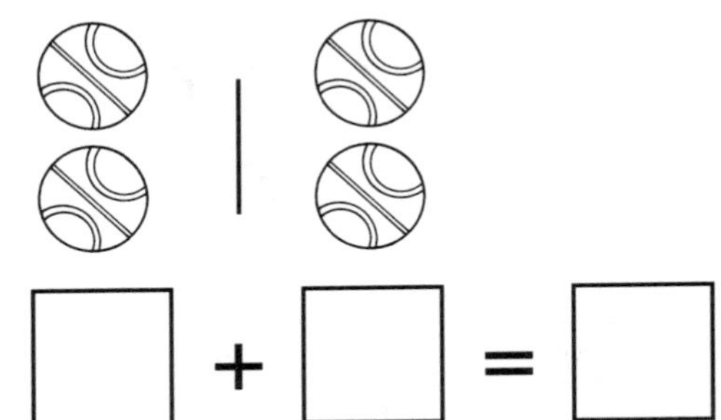

☐ + ☐ = ☐

16.

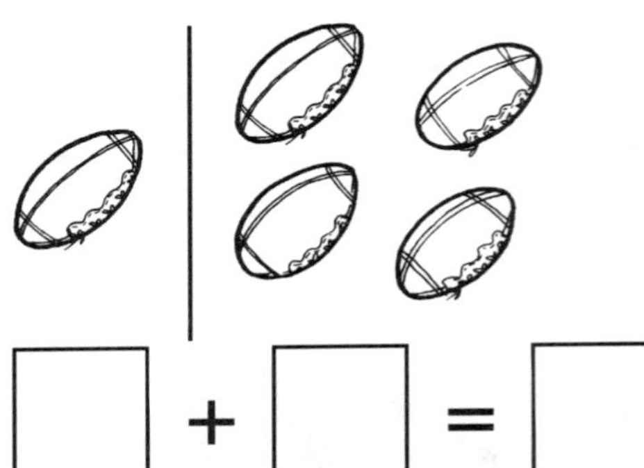

☐ + ☐ = ☐

17.

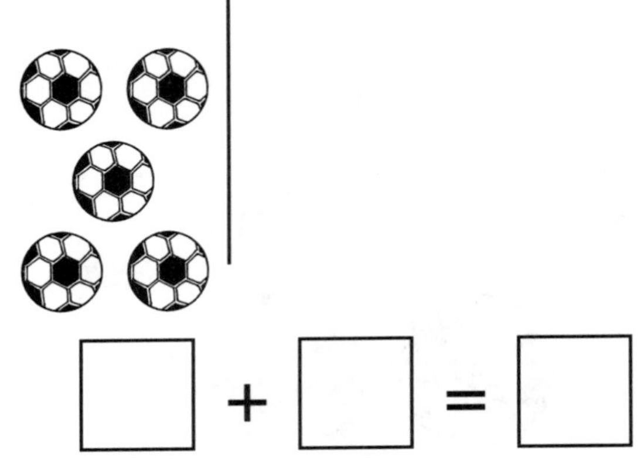

☐ + ☐ = ☐

Tell a story. Complete.

18.

$$\begin{array}{r} 3 \\ +\ 2 \\ \hline \square \end{array}$$

19.

$$\begin{array}{r} 4 \\ +\ 1 \\ \hline \square \end{array}$$

Name ______________________________

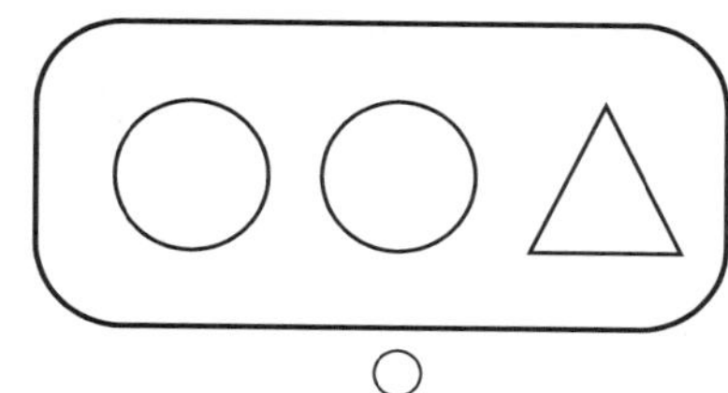

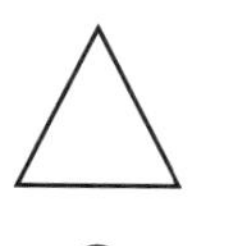

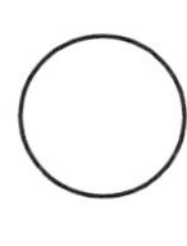

5

8 ○ 6 ○ 9 ○

4 ○ 3

$<$ ○ $>$ ○ $=$ ○

Solve. Mark the space for your answer.

$3 + 2 = \square$

4 ○ 5 ○ 6 ○

8

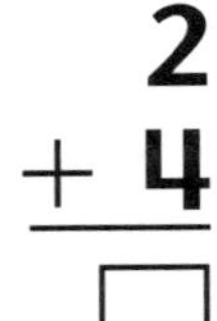

$$\begin{array}{r} 2 \\ +\ 4 \\ \hline \square \end{array}$$

4 ○ 5 ○ 6 ○

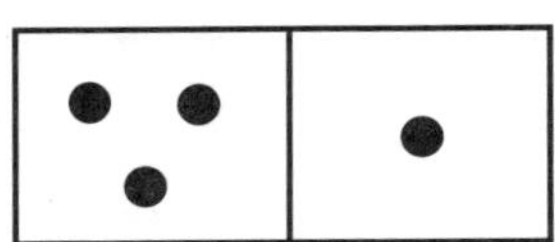

$3 + \square = 4$

3 ○ 2 ○ 1 ○

10

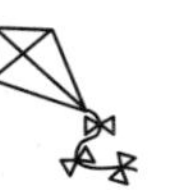

$$\begin{array}{r} 5 \\ +\ 0 \\ \hline \square \end{array}$$

0 ○ 6 ○ 5 ○

UNIT 4 • TABLE OF CONTENTS

Subtracting from 6 or Less

We will be using this vocabulary:

difference result of a subtraction problem

more and **fewer** to compare two groups

number sentence an equation, such as $6 - 2 = 4$

minus take away

Dear Family,

During the next few weeks our math class will be learning when and how to subtract. We will be subtracting from 6 or less.

You can expect to see homework that provides practice with both take away and comparison subtraction situations.

As we learn about subtraction, you may wish to keep the following sample as a guide.

Take Away Subtraction

$3 - 2 = \boxed{1}$

Comparison Subtraction

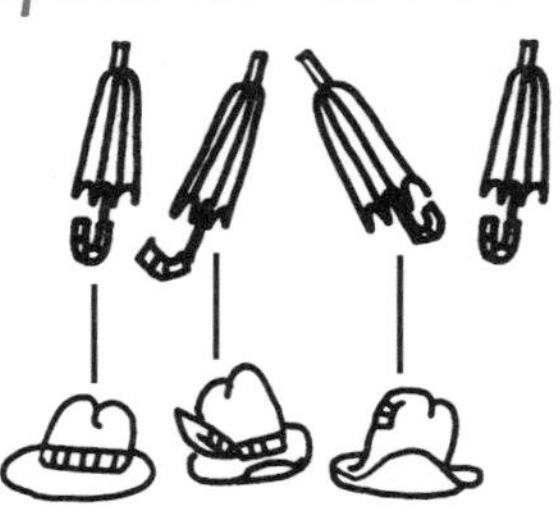

$4 - 3 = \boxed{1}$

1 more

Knowing how and when to subtract is an important mathematics skill.

Sincerely,

Name ______________________________

Listen.
Act out the story with your counters.
Write how many.

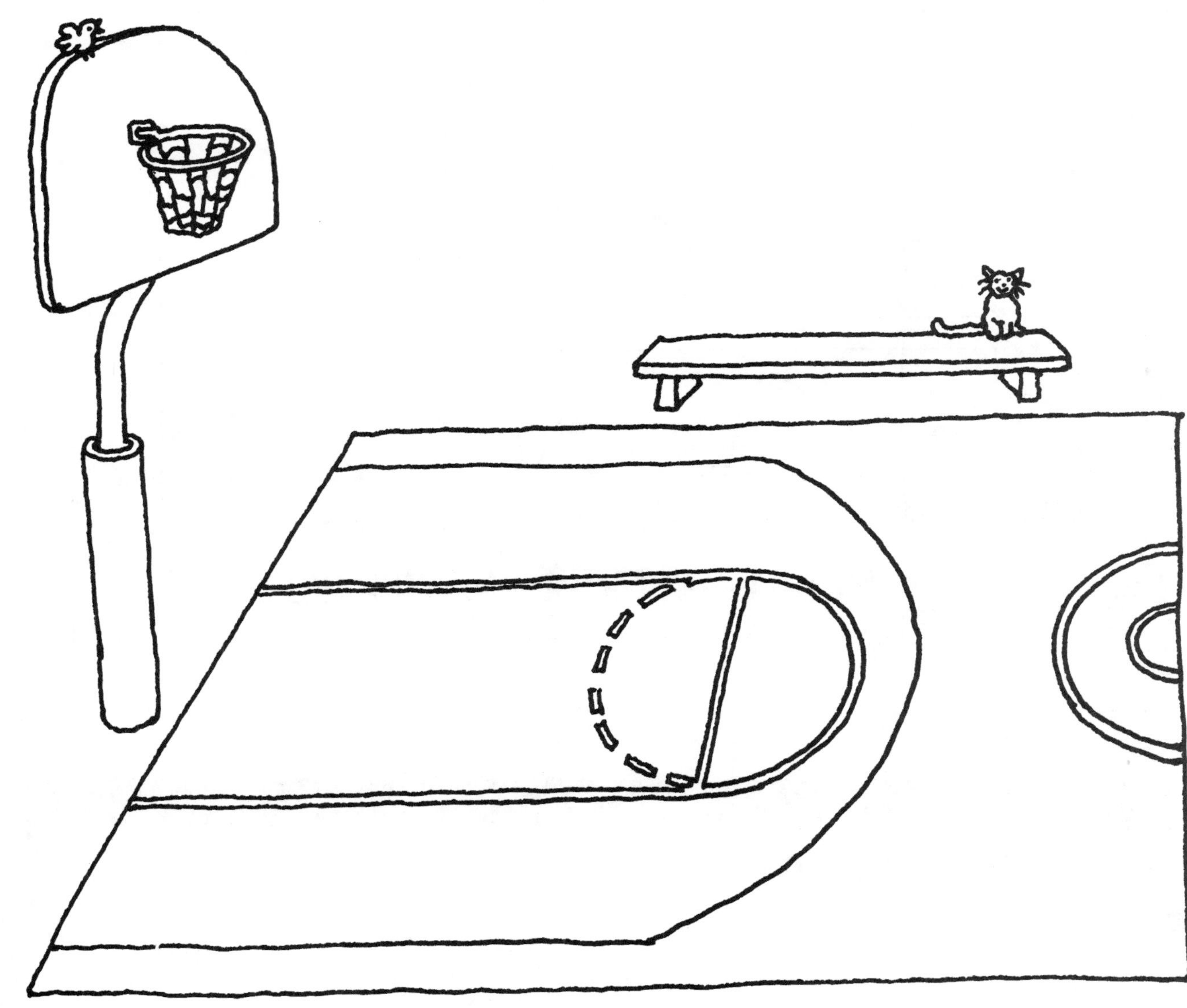

1. __2__ 2. ____ 3. ____

Listen.
Act out the story with counters.
Write how many.

4. ____ 5. ____ 6. ____

★ Test Prep

Listen. Mark the space under your answer.

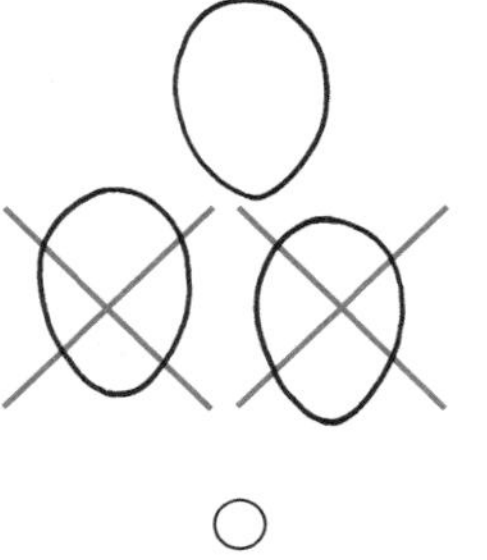

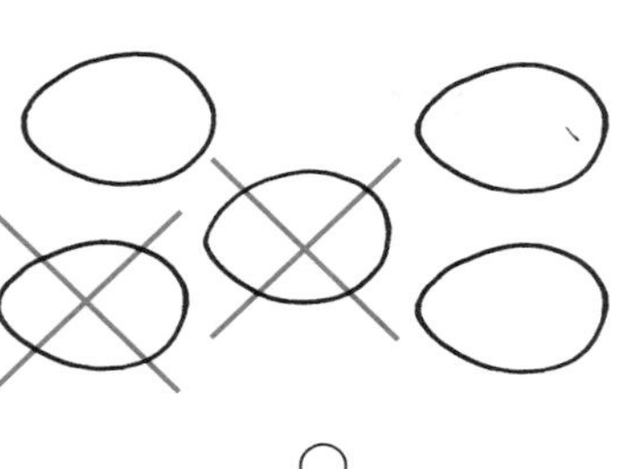

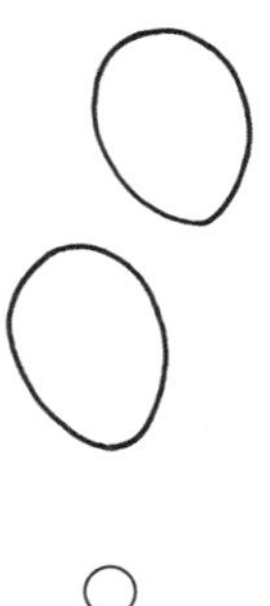

○ ○ ○

Name ______________________________

4 minus 1 = 3

4 − 1 = 3

$$\begin{array}{r} 4 \\ -\ 1 \\ \hline 3 \end{array}$$

difference

Cross out the objects to subtract.
Complete.

1.

2 − 1 = [1]

2.

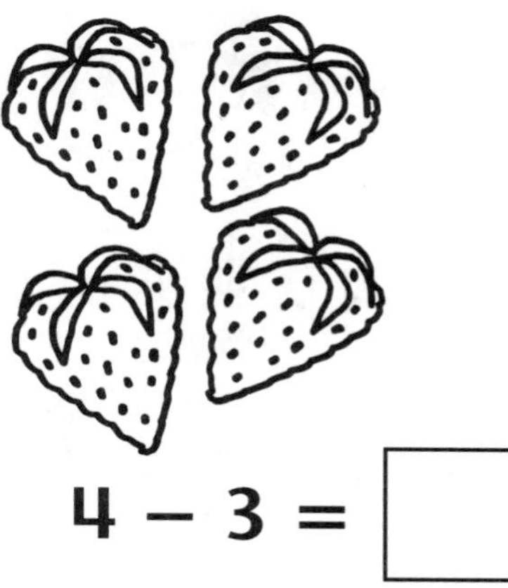

4 − 3 = [ ]

3.

2 − 2 = [ ]

4.

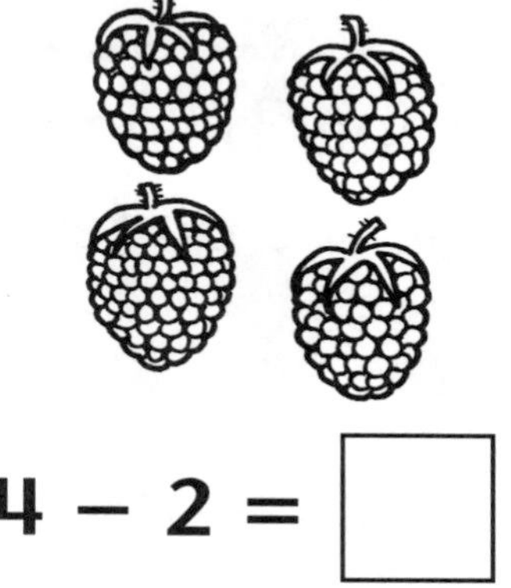

4 − 2 = [ ]

Cross out the objects to subtract.
Complete.

5.

3 − 2 = [ ]

6.

4 − 0 = [ ]

7.

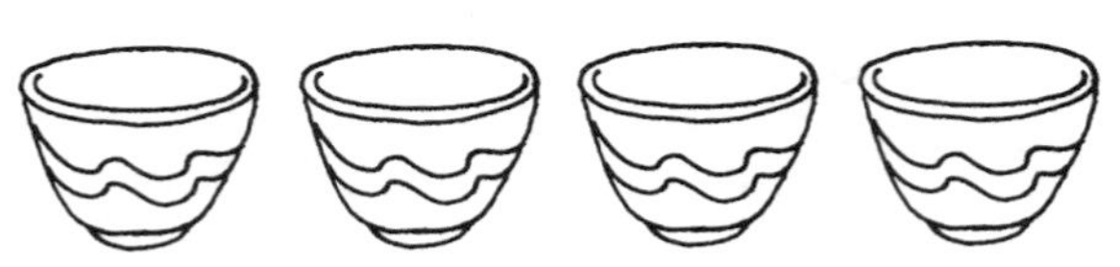

4 − 1 = [ ]

8.

2 − 1 = [ ]

9.

2 − 2 = [ ]

10.

5 − 4 = [ ]

Problem Solving Reasoning

How is subtraction different from addition?

★ Test Prep

Which number belongs in the box?
Mark the space under your answer.

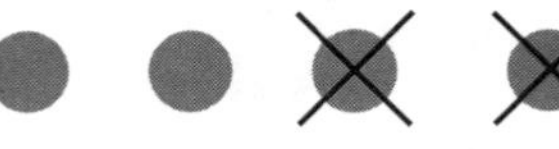

4 − 2 = [ ]

4	3	2
○	○	○

Name ____

Cross out to subtract.
Complete.

1.

$$\begin{array}{r} 2 \\ -\ 1 \\ \hline 1 \end{array}$$

2.

$$\begin{array}{r} 3 \\ -\ 2 \\ \hline \square \end{array}$$

3.

$$\begin{array}{r} 1 \\ -\ 1 \\ \hline \square \end{array}$$

4.

$$\begin{array}{r} 4 \\ -\ 4 \\ \hline \square \end{array}$$

5.

$$\begin{array}{r} 2 \\ -\ 1 \\ \hline \square \end{array}$$

6.

$$\begin{array}{r} 1 \\ -\ 0 \\ \hline \square \end{array}$$

7.

$$\begin{array}{r} 4 \\ -\ 3 \\ \hline \square \end{array}$$

8.

$$\begin{array}{r} 3 \\ -\ 1 \\ \hline \square \end{array}$$

9.

$$\begin{array}{r} 2 \\ -\ 0 \\ \hline \square \end{array}$$

10.

$$\begin{array}{r} 2 \\ -\ 2 \\ \hline \square \end{array}$$

Cross out to subtract.

Complete.

11.

$$\begin{array}{r} 2 \\ -\ 0 \\ \hline \boxed{2} \end{array}$$

12.

$$\begin{array}{r} 3 \\ -\ 0 \\ \hline \boxed{} \end{array}$$

Problem Solving Reasoning

Write the numbers 1, 4, and 5 in the boxes to make the problem true.

13.

$$\begin{array}{r} \boxed{} \\ -\ \boxed{} \\ \hline \boxed{} \end{array}$$

Quick Check

Complete.

1.

$3 - 1 = \boxed{}$

2.

$4 - 0 = \boxed{}$

3.

$$\begin{array}{r} 5 \\ -\ 2 \\ \hline \boxed{} \end{array}$$

Name ______________________________

Draw lines to match. Complete.
Tell how many more.

1.

$4 - 3 = $ [1]

1 more

2.

$4 - 4 = $ [ ]

_____ more

3.

$3 - 2 = $ [ ]

_____ more

4.

$3 - 1 = $ [ ]

_____ more

5.

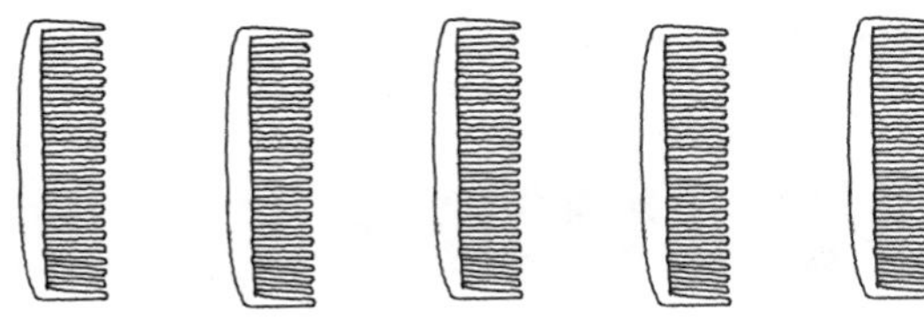

$5 - 2 = $ [ ]

_____ more

6.

$6 - 4 = $ [ ]

_____ more

Draw lines to match. Complete.

Tell how many fewer.

7.

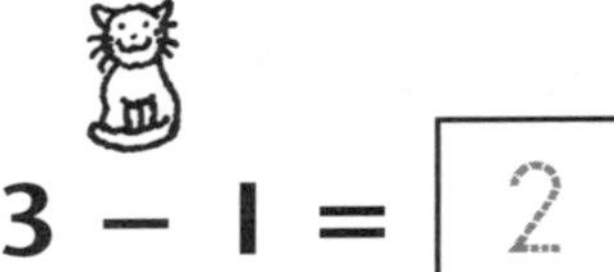

$3 - 1 = $ [2]

2 fewer

8.

$5 - 4 = $ [ ]

_____ fewer

9.

$6 - 2 = $ [ ]

_____ fewer

10.

$1 - 1 = $ [ ]

_____ fewer

Problem Solving
Reasoning

Look at the picture.

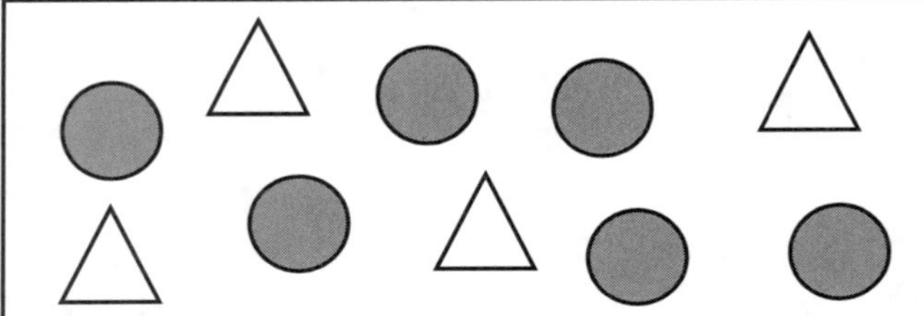

11. How many more  than △? ____ more 

★ Test Prep

How many fewer white squares? Mark your answer.

3 fewer	4 fewer	5 fewer
○		

STANDARD

Name ______________________________

Problem

What number sentence can you write for this picture?

1 **Understand**

2 **Decide**

3 **Solve** Write a number sentence for the picture.

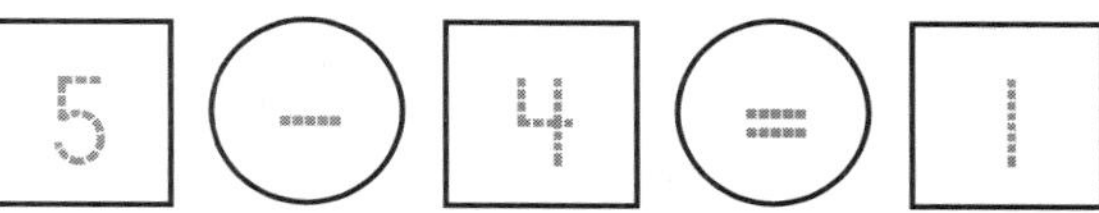

4 **Look back**

Write a number sentence for the picture.

1.

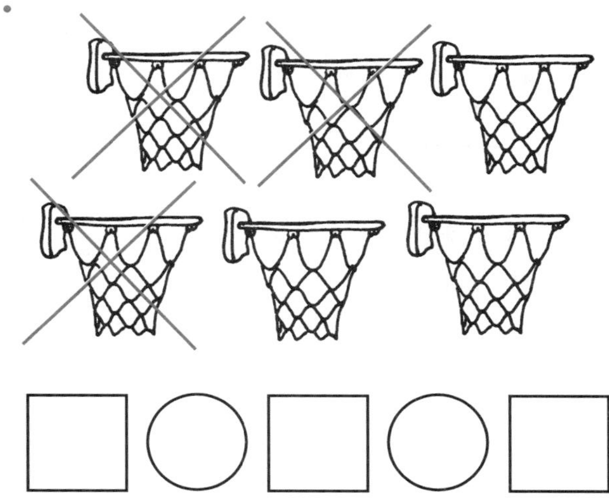

2.

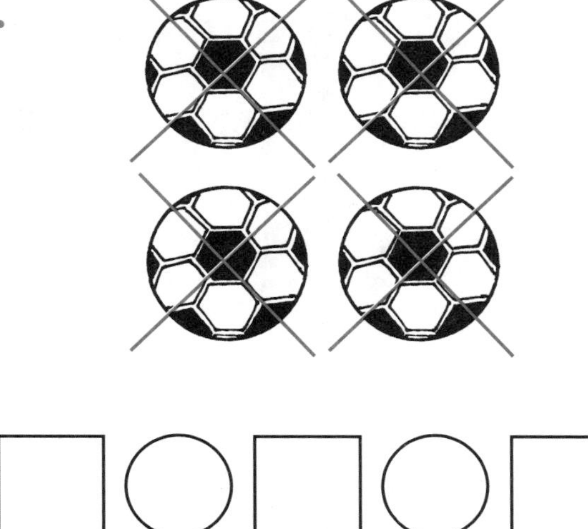

Write a number sentence for the picture.

3.

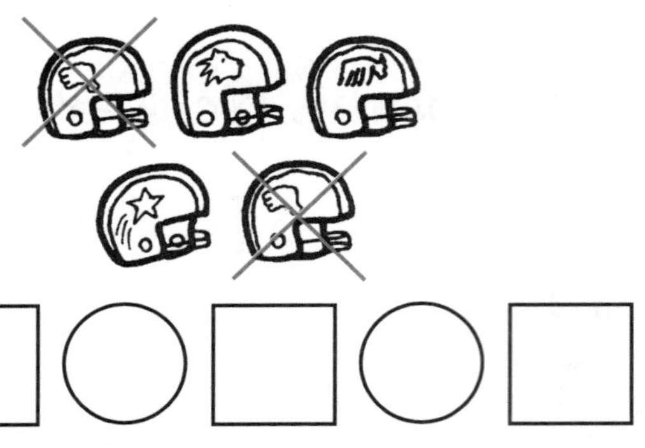

□ ○ □ ○ □

4.

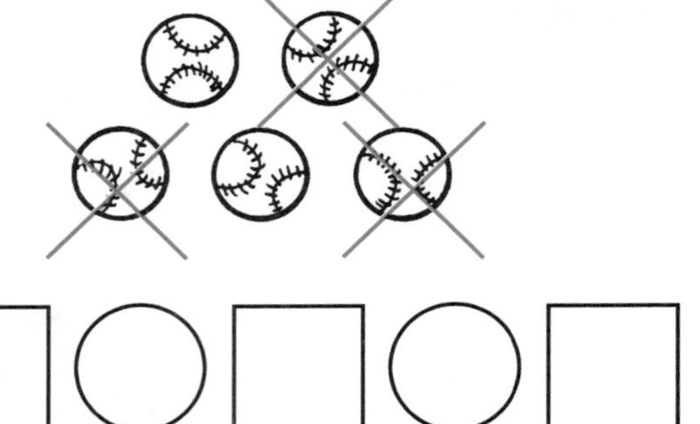

□ ○ □ ○ □

5.

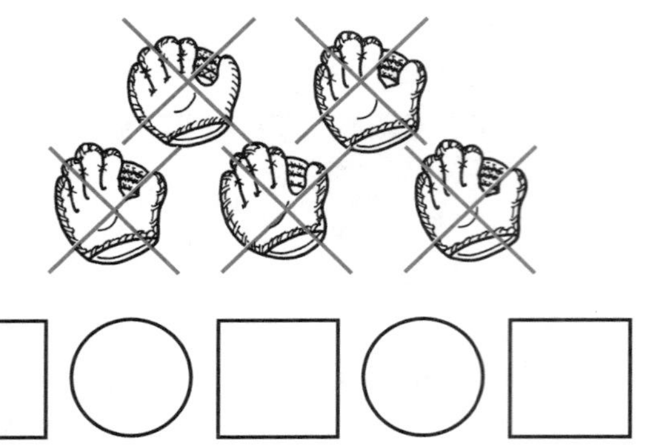

□ ○ □ ○ □

6.

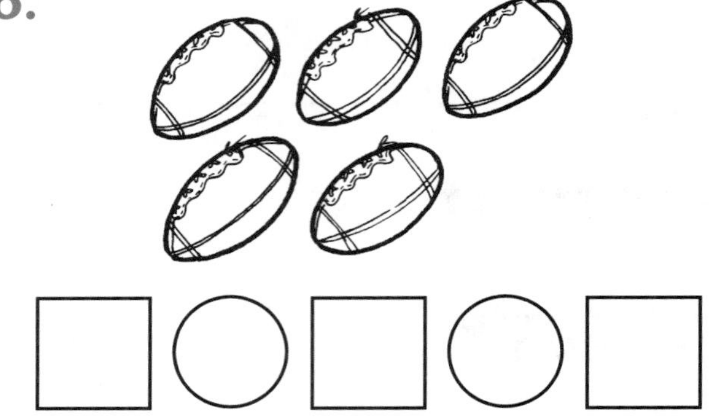

□ ○ □ ○ □

7.

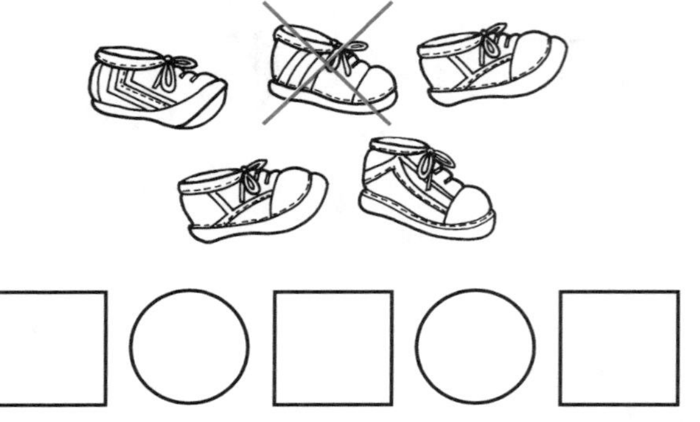

□ ○ □ ○ □

8.

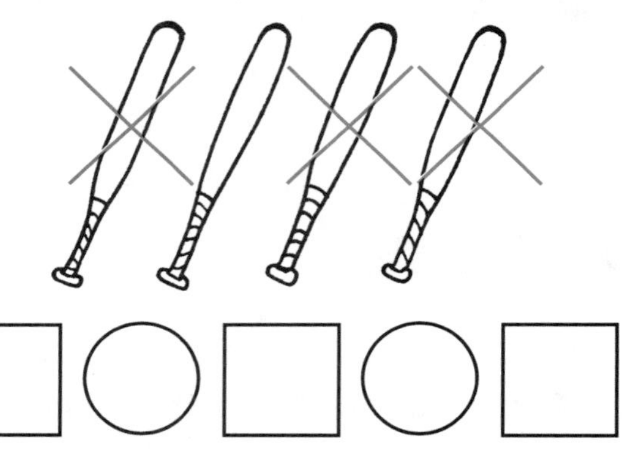

□ ○ □ ○ □

9. Draw a picture for the number sentence.

3 − 2 = 1

Name ______________________________

Cross out to subtract.
Complete.

1.

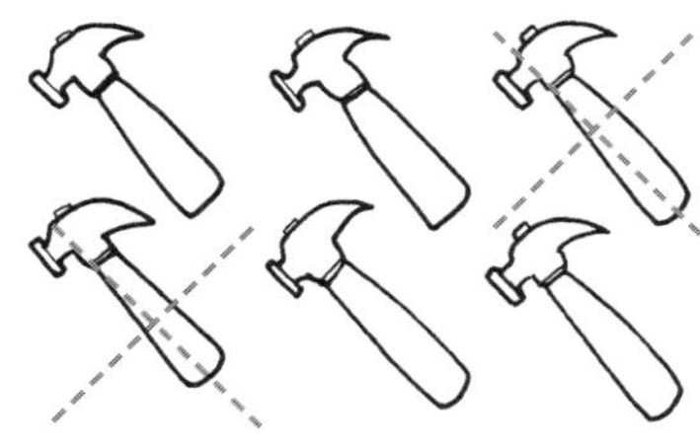

6 − 2 = 4

2.

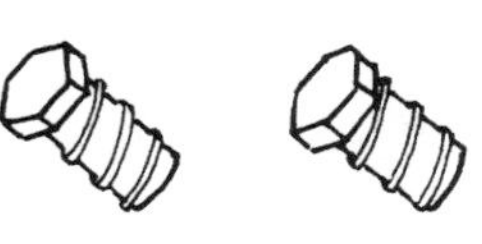

3 − 0 = ☐

3.

5 − 1 = ☐

4.

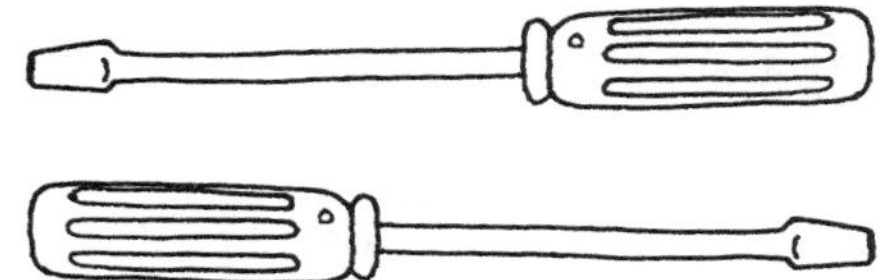

2 − 1 = ☐

5.

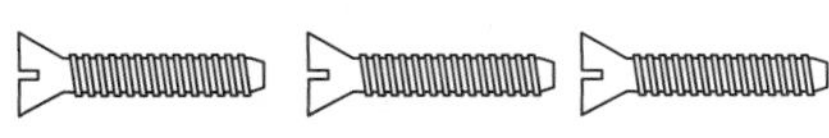

6 − 6 = ☐

6.

4 − 2 = ☐

7.

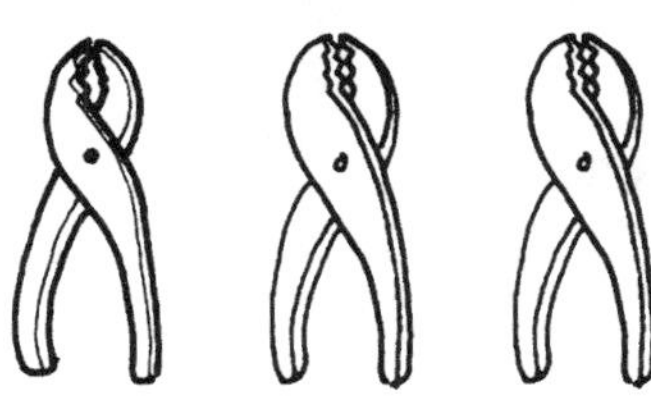

3 − 2 = ☐

8.

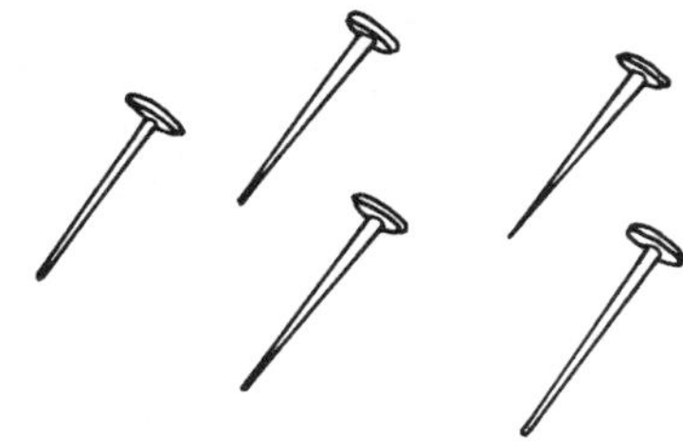

5 − 2 = ☐

Draw a picture.
Write the difference.

9.

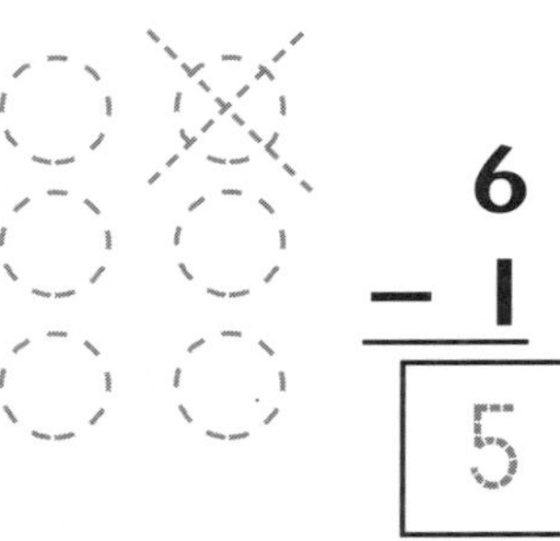

$$\begin{array}{r} 6 \\ -\ 1 \\ \hline 5 \end{array}$$

10.

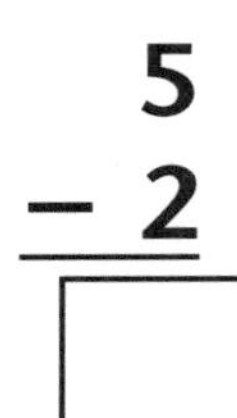

$$\begin{array}{r} 5 \\ -\ 2 \\ \hline \square \end{array}$$

11.

$$\begin{array}{r} 4 \\ -\ 3 \\ \hline \square \end{array}$$

12.

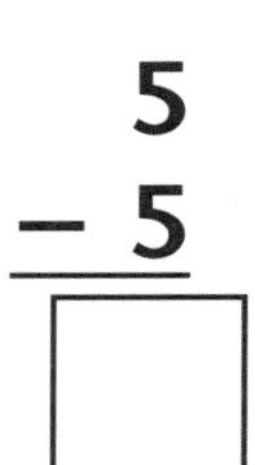

$$\begin{array}{r} 5 \\ -\ 5 \\ \hline \square \end{array}$$

13.

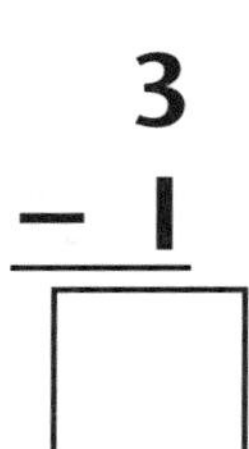

$$\begin{array}{r} 3 \\ -\ 1 \\ \hline \square \end{array}$$

14.

$$\begin{array}{r} 6 \\ -\ 2 \\ \hline \square \end{array}$$

Problem Solving Reasoning

Write the number sentence.

15.

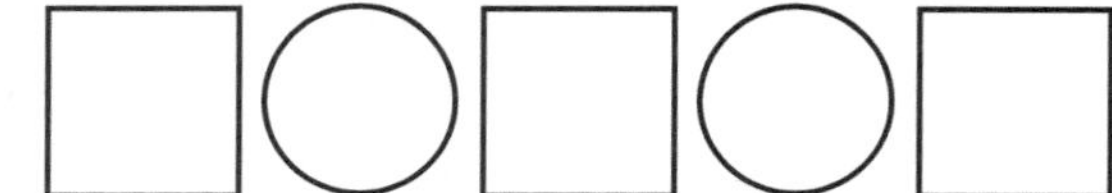

16.

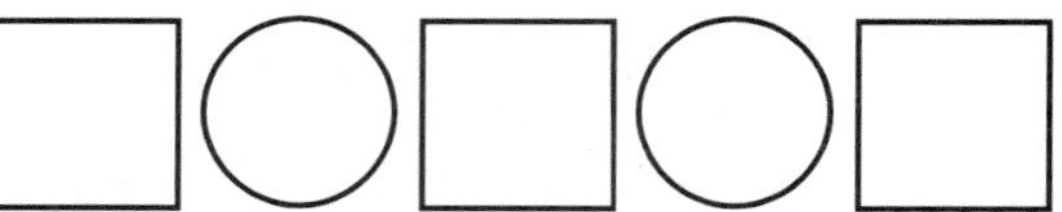

★ Test Prep

Solve. Mark the space under your answer.

$5 - 3 = \square$

2	3	5
○	○	○

Name ______________________________

Problem Solving Plan			
1. Understand	2. Decide	3. Solve	4. Look back

Tell a story for the pictures.
Ring the matching number sentence.

1.  

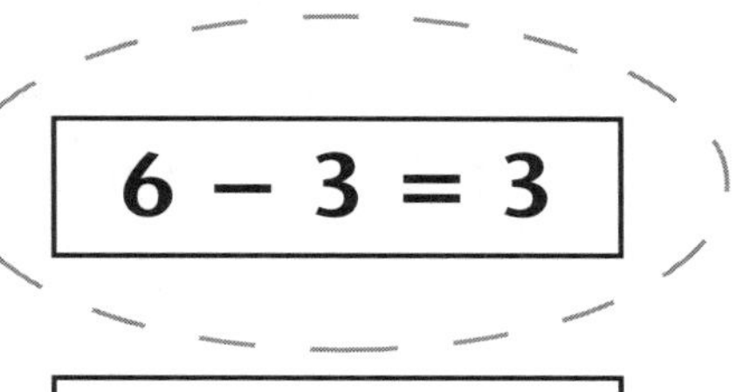

6 − 3 = 3

6 − 2 = 4

Think Does my answer match the pictures?

2.  

6 − 5 = 1

6 − 1 = 5

3. 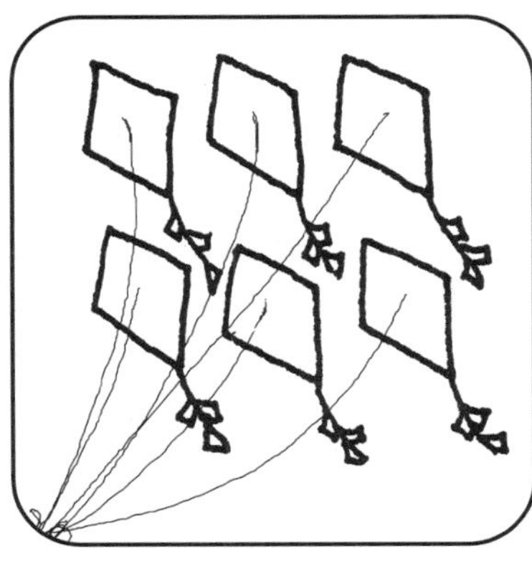 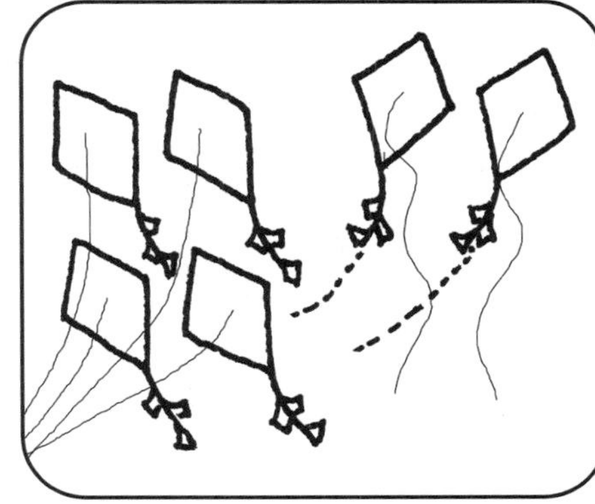

6 − 4 = 2

6 − 2 = 4

Tell a story for the pictures.
Ring the matching number sentence.

4.  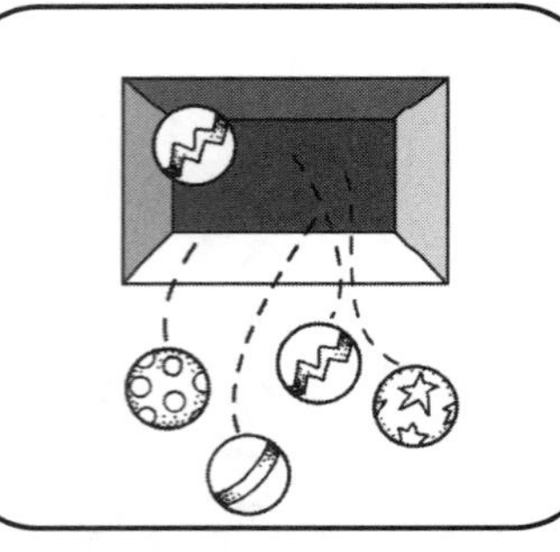

5 − 4 = 1

5 − 1 = 4

5. 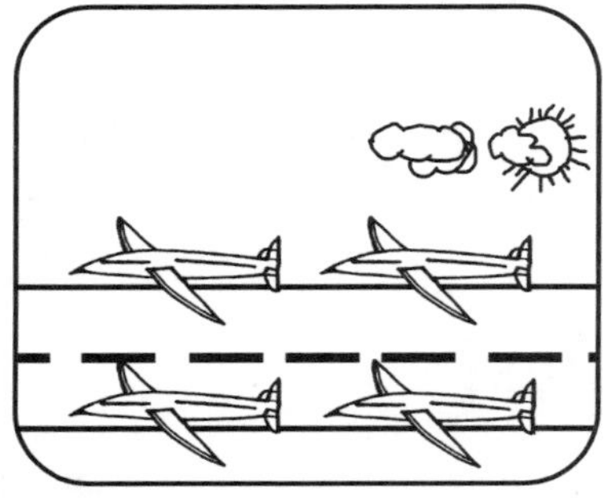 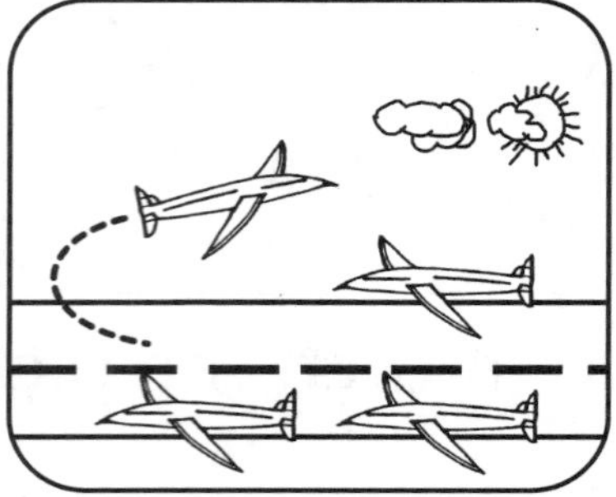

3 − 1 = 2

4 − 1 = 3

6. 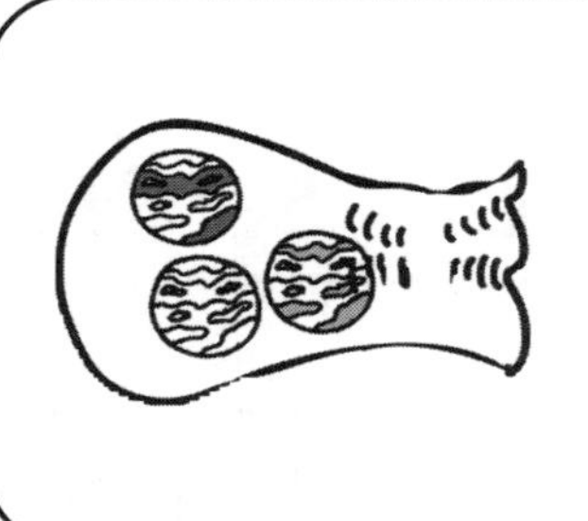 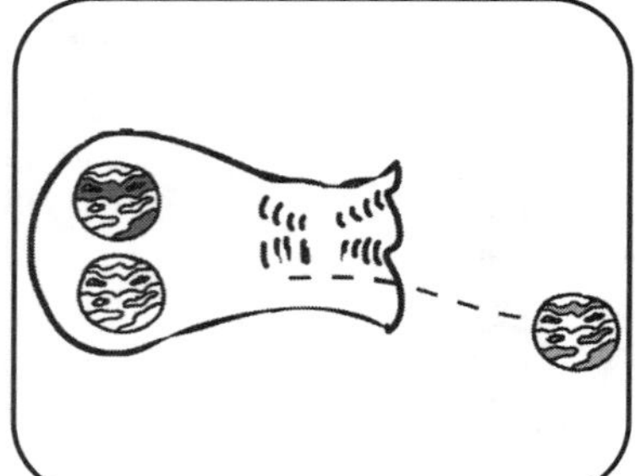

3 − 1 = 2

4 − 3 = 1

Extend Your Thinking

Draw pictures to match the number sentence.

7.  

4 − 3 = 1

Name ____________________

Cross out to subtract. Complete.

1\.

6¢
− 4¢
2¢

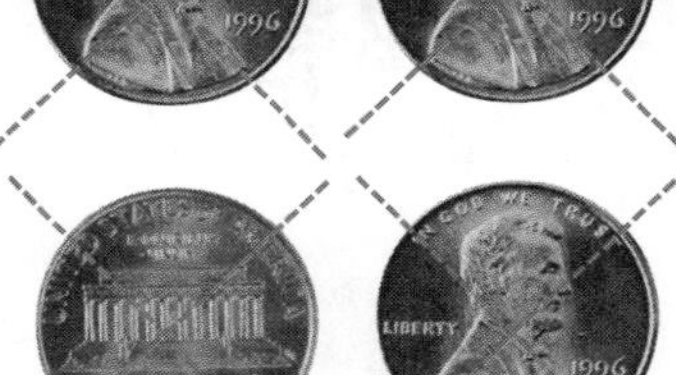

2\.

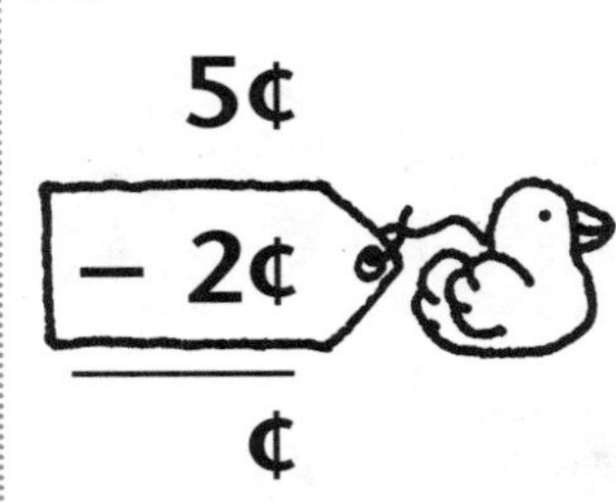

5¢
− 2¢
¢

3\.

3¢
− 1¢
¢

4\.

6¢
− 3¢
¢

5\.

6¢
− 2¢
¢

6\.

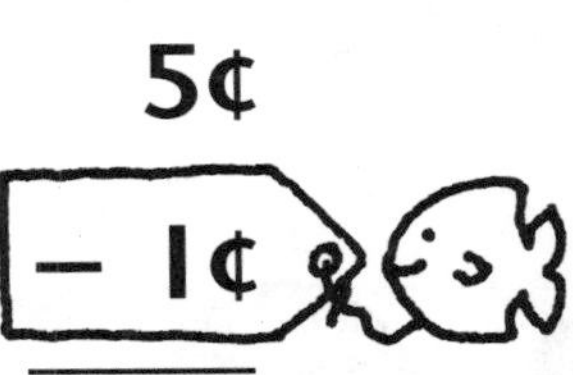

5¢
− 1¢
¢

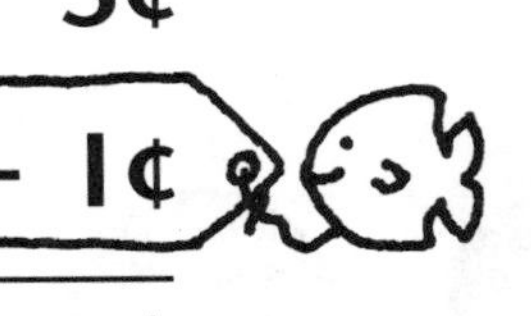

Cross out to subtract. Complete.

7. 6¢

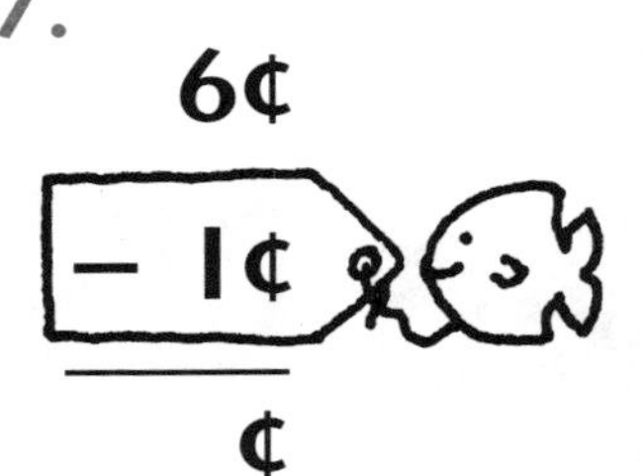

___ ¢

8. 6¢

___ ¢

Problem Solving Reasoning

Solve.

9. You have **2** pennies.

How many more do you need to buy 

?

_____ more pennies

Quick Check

How many more  ?

1.

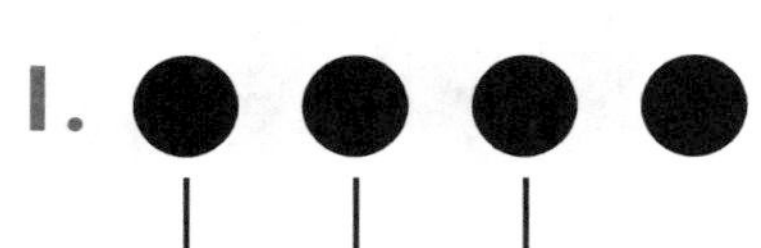

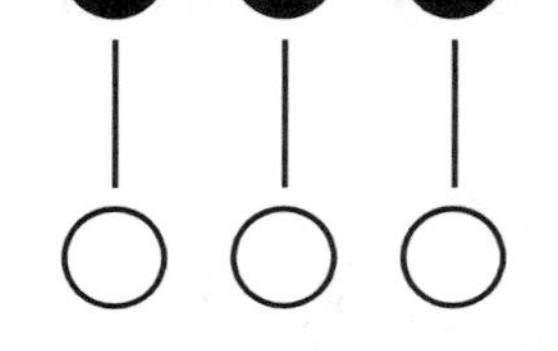

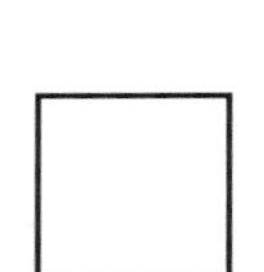

more

Solve.

2.

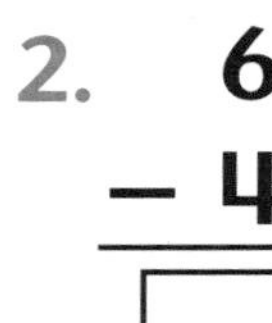

$$\begin{array}{r} 6 \\ -\ 4 \\ \hline \end{array}$$

Cross out to subtract.
Complete.

3.

$$\begin{array}{r} 3 \\ -\ 1 \\ \hline \end{array}$$

Name ____________________

Solve.

1. $\begin{array}{r} 2 \\ -\ 1 \\ \hline \end{array}$

2. $\begin{array}{r} 5 \\ -\ 2 \\ \hline \end{array}$

3. $\begin{array}{r} 6 \\ -\ 4 \\ \hline \end{array}$

4. $\begin{array}{r} 5 \\ -\ 0 \\ \hline \end{array}$

5. 4 − 4 = ____

6. 6 − 2 = ____

Cross out to subtract. Complete.

7. 4¢ − 1¢ = ____¢

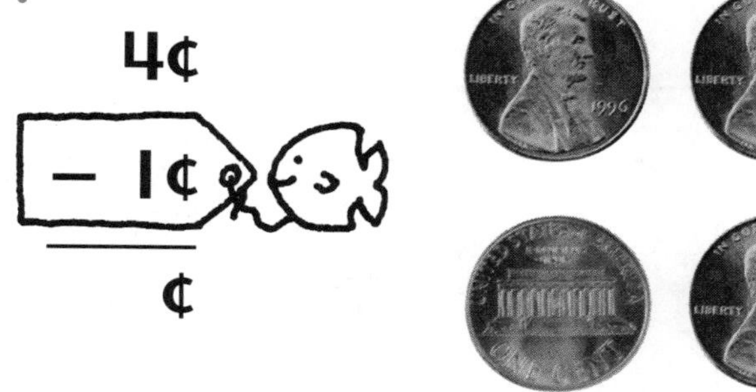

8. 6¢ − 5¢ = ____¢

Problem Solving Reasoning

Ring the number sentence that matches the pictures.

9.

3 − 1 = 2

4 − 1 = 3

Write a number sentence for the picture.

10.

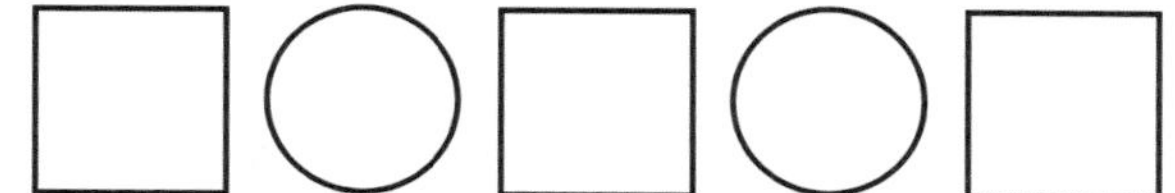

11.

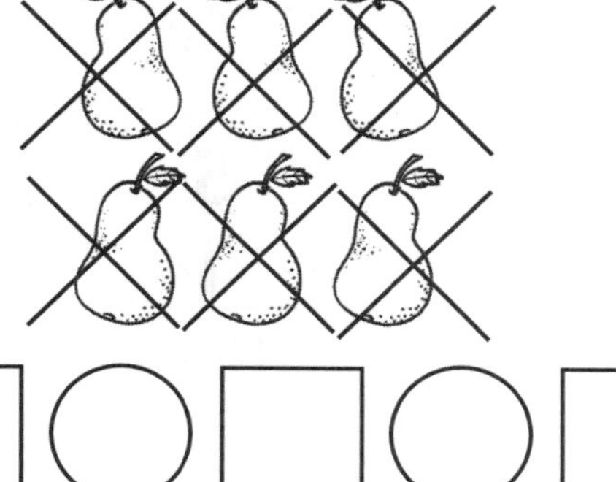

Name ______________________________

Cumulative Review

 ○

 ○

 ○

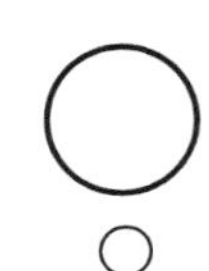		
○	○	○

6	8	9
○	○	○

6 ○ **9**

$<$	$<$	$=$
○	○	○

$$4 + 2 = \square$$

2	4	6
○	○	○

$$\begin{array}{r} 5 \\ -\ 1 \\ \hline \square \end{array}$$

4	1	3
○	○	○

UNIT 5 • TABLE OF CONTENTS

Addition and Subtraction Facts through 6

We will be using this vocabulary:

addend one of the numbers added in an addition problem
sum result of an addition problem
difference result of a subtraction problem
fact family the related addition and subtraction facts

Dear Family,

During the next few weeks our math class will be learning and practicing addition and subtraction facts through 6.

You can expect to see homework that provides practice with addition and subtraction facts.

As we learn about related facts and fact families you may wish to keep the following sample as a guide.

Related Facts

$3 + 1 = 4$ $\qquad$ $4 - 1 = 3$

Fact Family

$\begin{array}{r} 4 \\ +\ 2 \\ \hline 6 \end{array} \qquad \begin{array}{r} 2 \\ +\ 4 \\ \hline 6 \end{array} \qquad \begin{array}{r} 6 \\ -\ 2 \\ \hline 4 \end{array} \qquad \begin{array}{r} 6 \\ -\ 4 \\ \hline 2 \end{array}$

Knowing addition facts can help children learn the related subtraction facts.

Sincerely,

Name ______________________________

Add or subtract.

1. 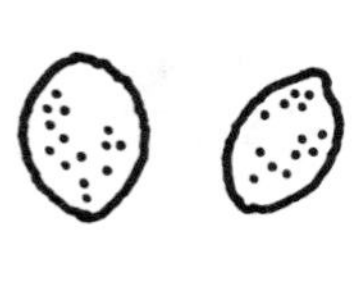 

2 + 1 = 3   3 − 1 = 2

2. 

2 + 2 = ☐   4 − 2 = ☐

3. 

3 + 1 = ☐   4 − 1 = ☐

4. 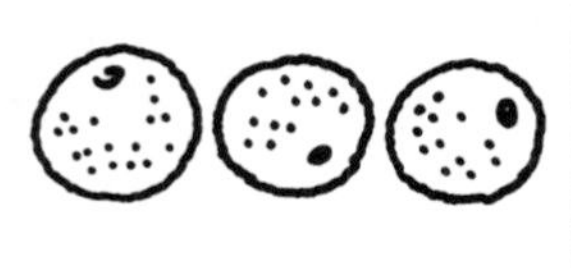

3 + 0 = ☐   3 − 0 = ☐

5. 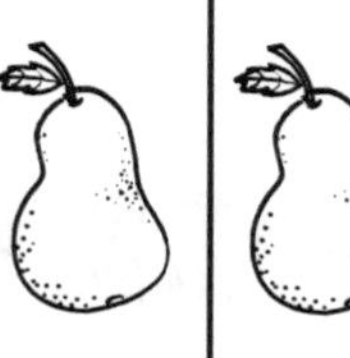

1 + 1 = ☐   2 − 1 = ☐

6. 

1 + 2 = ☐   3 − 2 = ☐

Add or subtract.

7.

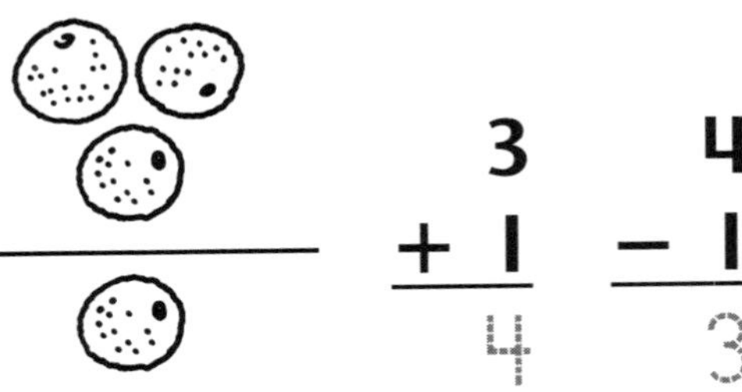

$$\begin{array}{r} 3 \\ +\ 1 \\ \hline 4 \end{array} \qquad \begin{array}{r} 4 \\ -\ 1 \\ \hline 3 \end{array}$$

8.

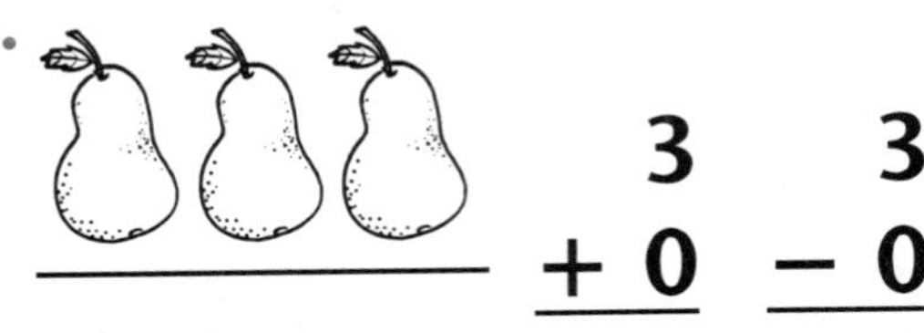

$$\begin{array}{r} 3 \\ +\ 0 \\ \hline \end{array} \qquad \begin{array}{r} 3 \\ -\ 0 \\ \hline \end{array}$$

Practice your facts.

9. $\begin{array}{r} 1 \\ +\ 2 \\ \hline \end{array}$ $\begin{array}{r} 3 \\ -\ 1 \\ \hline \end{array}$ $\begin{array}{r} 1 \\ +\ 3 \\ \hline \end{array}$ $\begin{array}{r} 0 \\ +\ 4 \\ \hline \end{array}$ $\begin{array}{r} 4 \\ -\ 0 \\ \hline \end{array}$

10. $\begin{array}{r} 1 \\ +\ 1 \\ \hline \end{array}$ $\begin{array}{r} 2 \\ -\ 1 \\ \hline \end{array}$ $\begin{array}{r} 1 \\ +\ 3 \\ \hline \end{array}$ $\begin{array}{r} 4 \\ -\ 3 \\ \hline \end{array}$ $\begin{array}{r} 3 \\ -\ 2 \\ \hline \end{array}$

Problem Solving
Reasoning

11. Which subtraction fact do you know if you know **2 + 1 = 3**? ______________________

★ Test Prep

Which number correctly completes the number sentence?
Mark the space under your answer.

3 − 1 = ☐

4	3	2
○	○	○

Name ______________________________

STANDARD

Complete the fact family.

1.

$1 + 3 = $ 4

$3 + 1 = $ 4

$4 - 1 = $ 3

$4 - 3 = $ 1

2.

$4 + 0 = $ ☐

$0 + 4 = $ ☐

$4 - 0 = $ ☐

$4 - 4 = $ ☐

3.

$2 + 2 = $ ☐

$4 - 2 = $ ☐

4.

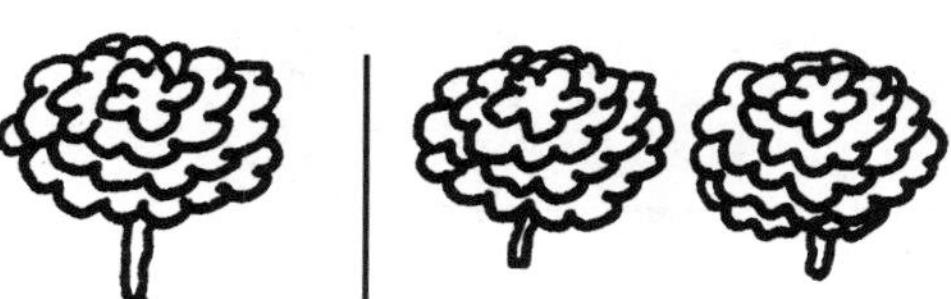

$1 + 2 = $ ☐

$2 + 1 = $ ☐

$3 - 1 = $ ☐

$3 - 2 = $ ☐

5.

$3 + 0 = $ ☐

$0 + 3 = $ ☐

$3 - 0 = $ ☐

$3 - 3 = $ ☐

Complete the fact family.

6.

$2 + 0 = \square$

$0 + 2 = \square$

$2 - 0 = \square$

$2 - 2 = \square$

7.

$1 + 0 = \square$

$0 + 1 = \square$

$1 - 0 = \square$

$1 - 1 = \square$

8.

$1 + 1 = \square$

$2 - 1 = \square$

9.

$0 + 0 = \square$

$0 - 0 = \square$

Problem Solving
Reasoning

10. Write 4 number sentences using only the numbers 4 and **0**. ______________________

★ Test Prep

Which subtraction sentence is related?
Mark the space under your answer.

11

 **3 − 1 = 2**

3 − 2 = 1	3 − 3 = 0	2 − 1 = 1
○	○	○

Name ____________________

Look at the pictures.
Write the fact family.

1.

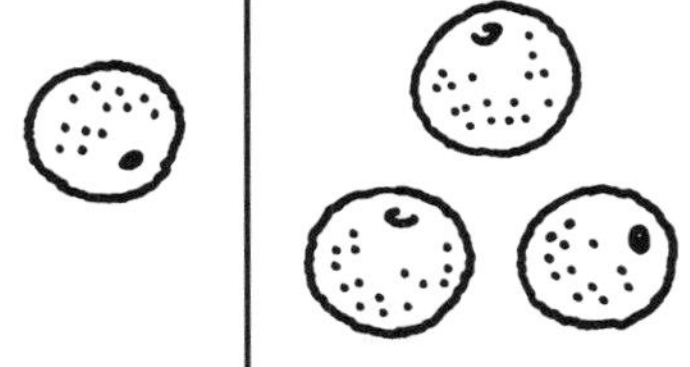

1	+	3	=	4
3	+	1	=	
4	−	3	=	
4	−	1	=	

2.

	+		=	
	+		=	
	−		=	
	−		=	

3.

	+		=	
	+		=	
	−		=	
	−		=	

4.

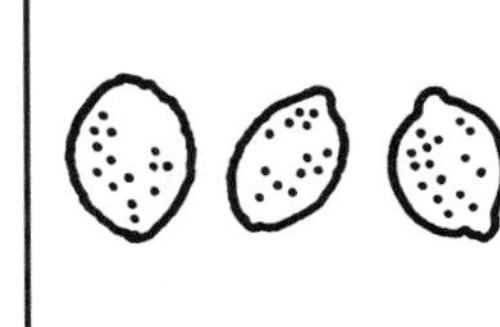

	+		=	
	+		=	
	−		=	
	−		=	

Complete.

5.

$$\begin{array}{r} 1 \\ +\ 2 \\ \hline \end{array} \qquad \begin{array}{r} 2 \\ +\ 1 \\ \hline \end{array}$$

$$\begin{array}{r} 3 \\ -\ 1 \\ \hline \end{array} \qquad \begin{array}{r} 3 \\ -\ 2 \\ \hline \end{array}$$

6.

$$\begin{array}{r} 4 \\ +\ 0 \\ \hline \end{array} \qquad \begin{array}{r} 0 \\ +\ 4 \\ \hline \end{array}$$

$$\begin{array}{r} 4 \\ -\ 0 \\ \hline \end{array} \qquad \begin{array}{r} 4 \\ -\ 4 \\ \hline \end{array}$$

Problem Solving Reasoning

7. How are the fact families for **0** + **0**; **1** + **1**; and **2** + **2** alike? How are they different?

Quick Check

Complete.

1. $3 + 0 = \square$

   $3 - 0 = \square$

2. $2 + 2 = \square$

   $4 - 2 = \square$

3. $1 + 3 = \square$

   $3 + 1 = \square$

   $\square - \square = \square$

   $\square - \square = \square$

Name ______________________

Problem

There are 4  .

3 fly away.

How many are left?

1 Understand

I need to find out how many birds are left.

2 Decide

I can draw a picture to solve the problem.

3 Solve

I can draw circles for the birds.

There is __1__ bird left.

4 Look back

I can use a number sentence to check.

Does $4 - 3 = 1$? ____________

My answer makes sense.

Draw a picture to solve.

1. There are 2 birds in a tree.

   3 more birds fly onto the tree.

   How many birds in all?

   ____ birds

2. There are 3 birds in a tree.

   1 bird flies away.

   How many  are there now?

   ____ birds

Tell a story to match the number sentence. Draw a picture.

3. $2 + 4 = 6$

Name ______________________________

Add or subtract.

1. 

$4 + 1 = $ 5 $5 - 1 = $ 4

2. 

$4 + 2 = $ ☐ $6 - 2 = $ ☐

3. 

$3 + 3 = $ ☐ $6 - 3 = $ ☐

4. 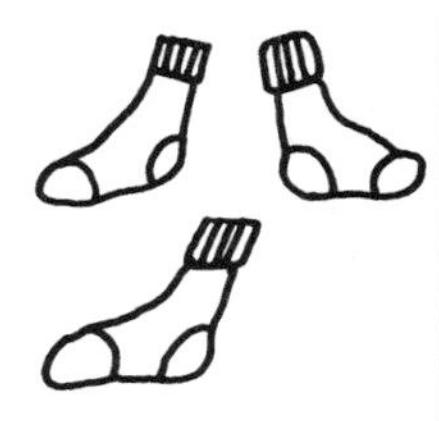 

$3 + 2 = $ ☐ $5 - 2 = $ ☐

5. 

$5 + 1 = $ ☐ $6 - 1 = $ ☐

6. 

$5 + 0 = $ ☐ $5 - 0 = $ ☐

Add or subtract.

7.

$$\begin{array}{r} 2 \\ +\ 4 \\ \hline \end{array} \qquad \begin{array}{r} 6 \\ -\ 4 \\ \hline \end{array}$$

8.

$$\begin{array}{r} 1 \\ +\ 5 \\ \hline \end{array} \qquad \begin{array}{r} 6 \\ -\ 5 \\ \hline \end{array}$$

Practice your facts.

9.

$$\begin{array}{r} 4 \\ -\ 1 \\ \hline \end{array} \qquad \begin{array}{r} 3 \\ +\ 1 \\ \hline \end{array} \qquad \begin{array}{r} 6 \\ -\ 5 \\ \hline \end{array} \qquad \begin{array}{r} 5 \\ +\ 1 \\ \hline \end{array} \qquad \begin{array}{r} 5 \\ -\ 5 \\ \hline \end{array}$$

10.

$$\begin{array}{r} 2 \\ +\ 1 \\ \hline \end{array} \qquad \begin{array}{r} 3 \\ -\ 1 \\ \hline \end{array} \qquad \begin{array}{r} 3 \\ +\ 2 \\ \hline \end{array} \qquad \begin{array}{r} 5 \\ -\ 2 \\ \hline \end{array} \qquad \begin{array}{r} 5 \\ -\ 0 \\ \hline \end{array}$$

Problem Solving
Reasoning

11. Which addition fact do you know if you know
$6 - 5 = 1$? ______________________

★ Test Prep

Which number correctly completes the number sentence?
Mark the space under your answer.

$5 - 3 = \square$

1	2	3
○	○	○

Name ____________________

Complete the fact family.

1.

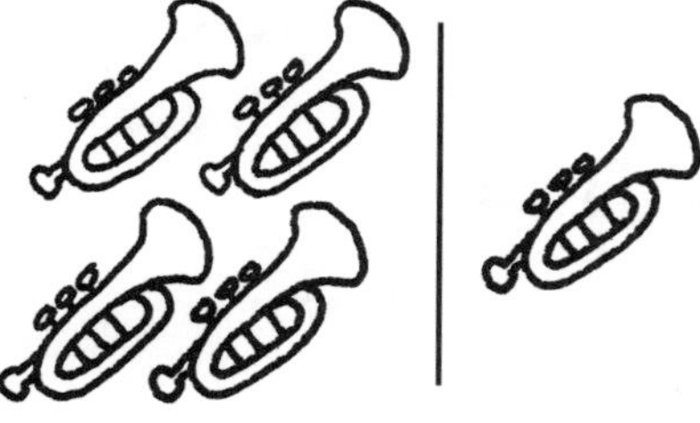

4 + 1 = 5

1 + 4 = 5

5 − 4 = 1

5 − 1 = 4

2.

2 + 3 = ☐

3 + 2 = ☐

5 − 3 = ☐

5 − 2 = ☐

3.

5 − 0 = ☐

5 − 5 = ☐

5 + 0 = ☐

0 + 5 = ☐

4.

5 − 1 = ☐

4 + 1 = ☐

1 + 4 = ☐

5 − 4 = ☐

5.

3 + 2 = ☐

2 + 3 = ☐

5 − 3 = ☐

5 − 2 = ☐

Complete the fact family.

6. 

$1 + 5 = \square$

$5 + 1 = \square$

$6 - 1 = \square$

$6 - 5 = \square$

7. 

$2 + 4 = \square$

$4 + 2 = \square$

$6 - 2 = \square$

$6 - 4 = \square$

8.  

$3 + 3 = \square$

$6 - 3 = \square$

Problem Solving
Reasoning

9. Write 4 number sentences using only the numbers **6** and **0**. ______________________

____

★ Test Prep

Which addition sentence is related?
Mark the space under your answer.

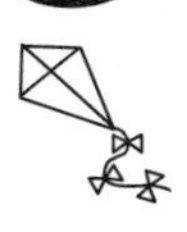

$4 + 2 = 6$ | $5 + 1 = 6$ ○ | $2 + 4 = 6$ ○ | $2 + 3 = 5$ ○

Name ____________________

STANDARD

3 (+) 1 = 4   3 (−) 1 = 2

Make true sentences.

Write + or −.

1. 2 ◯ 1 = 1   4 ◯ 2 = 6   3 ◯ 0 = 3

2. 3 ◯ 2 = 1   1 ◯ 5 = 6   1 ◯ 0 = 1

3. 0 ◯ 2 = 2   3 ◯ 3 = 6   1 ◯ 2 = 3

4. 2 ◯ 2 = 4   6 ◯ 4 = 2   1 ◯ 3 = 4

5. 4 ◯ 1 = 3   5 ◯ 3 = 2   3 ◯ 1 = 2

6. 2 ◯ 1 = 3   4 ◯ 4 = 0   1 ◯ 1 = 2

7. 4 ◯ 2 = 2   3 ◯ 1 = 4   2 ◯ 2 = 0

Use the pictures to make the sentence true.

Write + or −.

8.  

3 ◯ 2 = 1

9.  

2 ◯ 2 = 4

Problem Solving
Reasoning

10. How do you decide whether to put a + or − in a number sentence to make it true? ______________________

____

Quick Check

Complete with related facts.

1. 5 + 1 = ☐ 6 − 1 = ☐

2. 4 + 1 = ☐ 5 − 1 = ☐

1 + ☐ = ☐ ☐ − ☐ = ☐

Write + or −.

3. 2  2 = 4

Name ______________________________

Ring the correct card.

Problem Solving Plan
1. Understand 2. Decide 3. Solve 4. Look back

Think Do you add or subtract?

1. There are **4** cats.

2 cats walk away.

How many are left?

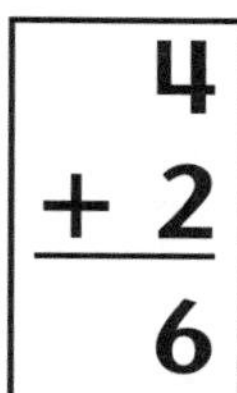

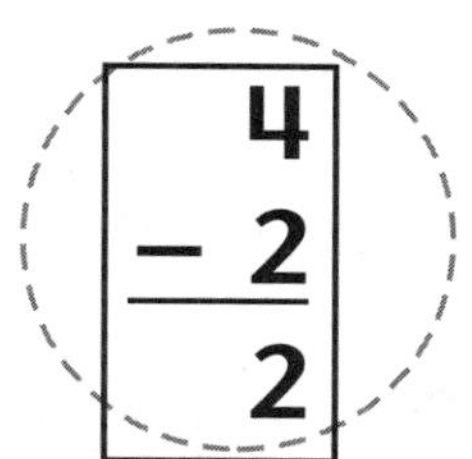

2. There are **4** dogs.

1 dog joins them.

How many in all?

4
− 1
3

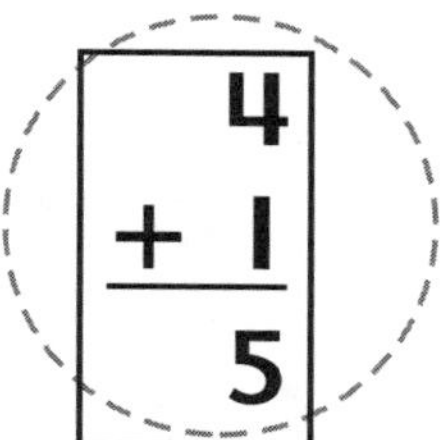

3. I have **3** starfish.

I find **2** starfish.

How many in all?

3
− 2
1

3
+ 2
5

4. I have **3** frogs.

3 frogs hop away.

How many are left?

3
+ 3
6

3
− 3
0

Solve.

Think Should I add or subtract?

5.

There are 2 pigs.

2  join them.

$$\begin{array}{r} 2 \\ + \; 2 \\ \hline 4 \end{array}$$

How many in all? 4

6.

There are 4 chickens.

4  fly away.

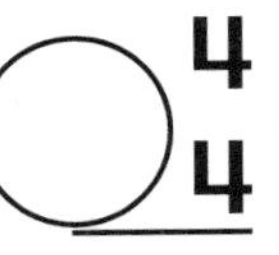

$$\begin{array}{r} 4 \\ \bigcirc \; 4 \\ \hline \square \end{array}$$

How many are left? ☐

7.

There are 5 squirrels.

1  joins them.

How many in all?

5 ◯ 1 = ☐

8.

There are 6 cats.

3  walk away.

How many are left?

6 ◯ 3 = ☐

Extend Your Thinking

Complete the problem and number sentence so that they match.

9. There are  .

 walk away.

How many are left?

___ ◯ ___ = ___

Name ______________________________

STANDARD

3¢
+ 1¢
4¢

How much for both?

1.

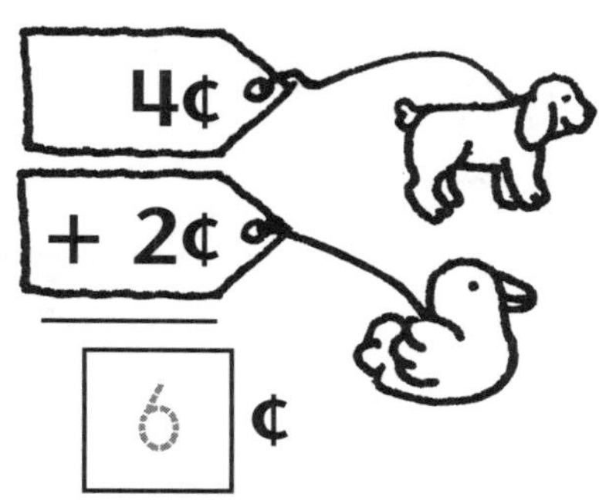

2.

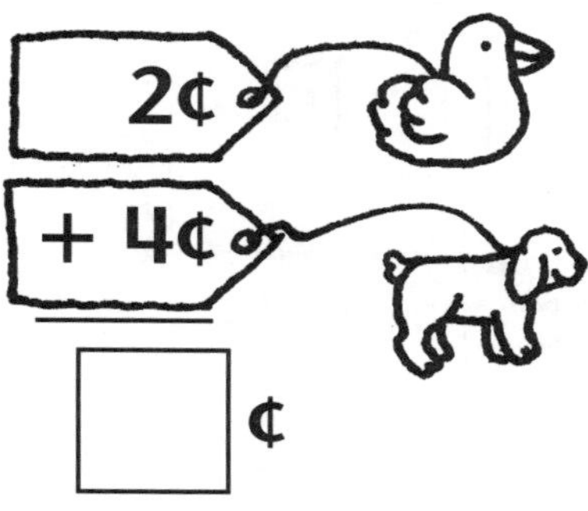

3.

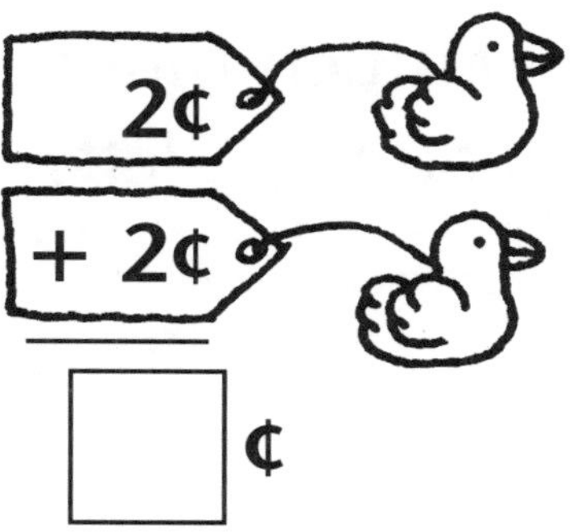

4.

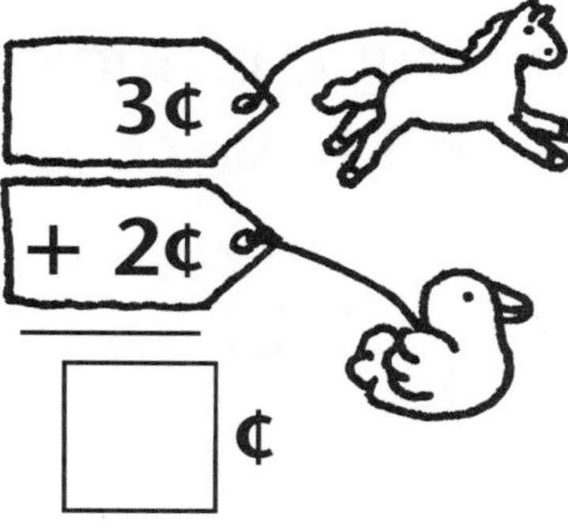

5.

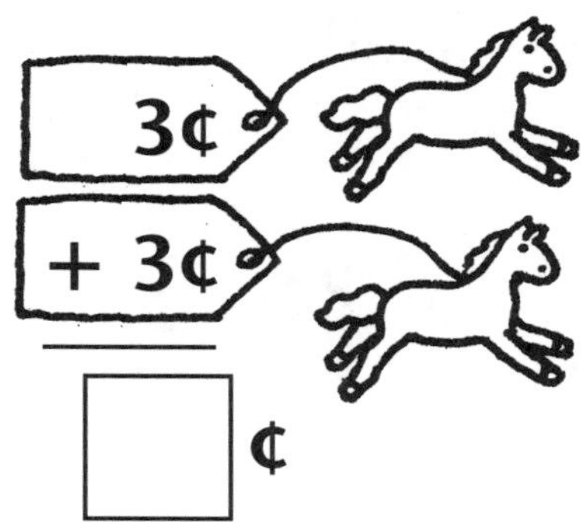

6.

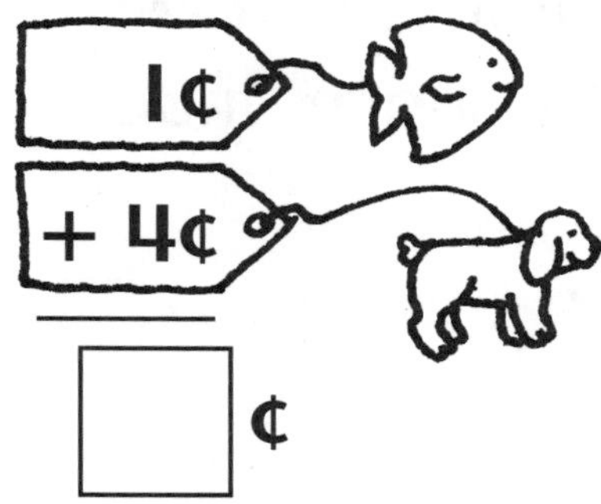

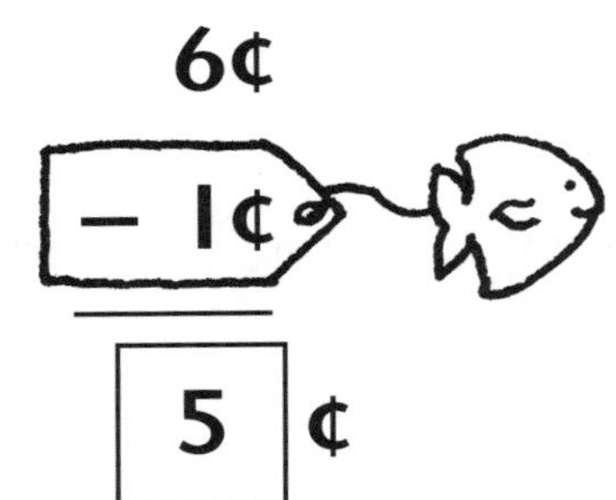

How much money is left?

7. 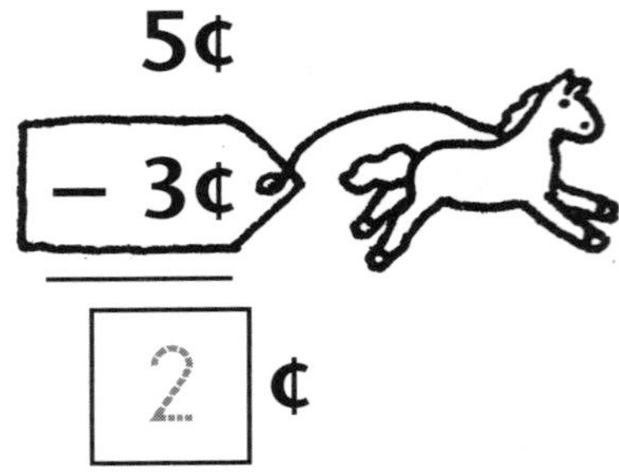

8. 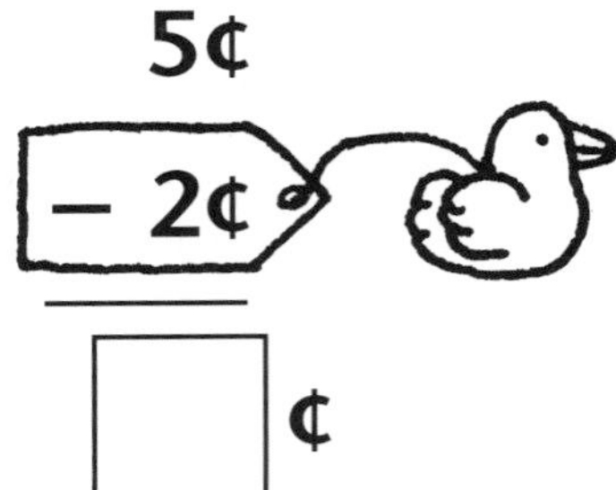

Problem Solving Reasoning Solve.

9. You have **3¢.**
You find **2¢** more.
How much money
do you have?

3¢ ◯ **2¢ =** ____¢

10. You have **5¢.**
You spend **1¢.**
How much money
do you have left?

5¢ ◯ **1¢ =** ____¢

★ Test Prep

Which amount shows how much money is left?
Mark the space under your answer.

11  **6¢ – 4¢ =** ☐

1¢	2¢	3¢
○	○	○

Name ______________________

Solve.

1. $\begin{array}{r} 6 \\ -\ 4 \\ \hline \end{array}$

2. $\begin{array}{r} 3 \\ +\ 2 \\ \hline \end{array}$

3. $\begin{array}{r} 4 \\ -\ 0 \\ \hline \end{array}$

4. $\begin{array}{r} 2 \\ +\ 2 \\ \hline \end{array}$

5. $\begin{array}{r} 4 \\ +\ 2 \\ \hline \end{array}$

Complete the fact family.

6. 5 + 1 = ☐

1 + ☐ = ☐

☐ − ☐ = ☐

☐ − ☐ = ☐

7. 3 + 2 = ☐

2 + ☐ = ☐

☐ − ☐ = ☐

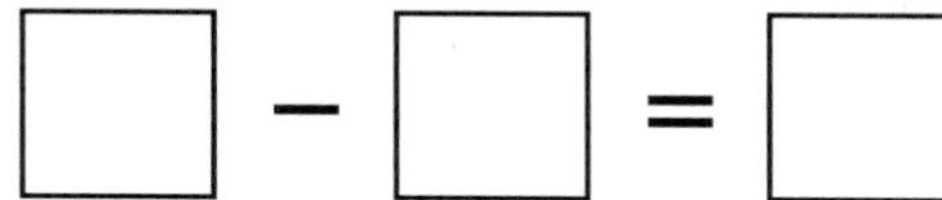

☐ − ☐ = ☐

Problem Solving Reasoning

Draw a picture. Solve.

8. 4 + 2 = ☐

9. 4 − 1 = ☐

Add or subtract to solve.

10. There are 5 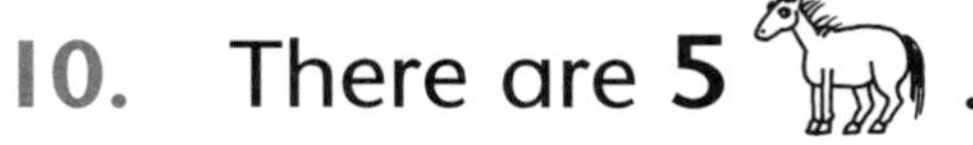 .

2  walk away.

How many are left?

5 ◯ 2 = ☐

11. There are 3 .

2 more  join them.

How many in all?

3 ◯ 2 = ☐

Name ____________________

★ Test Prep

1

8 ○ 9 ○ 10 ○

2

9 ○ 9

< ○ > ○ = ○

3

2 + 1 = 3
1 + 2 = 3
3 − 2 = 1
______

2 − 1 = 1 ○ 3 − 3 = 0 ○ 3 − 1 = 2 ○

4

3 − 2 = 1 ○ 3 + 2 = 5 ○ 3 − 3 = 0 ○

Solve.

$$\begin{array}{r} 4 \\ +\ 2 \\ \hline \end{array}$$

2 ○ 4 ○ 6 ○

$$\begin{array}{r} 5 \\ -\ 4 \\ \hline \end{array}$$

1 ○ 3 ○ 5 ○

UNIT 6 • TABLE OF CONTENTS

Addition and Subtraction Facts through 10

UNIT 6 • TABLE OF CONTENTS

We will be using this vocabulary:

fact family the related addition and subtraction facts

addend one of the numbers added in an addition problem

function tables A two-column chart of numbers in which the same number is added to or subtracted from each number in the first column resulting in the numbers in the second column

+3

1	4
2	5
3	6

Dear Family,

During the next few weeks our math class will be learning and practicing addition and subtraction facts through 10.

You can expect to see homework that provides practice with addition and subtraction facts.

As we learn about related facts and fact families you may wish to keep the following sample as a guide.

Related Facts

$7 + 3 = 10$ $10 - 3 = 7$

Fact Family

$4 + 2 = 6$ $6 - 4 = 2$

$2 + 4 = 6$ $6 - 2 = 4$

Knowing addition facts can help children learn the related subtraction facts.

Sincerely,

Name ______________________________

5 + 3 = 8   8 − 3 = 5

Complete.

1. 

6 + 1 = ☐   7 − 1 = ☐

2. 5 + 2 = ☐   7 − 2 = ☐

3. 4 + 4 = ☐   8 − 4 = ☐

4. 

2 + 6 = ☐   8 − 6 = ☐

5. 7 + 0 = ☐   7 − 0 = ☐

6. 

0 + 8 = ☐   8 − 8 = ☐

Solve.

7. $\begin{array}{r} 2 \\ +\ 6 \\ \hline \end{array}$

8. $\begin{array}{r} 8 \\ -\ 2 \\ \hline \end{array}$

9. $\begin{array}{r} 1 \\ +\ 3 \\ \hline \end{array}$

10. $\begin{array}{r} 4 \\ -\ 3 \\ \hline \end{array}$

11. $\begin{array}{r} 3 \\ +\ 3 \\ \hline \end{array}$

12. $\begin{array}{r} 6 \\ -\ 3 \\ \hline \end{array}$

13. $\begin{array}{r} 7 \\ -\ 5 \\ \hline \end{array}$

14. $\begin{array}{r} 5 \\ +\ 2 \\ \hline \end{array}$

Problem Solving Reasoning

Draw a picture. Solve.

15. There are **7** dishes on a table. **3** dishes fall. How many are left?

_____ dishes

★ Test Prep

Which number correctly completes the number sentence? Mark the space under your answer.

16  $3 + 5 = \square$

6	2	8
○	○	○

Name ______________________________

Complete the fact family.

1. 

7 + 0 = 7

0 + 7 = 7

7 − 0 = 7

7 − 7 = 0

2. 

1 + 6 = ☐

6 + 1 = ☐

7 − 1 = ☐

7 − 6 = ☐

3. 

3 + 4 = ☐

4 + 3 = ☐

7 − 3 = ☐

7 − 4 = ☐

4.  

2 + 5 = 7

☐ ○ ☐ ○ ☐

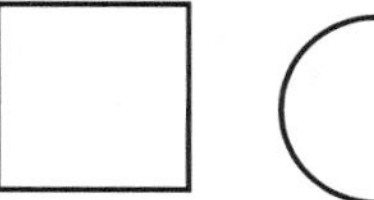 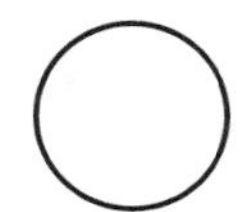 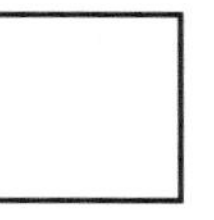 

☐ ○ ☐ ○ ☐

 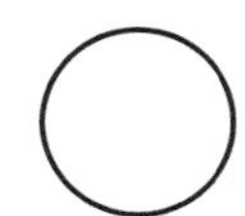 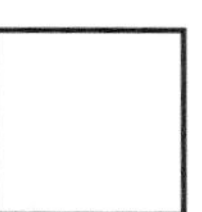 

☐ ○ ☐ ○ ☐

  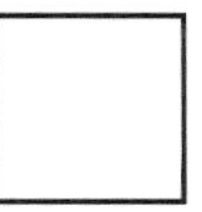  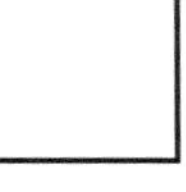

Complete the fact family.

5.

$2 + 6 = \square$ $8 - 2 = \square$

$6 + 2 = \square$ $8 - 6 = \square$

6.

$3 + 5 = \square$ $8 - 3 = \square$

$5 + 3 = \square$ $8 - 5 = \square$

7.

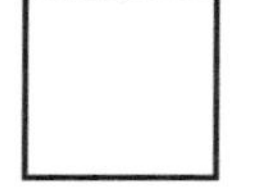
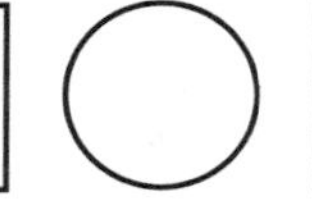
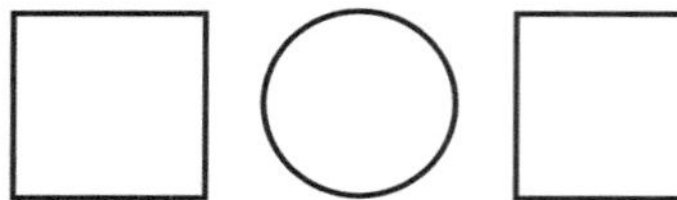

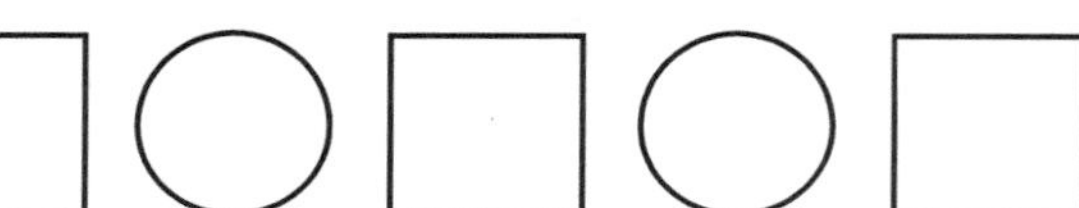

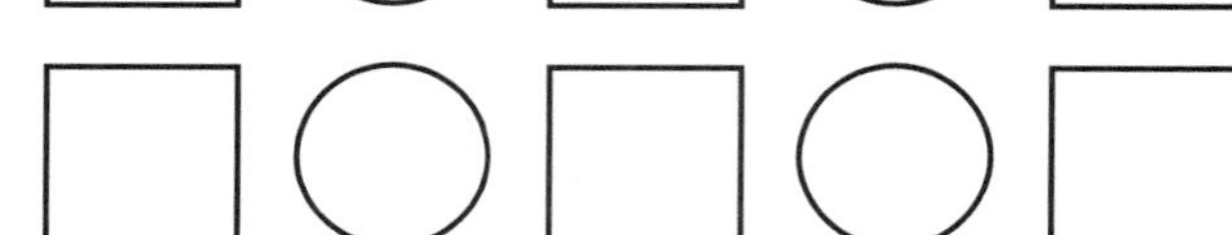

Problem Solving
Reasoning

Write 3 numbers that belong to the same fact family.

8. _____, _____, _____

★ Test Prep

Mark the space under the related number sentence.

9 $\mathbf{3 + 3 = 6}$

$3 + 2 = 5$	$6 - 3 = 3$	$3 - 3 = 0$
○	○	○

Name ______________________________

Add or subtract.

1. 

$8 + 2 =$ [10] $10 - 2 =$ [8]

2. 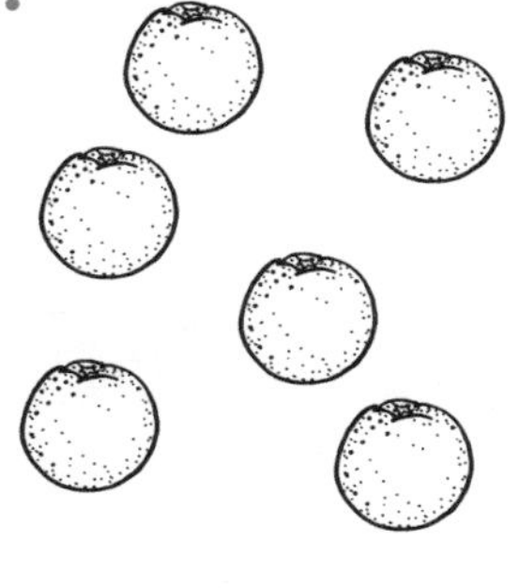

$6 + 3 =$ [ ] $9 - 3 =$ [ ]

3.  

$3 + 7 =$ [ ] $10 - 7 =$ [ ]

4. 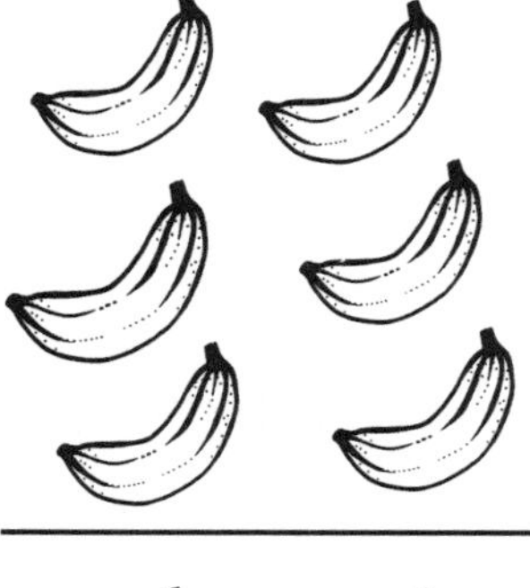 

$$\begin{array}{r} 6 \\ +\ 4 \\ \hline \end{array} \qquad \begin{array}{r} 10 \\ -\ 4 \\ \hline \end{array}$$

5. 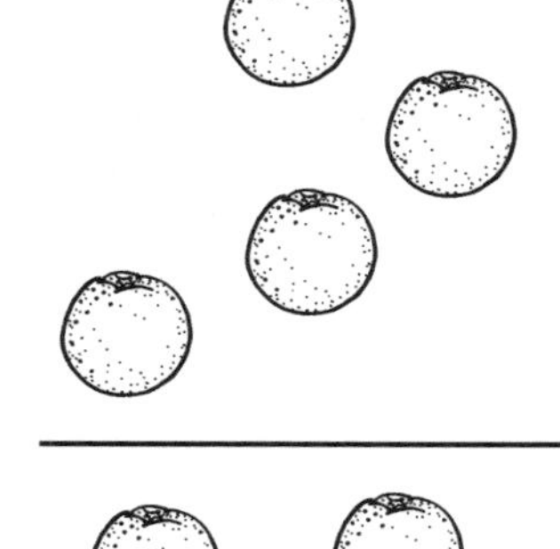 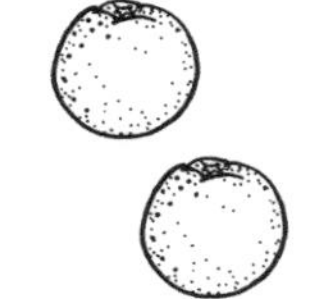

$$\begin{array}{r} 5 \\ +\ 4 \\ \hline \end{array} \qquad \begin{array}{r} 9 \\ -\ 4 \\ \hline \end{array}$$

Problem Solving
Reasoning

Solve.

6. There are **8** dogs.
1 dog joins them.
How many dogs are there in all?

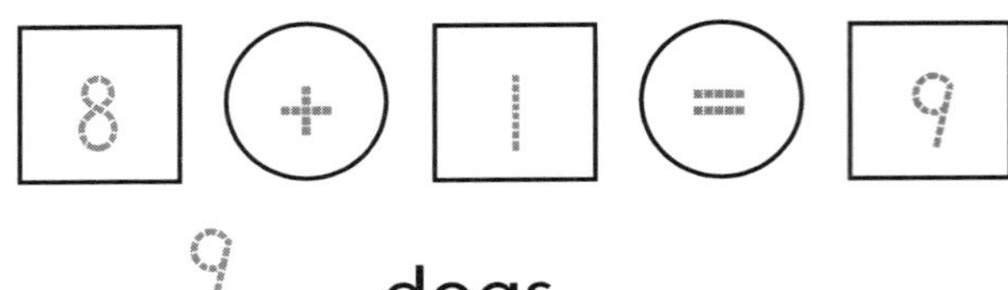

9 dogs

7. There are **9** frogs.
5 hop away.
How many frogs are left?

☐ ◯ ☐ ◯ ☐

_____ frogs

Quick Check

Write the fact family for the picture.

1.

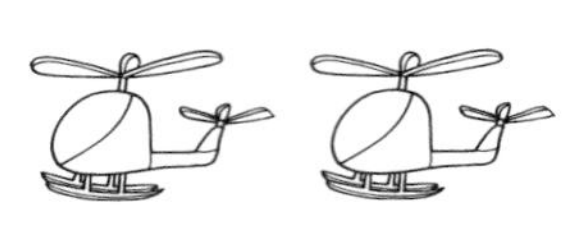

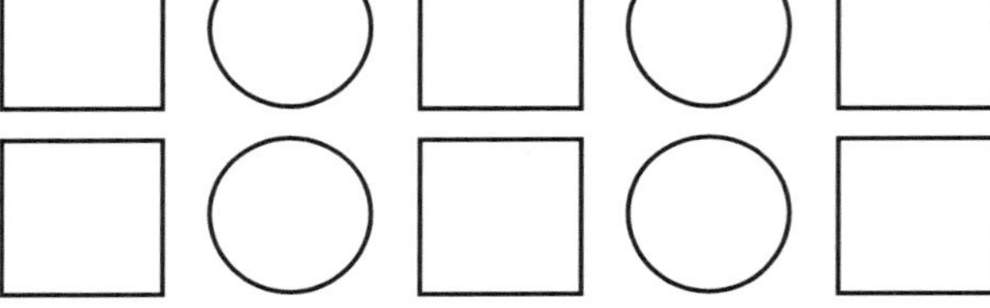

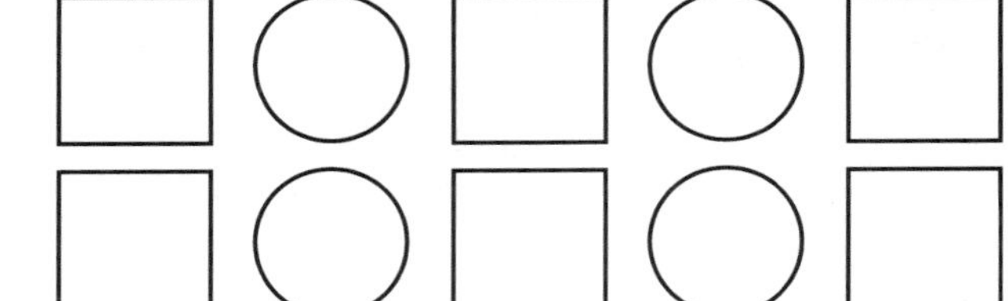

Add or subtract.

2. $\begin{array}{r} 2 \\ +\ 7 \\ \hline \end{array}$

3. $\begin{array}{r} 10 \\ -\ 4 \\ \hline \end{array}$

Name ______________________________

Complete the fact family.

1.

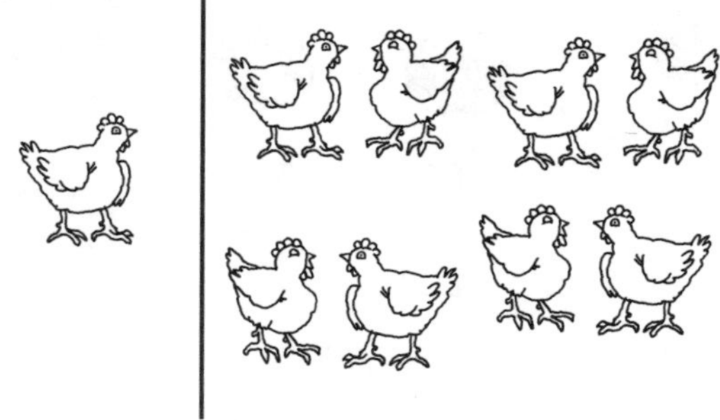

1 + 8 = 9

8 + 1 = 9

9 − 1 = 8

9 − 8 = 1

2.

2 + 7 = ☐

7 + 2 = ☐

9 − 2 = ☐

9 − 7 = ☐

3.

3 + 6 = ☐

6 + 3 = ☐

9 − 3 = ☐

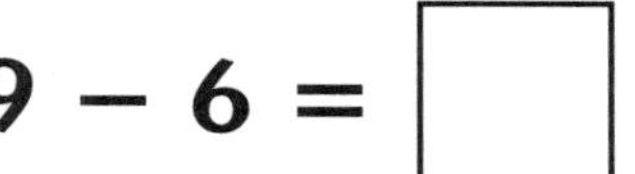

9 − 6 = ☐

4.

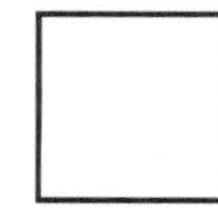

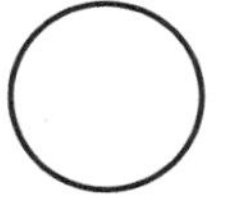

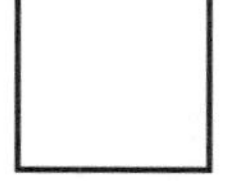

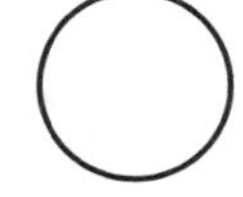

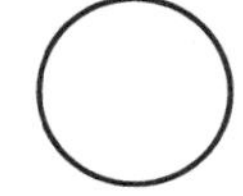

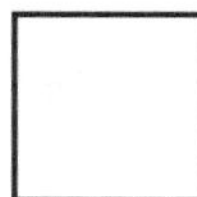

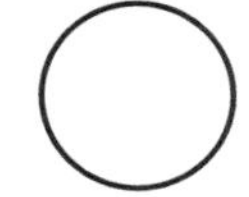

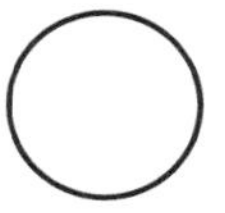

Complete the fact family.

5.

$1 + 9 =$ ☐

$9 + 1 =$ ☐

$10 - 1 =$ ☐

$10 - 9 =$ ☐

6.

☐ ◯ ☐ ◯ ☐

☐ ◯ ☐ ◯ ☐

☐ ◯ ☐ ◯ ☐

☐ ◯ ☐ ◯ ☐

Problem Solving Reasoning

Draw a picture. Solve.

7. There are **3** children.
7 more children join them.
How many in all?

_____ children

8. There are **10** children.
4 children walk away.
How many are left?

_____ children

★ Test Prep

Mark the space under the related number sentence.

9. **10 − 7 = 3**

$7 - 3 = 4$	$10 - 3 = 7$	$4 - 3 = 1$
◯	◯	◯

Name ____________________

Group the numbers and add.

1.

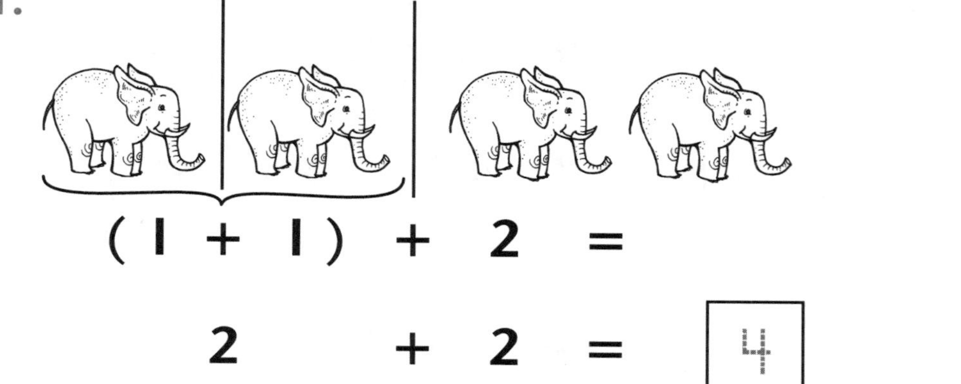

(1 + 1) + 2 =

2 + 2 = [4]

1) 2
1
+ 2
4

2.

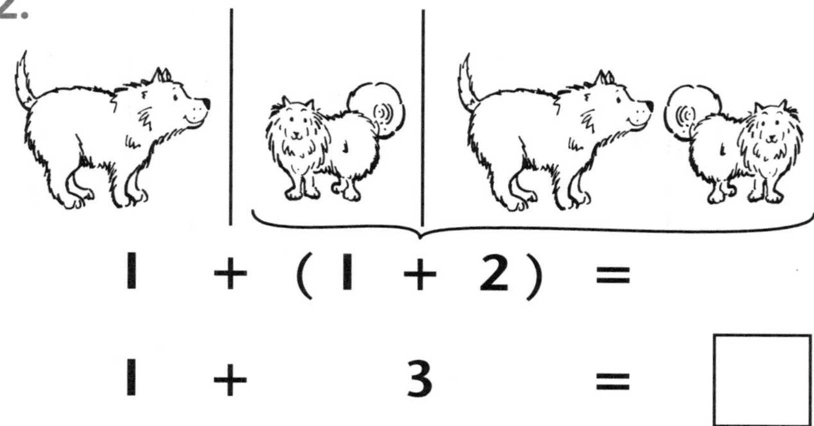

1 + (1 + 2) =

1 + 3 = [ ]

1
1) 3
+ 2

3.

(2 + 1) + 2 =

3 + 2 = [ ]

2)
1
+ 2

4. 2) 3
1
+ 1

5. 4
1)
+ 0

6. 3)
1
+ 1

7. 1
3)
+ 1

8. 2)
2
+ 1

Find the sum.

9. $(2 + 3) + 1 =$

$5 + 1 = \boxed{6}$

10. $2 + (3 + 1) =$

$2 + 4 = \square$

11.

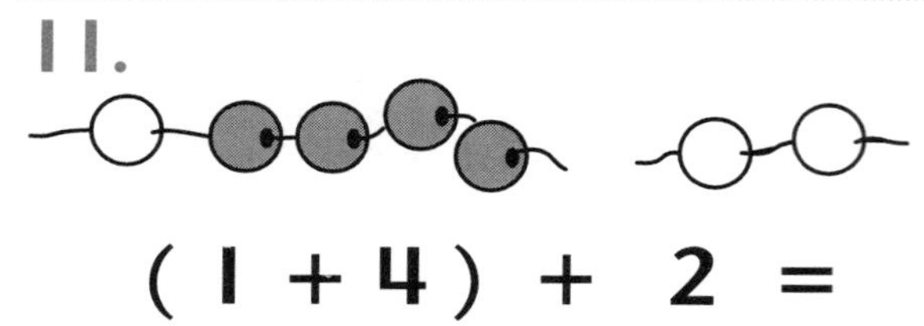

$(1 + 4) + 2 =$

$5 + 2 = \square$

12. $1 + (4 + 2) =$

$1 + 6 = \square$

13. $\begin{array}{r} 2 \\ 1 \\ +\ 3 \\ \hline \end{array}$

14. $\begin{array}{r} 1 \\ 2 \\ +\ 3 \\ \hline \end{array}$

15. $\begin{array}{r} 4 \\ 2 \\ +\ 1 \\ \hline \end{array}$

16. $\begin{array}{r} 1 \\ 3 \\ +\ 3 \\ \hline \end{array}$

17. $\begin{array}{r} 4 \\ 1 \\ +\ 1 \\ \hline \end{array}$

Problem Solving Reasoning

Solve.

18. There are 2 red crayons, 3 blue crayons, and 2 black crayons. How many in all? _____ crayons

★ Test Prep

Mark the space under the sum.

$2 + (2 + 2) = \square$

4	5	6
○	○	○

Name ______________________________

Group the numbers and add.

1.

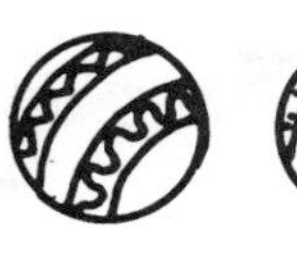

(3 + 4) + 1 = 3 + (4 + 1) =

7 + 1 = 8 3 + 5 = 8

2.

(1 + 5) + 3 = 1 + (5 + 3) =

____ + ____ = ☐ ____ + ____ = ☐

3.

(1 + 2) + 6 = 1 + (2 + 6) =

____ + ____ = ☐ ____ + ____ = ☐

4. $\begin{array}{r} 4 \\ 2 \\ +\ 2 \\ \hline \end{array}$

5. $\begin{array}{r} 7 \\ 0 \\ +\ 2 \\ \hline \end{array}$

6. $\begin{array}{r} 6 \\ 1 \\ +\ 1 \\ \hline \end{array}$

7. $\begin{array}{r} 4 \\ 3 \\ +\ 2 \\ \hline \end{array}$

8. $\begin{array}{r} 4 \\ 0 \\ +\ 4 \\ \hline \end{array}$

Group the numbers and add.

9.          

$(5 + 3) + 2 =$ $\qquad$ $5 + (3 + 2) =$

8 + 2 = ☐ $\qquad$ 5 + 5 = ☐

10.    

$(1 + 3) + 6 =$ $\qquad$ $1 + (3 + 6) =$

____ + ____ = ☐ $\qquad$ ____ + ____ = ☐

11. $\begin{array}{r} 4 \\ 4 \\ +\ 2 \\ \hline \end{array}$ 12. $\begin{array}{r} 3 \\ 4 \\ +\ 2 \\ \hline \end{array}$ 13. $\begin{array}{r} 4 \\ 4 \\ +\ 1 \\ \hline \end{array}$ 14. $\begin{array}{r} 1 \\ 4 \\ +\ 5 \\ \hline \end{array}$ 15. $\begin{array}{r} 0 \\ 4 \\ +\ 5 \\ \hline \end{array}$ 16. $\begin{array}{r} 1 \\ 3 \\ +\ 5 \\ \hline \end{array}$

Problem Solving
Reasoning

17. What 3 numbers have a sum of 10? ____, ____, ____

 **Quick Check**

Complete the fact family.

1. 6 + 4 = 10 $\qquad$ 10 − ☐ = ☐

☐ + 6 = ☐ $\qquad$ ☐ − ☐ = ☐

Solve.

2. $\begin{array}{r} 1 \\ 3 \\ +\ 2 \\ \hline \end{array}$ $\qquad$ 3. $\begin{array}{r} 3 \\ 3 \\ +\ 2 \\ \hline \end{array}$

Name ______________________________

Fill in each □ .

1. Put in 3 + Put in [3] more = 6 in all

2. Put in 6 + Put in □ more = 10 in all

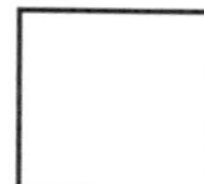

3. 7 + □ = 9 in all

4. 5 + □ = 8 in all

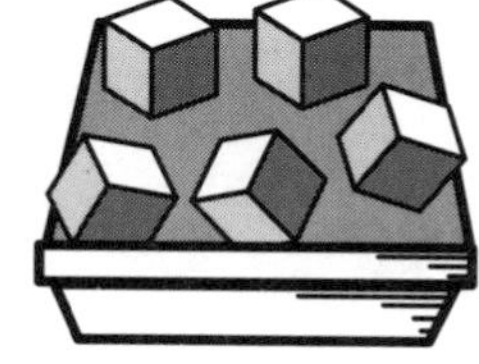

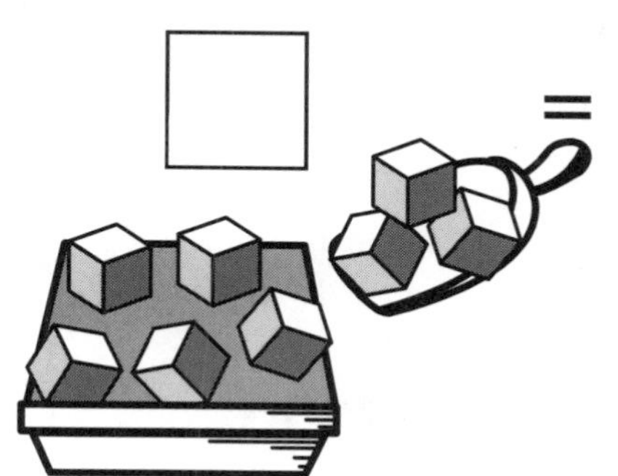

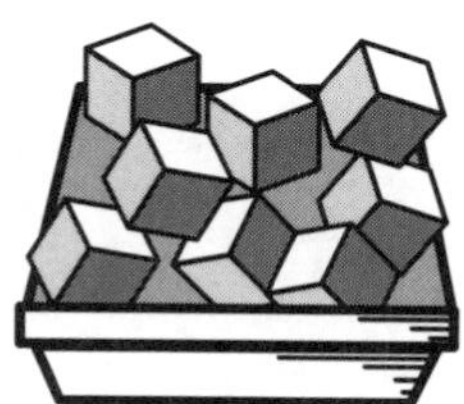

Write the missing number.

5.

$\square + 3 = 4$

6.

$\square + 2 = 3$

7.

$\square + 6 = 10$

$$\begin{array}{r} \square \\ +\ 6 \\ \hline 10 \end{array}$$

8.

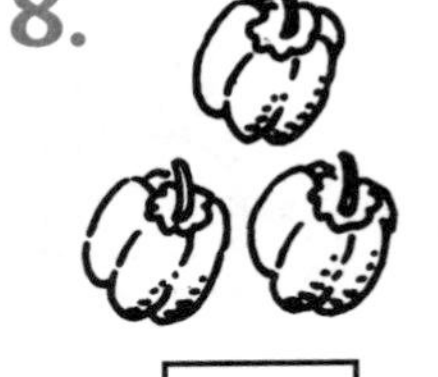

$\square + 4 = 7$

$$\begin{array}{r} \square \\ +\ 4 \\ \hline 7 \end{array}$$

9.
$$\begin{array}{r} 2 \\ +\ \square \\ \hline 8 \end{array}$$

10.

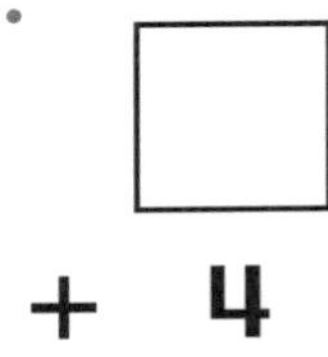

$$\begin{array}{r} \square \\ +\ 4 \\ \hline 8 \end{array}$$

11.
$$\begin{array}{r} 5 \\ +\ \square \\ \hline 9 \end{array}$$

12.
$$\begin{array}{r} \square \\ +\ 7 \\ \hline 10 \end{array}$$

13.
$$\begin{array}{r} 6 \\ +\ \square \\ \hline 7 \end{array}$$

Problem Solving Reasoning

Draw a picture. Solve.

14. There are **4** fish.
Some more fish join them.
Now there are **9** fish.
How many fish joined?

_____ fish

★ Test Prep

Mark under the number that makes the sentence true.

15. $\square + 3 = 8$

6	5	7
○	○	○

Name ______________________

Complete the table.

1. +2

2	4
3	5
4	6
5	7

2. +1

8	
7	
6	
5	

3. +3

3	
4	
5	
6	

4. −1

7	6
6	5
5	4
4	3

5. −3

4	
5	
6	
7	

6. −4

7	
6	
5	
4	

7. +2

7	
3	
8	
4	
2	
1	
5	

8. −2

9	
3	
7	
10	
5	
8	
4	

9. +4

5	
2	
4	
0	
3	
1	
6	

Complete the table.

10.

Rule + 4

In	3	1	2	4
Out	7	5	6	8

11.

Rule − 2

In	8	7	6	5
Out	6	5		

12.

Rule − 3

In	6	5	7	8
Out		2	4	

13.

Rule + 1

In	8	4	6	9
Out	9			10

Problem Solving Reasoning

Write the rule.

14.

Rule ____

In	1	2	3	4	5	6	7	8
Out	3	4	5	6	7	8	9	10

How can you check if the rule is right? ____________________

____

____

★ Test Prep

Mark the space under your answer to complete the table.

15 

+3

6	9
4	

7 ○ 8 ○ 5 ○

Name ____________________

Problem Solving Application: Use a Table

Problem Solving Plan
1. Understand 2. Decide 3. Solve 4. Look back

STANDARD

Favorite Fruit					
Number of Children	7	3	8	9	5

Use the table to answer the question.

Think Find the fruit in the table.
Look at the number of children.

1. How many children like  ? 9

2. How many children like  ? ____

3. How many children like  ? ____

Ring your answer.

4. Do more children like  than  ? yes no

5. Do fewer children like  than  ? yes no

Toy				
Cost	8¢	5¢	4¢	6¢

Look at the table. Write the cost of the toy.

Think Where is the object pictured?
How much does it cost?

6.  ______ ¢

7.  ______ ¢

Ring the coins needed to buy the toy.

8. 

9. 

Extend Your Thinking

10. Can you pay for the dog another way?
What coins could you use? ______________________

____

Name ______________________________

I penny	I nickel	I dime	I dime

I cent	5 cents	10 cents	10 cents
I¢	5¢	10¢	10¢

How much money?

I.

¢

2.

☐ ¢

3.

¢

4.

☐ ¢

Ring the coins needed.

5. 

Problem Solving
Reasoning

Show 10¢ in three different ways. Write how many of each coin you need.

6.

10 ¢	10 ¢	10 ¢
1		
0		
0		

Quick Check

Complete.

1. 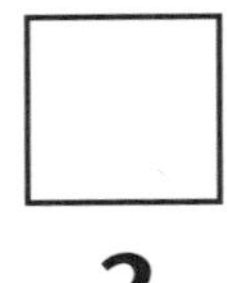

$$\begin{array}{r} \square \\ + \ 2 \\ \hline 7 \end{array}$$

2.

−4	
10	6
8	4
4	

3. How much?

   _____¢

Name ______________________________

How much for both?

1.

2.

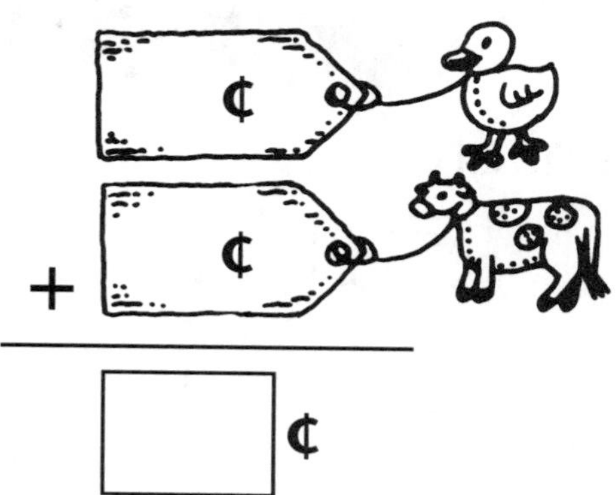

3.

4.

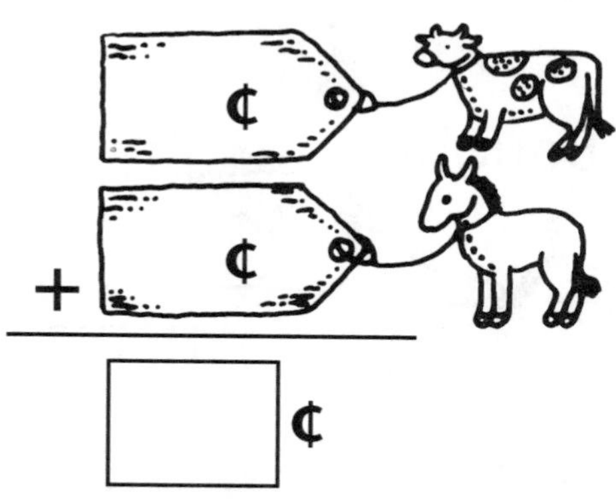

5.

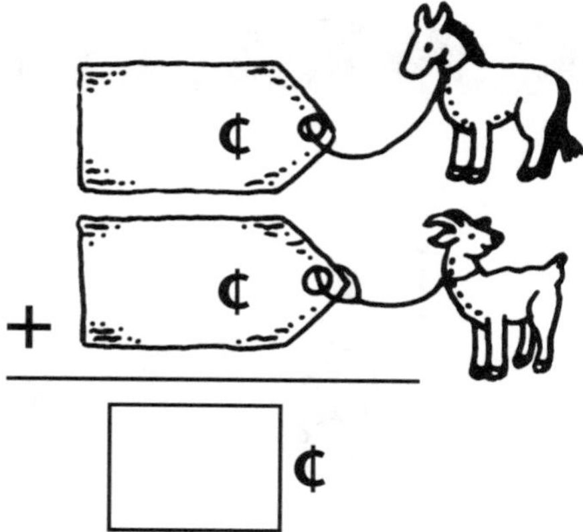

6.

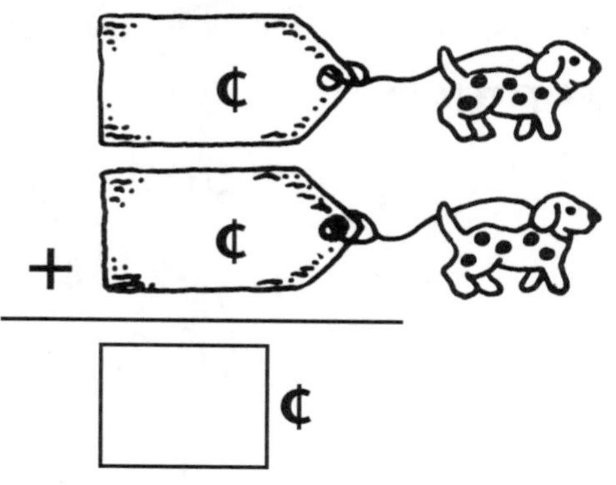

Add.

7.
 1¢
 2¢
+ 6¢
 9¢

8.
 8¢
 1¢
+ 1¢
 ¢

9.
 6¢
 1¢
+ 2¢
 ¢

10.
 4¢
 2¢
+ 3¢
 ¢

11.
 1¢
 5¢
+ 2¢
 ¢

How much money is left?

12. Had   

Bought

3 ¢ left

13. Had 

Bought

¢ left

14. Had 

Bought

¢ left

15. Had  

Bought

¢ left

★ Test Prep

How much do both cats cost in all?
Mark the space under your answer.

16 

 ○
 ○
 ○

Name ______________________________

Problem

You have     .

Can you buy the ball?

1 Understand

I need to know if I have enough money.

2 Decide

I will guess then check.

3 Solve

Can you buy the ball? no

4 Look back

Does my answer make sense?

Solve.

1. You have  . Can you buy the hat?

yes

Guess and check. Solve.

2. 

You have 

 .

Can you buy the top? ____________

3. 

You have  .

Can you buy the dog? ____________

4. 

You have  .

Can you buy the bear? ____________

5. 

You have  .

Can you buy the kite? ____________

6. 

You have  .

Can you buy the jump rope? ____________

How can you check if your answer is right? ____________

____

Name ______________________________

Complete the fact family.

1.
9 + 1 = ☐
1 + ☐ = ☐
10 − ☐ = ☐
☐ − ☐ = ☐

2.
5 + 3 = ☐
3 + ☐ = ☐
8 − ☐ = ☐
☐ − ☐ = ☐

Solve.

3. $10 - 7$

4. $6 + 4$

5. $4 + 4$

6. $3 + 2$

7. $1 + 8$

8. $8 - 5$

9. $3 + 3$

10. $7 - 6$

11. $9 - 4$

12. $6 - 0$

Add.

13. $5 + 2 + 2$

14. $3 + 4 + 1$

15. $6 + 0 + 4$

16. $3 + 1 + 3$

17. $4 + 2 + 2$

Write the missing number.

18. ☐ + 6 = 9

19. 4 + ☐ = 4

20. 2 + ☐ = 8

Ring the coins needed.

21. 

22. 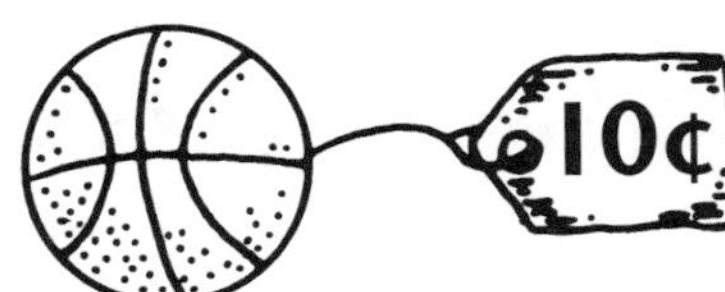

How much for both?

23. 

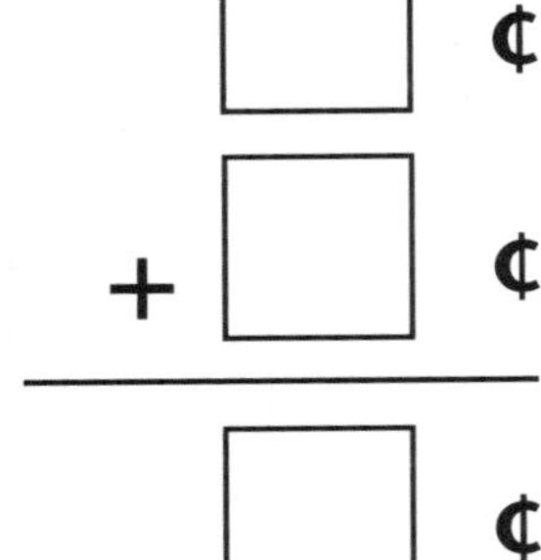

Problem Solving Reasoning Use the table to solve.

Figures	○	□	△	▭
Number of Figures	4	3	6	2

24. How many △ ? _____

25. How many 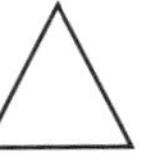 ? _____

Solve.

26. You have    .

Can you buy the ring? ___________

Name ____________________

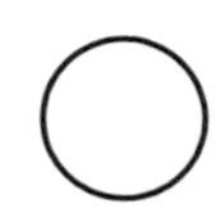

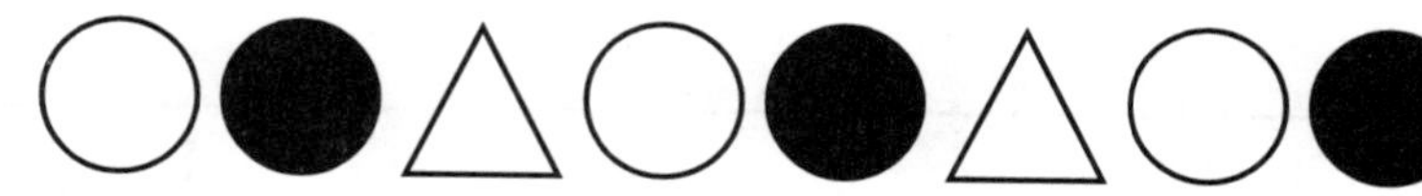

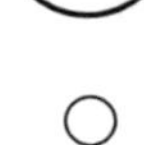

○ ○ ○

6 ○ 5

< > =

○ ○ ○

$7 - 3 = 4$ ○

$3 + 7 = 10$ ○

$7 + 0 = 7$ ○

$6 + 2 = 8$ ○

$6 - 2 = 4$ ○

$6 + 4 = 10$ ○

2 + 2 = 4 ○ 2 − 0 = 2 ○ 2 − 2 = 0 ○

7

10 − 3 = 7 | 7 − 3 = 4 ○ 7 + 3 = 10 ○ 4 + 3 = 7 ○

Solve.

3 + 5 = □

8 ○ 6 ○ 9 ○

9

5 + 3 = □

4 ○ 8 ○ 9 ○

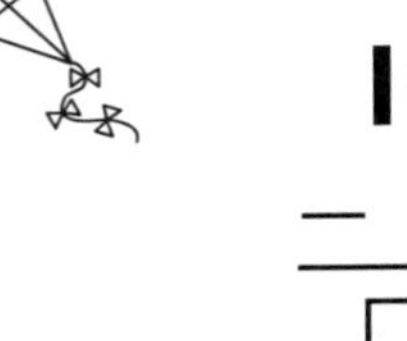

$$\begin{array}{r} 10 \\ -\ 7 \\ \hline \square \end{array}$$

6 ○ 3 ○ 4 ○

11

$$\begin{array}{r} 9 \\ -\ 7 \\ \hline \square \end{array}$$

2 ○ 5 ○ 3 ○

12

$$\begin{array}{r} 8 \\ -\ 4 \\ \hline \square \end{array}$$

6 ○ 2 ○ 4 ○

13

$$\begin{array}{r} 8 \\ -\ 8 \\ \hline \square \end{array}$$

8 ○ 6 ○ 0 ○

UNIT 7 • TABLE OF CONTENTS

Place Value through 99

We will be using this vocabulary:

1 ten ten objects in a group, 10 ones

ordinal numbers numbers used to show position or order:

1st	2nd	3rd	4th	5th
first	second	third	fourth	fifth

hundred chart a 10-by-10 grid that lists the numbers 1–100 in rows of ten

Dear Family,

During the next few weeks our math class will be learning and practicing place value through 99.

You can expect to see homework that provides practice with writing and counting numbers from 1 through 99.

As we learn about place value you may wish to keep the following sample as a guide.

The different forms of a number:

Word form: Fifteen

Standard form: 15

Place Value form:

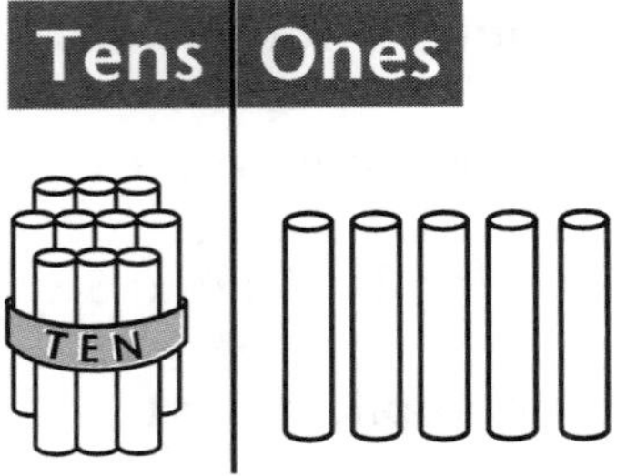

1 ten and 5 ones

Knowing place value can help children read, write, count, and compare greater numbers and quantities.

Sincerely,

Name ______________________________

10 objects in a group make 1 ten.

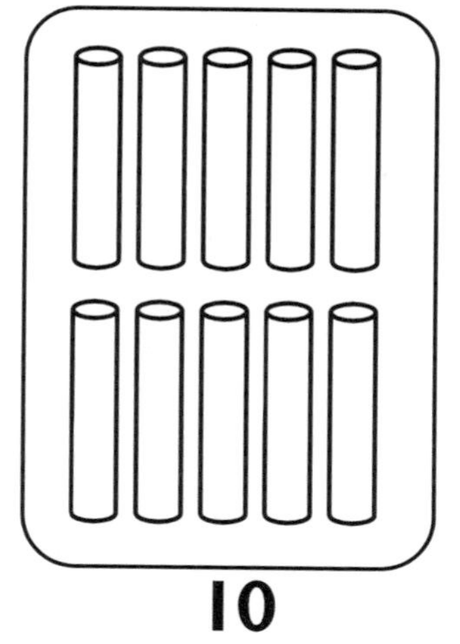

10

or

1 ten and  ones = **10**

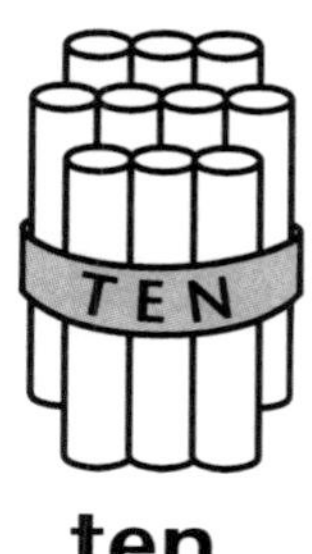

ten

Ring a group of ten.
Write how many tens and ones.
Write the number.

1.

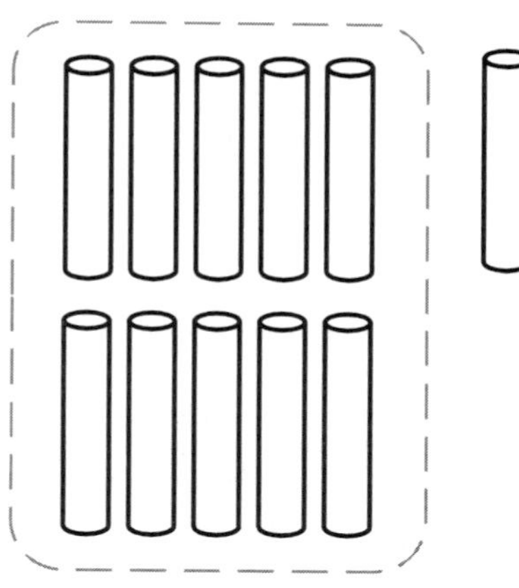

 ten and [1] one = [11]

eleven

2.

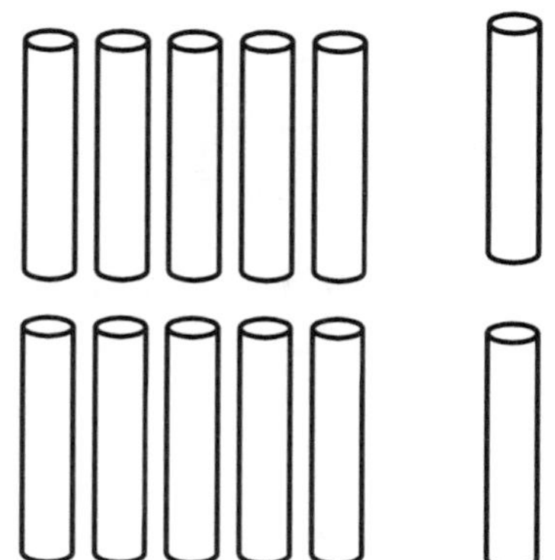

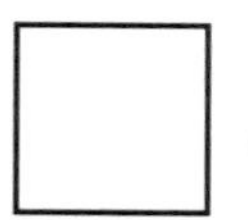 ten and [ ] ones = [ ]

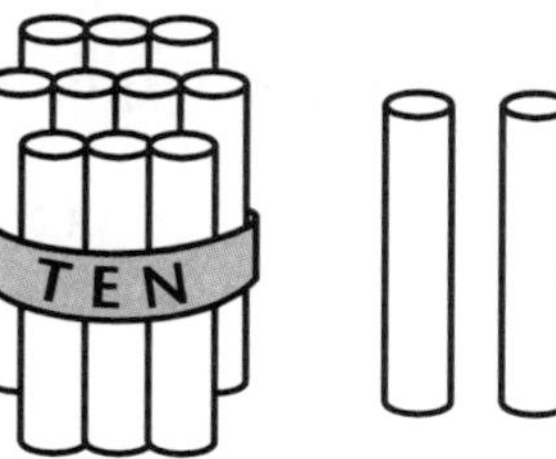

twelve

Ring a group of ten. Write how many tens and ones. Write the number.

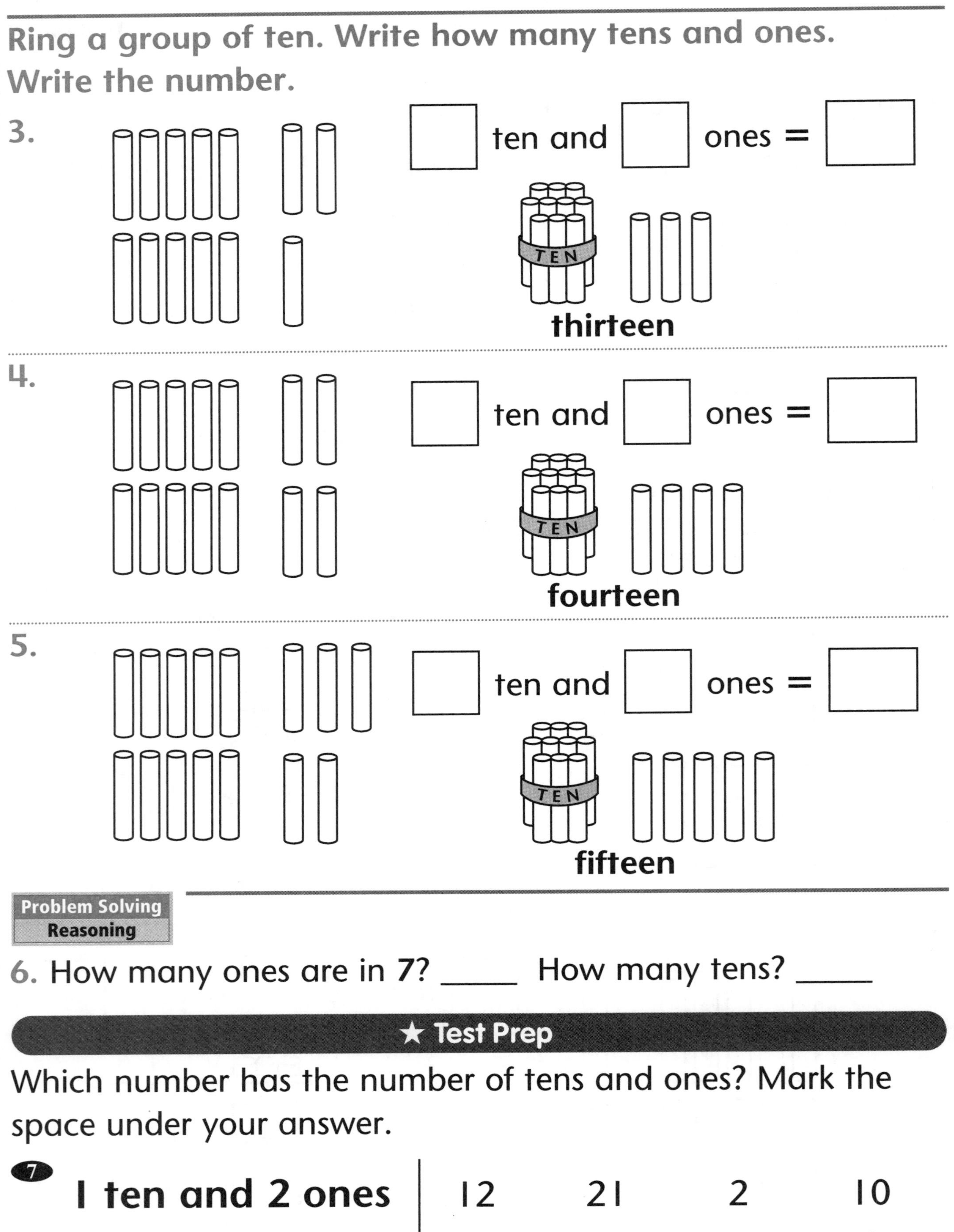

3. ☐ ten and ☐ ones = ☐

thirteen

4. ☐ ten and ☐ ones = ☐

fourteen

5. ☐ ten and ☐ ones = ☐

fifteen

Problem Solving Reasoning

6. How many ones are in **7**? _____ How many tens? _____

★ Test Prep

Which number has the number of tens and ones? Mark the space under your answer.

7 **1 ten and 2 ones** | 12 ○ | 21 ○ | 2 ○ | 10 ○

Name ______________________________

Write how many tens and ones.
Complete the number sentence.

1\.  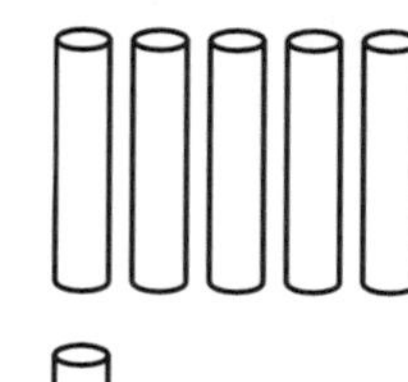 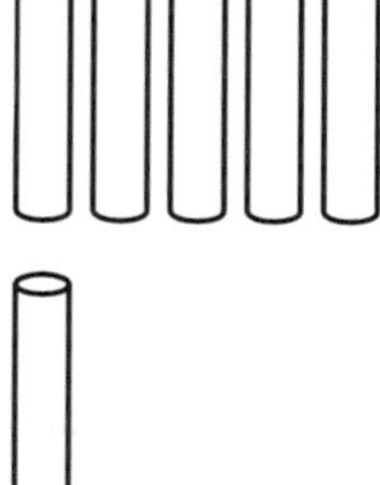

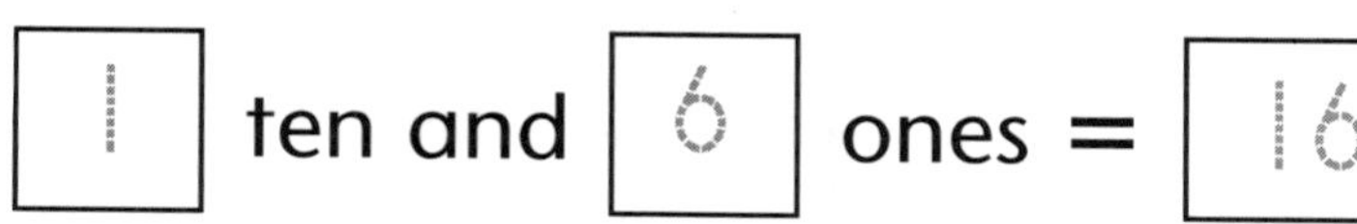

[1] ten and [6] ones = [16]

10 + [6] = 16

10 + 6 = [16] sixteen

2\.  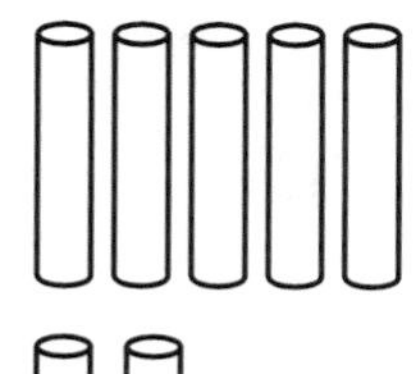 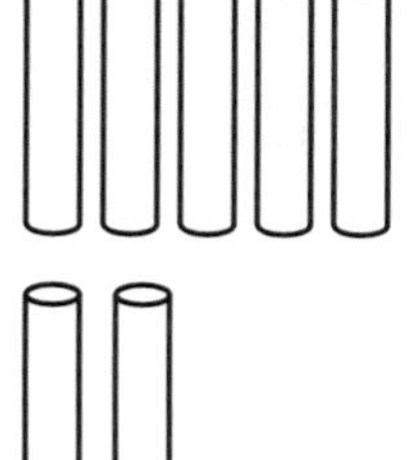

 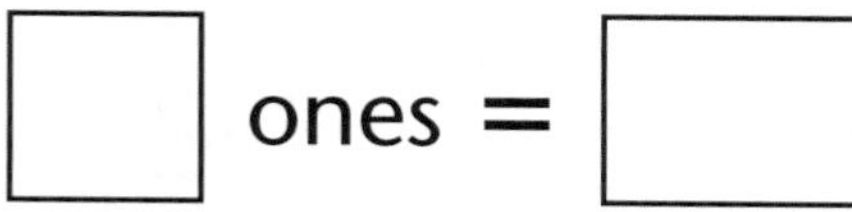

[ ] ten and [ ] ones = [ ]

10 + [ ] = 17

10 + 7 = [ ] seventeen

3\.  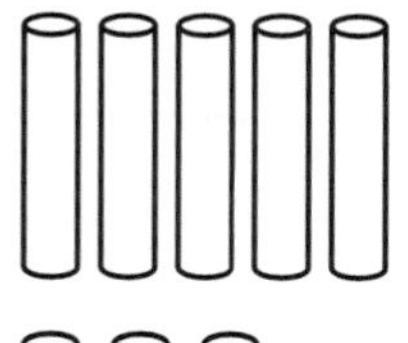 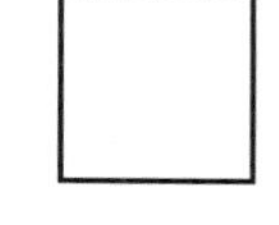

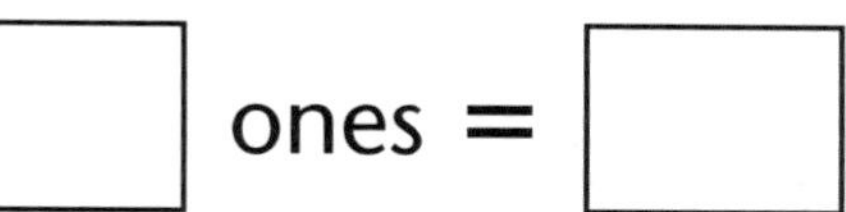

[ ] ten and [ ] ones = [ ]

10 + [ ] = 18

10 + 8 = [ ] eighteen

4\. 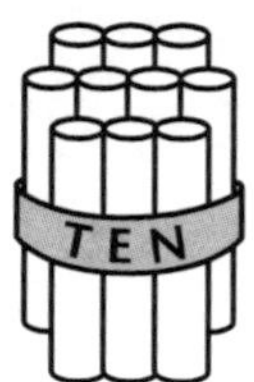 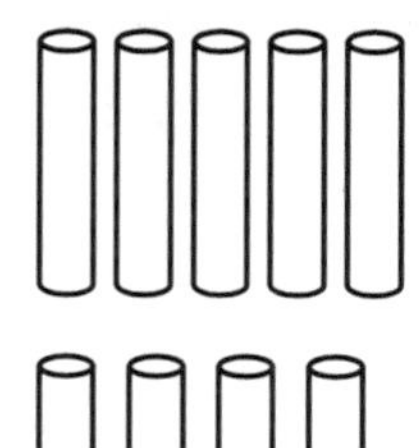

 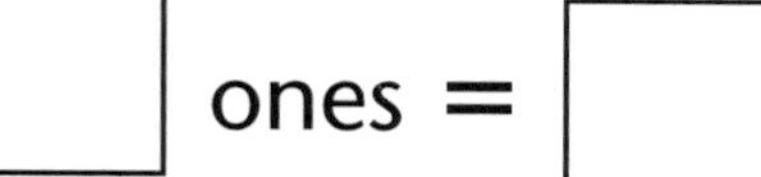

[ ] ten and [ ] ones = [ ]

10 + [ ] = 19

10 + 9 = [ ] nineteen

Complete.

5. 16 = ☐ ten and ☐ ones

6. ☐ ten and ☐ ones = 17

7. 14 = ☐ ten and ☐ ones

8. 10 + 8 = ☐

9. 19 = ☐ ten and ☐ ones

10. 10 + 5 = ☐

11. 15 = ☐ ten and ☐ ones

12. 10 + 4 = ☐

Problem Solving
Reasoning

13. What pattern do you see in the number word names?

★ Test Prep

I have **18** sticks. How many bundles of ten sticks can I make? Mark the space under your answer.

14

1	10	8	18
○	○	○	○

Name ______________________

Complete.

1. TEN

ten

1 ten

Tens	Ones
1	0

10

2. TEN TEN

twenty

☐ tens

Tens	Ones

☐

3. TEN TEN TEN

thirty

☐ tens

Tens	Ones

☐

4. TEN TEN TEN TEN

forty

☐ tens

Tens	Ones

☐

5. TEN TEN TEN TEN TEN

fifty

☐ tens

Tens	Ones

☐

Complete.

6. 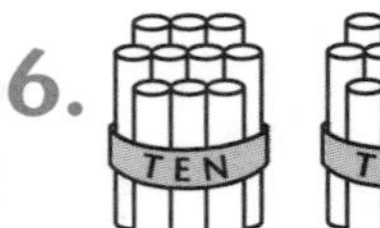 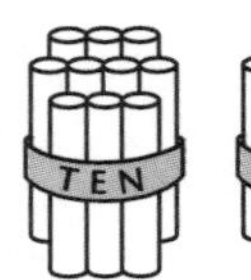 

sixty

60 = 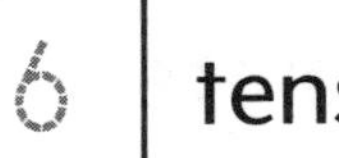 tens

6 tens = 

7. 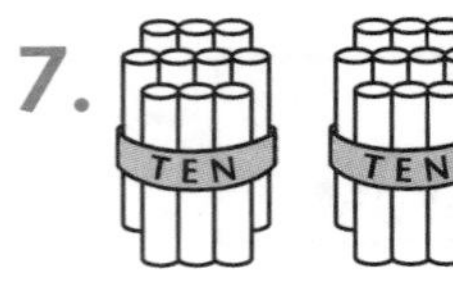 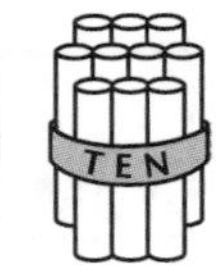 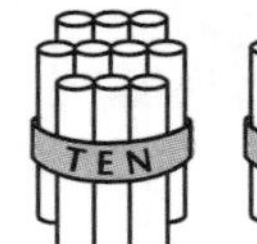 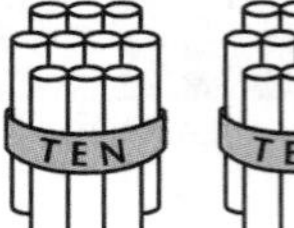  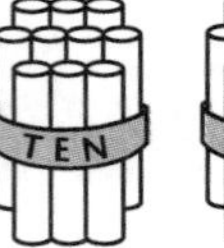   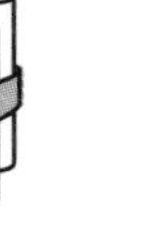

seventy

70 = ☐ tens

7 tens = 

8.  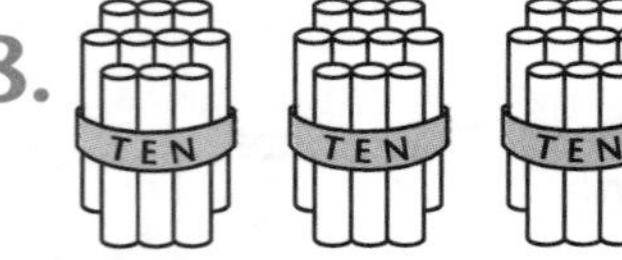  

eighty

80 = ☐ tens

8 tens = 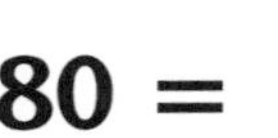

9.   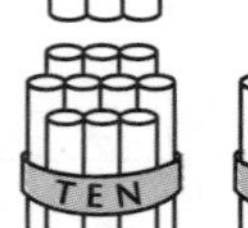 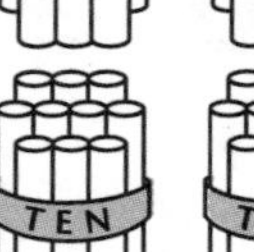 

ninety

90 = ☐ tens

9 tens = 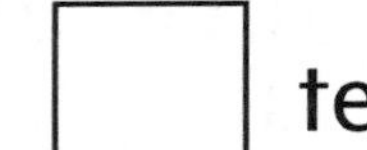

 Quick Check

Complete.

1.  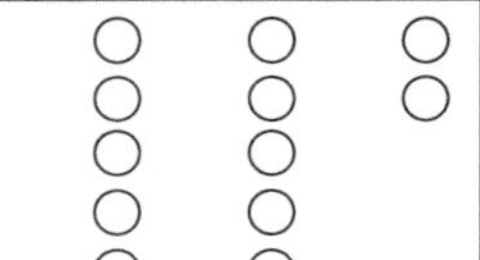  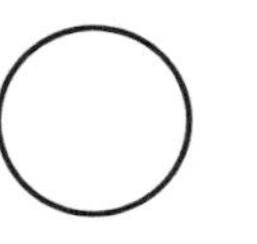 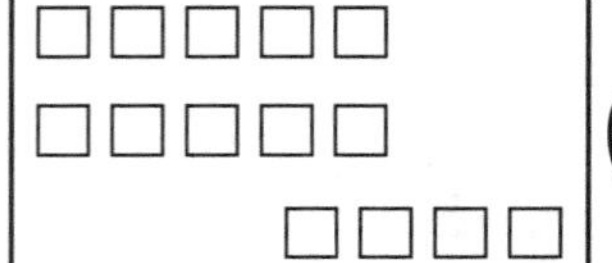 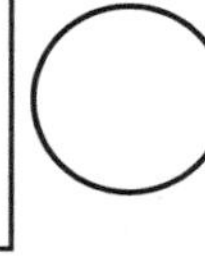

2.     

10		30	40		60	70	80	

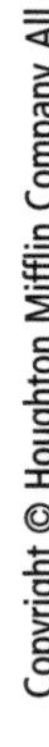

Name ______________________________

Complete.

1\.

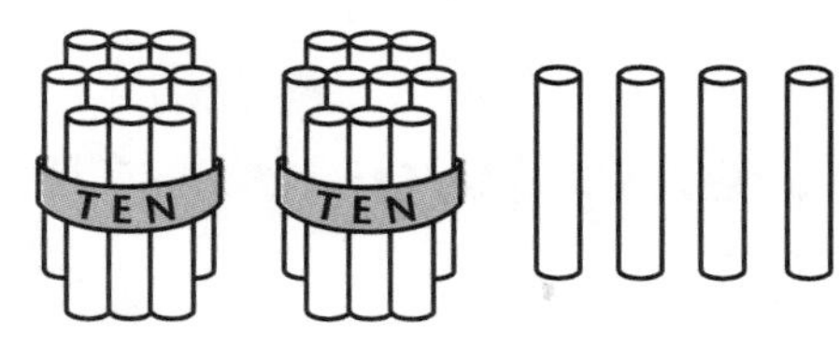

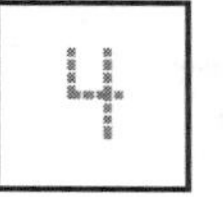

2 tens and 4 ones = 24

20 + 4 = 24

20 + 4 = 24

Tens	Ones
2	4

twenty-four

2\.

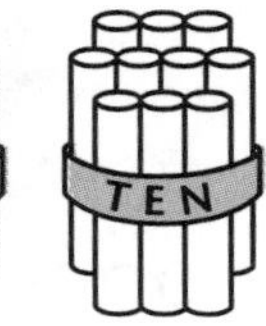

☐ tens and ☐ ones = ☐

30 + ☐ = 35

30 + 5 = ☐

Tens	Ones
3	5

thirty-five

3\.

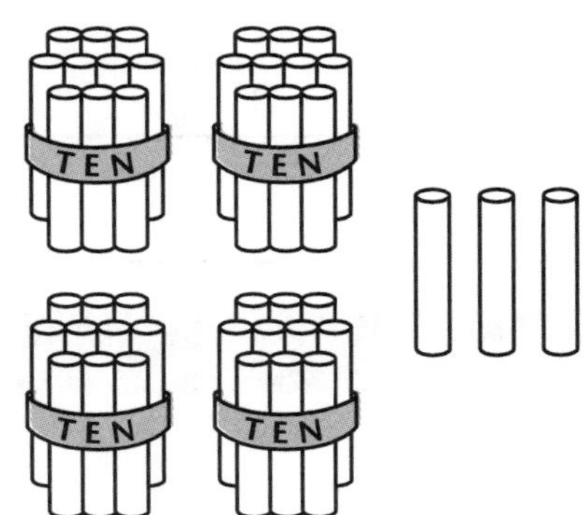

☐ tens and ☐ ones = ☐

40 + ☐ = 43

40 + 3 = ☐

Tens	Ones
4	3

forty-three

Complete.

4. ☐ tens and ☐ ones = **22**

twenty-two

5. ☐ tens and ☐ ones = **45**

forty-five

6. ☐ tens and ☐ ones = **32**

thirty-two

Problem Solving
Reasoning

7. How are the numbers **25** and **52** alike? How are they different? ____________________

____

★ Test Prep

Which number has **4** tens and **5** ones?
Mark the space under your answer.

8

405	40	54	45
○	○	○	○

Name ______________________________

Complete.

1.

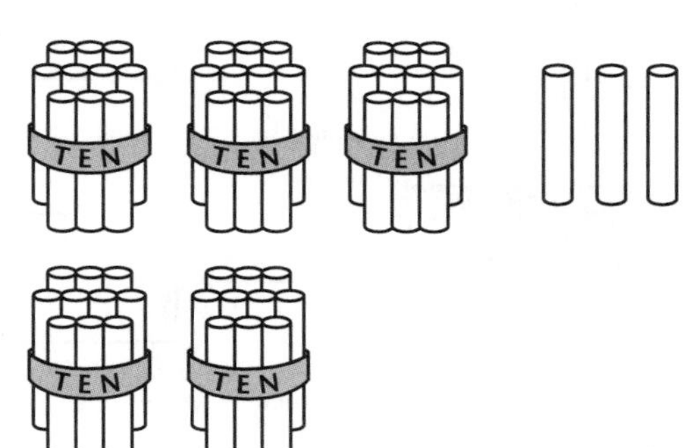

[5] tens and [3] ones = 53

50 + [3] = 53

50 + 3 = [53]

Tens	Ones
5	3

fifty-three

2.

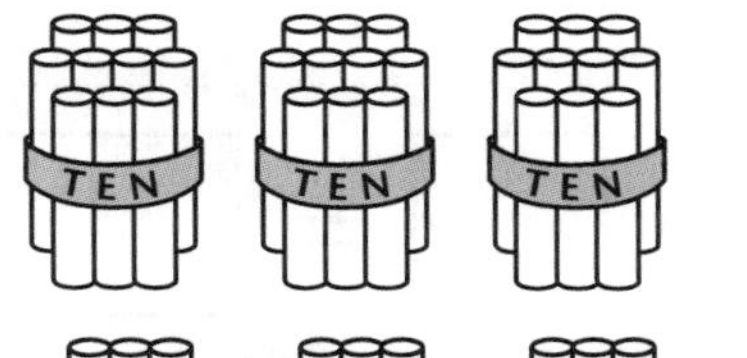

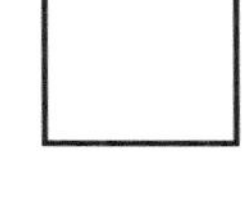

[ ] tens and [ ] ones = 68

60 + [ ] = 68

60 + 8 = [ ]

Tens	Ones
6	8

sixty-eight

3.

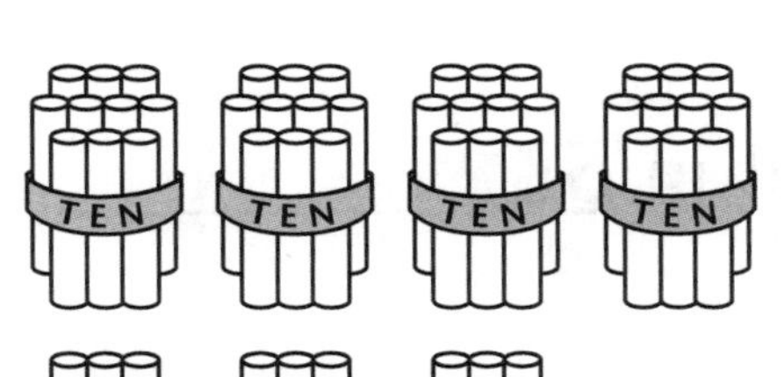

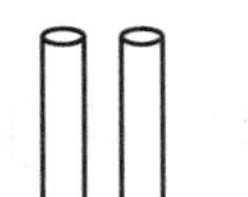

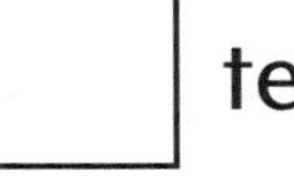

[ ] tens and [ ] ones = 75

70 + [ ] = 75

70 + 5 = [ ]

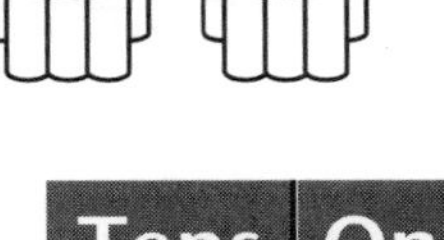

Tens	Ones
7	5

seventy-five

Complete.

4.

Tens	Ones
4	6

→ [46]

5.

Tens	Ones
5	9

→ [ ]

6.

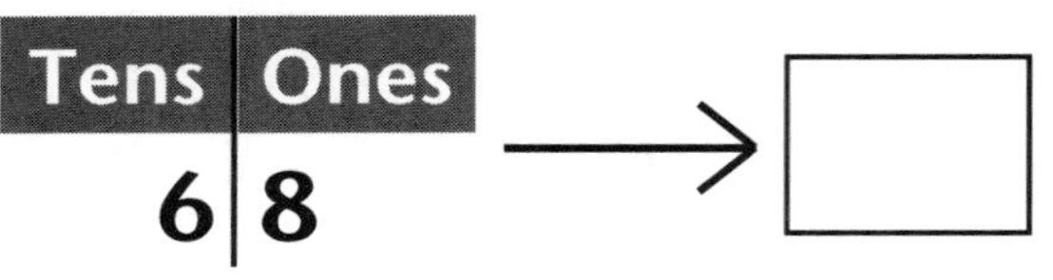

→ [ ]

7.

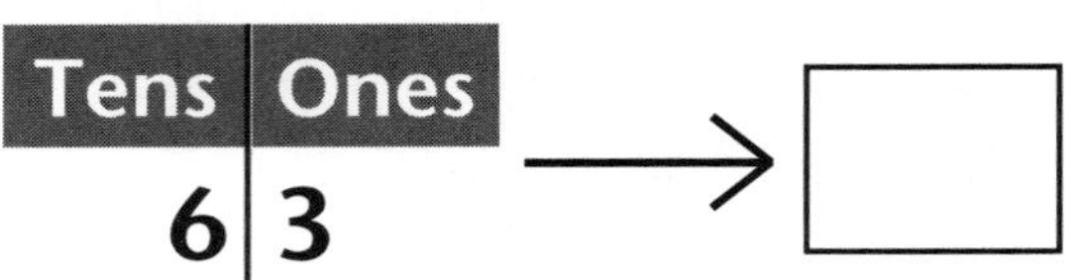

→ [ ]

8.

Tens	Ones
5	1

→ [ ]

9.

→ [ ]

10. **5** tens and **2** ones → **50 +** [ ] = [ ]

11. **5** tens and **4** ones → **50 +** [ ] = [ ]

12. **6** tens and **5** ones → **60 +** [ ] = [ ]

13. **7** tens and **3** ones → **70 +** [ ] = [ ]

Problem Solving
Reasoning

14. Write the value of the underlined digit in **<u>5</u>3**. ____________

★ Test Prep

What is the value of the underlined digit?
Mark the space under your answer.

15. <u>4</u>7

7	4	40	47
○	○	○	○

Name ____________________

Complete.

1. 

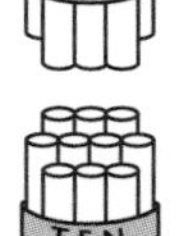

Tens	Ones
7	5

[7] tens and [5] ones = 75

70 + [5] = 75

70 + 5 = [75]

seventy-five

2. 

Tens	Ones
8	2

[ ] tens and [ ] ones = 82

80 + [ ] = 82

80 + 2 = [ ]

eighty-two

3. 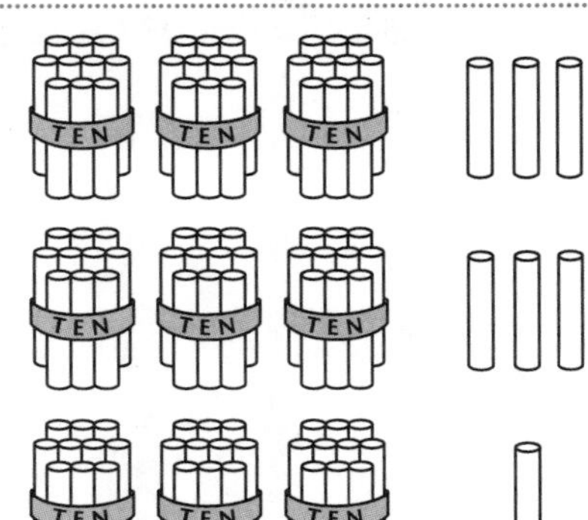

Tens	Ones
9	7

[ ] tens and [ ] ones = 97

90 + [ ] = 97

90 + 7 = [ ]

ninety-seven

Complete the tables.

4. 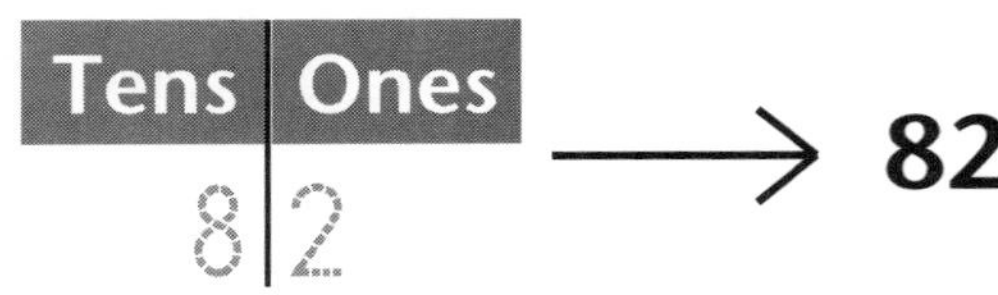

→ **82**

5. Tens | Ones → **89**

6. 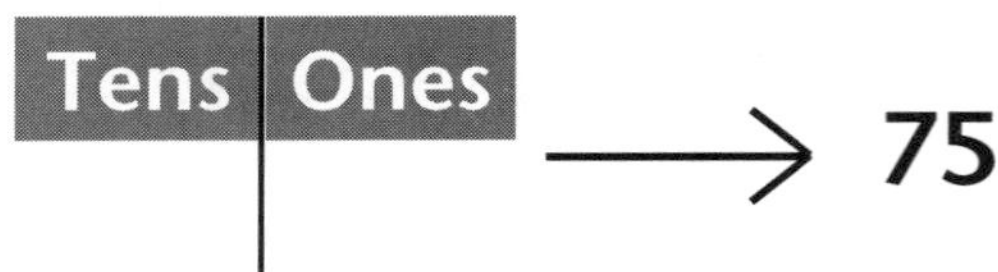

→ **75**

7. Tens | Ones → **95**

Complete.

8. **7** tens and **4** ones → **70 +** ☐ **=** ☐

9. **9** tens and **9** ones → **90 +** ☐ **=** ☐

10. **60 + 4 =** ☐

11. **70 + 1 =** ☐

Problem Solving
Reasoning

12. Write the value of the underlined digit in **<u>8</u>9**. ____________

Quick Check

Complete.

1.

Tens	Ones
4	3

= ______

2.

Tens	Ones
8	7

= ______

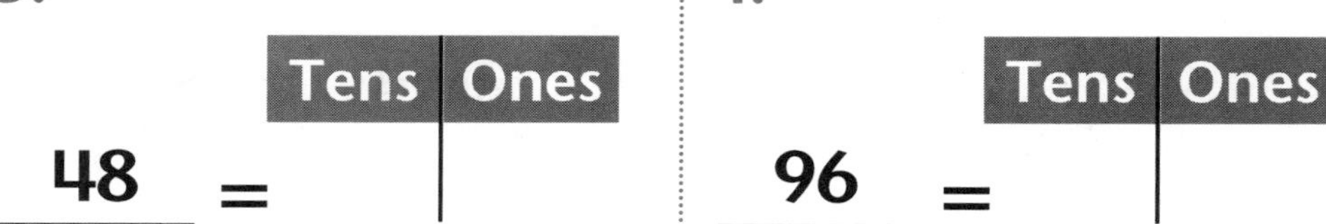

3. **48** = Tens | Ones

4. **96** = Tens | Ones

Name ______________________________

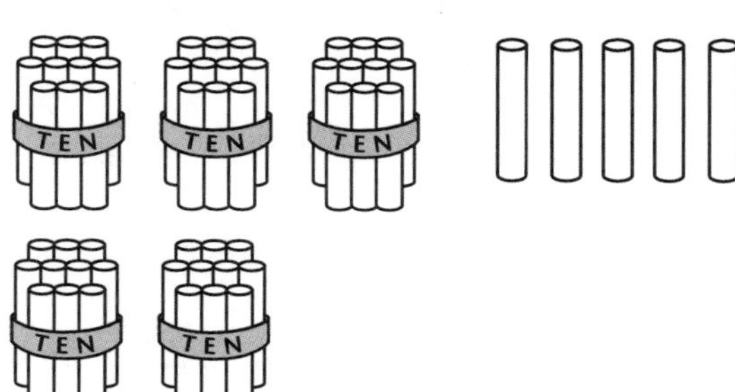

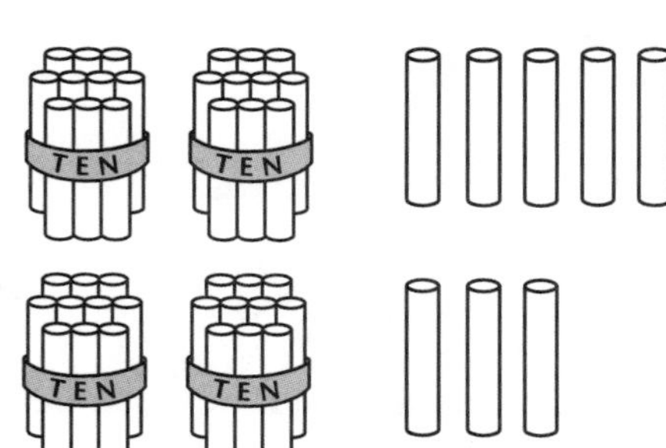

55 | **48**

55 is greater than **48**. | **48** is less than **55**.

55 > 48 | **48 < 55**

Ring the number that is greater.

1. 36 21
2. 67 87
3. 59 55
4. 73 91

Ring the number that is less.

5. 83 81
6. 62 79
7. 41 46
8. 92 93

Use >, <, or = .

9. 84 (>) 77
10. 42 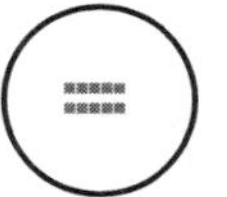 42
11. 30 + 3 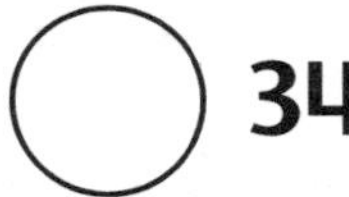 34
12. 91 ◯ 60
13. 56 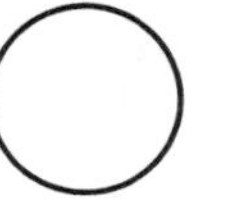 78
14. 50 + 1  54
15. 28 ◯ 28
16. 37 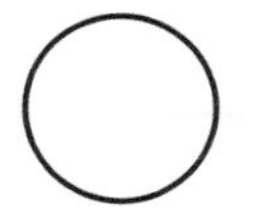 62
17. 90 + 0  90

Ring the greatest.

18.	70	26	82	19.	95	61	34
20.	47	58	69	21.	72	50	24

Ring the least.

22.	76	94	84	23.	23	31	40
24.	57	80	98	25.	49	20	66

Ring the least number.
Mark an X next to the greatest number.

26.

TEN TEN

23

TEN TEN TEN

32

TEN

15

Write the numbers in order.

27. __________ __________ __________

least greatest

Problem Solving
Reasoning

28. Jack says, "**39** is greater than **51**. I know because **9** is greater than **5** or **1**." Is Jack right? Why or why not? __________

____

____

Name ____________________

STANDARD

Read the numbers. Count on the number line. Write the missing numbers.

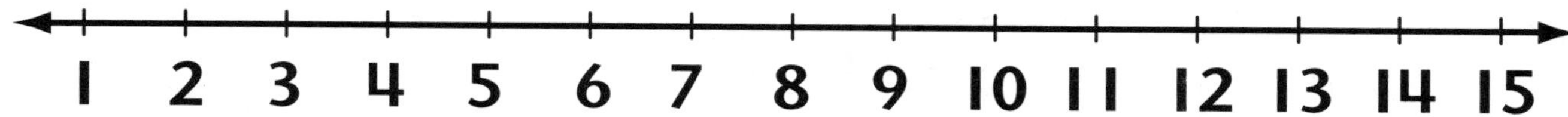

1. 1, [2], [3], 4, [ ], [ ], [ ], 8

2. 3, 4, [ ], [ ], [ ], [ ], [ ], 10

3. [ ], [ ], [ ], [ ], [ ], 7, [ ], [ ]

4. What number is **1** more than **9**? ______

5. What number is **1** less than **14**? ______

Complete.

After	Between	Before
6. 9, [10]	7. 7, [8], 9	8. [14], 15
9. 11, [ ]	10. 10, [ ], 12	11. [ ], 11
12. 8, [ ]	13. 4, [ ], 6	14. [ ], 7
15. 12, [ ]	16. 13, [ ], 15	17. [ ], 13

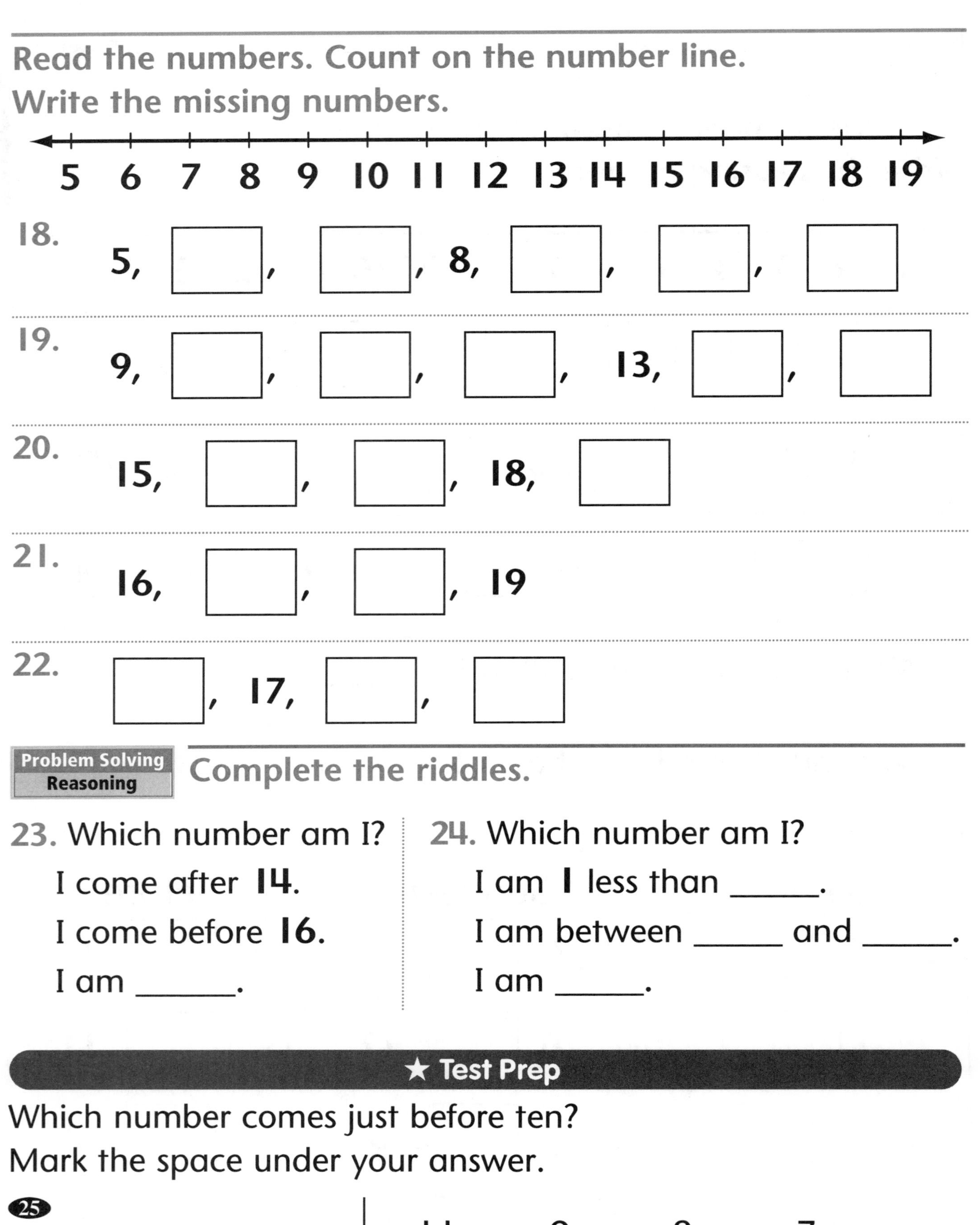

Read the numbers. Count on the number line.
Write the missing numbers.

5 6 7 8 9 10 11 12 13 14 15 16 17 18 19

18. 5, ☐, ☐, 8, ☐, ☐, ☐

19. 9, ☐, ☐, ☐, 13, ☐, ☐

20. 15, ☐, ☐, 18, ☐

21. 16, ☐, ☐, 19

22. ☐, 17, ☐, ☐

Problem Solving
Reasoning

Complete the riddles.

23. Which number am I?
I come after **14**.
I come before **16**.
I am ______.

24. Which number am I?
I am **1** less than ______.
I am between ______ and ______.
I am ______.

★ Test Prep

Which number comes just before ten?
Mark the space under your answer.

25

☐, 10

11	9	8	7
○	○	○	○

Name ______________________

Read the numbers. Count on the number line. Write the missing numbers.

10 11 12 13 14 15 16 17 18 19 20

After	Between	Before
1. 11, 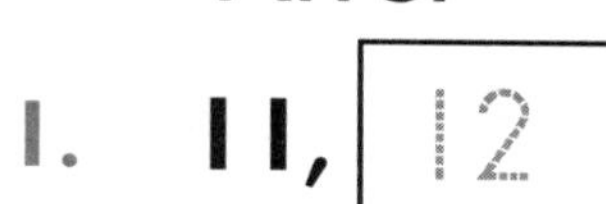	2. 15, [16], 17	3. [19], 20
4. 16, ☐	5. 10, ☐, 12	6. ☐, 12
7. 19, ☐	8. 18, ☐, 20	9. ☐, 16
10. 14, ☐	11. 13, ☐, 15	12. ☐, 18

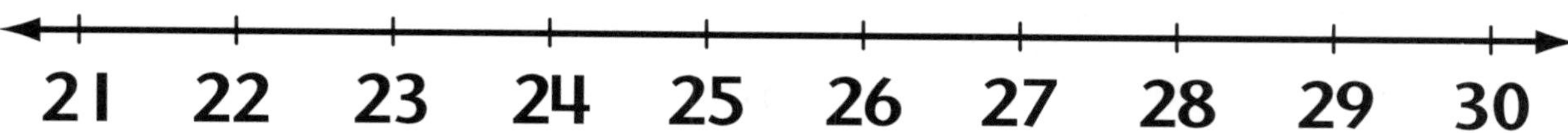

After	Between	Before
13. 22, ☐	14. 28, ☐, 30	15. ☐, 30
16. 27, ☐	17. 21, ☐, 23	18. ☐, 23
19. 25, ☐	20. 26, ☐, 28	21. ☐, 27
22. 29, ☐	23. 24, ☐, 26	24. ☐, 29

Read the numbers. Count on the number line.
Write the missing numbers.

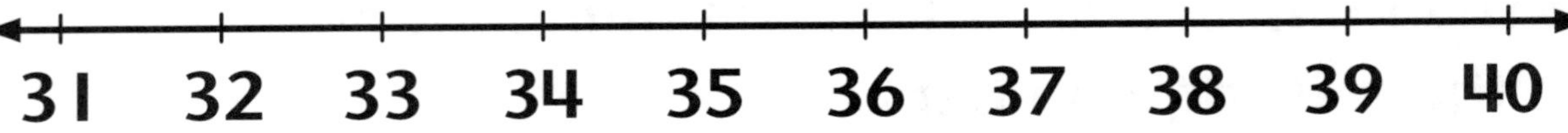

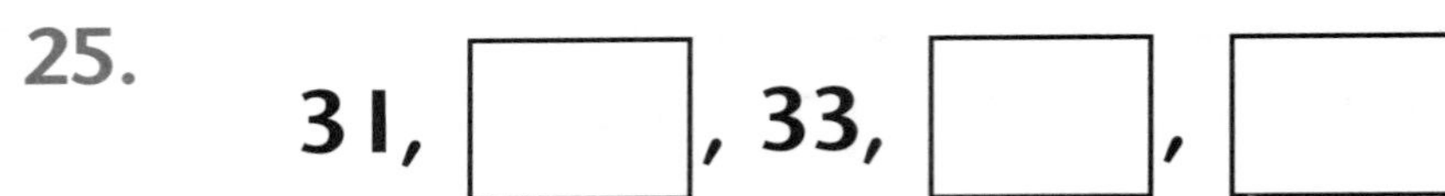

25. 31, ☐, 33, ☐, ☐

26. ☐, ☐, ☐, ☐, 37

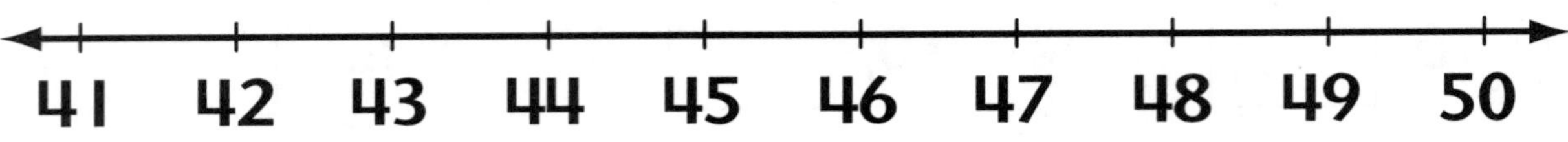

27. 46, ☐, ☐, ☐, 50

28. ☐, 43, ☐, ☐, ☐

Count by 10's to complete.

29. | 10 | ☐ | 30 | ☐ | 50 |

✓ Quick Check

Write <, >, or =. Complete.

1. 30 ◯ 27

2. 85 ◯ 86

3. ☐, 17, ☐, ☐, 20

4. 39, ☐, 41

Name ____________________

Read the numbers. Count on the number line. Write the missing numbers.

51 52 53 54 55 56 57 58 59 60

After	Between	Before
1. 55, [56]	2. 51, [52], 53	3. [51], 52
4. 59, [ ]	5. 56, [ ], 58	6. [ ], 55
7. 52, [ ]	8. 52, [ ], 54	9. [ ], 60
10. 57, [ ]	11. 58, [ ], 60	12. [ ], 58

61 62 63 64 65 66 67 68 69 70

After	Between	Before
13. 62, [ ]	14. 61, [ ], 63	15. [ ], 65
16. 68, [ ]	17. 67, [ ], 69	18. [ ], 70
19. 65, [ ]	20. 64, [ ], 66	21. [ ], 63
22. 69, [ ]	23. 62, [ ], 64	24. [ ], 68

Read the numbers. Count on the number line.
Write the missing numbers.

71 72 73 74 75 76 77 78 79 80

25. ☐, ☐, 78, ☐, ☐

81 82 83 84 85 86 87 88 89 90

26. 86, ☐, ☐, ☐, ☐

91 92 93 94 95 96 97 98 99 100

27. ☐, ☐, ☐, ☐, 100

Problem Solving
Reasoning

28. Which numbers are between **87** and **93**?

★ Test Prep

Which number does not come after **71**?
Mark the space under your answer.

74	80	69	92
○	○	○	○

Name ______________________

Count forward and backward by 2's, 5's, and 10's on the hundred chart. Use the key to color what you count.

1.

1	2	3	4	5	6	7	8	9	10
11	12	13	14	15	16	17	18	19	20
21	22	23	24	25	26	27	28	29	30
31	32	33	34	35	36	37	38	39	40
41	42	43	44	45	46	47	48	49	50
51	52	53	54	55	56	57	58	59	60
61	62	63	64	65	66	67	68	69	70
71	72	73	74	75	76	77	78	79	80
81	82	83	84	85	86	87	88	89	90
91	92	93	94	95	96	97	98	99	100

Count by	Color
2's	blue
5's	yellow
10's	red

Write the number.

2. **10** more than **64** is 74.
3. **10** less than **77** is 67.
4. **1** less than **22** is ______.
5. **1** more than **43** is ______.
6. **10** more than **32** is ______.
7. **10** less than **55** is ______.
8. **1** less than **86** is ______.
9. **1** more than **91** is ______.
10. **10** more than **68** is ______.
11. **10** less than **29** is ______.

STANDARD

Name ________________________

Count by 2's.

1.

2, 4, 6, 8, ____, ____, ____, ____, ____, 20

2.

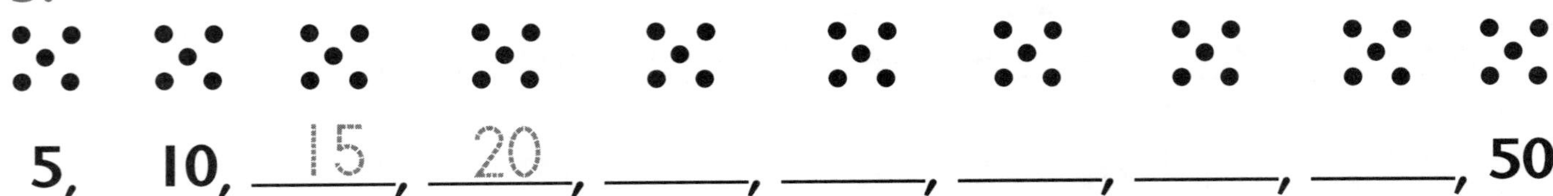

22, ____, ____, ____, ____, ____, ____, ____, ____, 40

Count by 5's.

3.

5, 10, 15, 20, ____, ____, ____, ____, ____, 50

Quick Check

Complete.

1. 49 , ____, 51

2.

60	70	80	

3.

85		95	100

Name ______________________________

Problem Solving Plan
1. Understand 2. Decide 3. Solve 4. Look back

Use this picture to help solve the problem.

10 stars

Guess how many stars are in the box.
Ring your guess.

1. **20** **40** **60**

Think Does my guess make sense?
Ring groups of **10** to count.

How many tens? ______

How many ones? ______

Write the number. ______

Guess how many.
Ring groups of **10** to count.
Write how many tens and ones.
Write the number.

10 stars

2. Guess. **10** **30** **50**

Tens ______ Ones ______

Number ______

3. Guess. **50** **70** **90**

Tens ______ Ones ______

Number ______

Extend Your Thinking

4. How did the picture of **10** stars help you guess? ____________

Name ______________________________

1st	2nd	3rd	4th	5th	6th	7th
first	second	third	fourth	fifth	sixth	seventh

Look at the ordinal number. Ring the object.

1. **5th**

2. **2nd**

3. **6th**

4. **1st**

5. **3rd**

6. **4th**

Complete the ordinal numbers.

7.

____st ____nd ____rd ____th ____th ____th ____th

Read the ordinal numbers.
Match objects.

8. 1st □ to 4th ■

□ □ □ □ □ □ □

■ ■ ■ ■ ■ ■ ■

9. 7th to 7th

10. 4th to 5th

11. 2nd □ to 7th ●

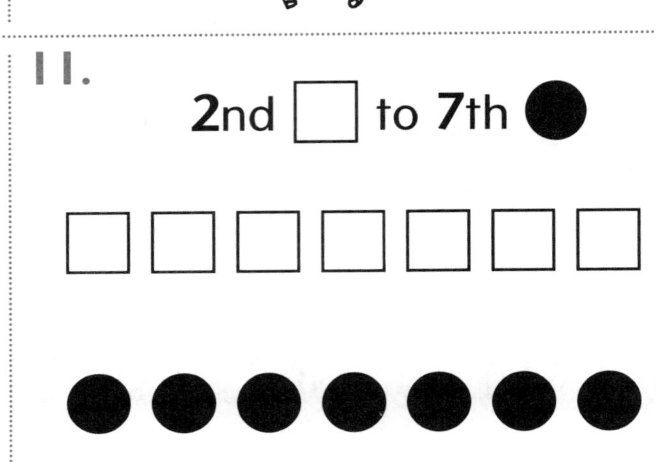

□ □ □ □ □ □ □

● ● ● ● ● ● ●

Problem Solving Reasoning Use the picture to solve.

12. Who is 4th in line?

_______________ is 4th

Pat **Matt** **Cal** **Sal** **Hal**

★ Test Prep

Which box is black?
Mark the space under your answer.

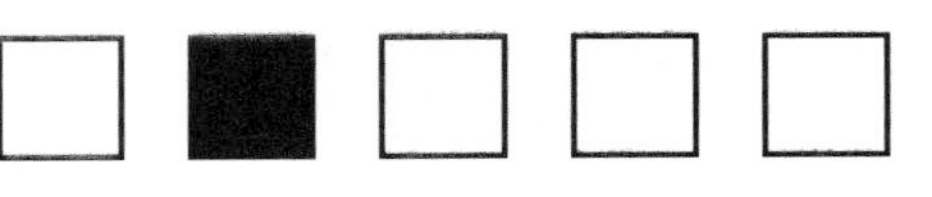

1st	2nd	3rd	5th
○	○	○	○

Name ______________________________

STANDARD

Problem

15, 25, 35, 45, 55, ___?___

What number comes next?

1 Understand I need to find the number that comes next.

2 Decide I can shade the hundred chart to help.

3 Solve

1	2	3	4	5	6	7	8	9	10
11	12	13	14	15	16	17	18	19	20
21	22	23	24	25	26	27	28	29	30
31	32	33	34	35	36	37	38	39	40
41	42	43	44	45	46	47	48	49	50
51	52	53	54	55	56	57	58	59	60
61	62	63	64	65	66	67	68	69	70
71	72	73	74	75	76	77	78	79	80
81	82	83	84	85	86	87	88	89	90
91	92	93	94	95	96	97	98	99	100

What number comes next? ___65___

4 Look back Does my answer make sense?

Solve.

1. **4, 8, 12, 16, ___?___**

   What number comes next? ______

Use the hundred chart to help find patterns.

1	2	3	4	5	6	7	8	9	10
11	12	13	14	15	16	17	18	19	20
21	22	23	24	25	26	27	28	29	30
31	32	33	34	35	36	37	38	39	40
41	42	43	44	45	46	47	48	49	50
51	52	53	54	55	56	57	58	59	60
61	62	63	64	65	66	67	68	69	70
71	72	73	74	75	76	77	78	79	80
81	82	83	84	85	86	87	88	89	90
91	92	93	94	95	96	97	98	99	100

What numbers come next?
Continue the pattern.

2. **25, 26, 27, 28,** _____, _____, _____, _____

3. **90, 80, 70, 60,** _____, _____, _____, _____

4. **59, 58, 57, 56,** _____, _____, _____, _____

Solve.

5. What number is **10** more than **19**? _____

6. What number is **1** less than **75**? _____

7. What number is **10** less than **41**? _____

8. What number is **1** more than **81**? _____

Name ____________________

Complete.

1. ______ , ______ , **37, 38, 39,** ______

2. **77,** ______ , ______ , ______ , ______ , **82**

Write the number.

3.

Tens	Ones
3	2

→ ☐

4.

Tens	Ones
7	0

→ ☐

5.

Tens	Ones

→ **95**

6.

Tens	Ones

→ **66**

Complete.

7. **1** more than **18** is ______ .

8. **1** less than **20** is ______ .

9. **10** more than **12** is ______ .

10. **10** less than **39** is ______ .

Count by 2's.

11. **12, 14, 16,** ______ , ______ , ______

Count by 5's.

12. **20, 25, 30, 35,** ______ , ______ , ______

Count by 10's.

13. **40, 50, _____, _____, _____, 90**

Write <, >, or = to make the sentence true.

14. **17** 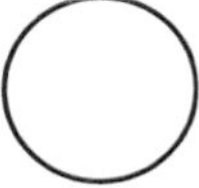 **17**

15. **23** 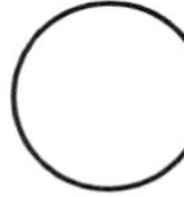 **32**

Ring the 2nd figure. (7F)

16.    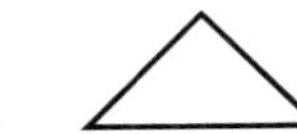   

Problem Solving Reasoning Use the hundred chart. Complete.

1	2	3	4	5	6	7	8	9	10
11	12	13	14	15	16	17	18	19	20
21	22	23	24	25	26	27	28	29	30
31	32	33	34	35	36	37	38	39	40
41	42	43	44	45	46	47	48	49	50
51	52	53	54	55	56	57	58	59	60
61	62	63	64	65	66	67	68	69	70
71	72	73	74	75	76	77	78	79	80
81	82	83	84	85	86	87	88	89	90
91	92	93	94	95	96	97	98	99	100

17. **1, 11, 21, 31, _____, _____, _____**

18. **80, 79, 78, 77, _____, _____, _____**

Name ______________________

1

○ 4 − 0 = 4 ○ 6 + 4 = 10

○ 6 − 4 = 2 ○ 4 + 2 = 6

2

7 + 3 = 10

3 + 7 = 10

10 − 7 = 3

○ 10 − 3 = 7 ○ 10 − 10 = 0

○ 4 + 3 = 7 ○ 10 + 3 = 13

3

66, 67, 68, 69, ____

65	70	71	80
○	○	○	○

4

97

Tens	Ones	Tens	Ones	Tens	Ones	Tens	Ones
7	7	7	9	9	7	0	9
○		○		○		○	

5

16, 18, ____

19	17	20	18
○	○	○	○

6

35, 40, 45, ____

46	48	47	50
○	○	○	○

7

40, ____, 60, 70

80	50	30	41
○	○	○	○

8

44 ◯ 39

>	<	=	+
○	○	○	○

9

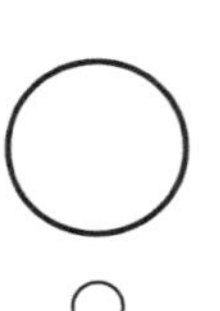

10

18	27	38	29
○	○	○	○

31	32	33	34	35	36	37	38	39	40
41	42	43	44	45	46	47	48	49	50

11

43, 42, 41, 40, ____

41	39	38	42
○	○	○	○

Decide on an answer. Mark the space for your answer.
If the answer is **not here**, mark the space for **NH**.

12

10 − 6 = □

0	4	6	NH
○	○	○	○

13

10 − 4 = □

4	0	8	NH
○	○	○	○

UNIT 8 • TABLE OF CONTENTS

Time and Money

UNIT 8 • TABLE OF CONTENTS

We will be using this vocabulary:

minute a unit of time that is 60 seconds
hour a unit of time that is 60 minutes

Dear Family,

During the next few weeks our math class will be learning about time and money.

You can expect to see homework that provides practice with telling time and counting money amounts using pennies, nickels, and dimes.

As we learn about time and money you may wish to keep the following samples as a guide.

Knowing how to tell time and count money will help children with real life skills.

Sincerely,

Name ________________________________

Write 1, 2, and 3 to show the correct order.

1.

2

1

3

2.

____

____

____

3.

____

____

____

★ Test Prep

Which picture shows what happened after the event at the beginning of the row? Mark your answer.

4

○

○

○

Name ______________________________

Watch a game.

hours

Eat a hot dog.

minutes

About how long? Ring minutes or hours.

1.

Brush your teeth.

hours

minutes

2.

Cook a turkey.

hours minutes

3.

See a play.

hours minutes

4.

Wash your face.

hours minutes

★ Test Prep

About how long? Mark next to your answer.

5

Bake a cake.

○ hours ○ seconds

○ minutes ○ days

Name ______________________

Write the correct time.

1\. 

7 o'clock

2\. 

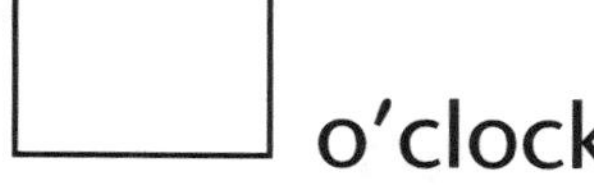

o'clock

3\. 

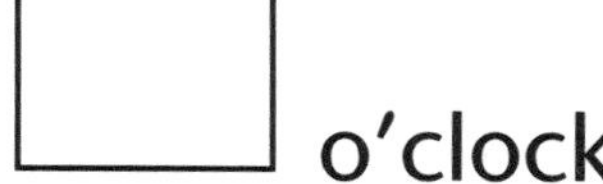

o'clock

4\. 

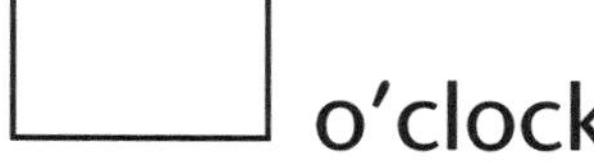

o'clock

5\. 

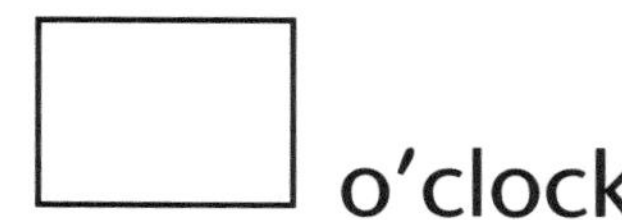

o'clock

6\. 

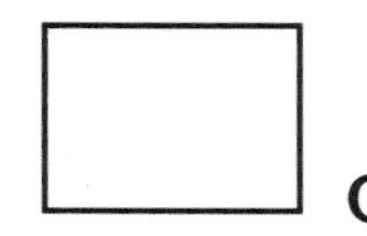

o'clock

Write the time.

7.

______ o'clock

8.

______ :00

9.

______ o'clock

10.

______ o'clock

11.

______ :00

12.

______ o'clock

Quick Check

Write 1, 2, and 3 to show order.

1.

Water seeds. ______

Plant seeds. ______

Seeds sprout. ______

Ring the event that takes hours.

2.

Tie your shoes.

Watch a movie.

Pour a drink.

Complete.

3.

______ :00

Name ______________________________

What time is it?

half past **12** or **12:30**

Write the correct time.

1. 

7 **:30**

2. 

half past ______

3. 

______ **:30**

4. 

______ **:30**

5. 

half past ______

6. 

______ **:30**

7. 

half past ______

8. 

______ **:30**

9. 

half past ______

hour hand

minute hand

Write the correct time.

10.

half past ____

11.

half past ____

12.

half past ____

13.

____ :00

14.

____ :30

15.

____ :30

Problem Solving Reasoning

Tell how you would change a clock that says 3:00 to 3:30.

★ Test Prep

Which clock shows 5:30? Mark the space under your answer.

16

○ ○ ○ ○

Name ____________________

Match.

1. 

6:00

11 o'clock

2. 

half past **2**

3. 

6 o'clock

4. 

half past **8**

★ Test Prep

Which digital clock shows the same time?
Mark next to your answer.

○ 

○ 

○ 9:30

○ 6:30

Name ______________________

STANDARD

Write the times. Answer the question.

1. 

3:00

3:30

4:00

How long did the boys play? 1 hour

2. 

___ : ___

___ : ___

___ : ___

How long did the girl rake? __________

Quick Check

Write the time.

1.

_____ :30

Ring the same time.

2. 

3. 

How long to the finish? _______

Name ______________________

Problem Solving Plan
1. Understand 2. Decide 3. Solve 4. Look back

Use the table to answer the question.

Morning Schedule

Time	Subject
9:00	Reading
10:00	Math
11:00	Science
11:30	Lunch
12:00	Recess

Think What does the question ask me to find out?

1. What time does math begin? 10:00
2. What time does science begin? ___:___
3. How long is reading? __________

Afternoon Schedule

Time	Subject
12:30	Music
1:00	Social Studies
2:00	Computers
3:00	Go home

4. Which subject begins at half past **12**? __________
5. When do the students go home? ___:___
6. How long is social studies? __________

Use the table to answer the question.

Ticket Counter Lines

Number of People	Time
10	12:00
7	12:30
5	1:00
1	1:30

7. How many more people are in line at **1:00** than at **1:30**?
____ more people

8. At what time were the most people in line? ____:____

9. How many people were in line at **1** o'clock?
____ people

Extend Your Thinking

10. Make up your own problem about the table.
Ask a friend to solve it.

____

____

____

____

Name ______________________________

Look at the calendar. Answer the question.

January						
Sunday	Monday	Tuesday	Wednesday	Thursday	Friday	Saturday
		1	2	3	4	5
6	7	8	9	10	11	12
13	14	15	16	17	18	19
20	21	22	23	24	25	26
27	28	29	30	31		

1. How many

Mondays? 4 birthdays? 5

days in this month? 31 weekend days? 8

2. What is the name of this month? ____________

3. How many days are in one week? ____

4. What date of the month is

the **fourth** Tuesday? _____

the **third** Sunday? _____

Write in the name of this month.

Number the days like the calendar in your classroom.

5\. Month ____________________

Sunday	Monday	Tuesday	Wednesday	Thursday	Friday	Saturday

January	April	July	October
February	May	August	November
March	June	September	December

★ Test Prep

Which day of the week is just before Sunday?

Mark the space under your answer.

6 Monday ○ Thursday ○ Friday ○ Saturday ○

Name ______________________

Remember:

 = 1¢

1 penny

    or = 5¢

5 pennies

1 nickel

Count by 5's. Write the amount.

1.

[10] ¢

2.

[ ] ¢

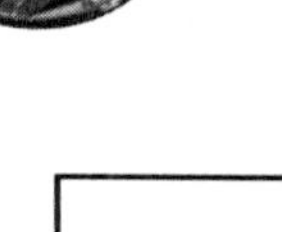

3.

[ ] ¢

4.

[ ] ¢

5.

[ ] ¢

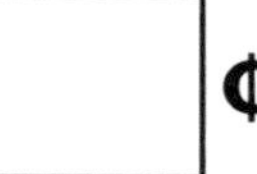

6.

[ ] ¢

Count by 5's.
Then count on by 1's. Write the amount.

7. 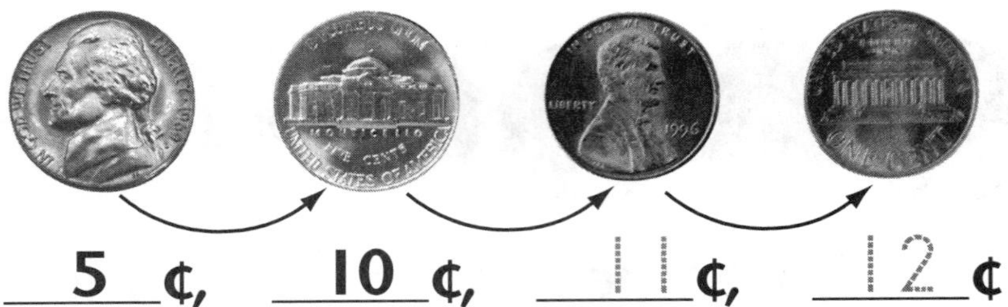

5 ¢, 10 ¢, 11 ¢, 12 ¢ — 12 ¢

8. 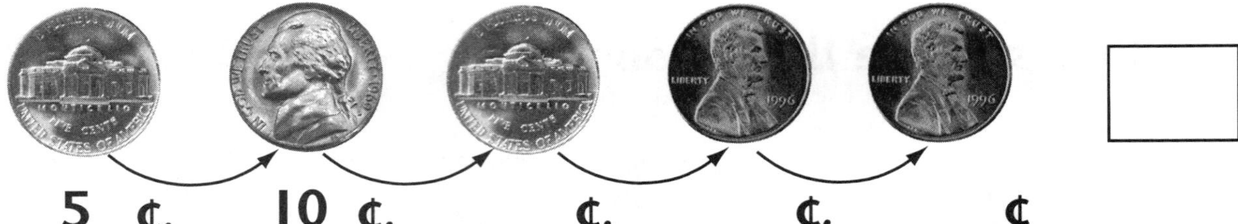

5 ¢, 10 ¢, ____ ¢, ____ ¢, ____ ¢ — ____ ¢

9.    

____ ¢, ____ ¢, ____ ¢, ____ ¢ — 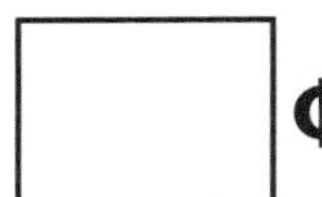 ¢

10.     

____ ¢, ____ ¢, ____ ¢, ____ ¢, ____ ¢ — ____ ¢

Problem Solving
Reasoning

11. How much money?

____ ¢

★ Test Prep

Which shows the amount? Mark the space under your answer.

12.  

7¢	10¢	11¢	15¢
○	○	○	○

Name ______________________________

STANDARD

Remember:

10 pennies
10¢

I dime
10¢

Count by 10's. Write the amount.

I. 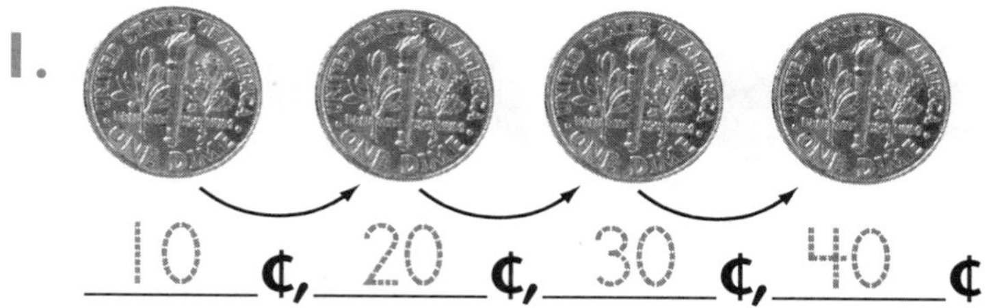

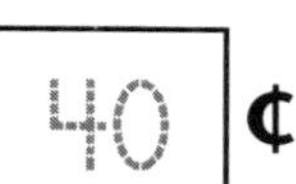

10 ¢, 20 ¢, 30 ¢, 40 ¢

40 ¢

2.       

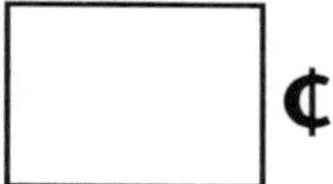

____¢, ____¢, ____¢, ____¢, ____¢, ____¢, ____¢

☐ ¢

Count by 10's.
Then count on by I's. Write the amount.

3. 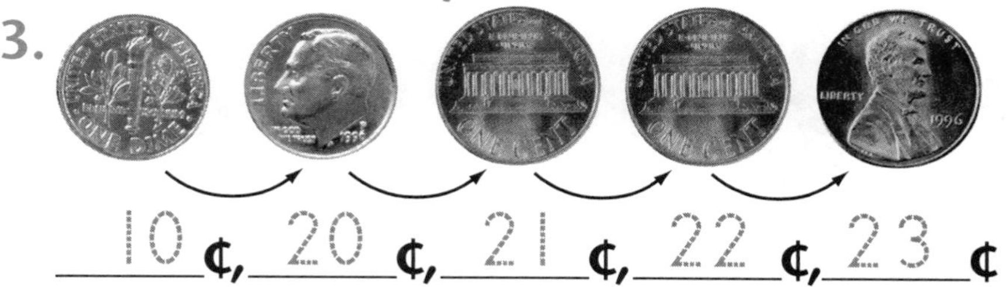

10 ¢, 20 ¢, 21 ¢, 22 ¢, 23 ¢

23 ¢

4.      

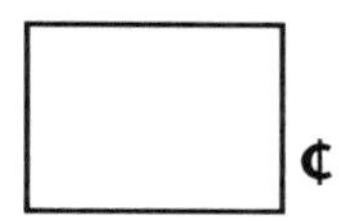

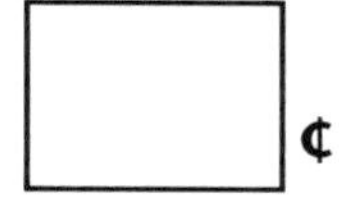

____¢, ____¢, ____¢, ____¢, ____¢, ____¢

☐ ¢

Count by 10's.
Then count by 5's. Write the amount.

5.

10 ¢, 20 ¢, 25 ¢, 30 ¢ 30 ¢

6. 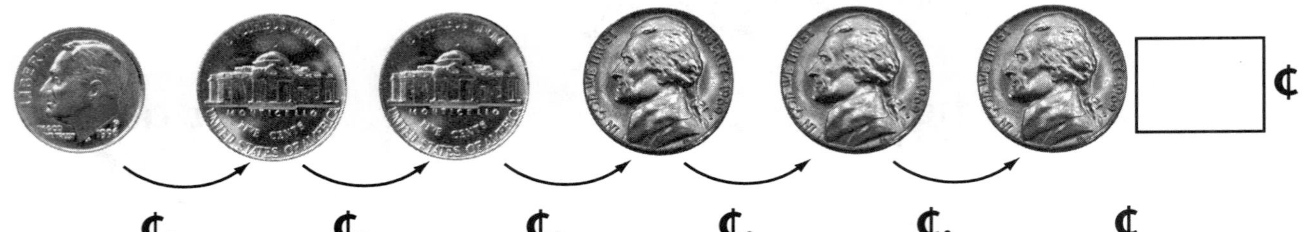

_____ ¢, _____ ¢, _____ ¢, _____ ¢, _____ ¢, _____ ¢   _____ ¢

7.      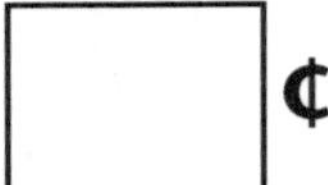

_____ ¢, _____ ¢, _____ ¢, _____ ¢, _____ ¢, _____ ¢   _____ ¢

 **Quick Check**

Solve.

1. How many days in a week? _____

Count the money. Write the amount.

2.   

_____ ¢, _____ ¢, _____ ¢, _____ ¢   _____ ¢

3.     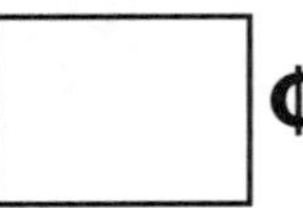

_____ ¢, _____ ¢, _____ ¢, _____ ¢   _____ ¢

Name ______________________________

Remember!

I penny

I nickel

I dime

Ring the amount.

I.

II¢

I3¢

I2¢

2.

I6¢

I3¢

I4¢

3.

I7¢

II¢

I4¢

4.

20¢

I5¢

I4¢

5.

I3¢

I8¢

I7¢

6.

I5¢

I2¢

20¢

Ring the coins needed to buy each toy.

7.

8.

Problem Solving Reasoning Solve.

9. I have some dimes, some nickels, and some pennies in my pocket. I take out **2** coins. How much money could I have? Write all the possible amounts.

_____ ¢, _____ ¢, _____ ¢, _____ ¢, _____ ¢, _____ ¢

★ Test Prep

How much money?
Mark the space for your answer.

10

22¢	26¢	31¢	30¢
○	○	○	○

Name ____________________

25¢

I quarter

25 cents

Use coins.

Find ways to make 25¢. Complete the chart.

I.

Ways to Make 25¢									
	2	2							
	I	0							
	0	5							

Solve.

2. Can you make **25¢** using only **I** coin? ____________

If yes, write the name of the coin. ____________

Write the amount.

3. 

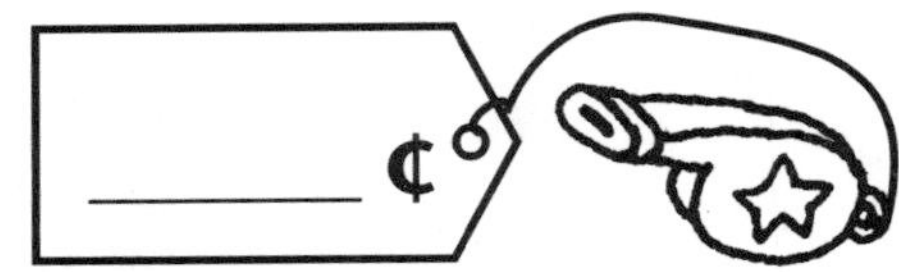

_____ ¢

4. 

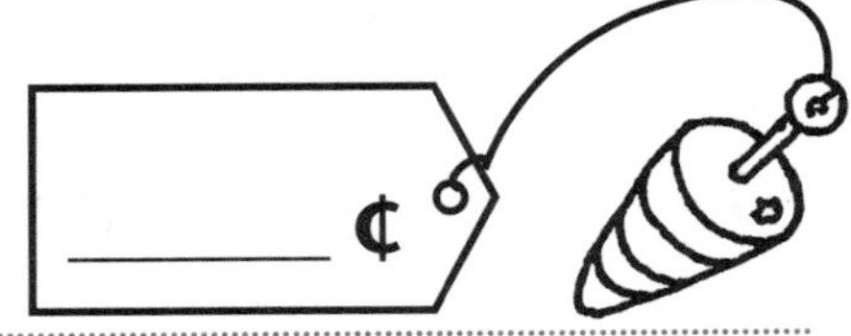

_____ ¢

5.     

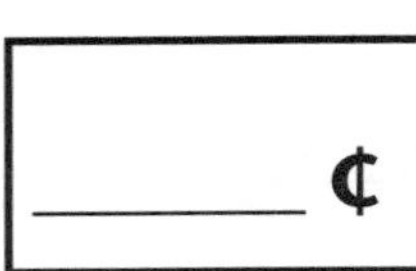 

_____ ¢

6.  

_____ ¢

7.  

_____ ¢

Problem Solving Reasoning

Solve.

8. You have **1**  , **1** , **1** , and **3** 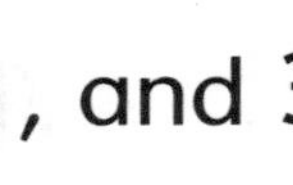 .

How much money do you have? _____ ¢

★ Test Prep

Which group of coins does not have a value of **25¢**?
Mark the space for your answer.

 ○

 ○

 ○

 ○

STANDARD

Name ________________________________

Problem

Emily spends **5¢**.
Which stamps does she buy?

1 **Understand**

I need to know which stamps Emily buys.

2 **Decide**

I can guess which stamps, then check.

3 **Solve**

Guess: 2¢ + 4¢ = 6¢

Check: 6¢ is not what Emily spends.

Guess: 2¢ + 3¢ = 5¢

Check: Emily spends **5¢**.

Answer Emily buys a **2¢** stamp and a **3¢** stamp.

4 **Look back**

I can check that I added the amounts right.

2¢ + 3¢ = 5¢.

My answer makes sense.

Guess and check to solve.

1. Ellen spends **7¢**.
   Ring the stamps
   she buys.

2. Allan spends **8¢**.
   Ring the stamps
   he buys.

3. Marie spends **6¢**.
   Ring the stamps
   she buys.

4. Bill spends **9¢**.
   Ring the stamps
   he buys.

5. Mario spends **7¢**.
   Ring the stamps
   he buys.

6. Sylvia spends **10¢**.
   Ring the stamps
   she buys.

Name ______________________________

Match.

1. 

6:30

2. 

3. 

Ring minutes or hours.

4. 

Put on mittens.

minutes hours

5. 

Work at school.

minutes hours

Answer the question.

6. How many days in a week? _____ days

7. How many months in a year? _____ months

Write the amount.

8. 

_______¢

9. 

_______¢

Ring the coins needed.

10. **16¢**

11. **32¢**

Problem Solving Reasoning

Use the table to answer the question.

Bus Schedule

Leaves at	From
9:00	Bean Town
10:30	Greenvale
11:00	Middle Village
12:30	Mine City

12. What time does the bus leave Greenvale? ___:___

13. Where will the bus leave from at **11** o'clock?

____

Use guess and check to solve.

14.

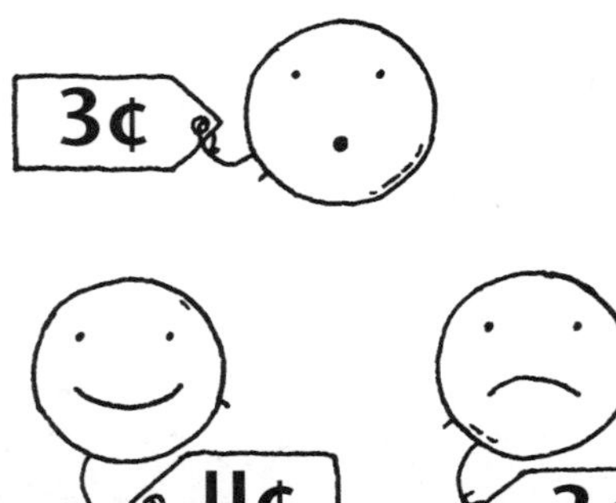

Bill spends **6¢**.
Ring the pins he buys.

15.

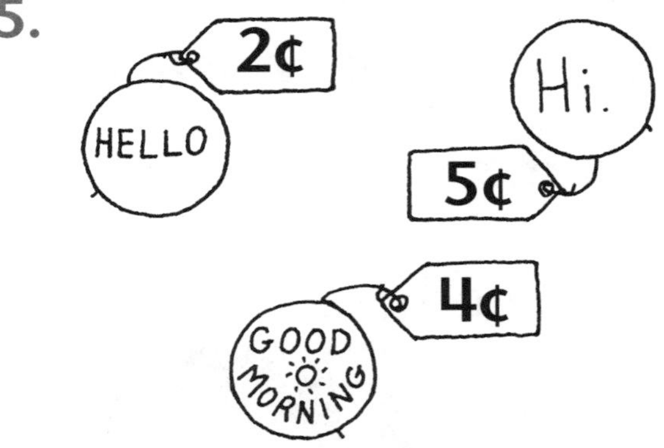

Ann spends **6¢**.
Ring the pins she buys.

Name ______________________

1

72, 71, ______ , 69, 68

75	66	70	67
○	○	○	○

2

40

○ 4 tens, 4 ones ○ 4 tens, 0 ones

○ 0 tens, 4 ones ○ 4 tens, 10 ones

3

20, ______ , 30, 35

15	21	35	25
○	○	○	○

4

23 ○ 32

<	>	=	+
○	○	○	○

5

A B C D E F G

B	E	F	G
○	○	○	○

6

○ $9 - 1 = 8$ ○ $9 + 1 = 10$

○ $8 - 1 = 7$ ○ $9 - 8 = 1$

7

50, 48, 46, 44, ____

40	41	42	43
○	○	○	○

8

6:00	6:30	12:30	1:30
○	○	○	○

9

Close a door.	Open a can.	Play a game of ball.
○	○	○

10

Start

Finish

○ a half hour ○ 1 hour

○ 9 hours ○ 1 minute

11

46¢	41¢	36¢	26¢
○	○	○	○

UNIT 9 • TABLE OF CONTENTS

2-Digit Addition and Subtraction

UNIT 9 • TABLE OF CONTENTS

We will be using this vocabulary:

2-digit numbers from 10 through 99
table a chart that contains data in an organized way
addend one of the numbers added in an addition problem

Dear Family,

During the next few weeks our math class will be learning and practicing addition and subtraction of 2-digit numbers.

You can expect to see homework that provides practice with addition and subtraction of numbers through 99.

As we learn about how to add and subtract 2-digit numbers, you may wish to keep the following sample as a guide.

Adding 2-Digit Numbers

Models

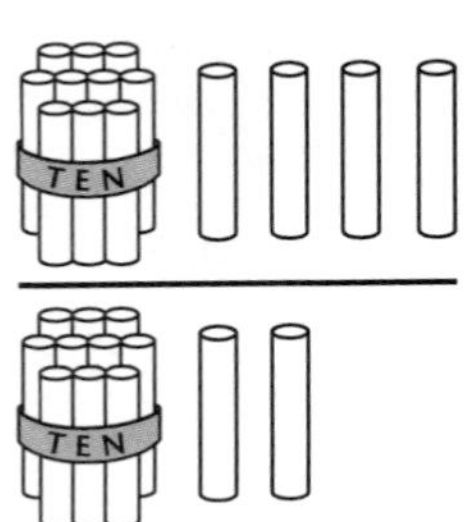

Place-Value Chart

Tens	Ones
1	4
+ 1	2
2	6

$$\begin{array}{r} 14 \\ +\ 12 \\ \hline 26 \end{array}$$

Subtracting 2-Digit Numbers

Models

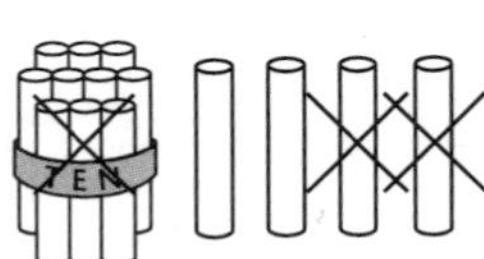

Place-Value Chart

Tens	Ones
1	4
− 1	2
	2

$$\begin{array}{r} 14 \\ -\ 12 \\ \hline 2 \end{array}$$

Knowing how to add and subtract 2-digit numbers can help children learn how to solve more complex problems.

Sincerely,

Name ____________________

Add the ones. Add the tens.

1.

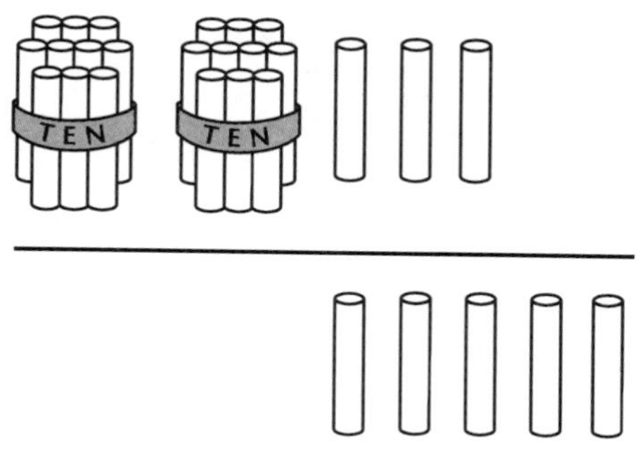

	Tens	Ones
	2	3
+		5
	2	8

$$\begin{array}{r} 23 \\ +\ 5 \\ \hline \end{array}$$

2.

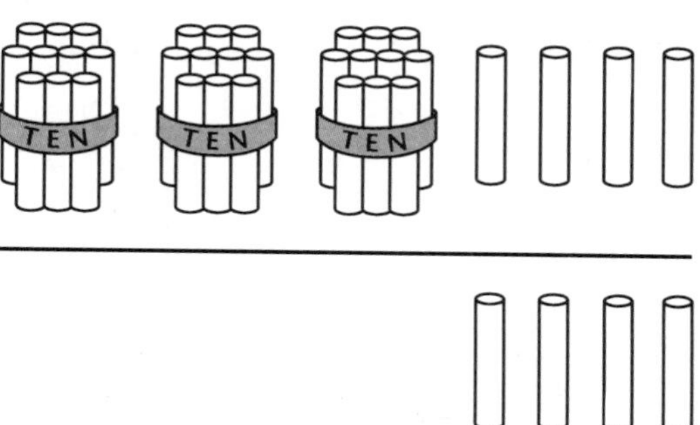

	T	O
	3	4
+		4

$$\begin{array}{r} 34 \\ +\ 4 \\ \hline \end{array}$$

3.

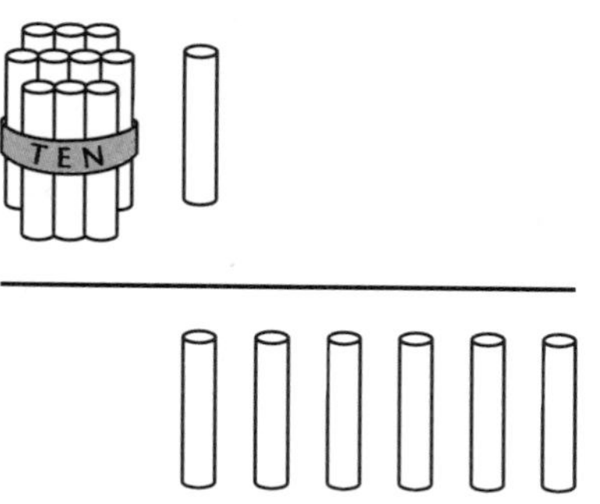

	T	O
	1	1
+		6

$$\begin{array}{r} 11 \\ +\ 6 \\ \hline \end{array}$$

4.

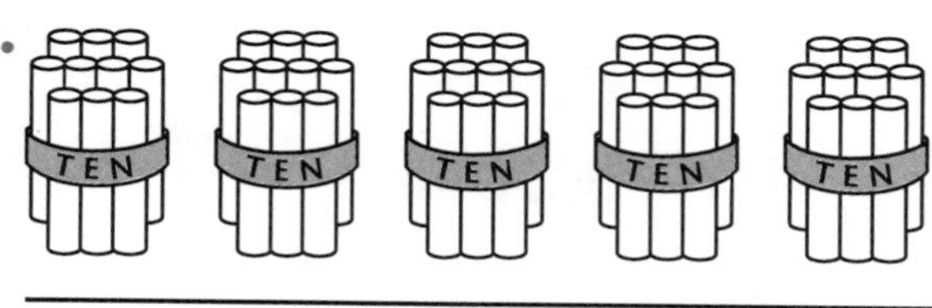

	T	O
	5	0
+		2

$$\begin{array}{r} 50 \\ +\ 2 \\ \hline \end{array}$$

Add the ones. Add the tens.

5.  

	T	O
	3	1
+		8
	3	9

$$\begin{array}{r} 31 \\ +\ 8 \\ \hline 39 \end{array}$$

6.

	T	O
	6	6
+		3

7.

	T	O
	5	2
+		7

8.

	T	O
	7	4
+		2

9.

	T	O
	4	0
+		6

10. $\begin{array}{r} 83 \\ +\ 5 \\ \hline \end{array}$

11. $\begin{array}{r} 41 \\ +\ 4 \\ \hline \end{array}$

12. $\begin{array}{r} 90 \\ +\ 9 \\ \hline \end{array}$

13. $\begin{array}{r} 53 \\ +\ 1 \\ \hline \end{array}$

14. $\begin{array}{r} 32 \\ +\ 6 \\ \hline \end{array}$

15. $\begin{array}{r} 42 \\ +\ 7 \\ \hline \end{array}$

16. $\begin{array}{r} 30 \\ +\ 5 \\ \hline \end{array}$

17. $\begin{array}{r} 25 \\ +\ 4 \\ \hline \end{array}$

Problem Solving Reasoning Solve.

18. There are **25** children in class.
2 more children join them.
How many children are in class now? ______ children

Name ______________________________

Add the ones. Add the tens

1.

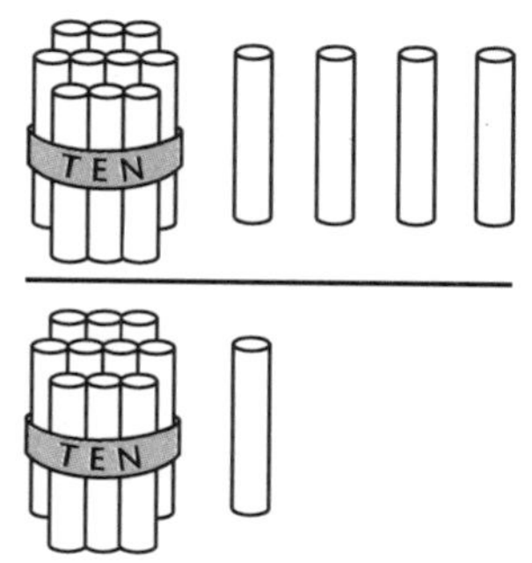

T	O
1	4
+ 1	1
2	5

$$\begin{array}{r} 14 \\ +\ 11 \\ \hline 25 \end{array}$$

2.

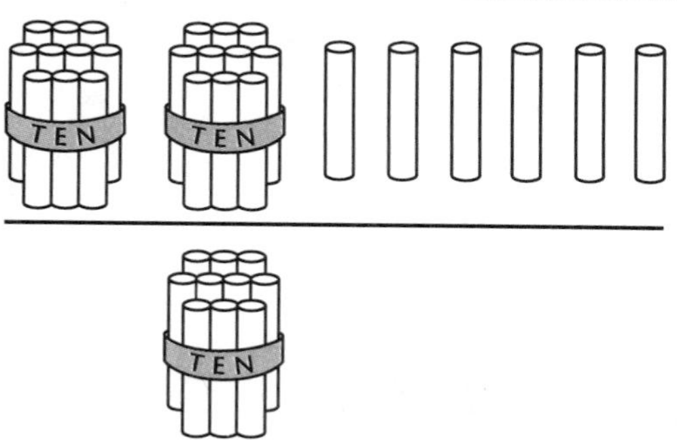

T	O
2	6
+ 1	0

$$\begin{array}{r} 26 \\ +\ 10 \\ \hline \end{array}$$

3.

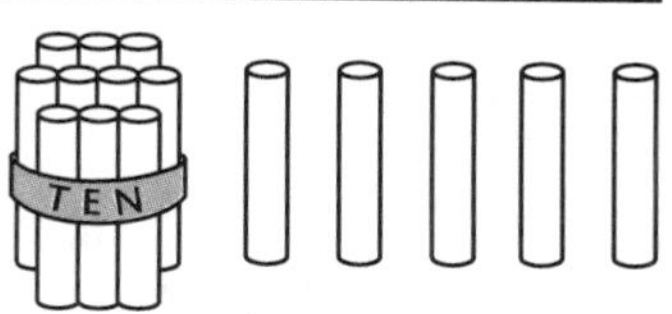

T	O
4	1
+ 1	5

$$\begin{array}{r} 41 \\ +\ 15 \\ \hline \end{array}$$

4.

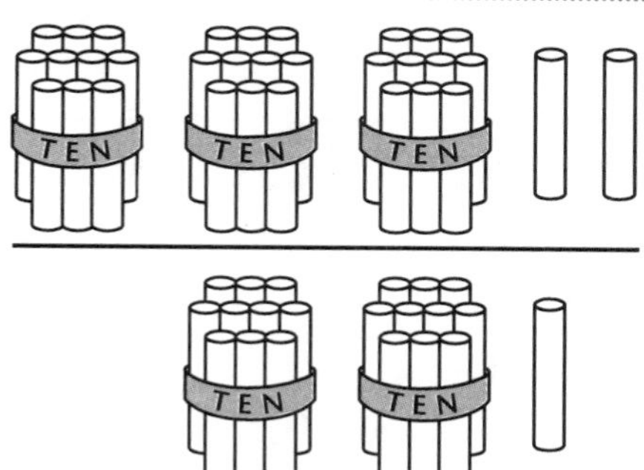

T	O
3	2
+ 2	1

$$\begin{array}{r} 32 \\ +\ 21 \\ \hline \end{array}$$

5.

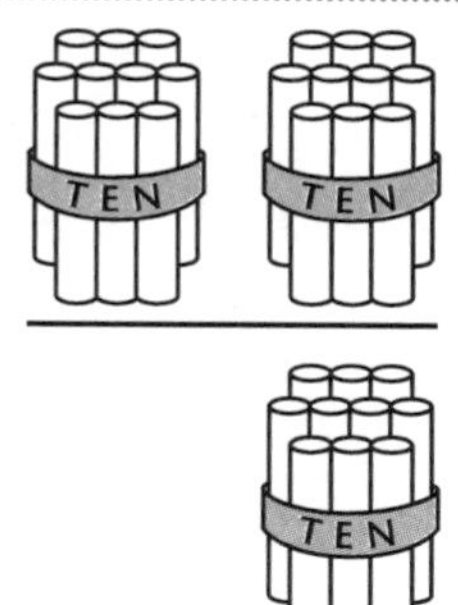

T	O
2	0
+ 1	0

$$\begin{array}{r} 20 \\ +\ 10 \\ \hline \end{array}$$

Add the ones. Add the tens.

6. 

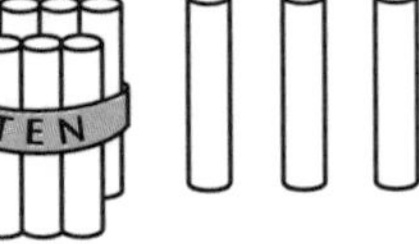

T	O
5	2
+ 1	3
6	5

$$\begin{array}{r} 52 \\ +\ 13 \\ \hline 65 \end{array}$$

7.

T	O
1	2
+ 3	1

8.

T	O
3	0
+ 4	7

9.

T	O
6	0
+ 2	4

10.

T	O
7	3
+ 2	6

11.

T	O
8	4
+ 1	0

12.

T	O
4	6
+ 2	2

13.

T	O
4	1
+ 3	5

14.

T	O
2	5
+ 4	3

15. $\begin{array}{r} 61 \\ +\ 34 \\ \hline \end{array}$

16. $\begin{array}{r} 44 \\ +\ 20 \\ \hline \end{array}$

17. $\begin{array}{r} 10 \\ +\ 53 \\ \hline \end{array}$

18. $\begin{array}{r} 52 \\ +\ 27 \\ \hline \end{array}$

19. $\begin{array}{r} 24 \\ +\ 20 \\ \hline \end{array}$

20. $\begin{array}{r} 63 \\ +\ 11 \\ \hline \end{array}$

21. $\begin{array}{r} 14 \\ +\ 70 \\ \hline \end{array}$

22. $\begin{array}{r} 56 \\ +\ 33 \\ \hline \end{array}$

Problem Solving
Reasoning

Solve.

23. What number can you add to **20** so that the sum has a **0** in the ones? ______________________

STANDARD

Name ______________________________

You need a place-value mat and tens and ones models.

29 + 4
Show **29.**
Add **4.**

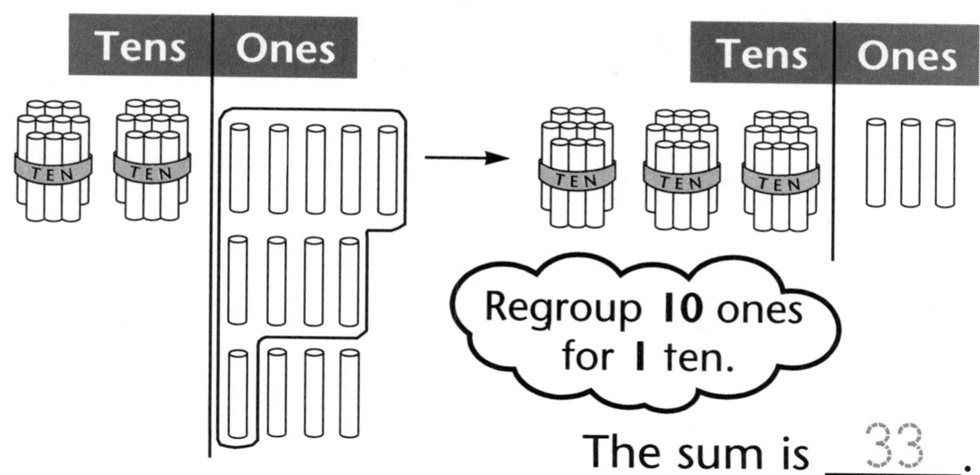

The sum is 33.

Show the addends. Regroup.
Add. Write the sum.

1. **43 + 8**

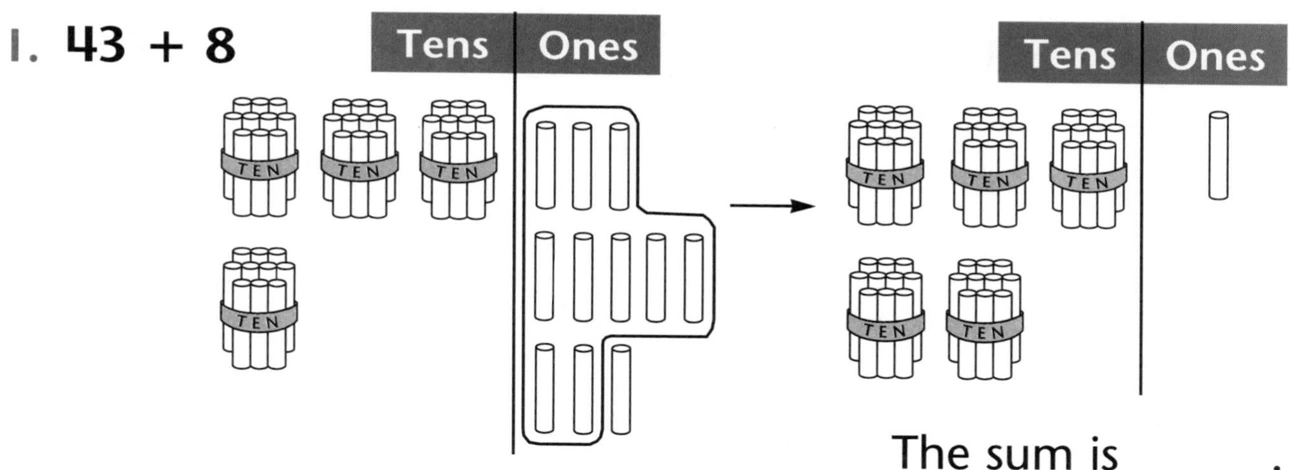

The sum is ______.

2. **38 + 5**

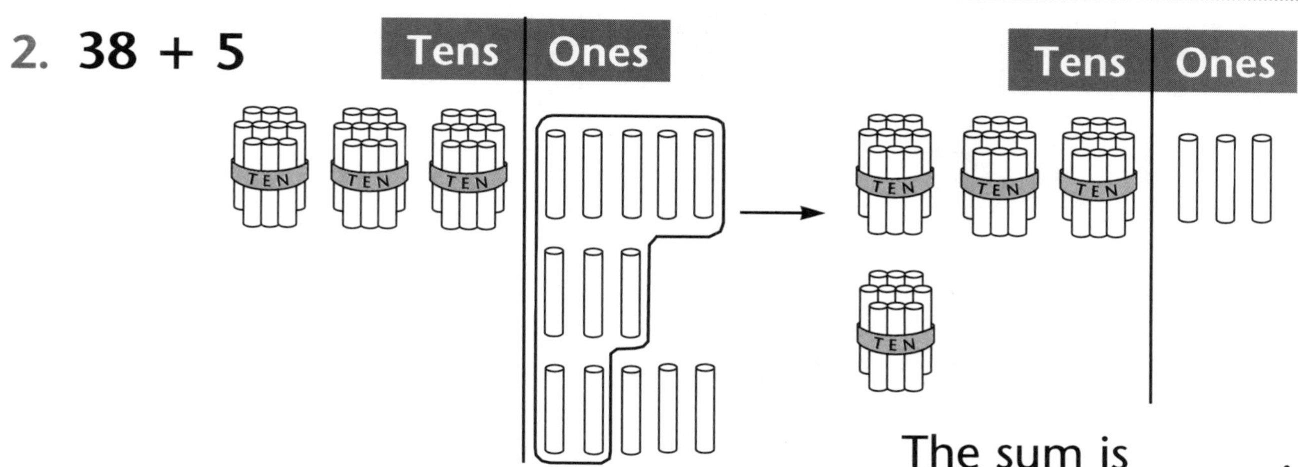

The sum is ______.

Show the addends. Regroup.
Add. Write the sum.

3. 7 + 54

Tens	Ones

Tens	Ones

The sum is ______.

Quick Check

Add.

1. $\begin{array}{r} 41 \\ +\ 7 \\ \hline \end{array}$

2. $\begin{array}{r} 50 \\ +\ 37 \\ \hline \end{array}$

3. $\begin{array}{r} 47 \\ +\ 22 \\ \hline \end{array}$

Write the sum.

4. 17 + 6

Tens	Ones

Tens	Ones

The sum is ______.

Name ______________________________

Subtract the ones. Subtract the tens.

1.

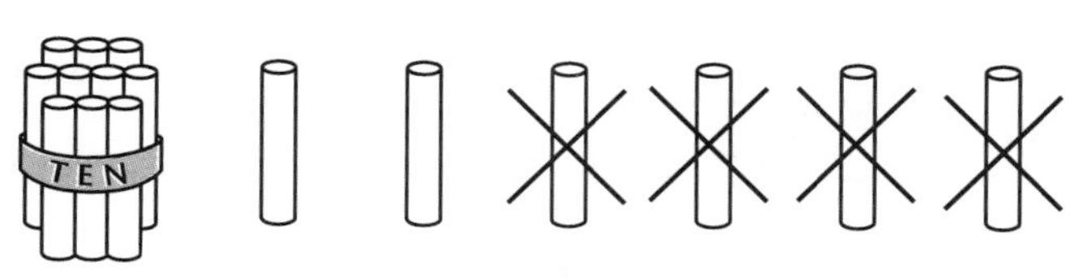

Tens	Ones
1	6
−	4
1	2

$$\begin{array}{r} 16 \\ -\ \ 4 \\ \hline 12 \end{array}$$

2.

T	O
3	2
−	1

$$\begin{array}{r} 32 \\ -\ \ 1 \\ \hline \end{array}$$

3.

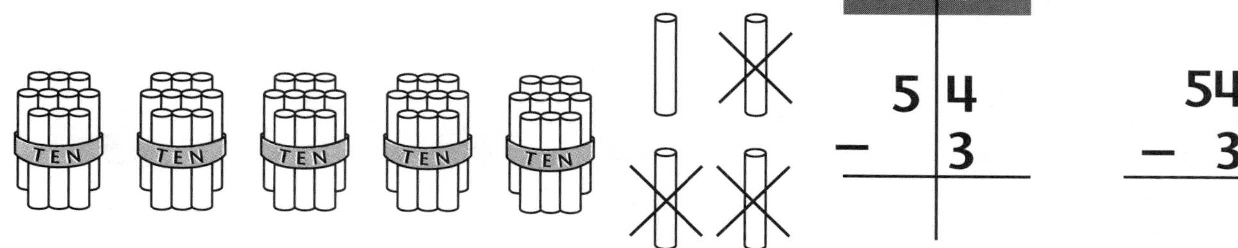

T	O
5	4
−	3

$$\begin{array}{r} 54 \\ -\ \ 3 \\ \hline \end{array}$$

4.

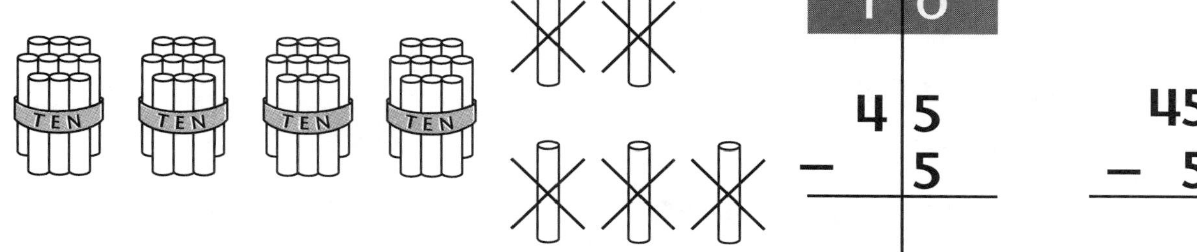

T	O
4	5
−	5

$$\begin{array}{r} 45 \\ -\ \ 5 \\ \hline \end{array}$$

Subtract the ones. Subtract the tens.

5.  

T	O
2	3
−	2
2	1

$$\begin{array}{r} 23 \\ -\ 2 \\ \hline 21 \end{array}$$

6.

T	O
4	4
−	2

7.

T	O
3	1
−	1

8.

T	O
5	6
−	5

9.

T	O
2	4
−	4

10. $\begin{array}{r} 47 \\ -\ 6 \\ \hline \end{array}$

11. $\begin{array}{r} 78 \\ -\ 3 \\ \hline \end{array}$

12. $\begin{array}{r} 67 \\ -\ 4 \\ \hline \end{array}$

13. $\begin{array}{r} 29 \\ -\ 7 \\ \hline \end{array}$

14. $\begin{array}{r} 75 \\ -\ 2 \\ \hline \end{array}$

15. $\begin{array}{r} 88 \\ -\ 6 \\ \hline \end{array}$

16. $\begin{array}{r} 63 \\ -\ 1 \\ \hline \end{array}$

17. $\begin{array}{r} 95 \\ -\ 3 \\ \hline \end{array}$

Problem Solving Reasoning Solve.

18. There are **36** crayons in a box.
4 are broken.
How many are not broken? ______ crayons

Name ______________________________

Subtract the ones. Subtract the tens.

1.

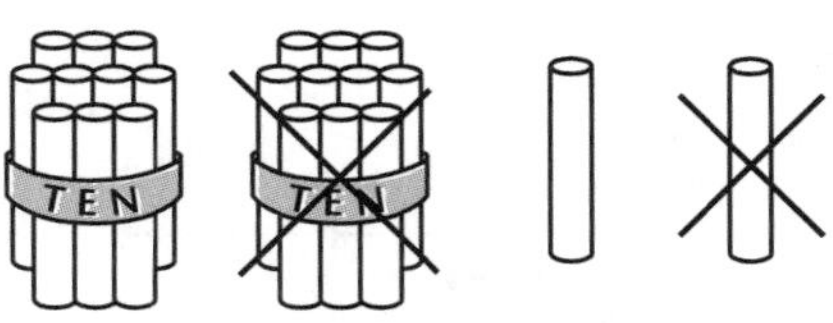

T	O
2	2
− 1	1
1	1

$$\begin{array}{r} 22 \\ -\ 11 \\ \hline 11 \end{array}$$

2.

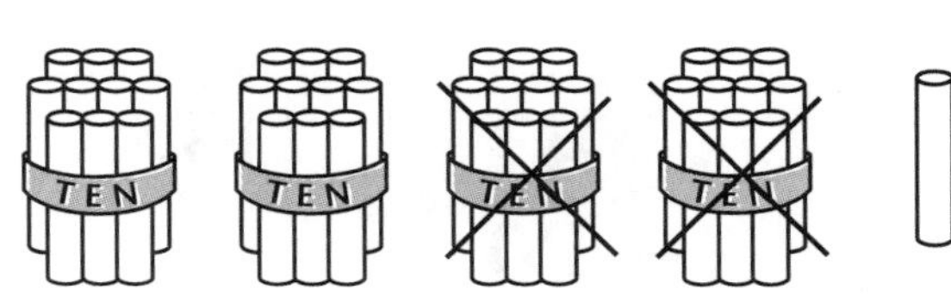

T	O
4	1
− 2	0

$$\begin{array}{r} 41 \\ -\ 20 \\ \hline \end{array}$$

3.

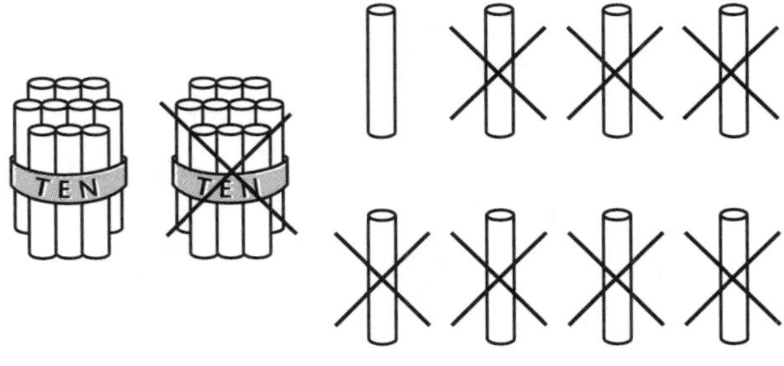

T	O
2	8
− 1	7

$$\begin{array}{r} 28 \\ -\ 17 \\ \hline \end{array}$$

4.

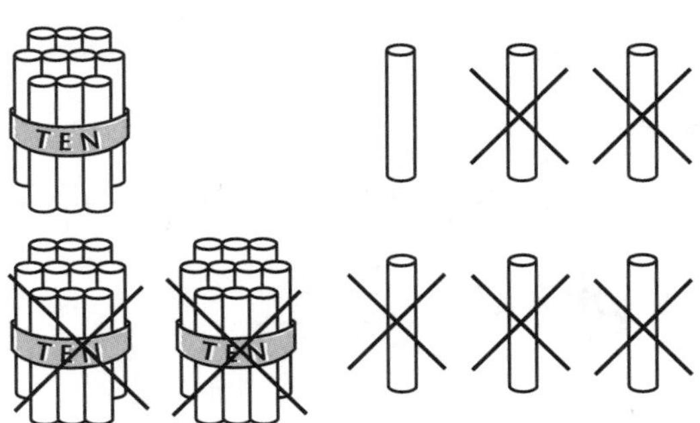

T	O
3	6
− 2	5

$$\begin{array}{r} 36 \\ -\ 25 \\ \hline \end{array}$$

Subtract the ones. Subtract the tens.

5\. 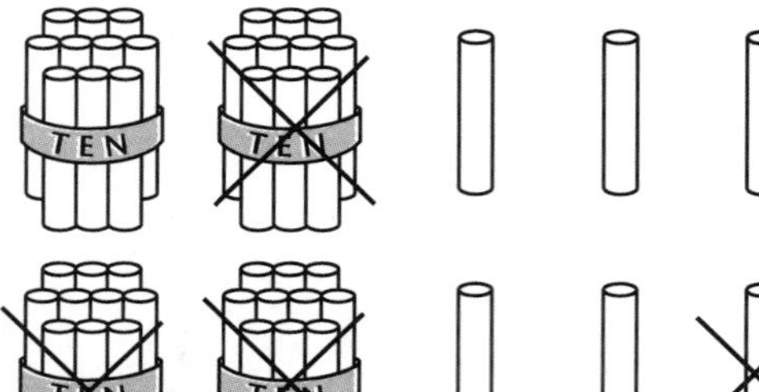

T	O
5	6
− 4	1
1	5

$$\begin{array}{r} 56 \\ -\ 41 \\ \hline 15 \end{array}$$

6\.

T	O
3	2
− 1	0

7\.

T	O
8	5
− 5	1

8\.

T	O
5	8
− 4	6

9\.

T	O
6	4
− 3	4

10\. $\begin{array}{r} 84 \\ -\ 62 \\ \hline \end{array}$

11\. $\begin{array}{r} 76 \\ -\ 53 \\ \hline \end{array}$

12\. $\begin{array}{r} 43 \\ -\ 20 \\ \hline \end{array}$

13\. $\begin{array}{r} 94 \\ -\ 72 \\ \hline \end{array}$

14\. $\begin{array}{r} 44 \\ -\ 31 \\ \hline \end{array}$

15\. $\begin{array}{r} 54 \\ -\ 10 \\ \hline \end{array}$

16\. $\begin{array}{r} 97 \\ -\ 65 \\ \hline \end{array}$

17\. $\begin{array}{r} 83 \\ -\ 30 \\ \hline \end{array}$

18\. $\begin{array}{r} 90 \\ -\ 40 \\ \hline \end{array}$

19\. $\begin{array}{r} 78 \\ -\ 26 \\ \hline \end{array}$

20\. $\begin{array}{r} 67 \\ -\ 15 \\ \hline \end{array}$

21\. $\begin{array}{r} 92 \\ -\ 70 \\ \hline \end{array}$

Problem Solving Reasoning Solve.

22\. What number can you subtract from **45** so that the difference has a **0** in the ones place? ______

Name ______________________________

You need a place-value mat and tens and ones models.

44 – 5
Show **44**.
Subtract **5**.

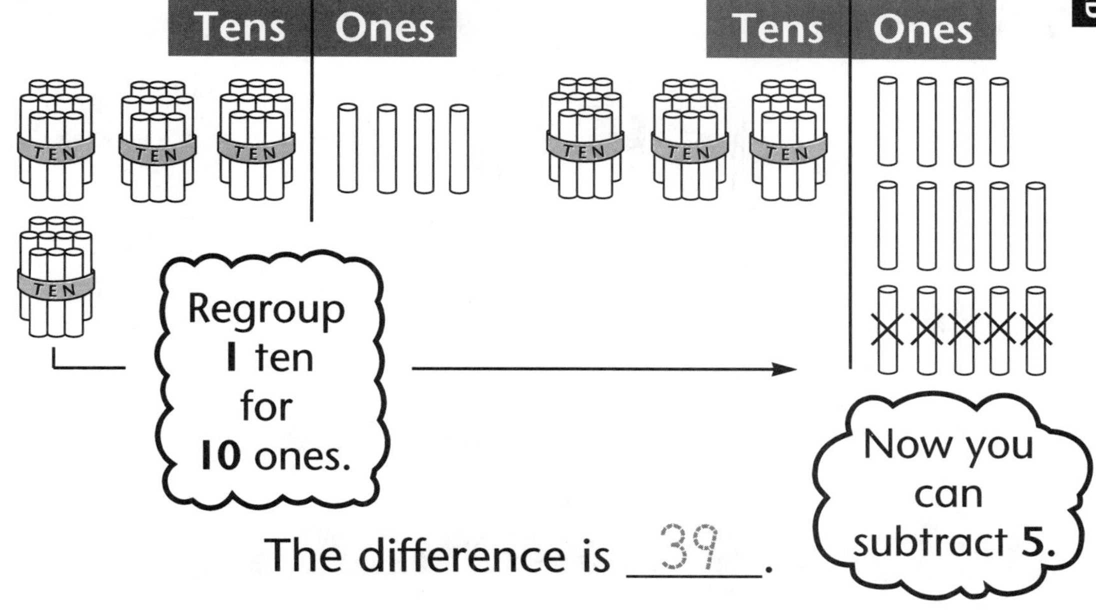

The difference is 39.

Show the number. Regroup.
Subtract. Write the difference.

1. **31 – 4**

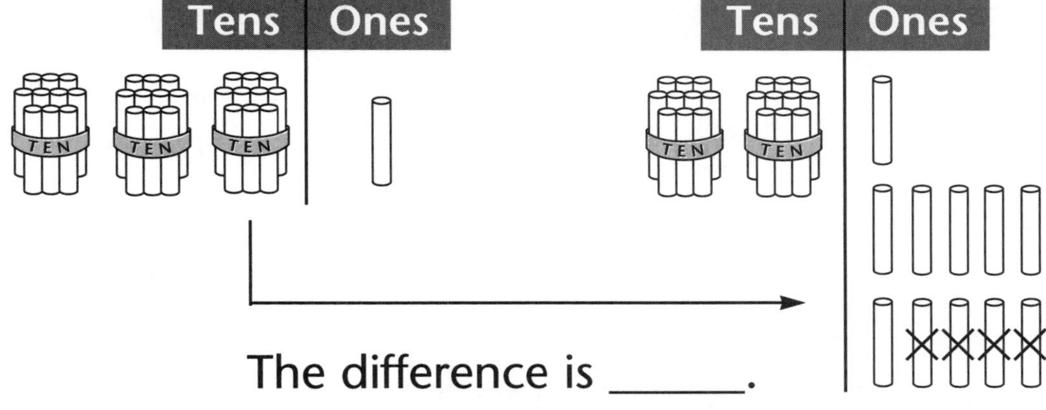

The difference is ______.

2. **53 – 7**

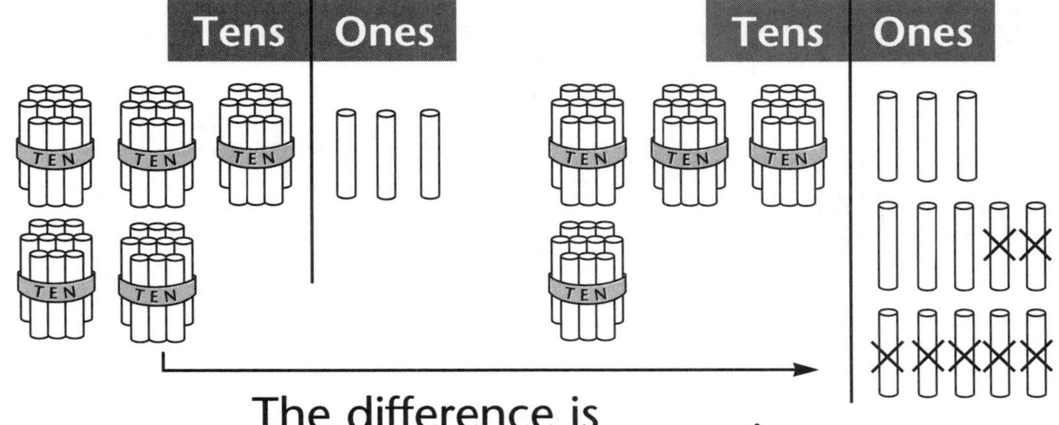

The difference is ______.

Show the number. Regroup.
Subtract. Write the difference.

3. **62 − 6**

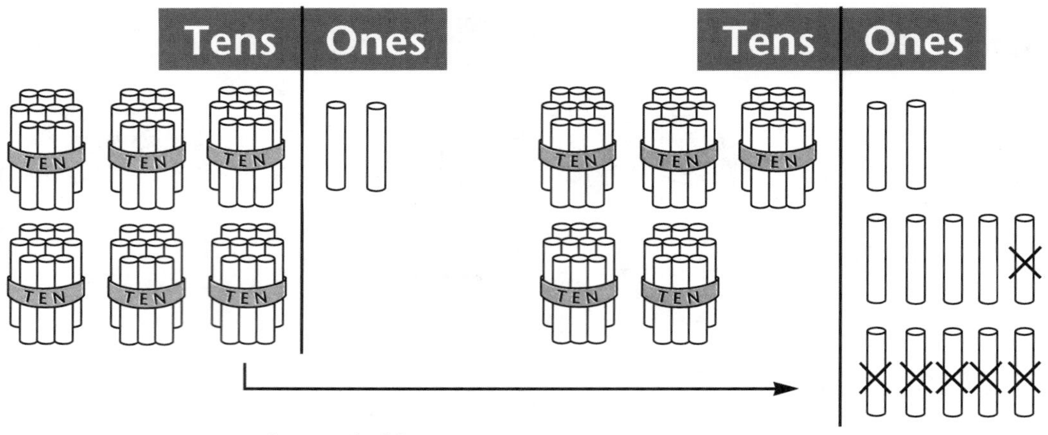

The difference is ______.

☑ Quick Check

Subtract.

1.
$$\begin{array}{r} 89 \\ -\ \ 6 \\ \hline \end{array}$$

2.
$$\begin{array}{r} 94 \\ -\ 60 \\ \hline \end{array}$$

3.
$$\begin{array}{r} 79 \\ -\ 54 \\ \hline \end{array}$$

Write the difference.

4. **41 − 5**

Tens | Ones

Tens | Ones

The difference is ______.

Name ____________________

Count the dimes.
Add or subtract.

1.

	5 dimes	50¢
and	3 dimes	+ 30¢
	8 dimes	80¢

2.

	4 dimes	40¢
and	5 dimes	+ 50¢
	____ dimes	____¢

3.

	8 dimes	80¢
take away	6 dimes	− 60¢
	____ dimes	____¢

4.

	9 dimes	90¢
take away	5 dimes	− 50¢
	____ dimes	____¢

Add or subtract.

5. $\begin{array}{r} 35¢ \\ +\ 43¢ \\ \hline 78¢ \end{array}$

6. $\begin{array}{r} 26¢ \\ +\ 31¢ \\ \hline \end{array}$

7. $\begin{array}{r} 42¢ \\ +\ 53¢ \\ \hline \end{array}$

8. $\begin{array}{r} 40¢ \\ +\ 20¢ \\ \hline \end{array}$

9. $\begin{array}{r} 84¢ \\ -\ 21¢ \\ \hline 63¢ \end{array}$

10. $\begin{array}{r} 67¢ \\ -\ 32¢ \\ \hline \end{array}$

11. $\begin{array}{r} 58¢ \\ -\ 24¢ \\ \hline \end{array}$

12. $\begin{array}{r} 73¢ \\ -\ 52¢ \\ \hline \end{array}$

13. $\begin{array}{r} 57¢ \\ +\ 12¢ \\ \hline \end{array}$

14. $\begin{array}{r} 41¢ \\ +\ 58¢ \\ \hline \end{array}$

15. $\begin{array}{r} 32¢ \\ +\ 17¢ \\ \hline \end{array}$

16. $\begin{array}{r} 65¢ \\ +\ 20¢ \\ \hline \end{array}$

Problem Solving Reasoning

Solve.

17. Ann has **67¢**. Bob has **57¢**. How much more money does Ann have than Bob? ______

18. Juan has **60¢**. Rita has **24¢**. How much money do they have in all?

______

★ Test Prep

Decide on an answer. Mark the space for your answer. If the answer is **not here**, mark the space for **NH**.

19. $\begin{array}{r} 11¢ \\ +\ 52¢ \\ \hline \square \end{array}$

36¢	64¢	41¢	NH
○	○		○

Name ______________________

Problem Solving Plan			
1. Understand	2. Decide	3. Solve	4. Look back

Write + or – in the ◯. Solve.

1. Pablo has **32** shells.
He found **17** more.
How many shells in all?

Think Do you need to add or subtract?

add

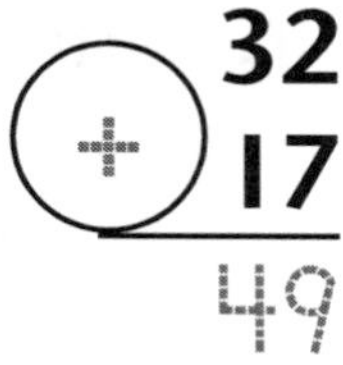

32
+ 17
49

49 shells

2. There are **29** toads.
13 hop away.
How many are left?

Think Do you need to add or subtract?

______

◯ 29
13

______ toads

3. There are **46** fish.
22 fish swim away.
How many are left?

Think Do you need to add or subtract?

______

46
22

______ fish

4. You have **18** starfish.
You get **11** more starfish.
How many in all?

Think Do you need to add or subtract?

______

◯ 18
11

______ starfish

Solve.

5. You have **35** toy cars.
You buy **11** more.
How many toy cars in all?

$$\begin{array}{r} 35 \\ \bigcirc\ 11 \\ \hline \end{array}$$

_____ toy cars

6. There are **42** chicks.
12 fly away.
How many chicks are left?

$$\begin{array}{r} 42 \\ \bigcirc\ 12 \\ \hline \end{array}$$

_____ chicks

7. There are **64** rabbits.
13 rabbits join them.
How many in all?

$$\begin{array}{r} 64 \\ \bigcirc\ 13 \\ \hline \end{array}$$

_____ rabbits

8. There are **75** blue airplanes and **31** red airplanes.
How many more airplanes are blue?

$$\begin{array}{r} 75 \\ \bigcirc\ 31 \\ \hline \end{array}$$

_____ airplanes

Extend Your Thinking

9. Draw a picture to show one of the problems. Have a friend guess which problem.

Name ______________________

STANDARD

Problem

How many wheels are there on **4** bicycles?

1 Understand

I need to find out how many wheels are on **4** bicycles.

2 Decide

I can make a table to count by **2**'s.
Then I can use the table to solve the problem.

3 Solve

Bicycles	1	2	3	4
Wheels	2	4	6	8

8 wheels

4 Look back

I can recheck the table to see if **4** bicycles have **8** wheels. They do.
My answer makes sense.

Fill in the table.
Solve.

Hands	1	2	3	4	5
Fingers	5				

1. How many fingers on **2** hands? ______

2. How many fingers on **3** hands? ______

3. How many hands if there are **20** fingers? ______

4. How many fingers on **5** hands? ______

5. What other strategy could you have used to solve problem **4**?

____

____

Name ____________________

Add.

1. 16 + 12 = ____

2. 72 + 13 = ____

3. 34 + 34 = ____

4. 30 + 20 = ____

Subtract.

5. 38 − 15 = ____

6. 49 − 23 = ____

7. 80 − 50 = ____

8. 78 − 5 = ____

Show the addends Regroup. Add. Write the sum.

9. 25 + 6

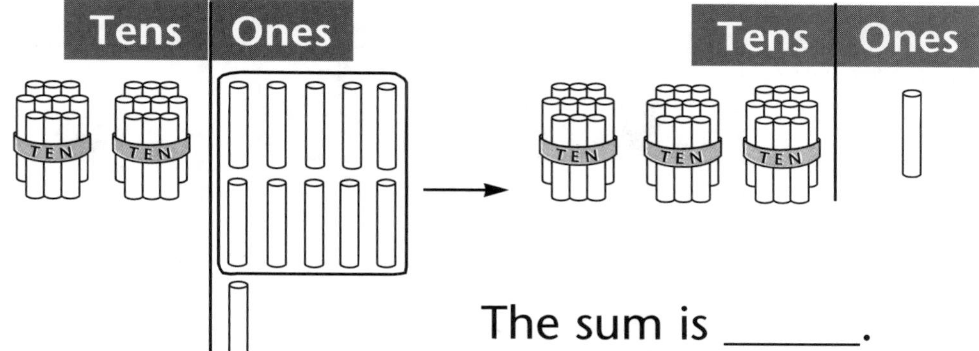

The sum is ______.

Show the number. Regroup. Subtract. Write the difference.

10. 32 − 3

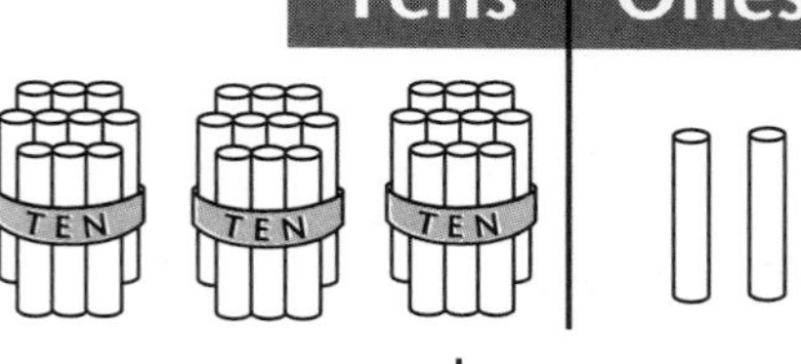

Tens | Ones

TEN TEN

The difference is ______.

Add or subtract.

11. 25¢ − 11¢ = ____

12. 63¢ + 2¢ = ____

13. 34¢ + 20¢ = ____

14. 70¢ − 30¢ = ____

Problem Solving Reasoning

Solve.

15. There are **23** chicks.
16 more chicks join them.
How many in all?

$$\begin{array}{r} 23 \\ \bigcirc\ 16 \\ \hline \end{array}$$

_____ chicks

16. There are **48** ducks.
15 fly away.
How many are left?

$$\begin{array}{r} 48 \\ \bigcirc\ 15 \\ \hline \end{array}$$

_____ ducks

Fill in the table. Solve.

17.

Bicycles	1	2	3	4	5	6
Wheels	2	4				

18. How many wheels on **5** bicycles? _____

19. How many wheels on **6** bicycles? _____

20. How many bicycles if there are **6** wheels? _____

Name ______________________________

1

10, 2, 8

○ 10 − 3 = 6 ○ 10 − 8 = 2

○ 6 + 2 = 8 ○ 10 − 4 = 6

2

twenty

12	2	20	02
○	○	○	○

3

3 tens and 7 ones

73	307	03	37
○	○	○	○

4

4, 6, 8, _____, 12, 14

9	10	11	15
○	○	○	○

5

65 ○ 56

<	>	=	+
○	○	○	○

6

○

○

○

52¢ ○ 37¢ ○ 32¢ ○ 17¢ ○

Decide on an answer. Mark the space for your answer.
If the answer is **not here**, mark the space for **NH**.

8

$8 + 2 = \square$

6 ○ 8 ○ 10 ○ NH ○

9

$$\begin{array}{r} 10 \\ -\ 8 \\ \hline \square \end{array}$$

2 ○ 6 ○ 8 ○ NH ○

10

$$\begin{array}{r} 35 \\ +\ 4 \\ \hline \square \end{array}$$

31 ○ 49 ○ 38 ○ NH ○

11

$$\begin{array}{r} 23 \\ +\ 30 \\ \hline \square \end{array}$$

13 ○ 62 ○ 53 ○ NH ○

12

$$\begin{array}{r} 45 \\ -\ 42 \\ \hline \square \end{array}$$

3 ○ 83 ○ 87 ○ NH ○

13

$$\begin{array}{r} 74 \\ -\ 34 \\ \hline \square \end{array}$$

44 ○ 40 ○ 48 ○ NH ○

UNIT 10 • TABLE OF CONTENTS

Fractions and Measurement

UNIT 10 • TABLE OF CONTENTS

Dear Family,

During the next few weeks our math class will be learning about fractions and measurement.

You can expect to see homework that provides practice with naming and recognizing fractions such as one half, one fourth, and one third as well as measuring length and comparing weight and capacity.

We will be using this vocabulary:

centimeter a unit of length in metric measurement

inch a unit of length in customary measurement

one fourth $\frac{1}{4}$ means 1 of 4 equal parts

one half $\frac{1}{2}$ means 1 of 2 equal parts

one third $\frac{1}{3}$ means 1 of 3 equal parts

shorter/longer used to compare length

heavier/lighter used to compare weight

As we learn about fractions of a region you may wish to keep the following samples as a guide.

Fractions

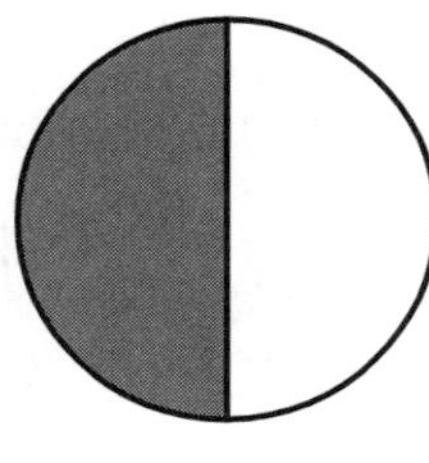

$\frac{1}{2}$

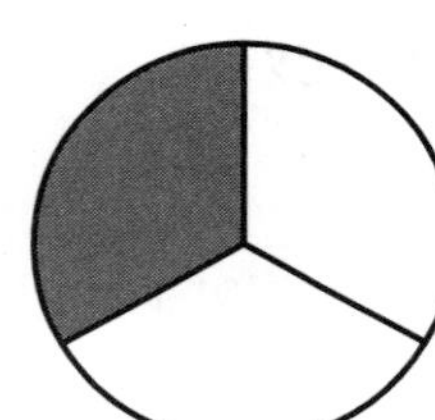

$\frac{1}{3}$

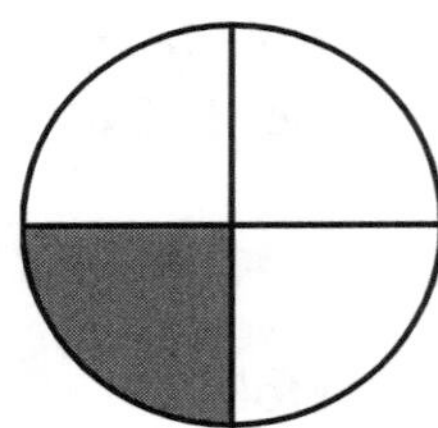

$\frac{1}{4}$

Knowing about fractions and measurement can help children find length, weight, and capacity in everyday life.

Sincerely,

Name ____________________

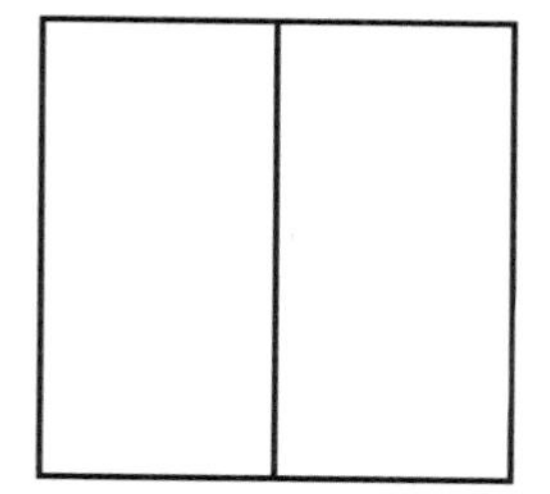

2 equal parts

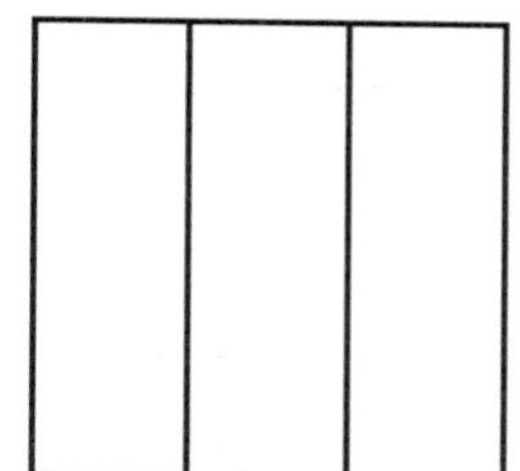

3 equal parts

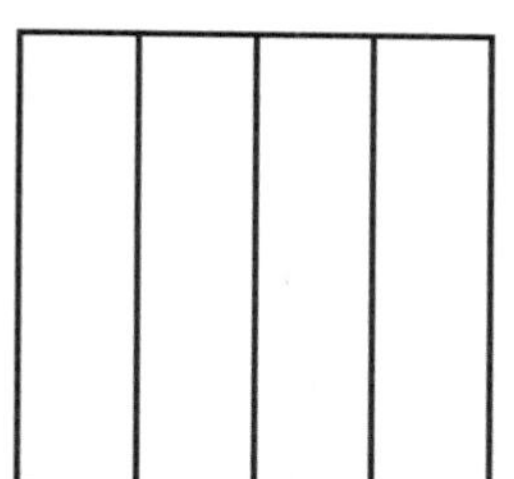

4 equal parts

Ring the figures with equal parts.

1.

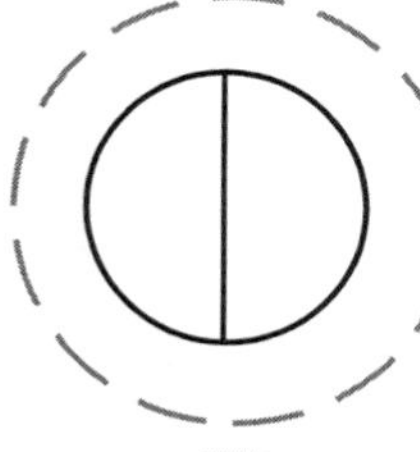

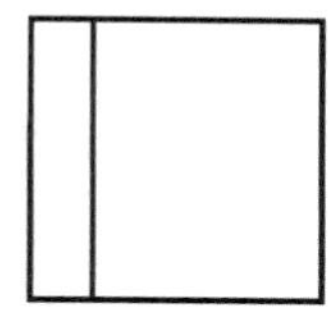

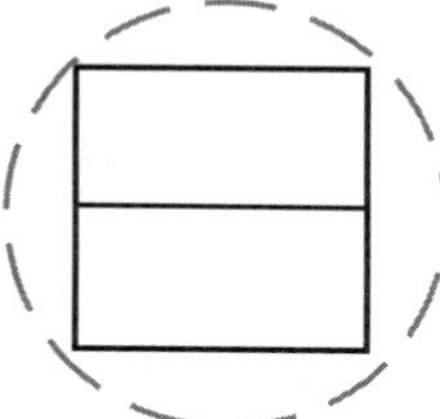

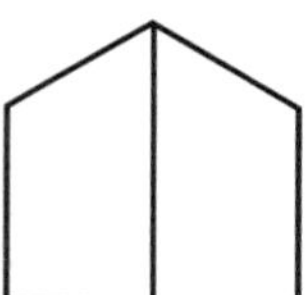

2.

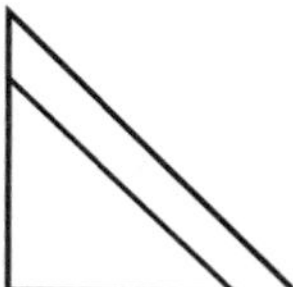

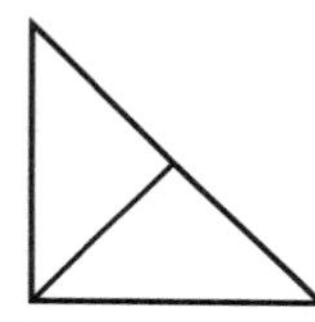

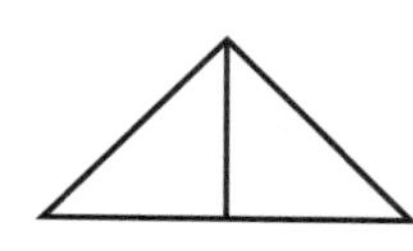

3.

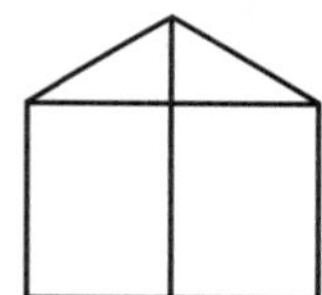

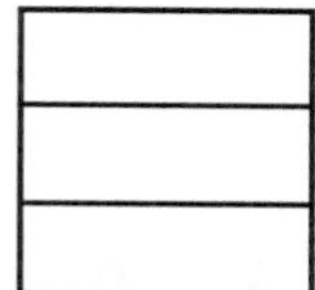

4.

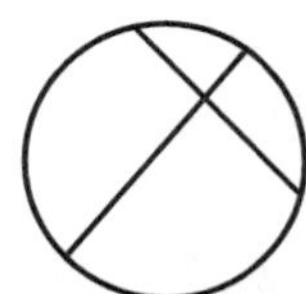

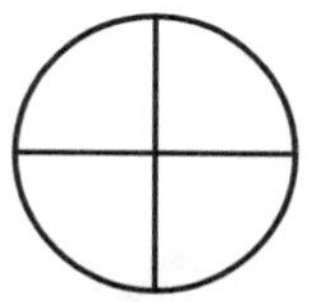

Color one equal part for each figure.

5.

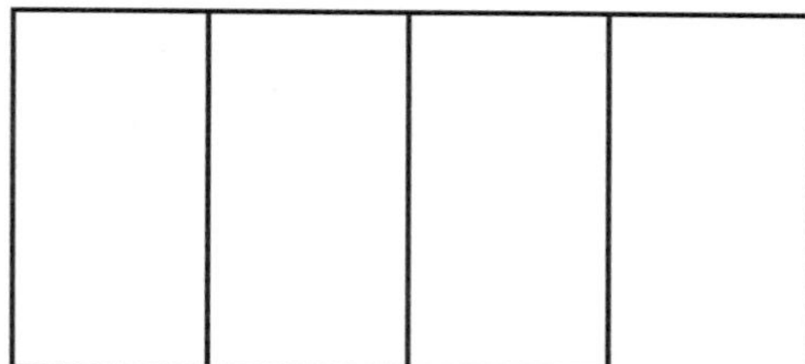

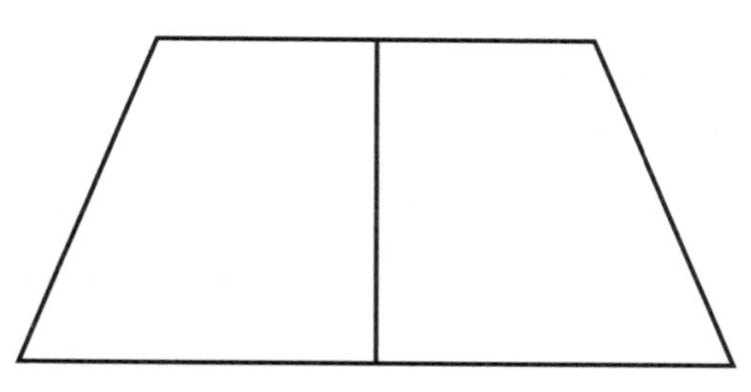

Count the equal parts. Write how many.

6.
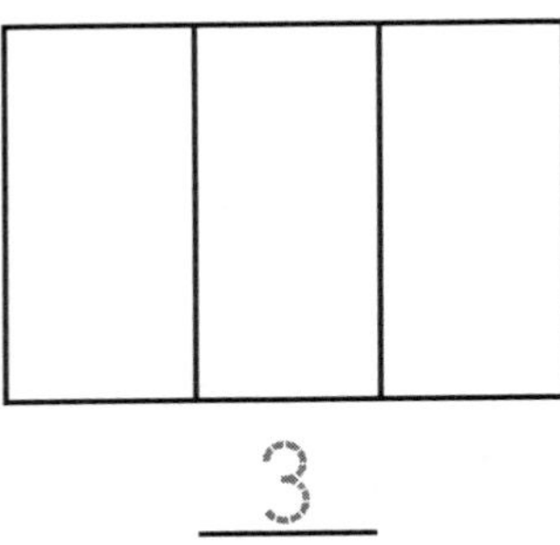
3

7.

____

8.

____

9.
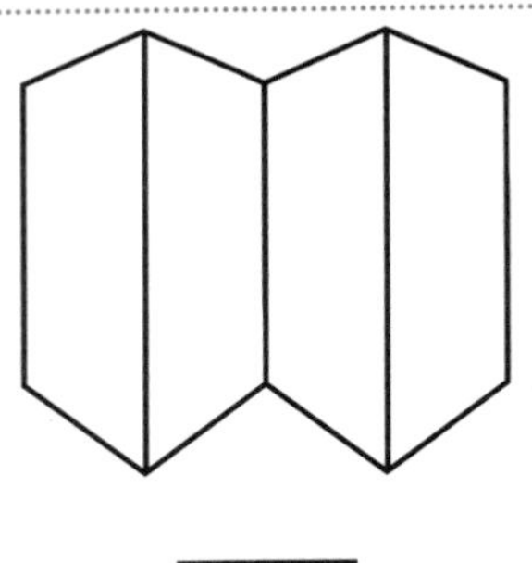
____

10.
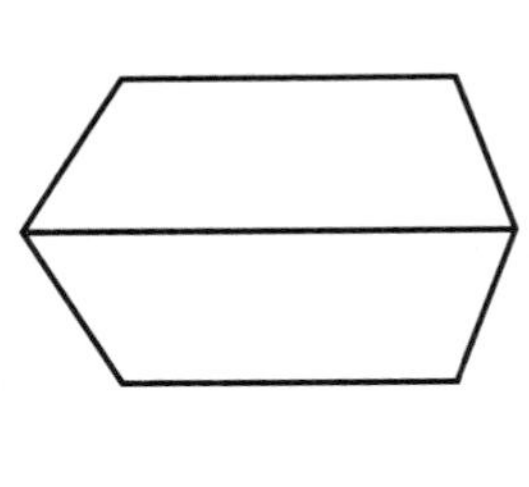
____

11.
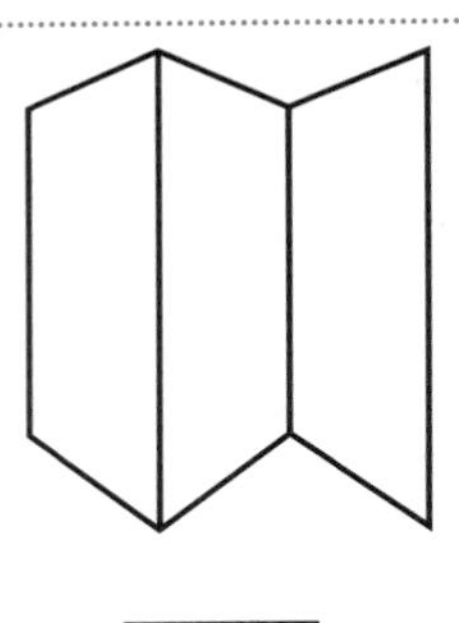
____

Draw lines to show equal parts.

12.
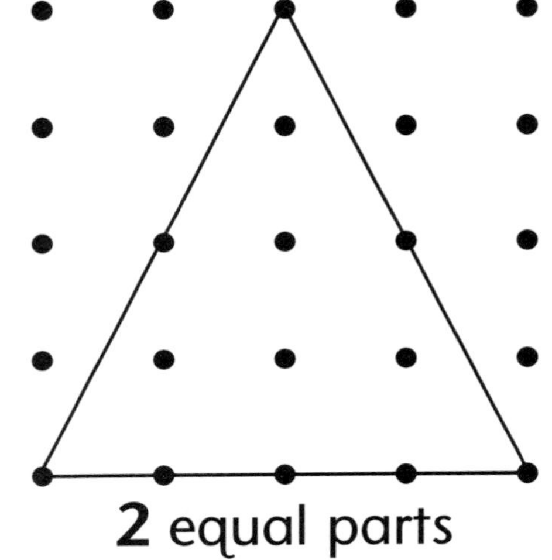
2 equal parts

13.
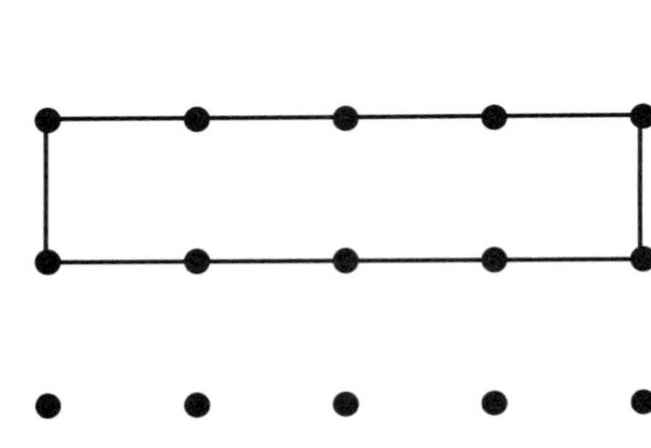
4 equal parts

★ Test Prep

Which figure has **3** equal parts? Mark the space under your answer.

14
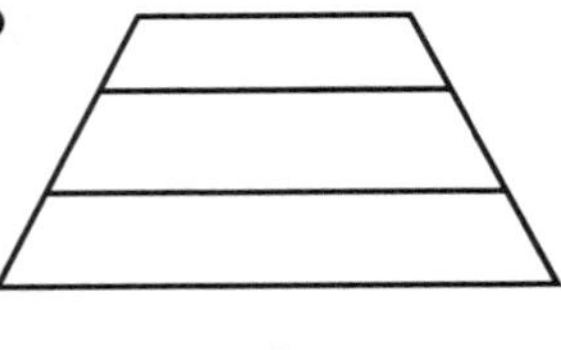
○
○
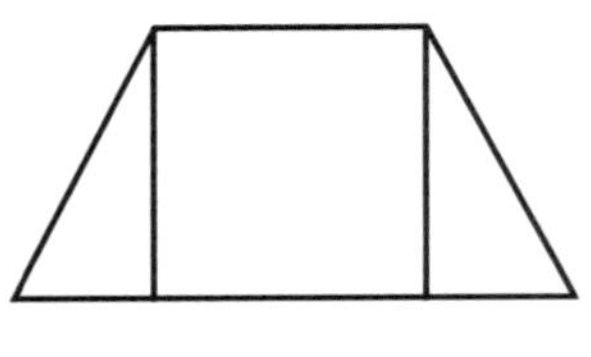
○
○

Name ____________________

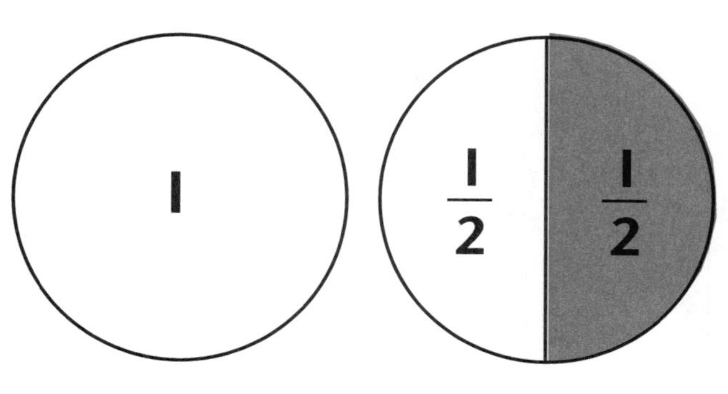

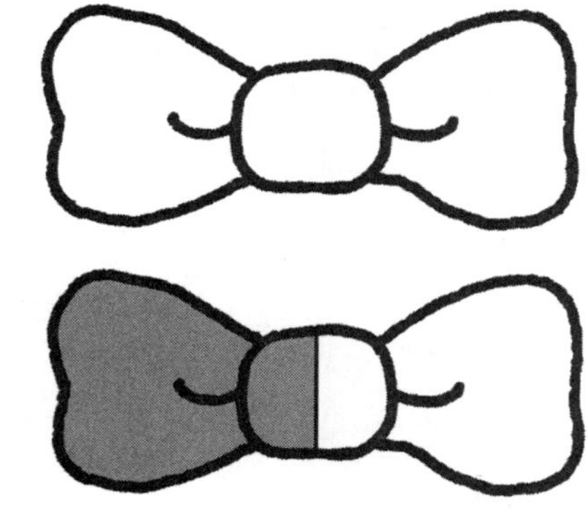

Color one half of the picture.

1. 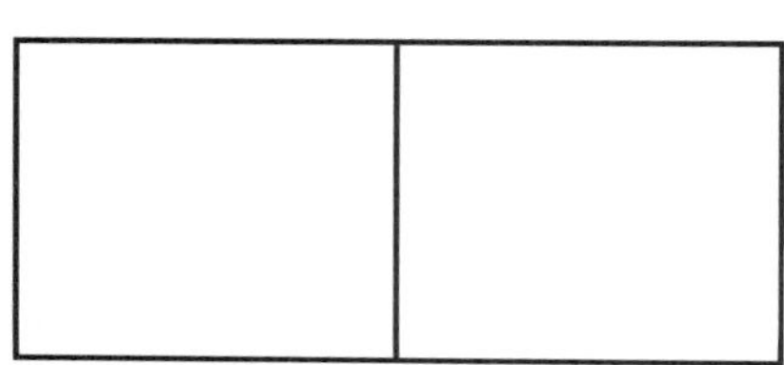

2. 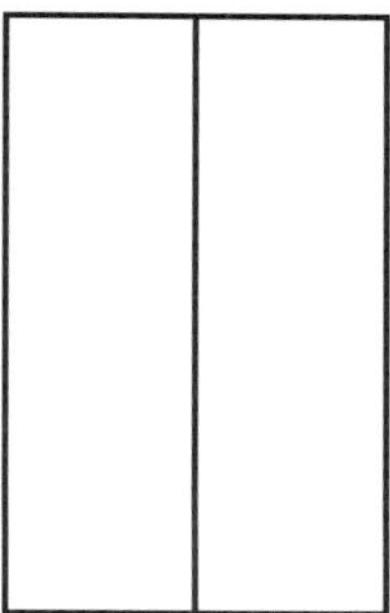

3. 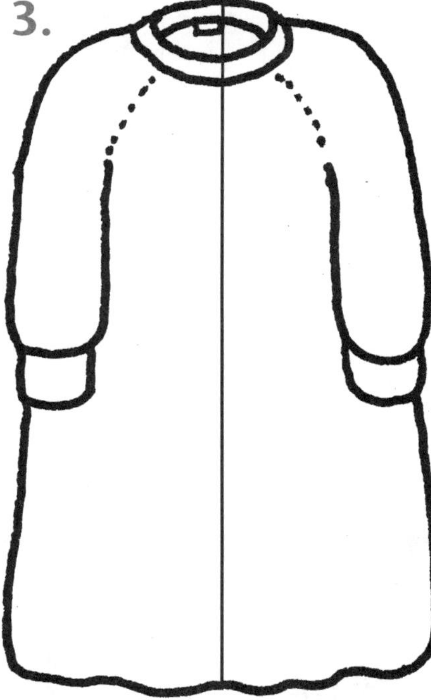

4. 

5. 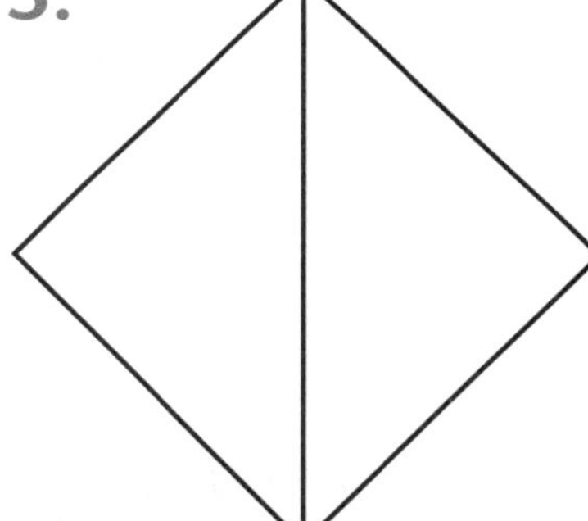

6. 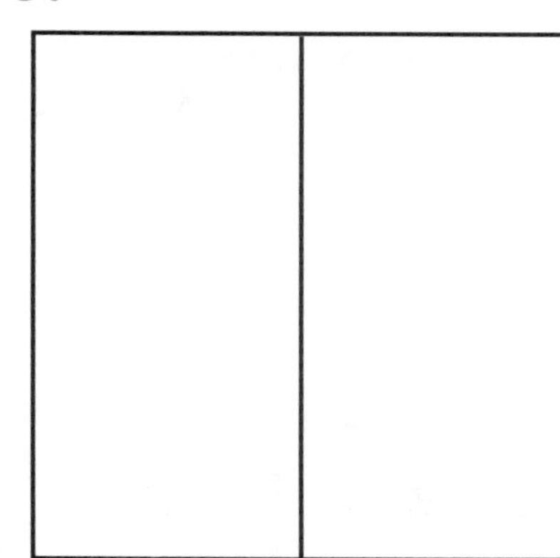

7. 

8.

Color $\frac{1}{2}$ of the picture.

9. 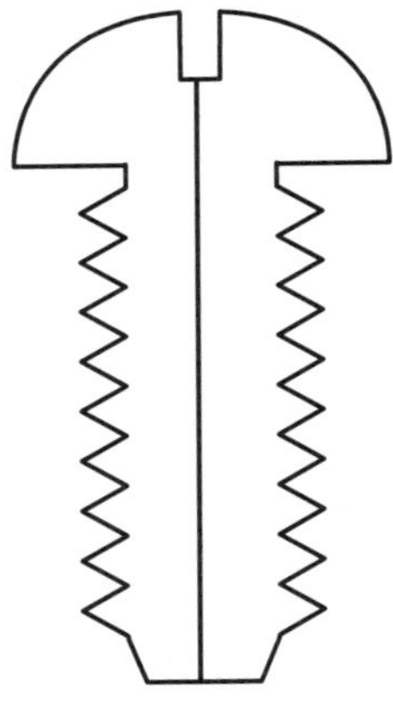

10. 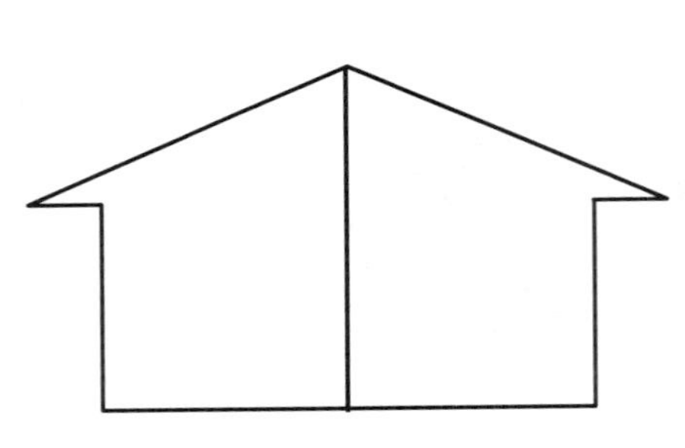

11. 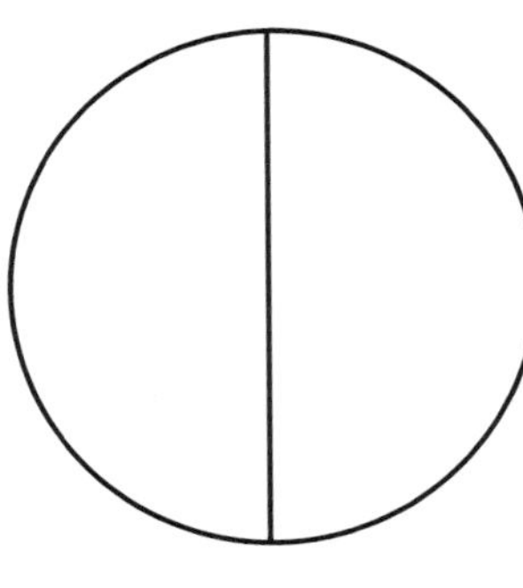

12. 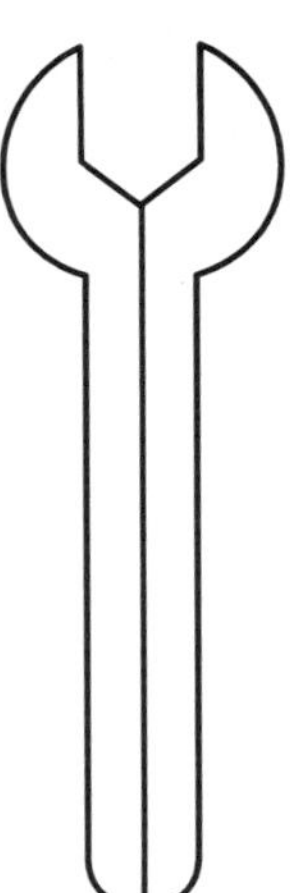

13. 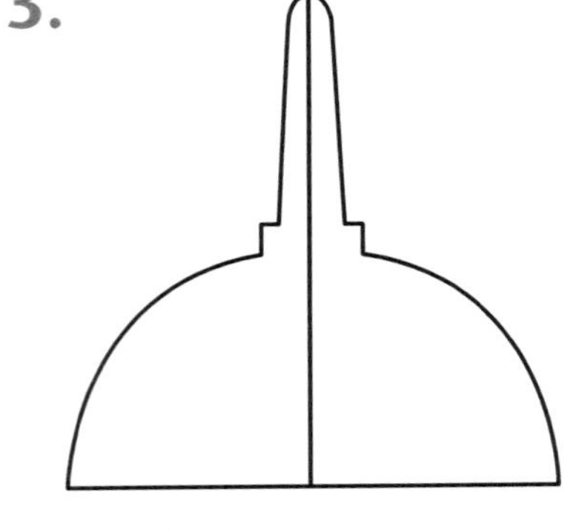

14. 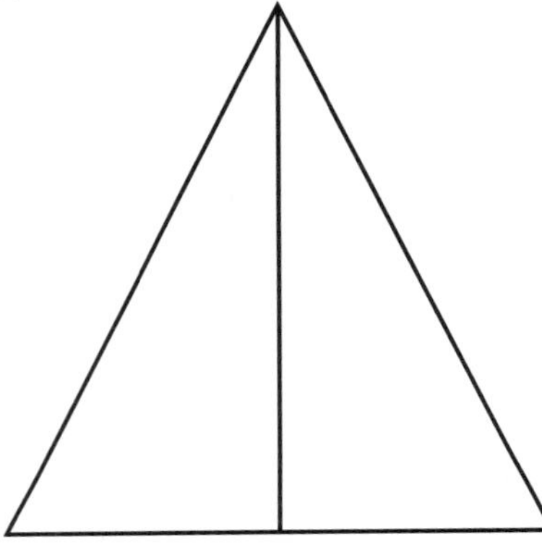

Problem Solving Reasoning Solve.

15. Maia broke a fruit bar in half. How many equal parts does she have? _____

★ Test Prep

Which figure shows $\frac{1}{2}$ colored? Mark the space under your answer.

16 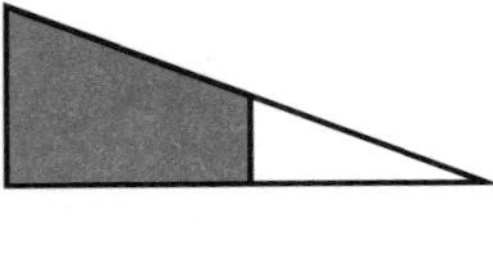 ○ 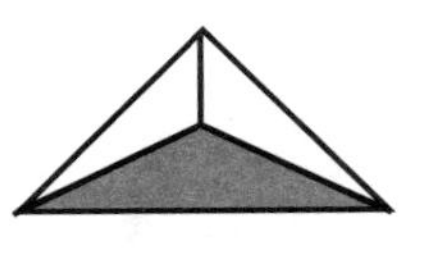 ○ ○ 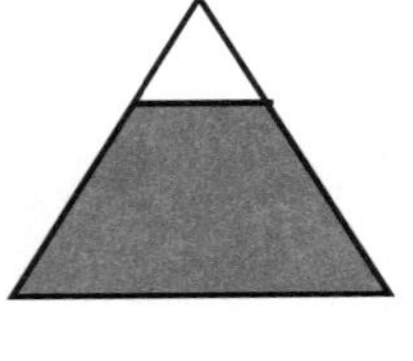 ○

Name ______________________________

1

$\frac{1}{4}$	$\frac{1}{4}$
$\frac{1}{4}$	$\frac{1}{4}$

Color one fourth of the picture.

1. 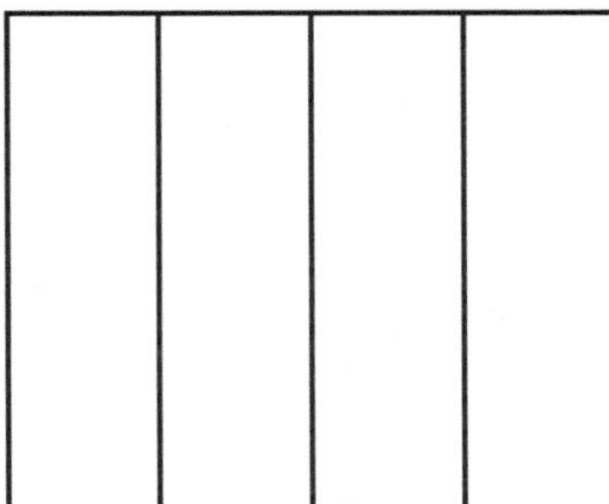

2. 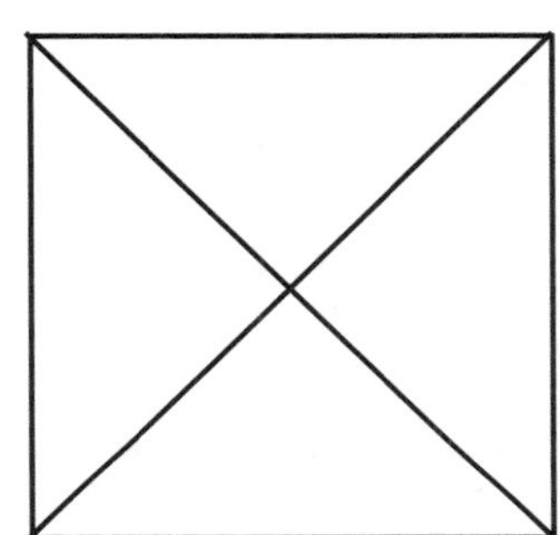

3. 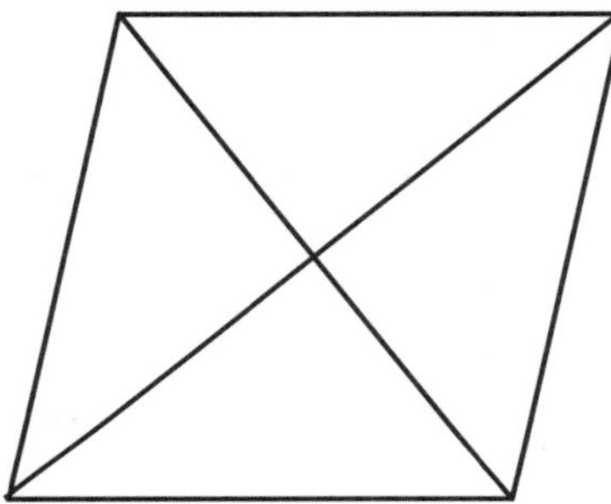

4. 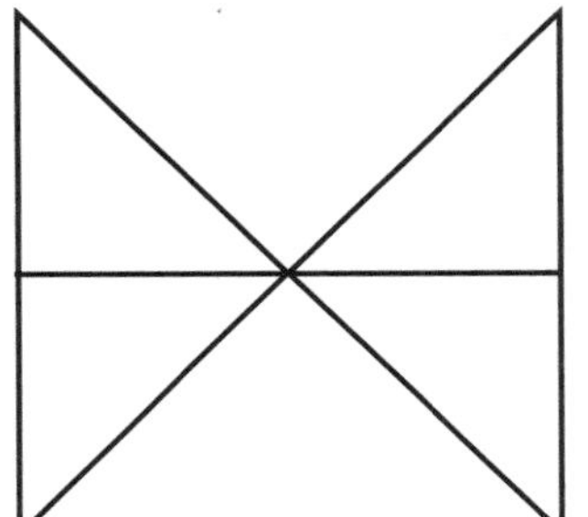

5. 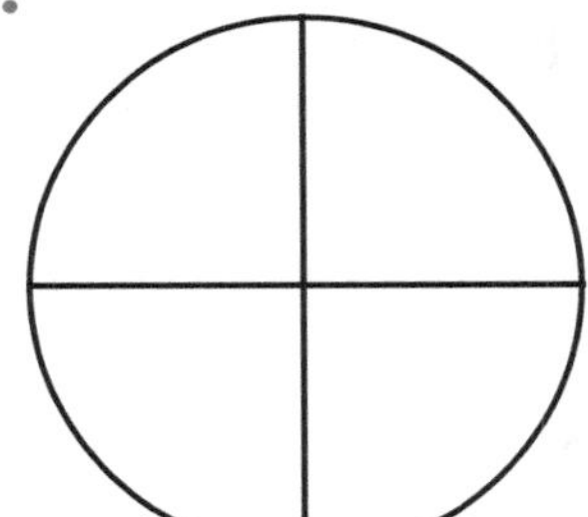

6. 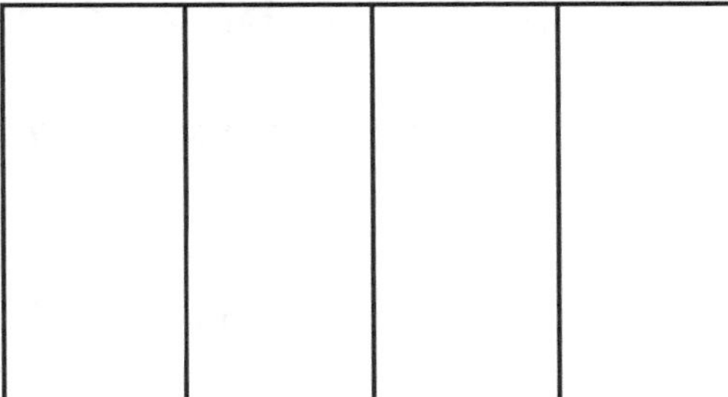

7. 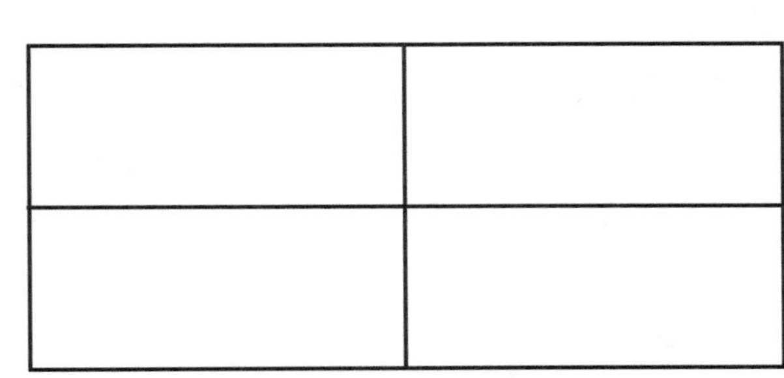

8. 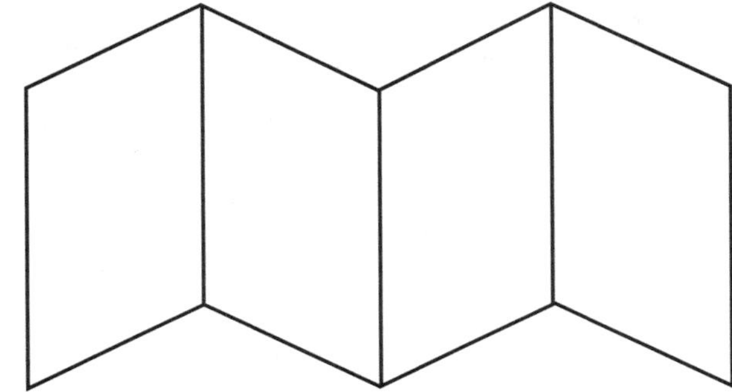

Color $\frac{1}{4}$ of the picture.

9.

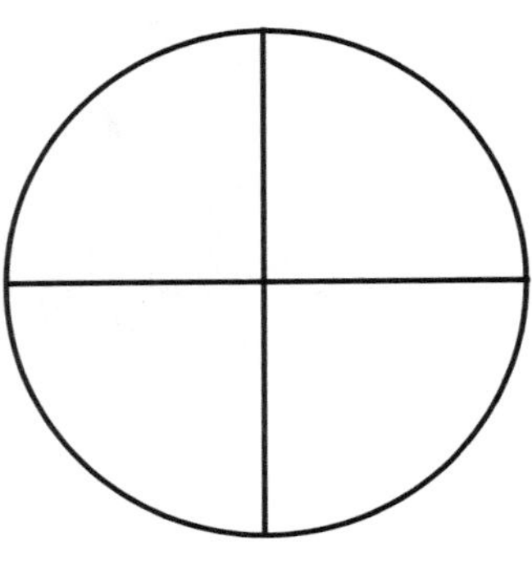

10.

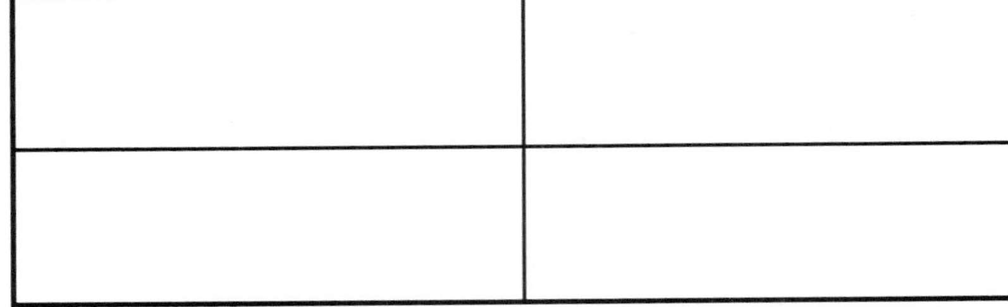

11.

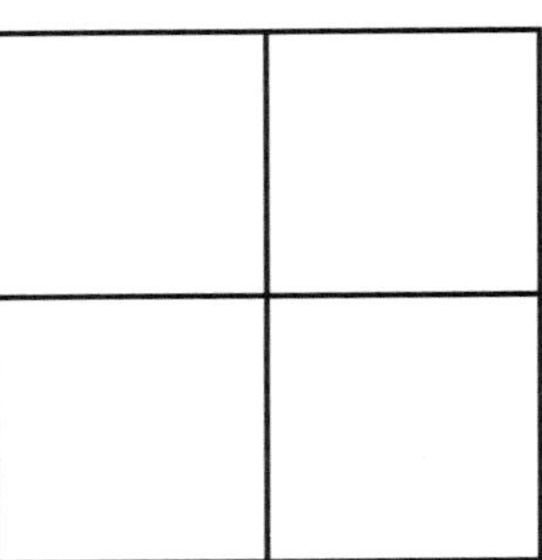

12.

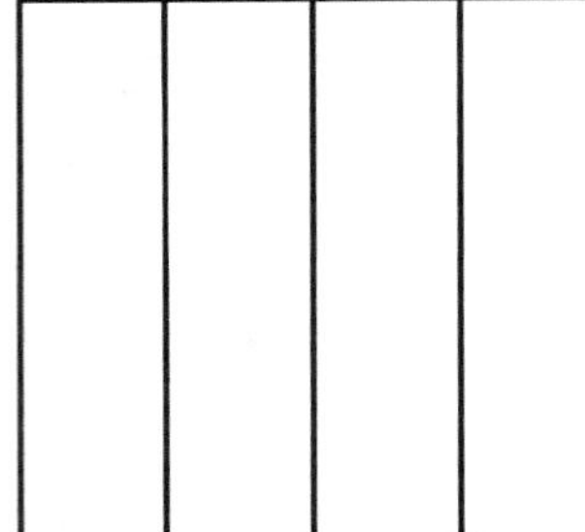

13.

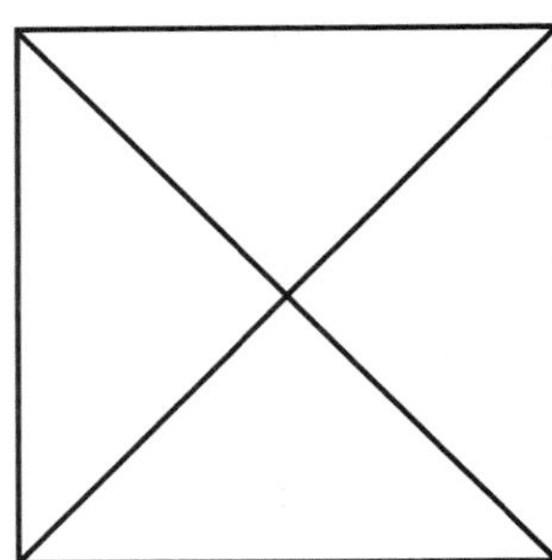

Quick Check

Draw lines to show **3** equal parts.

1.

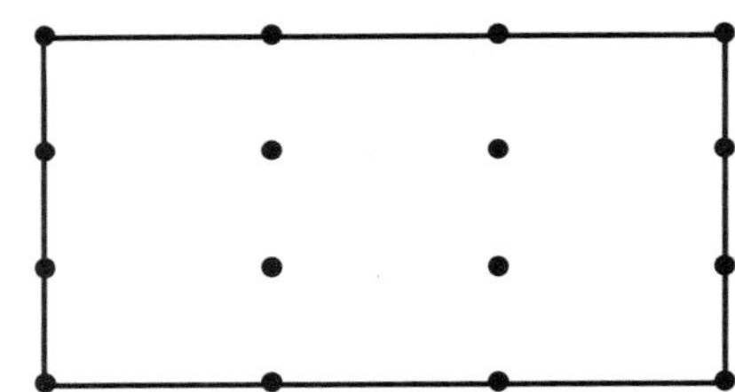

Color to match the fraction.

2. $\frac{1}{2}$

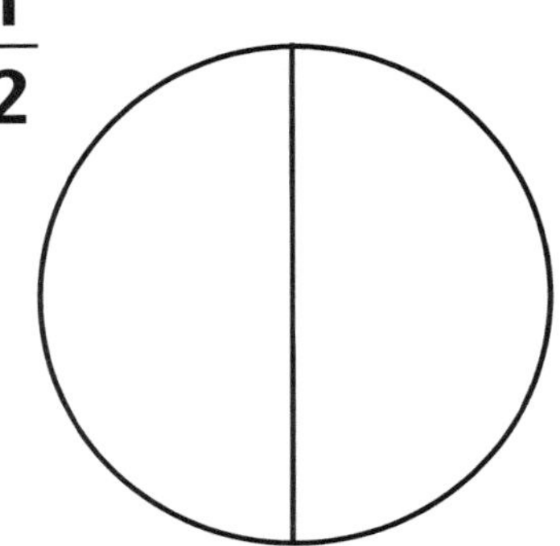

3. $\frac{1}{4}$

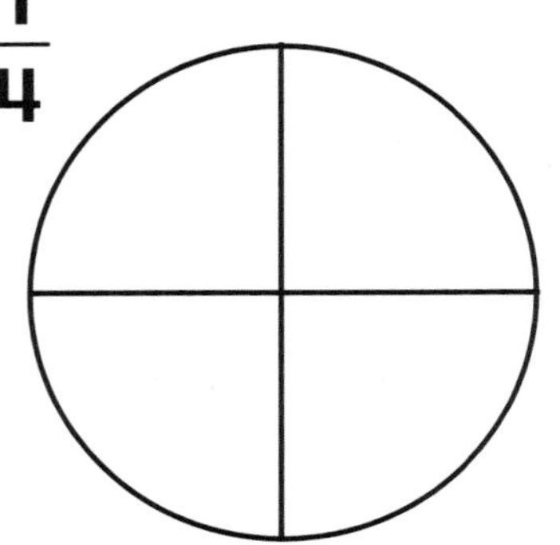

Name ______________________________

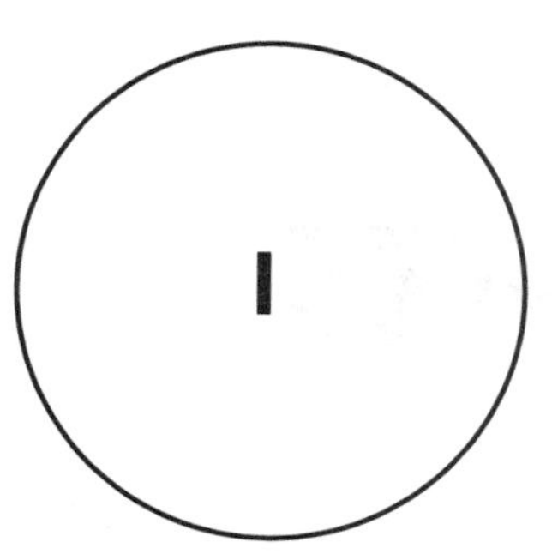

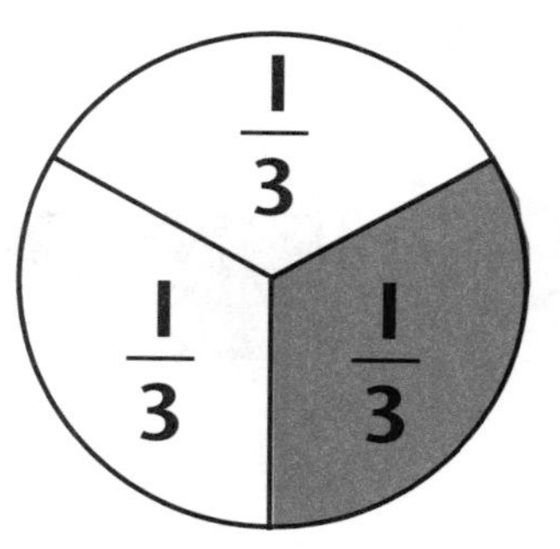

Color one third of the picture.

1. 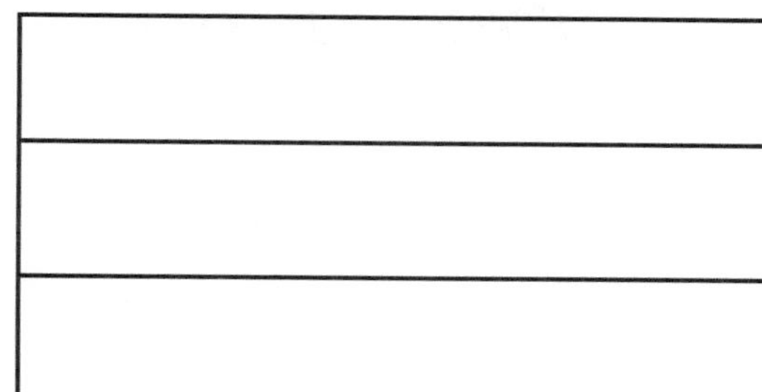

2. 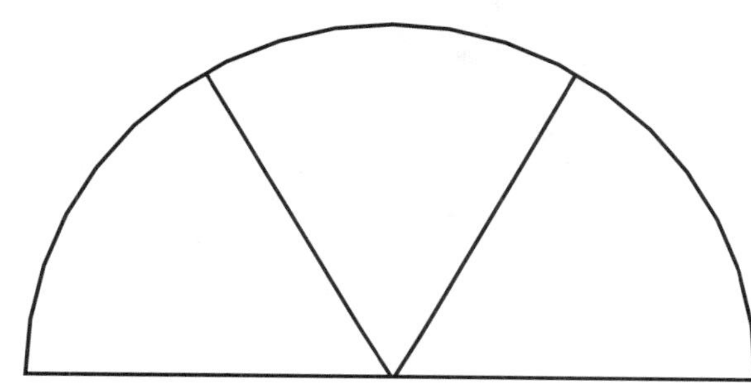

3. 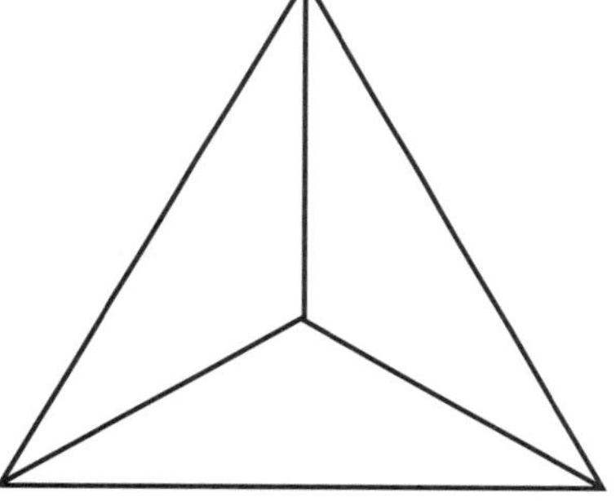

4. 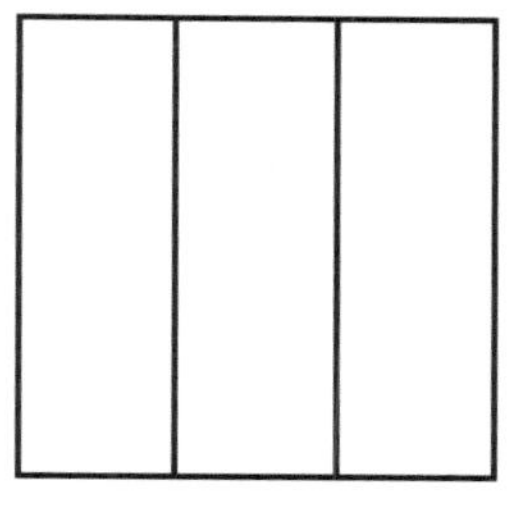

5. 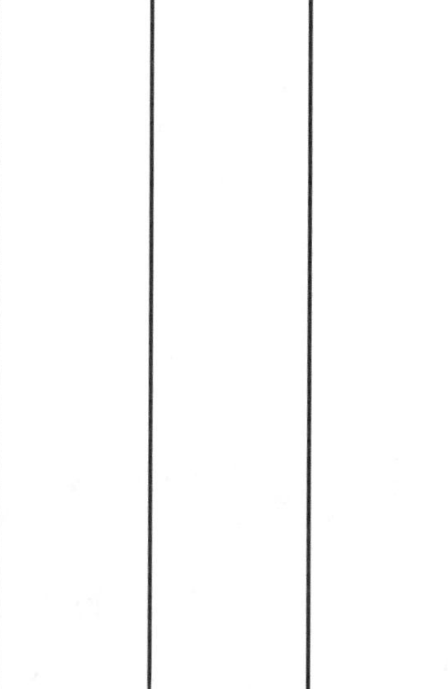

6. 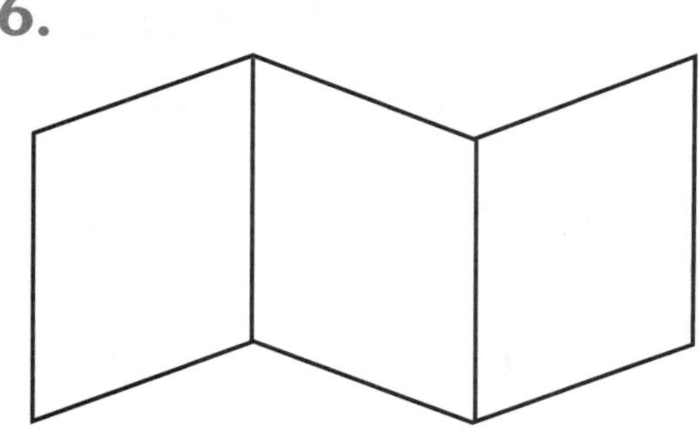

7. 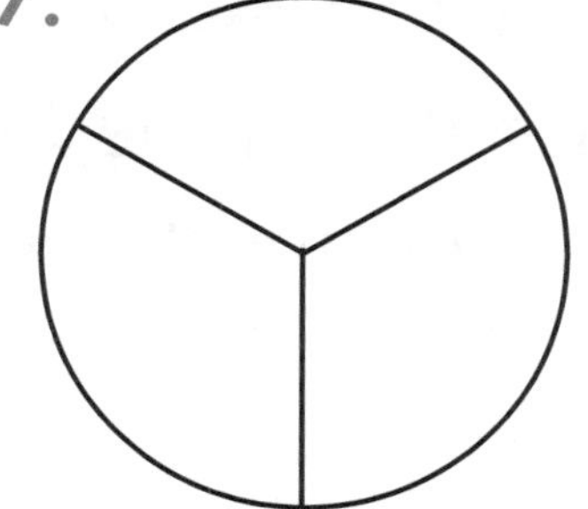

Ring the fraction.

8.

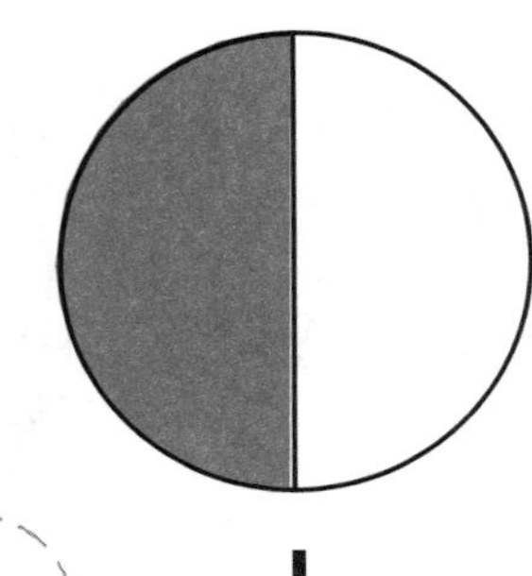

$\frac{1}{2}$ $\frac{1}{3}$ $\frac{1}{4}$

9.

$\frac{1}{2}$ $\frac{1}{3}$ $\frac{1}{4}$

10.

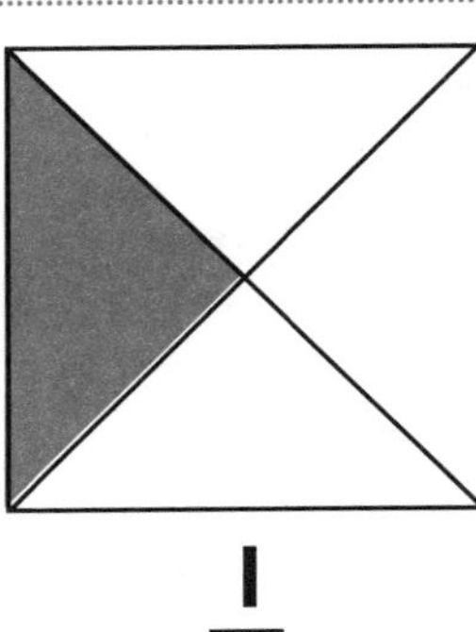

$\frac{1}{2}$ $\frac{1}{3}$ $\frac{1}{4}$

11.

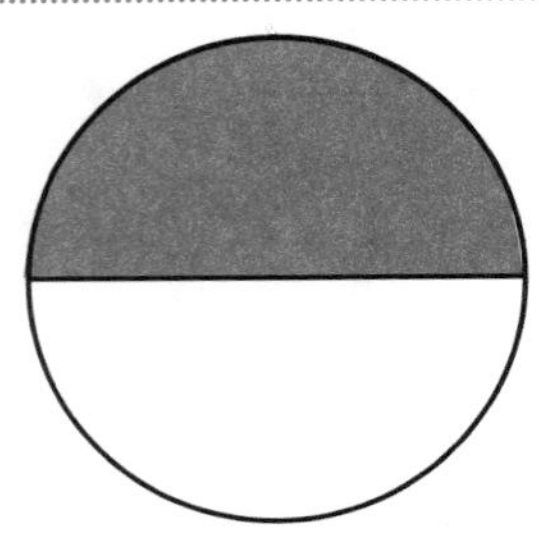

$\frac{1}{2}$ $\frac{1}{3}$ $\frac{1}{4}$

12.

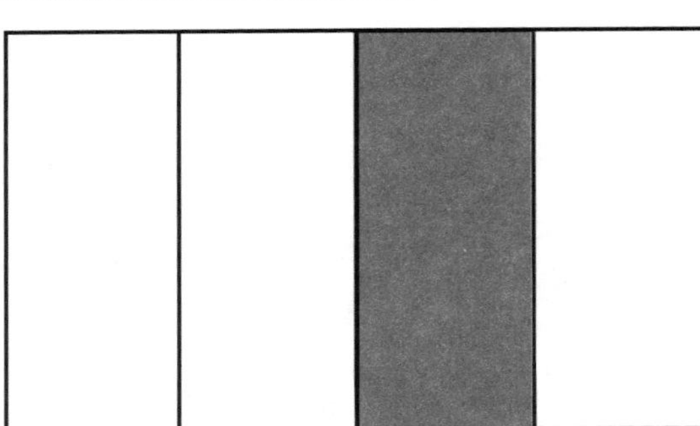

$\frac{1}{2}$ $\frac{1}{3}$ $\frac{1}{4}$

★ Test Prep

Which fraction names the shaded part? Mark your answer.
If the answer is **not here**, mark the space for **NH**.

13

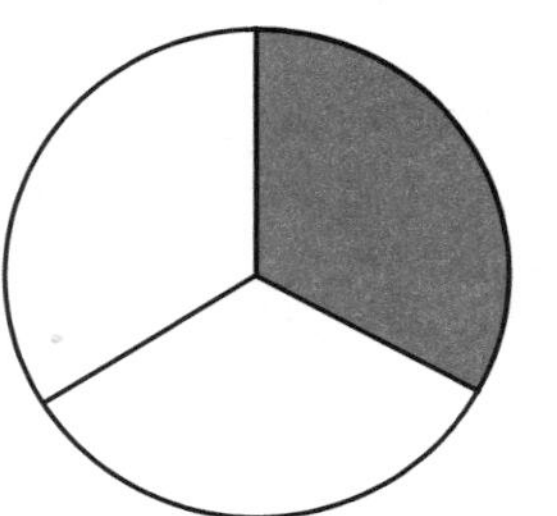

$\frac{1}{2}$ ○ $\frac{1}{3}$ ○ $\frac{1}{4}$ ○ NH ○

Name ______________________________

This desk is about 6 erasers long.

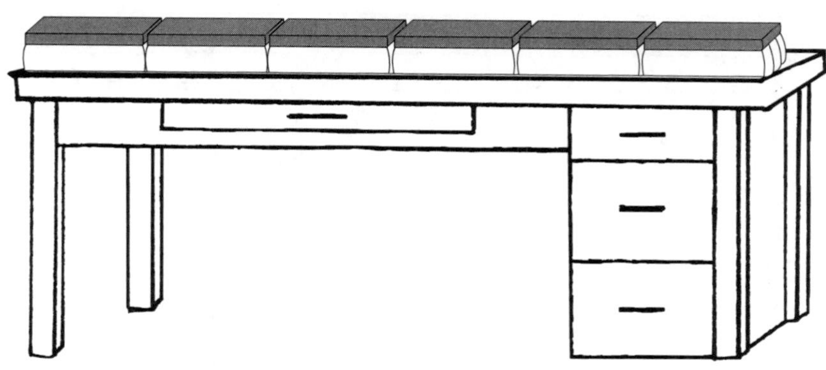

Measure in your classroom.

Use 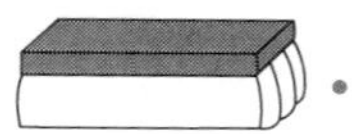.

1. your teacher's desk

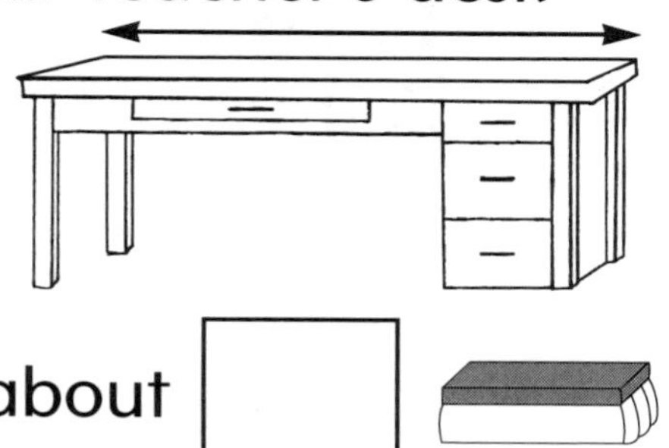

about ☐

2. a door

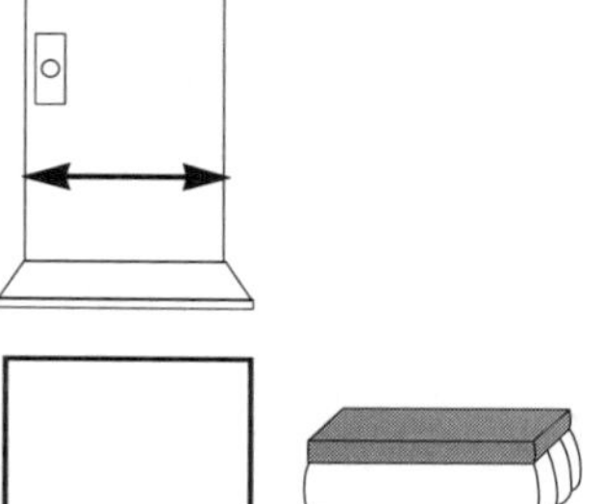

about ☐

3. Which is longer?

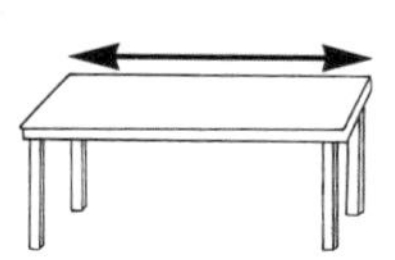

or

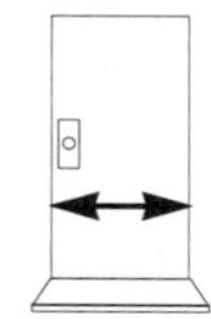

4. a window

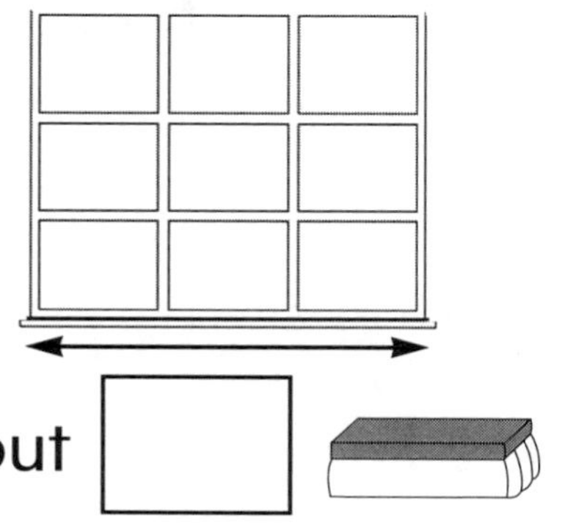

about ☐

5. your desk

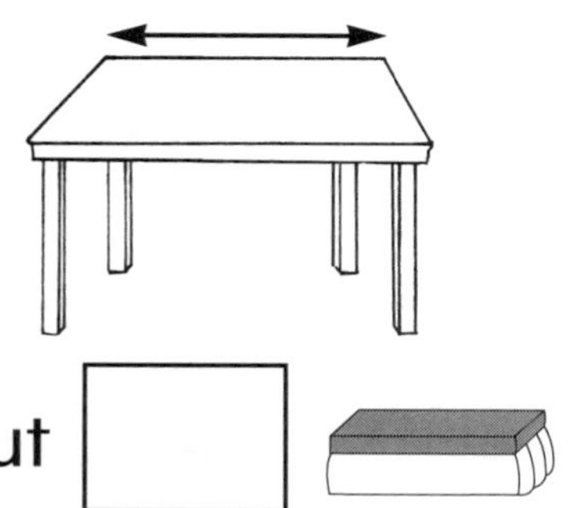

about ☐

6. Which is longer?

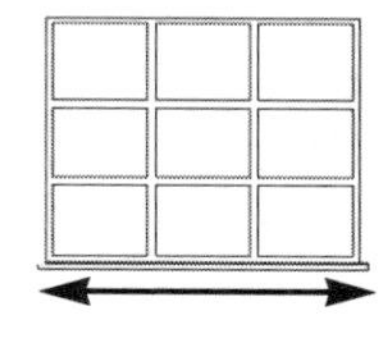

or

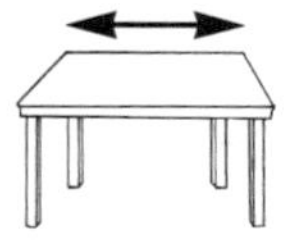

How long is this pencil?

7\.

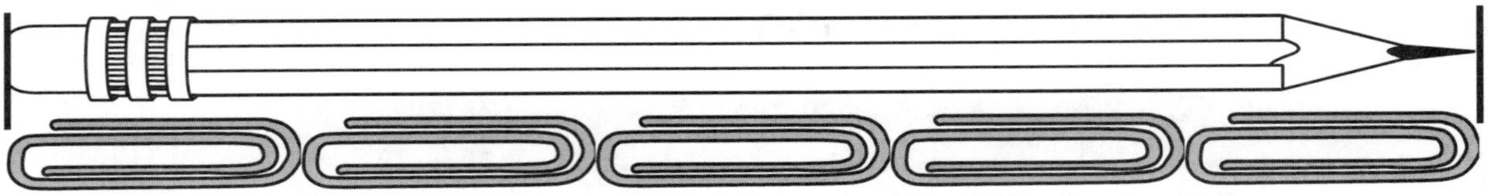

about 5

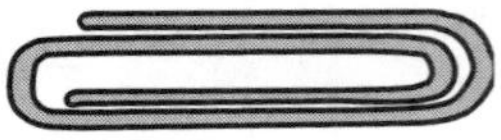

How long? Use small .

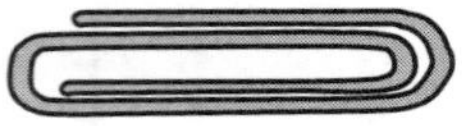

8\.

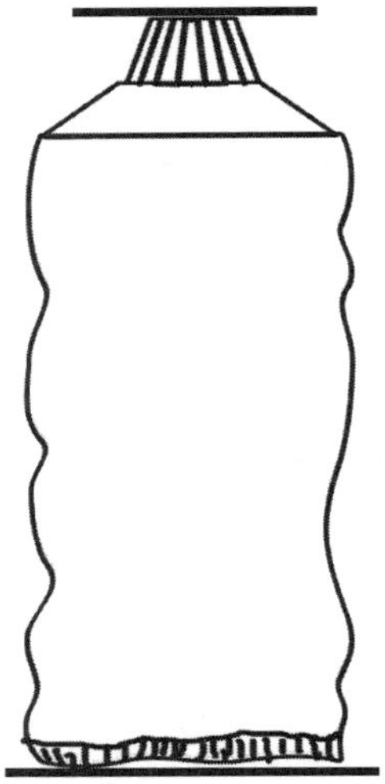

about

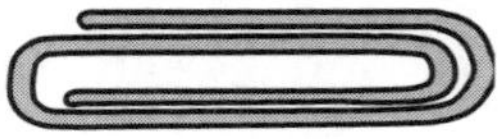

9\.

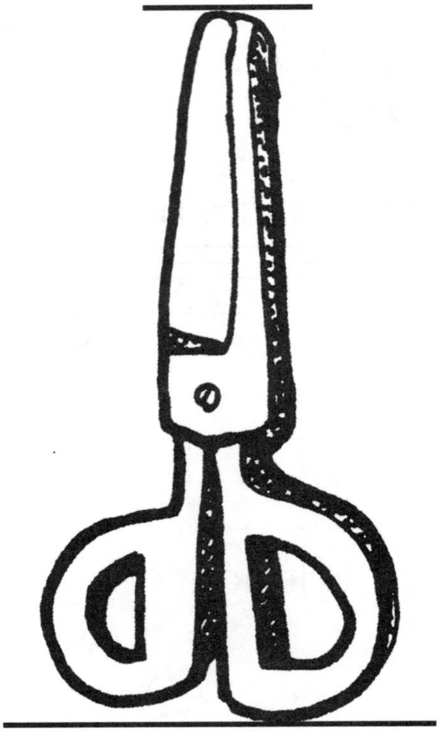

about

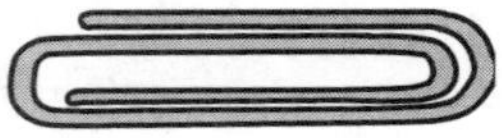

10\. Ring which is longer. tube or scissors

★ Test Prep

About how many paper clips long is the line at the beginning of the row? Mark the space under your answer.

11

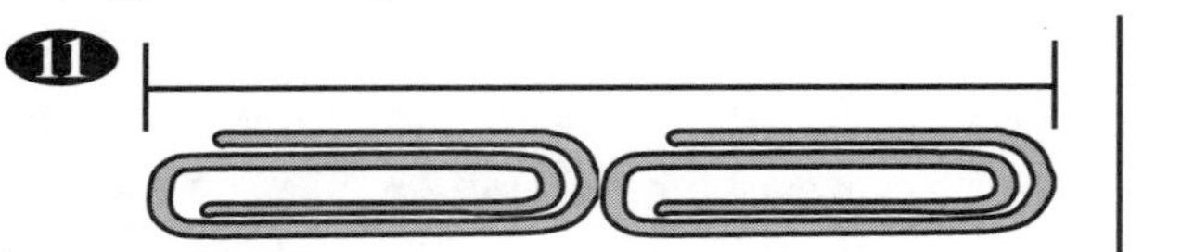

1	2	3	4
○	○	○	○

Name ____________________

STANDARD

Problem Solving Plan
1. Understand **2.** Decide **3.** Solve **4.** Look back

Object	Length in Paper Clips
pencil	about 4
crayon	about 3
stapler	about 7
eraser	about 6

Use the chart to solve.

1. Which is the shortest object?

   crayon

2. Which is the longest object?

   ____

3. Which is longer, the crayon or the pencil?

   ____

4. Which object is about **6** paper clips long?

   ____

Object	Length in Paper Clips	Length in Erasers
across a desk	about 36	about 6
across a window	about 31	about 5
across a shelf	about 26	about 4

Use the chart to solve.

5. About how many paper clips long is the shelf?

_____ paper clips

6. Which is the shortest object?

____

7. Which object is about **6** erasers long?

____

8. Which is longer, the window or desk?

____

Extend Your Thinking

Why are two different numbers used to tell how long the same object is?

Name ______________________

These blocks are 1 inch long.

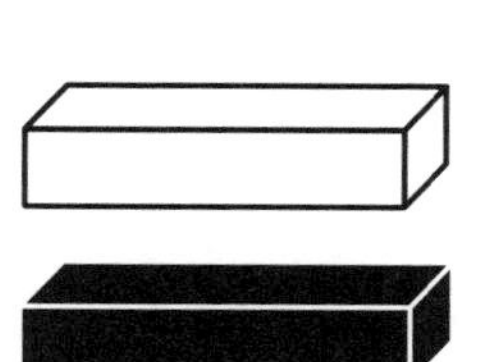

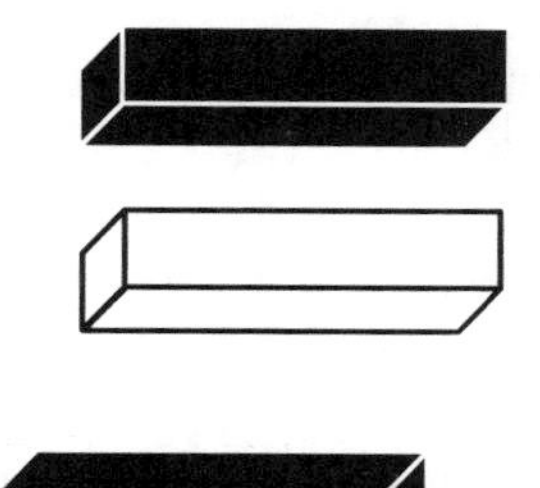

How many inches long?

1.

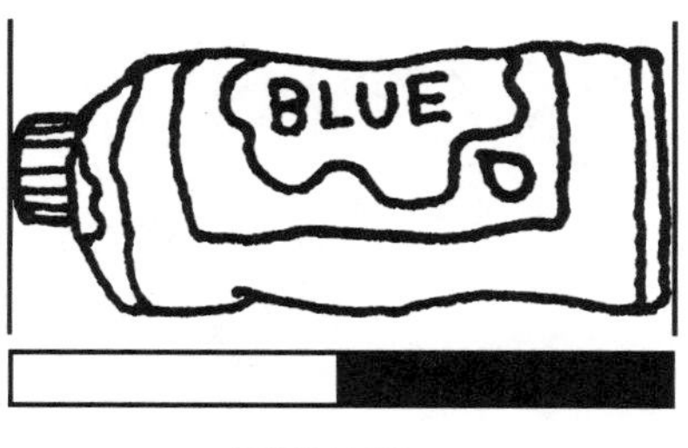

about ☐ inches

2.

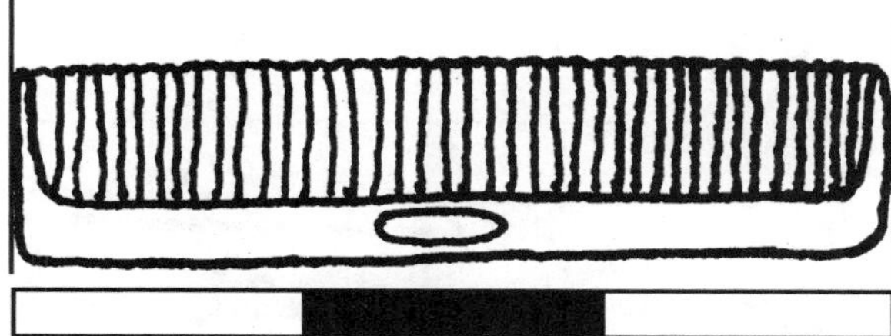

about ☐ inches

3.

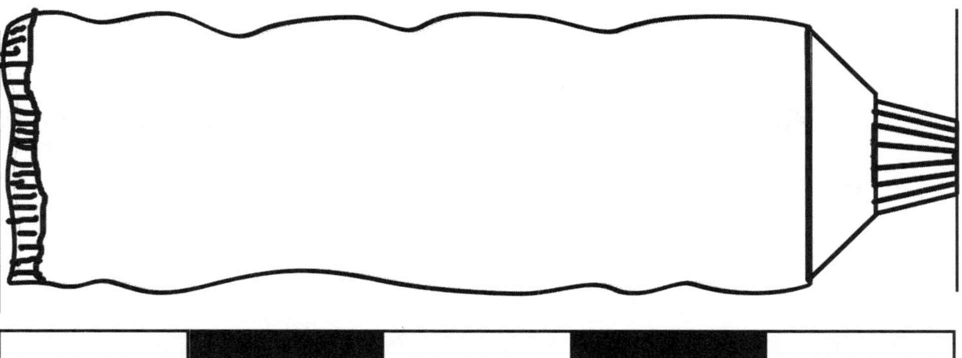

about ☐ inches

4.

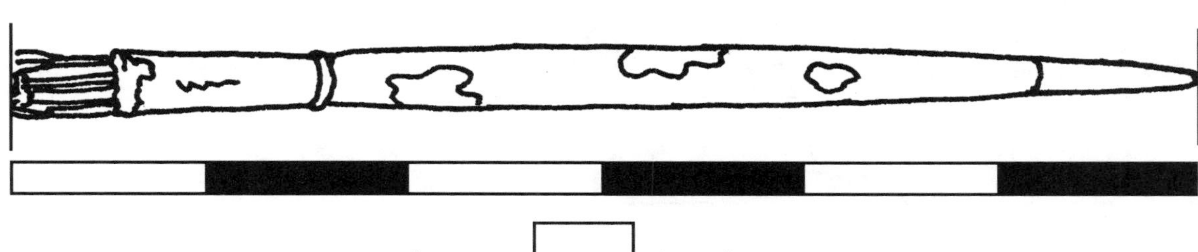

about ☐ inches

About how long is the picture?

5.

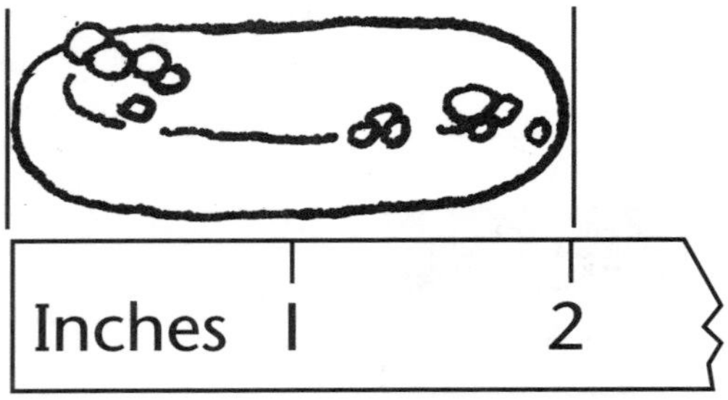

Inches	1	2

about ☐ inches

6.

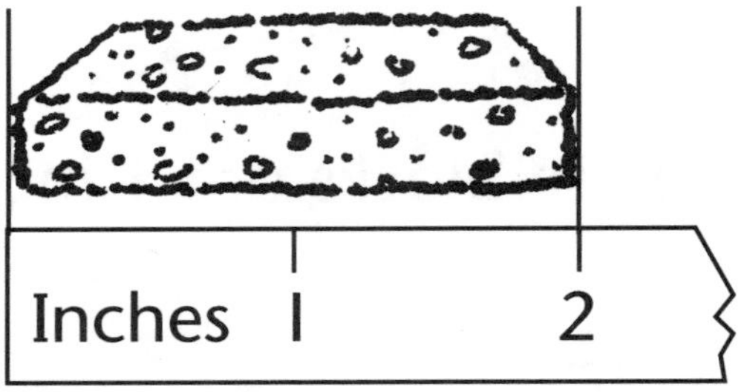

Inches	1	2

about ☐ inches

7.

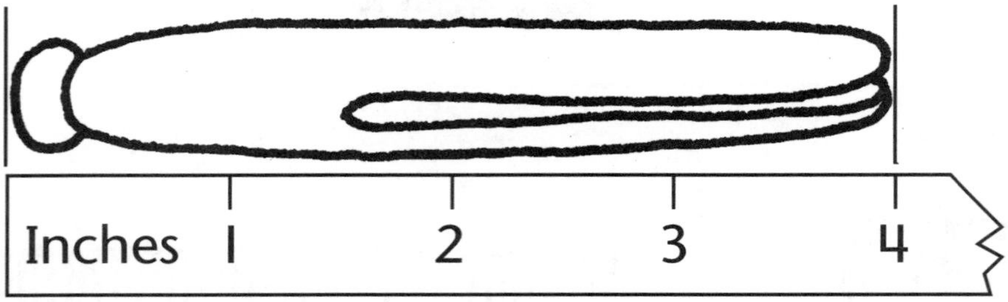

Inches	1	2	3	4

about ☐ inches

8.

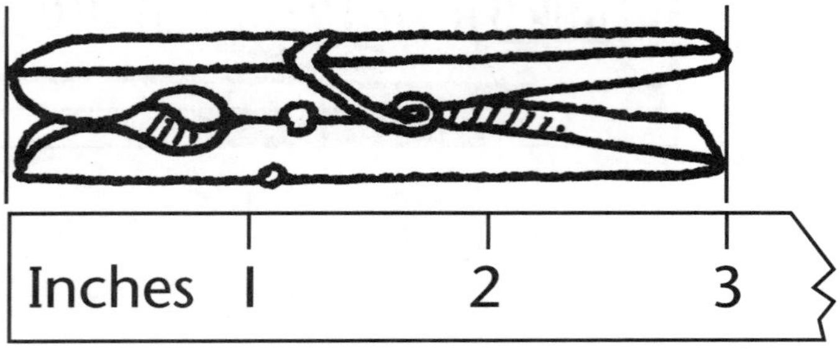

Inches	1	2	3

about ☐ inches

Quick Check

Ring the fraction.

1. 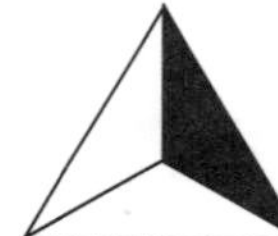

$\frac{1}{2}$ $\frac{1}{3}$ $\frac{1}{4}$

About how long?

2.

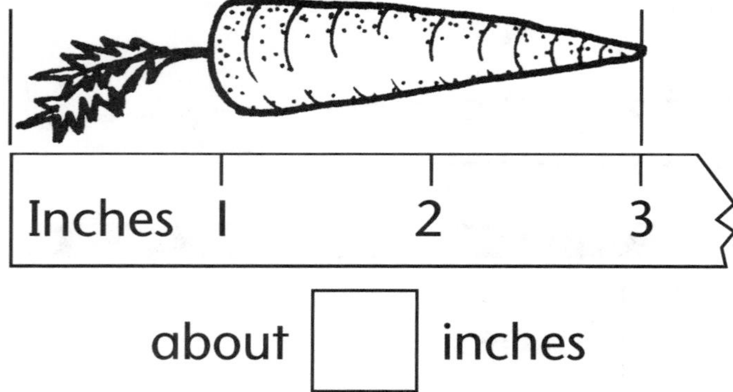

about ☐ inches

Name ______________________________

These blocks are **1** centimeter long.

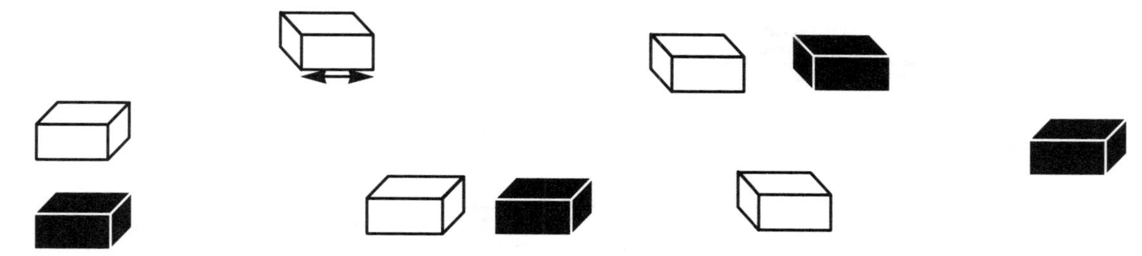

How many centimeters long?

1.

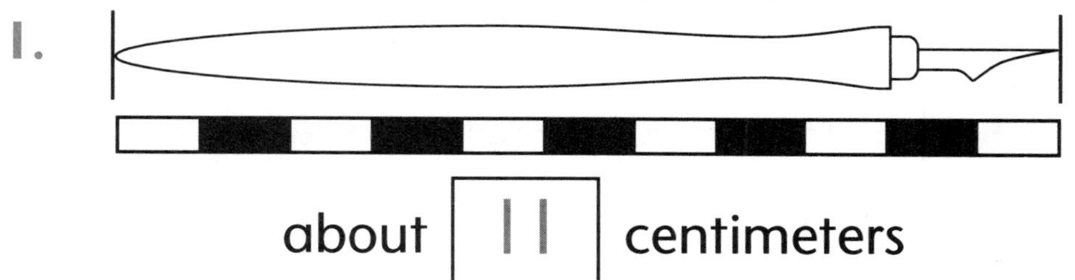

about 11 centimeters

2.

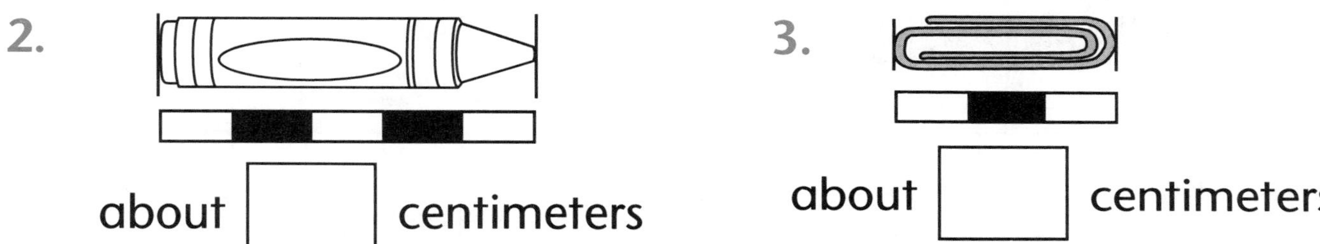

about ☐ centimeters

3.

about ☐ centimeters

4.

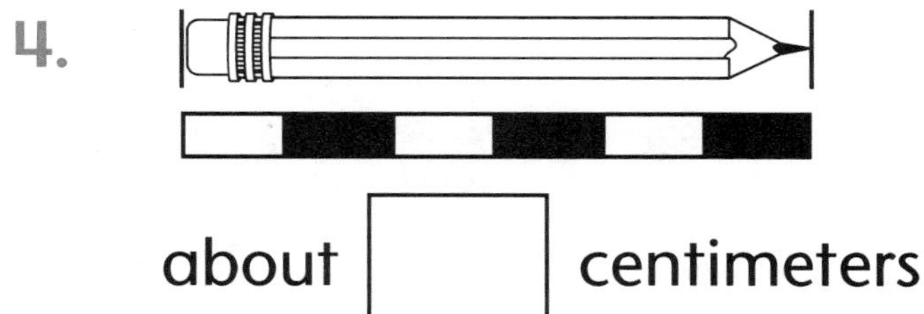

about ☐ centimeters

5.

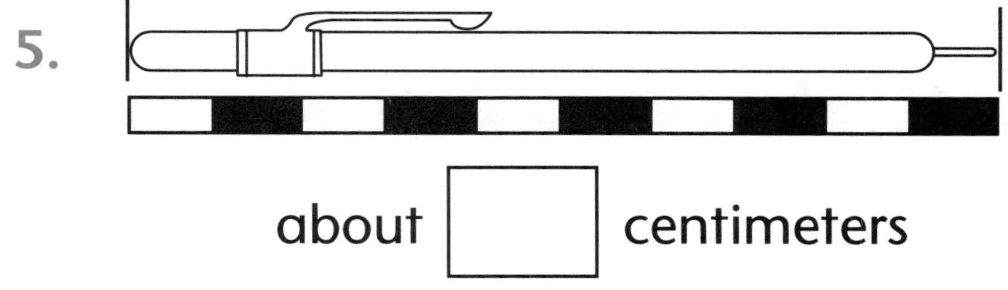

about ☐ centimeters

About how long is the picture?

6.

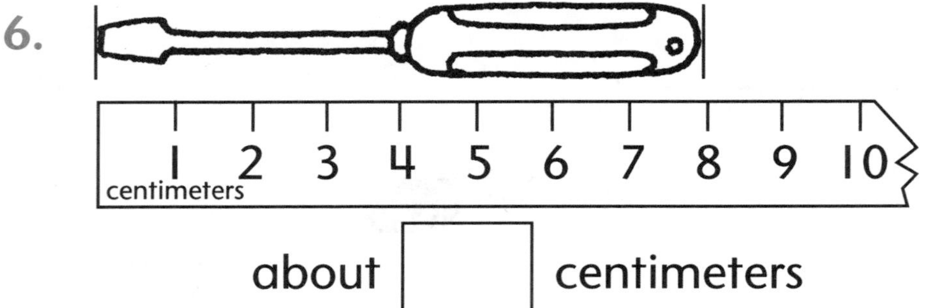

about ☐ centimeters

7.

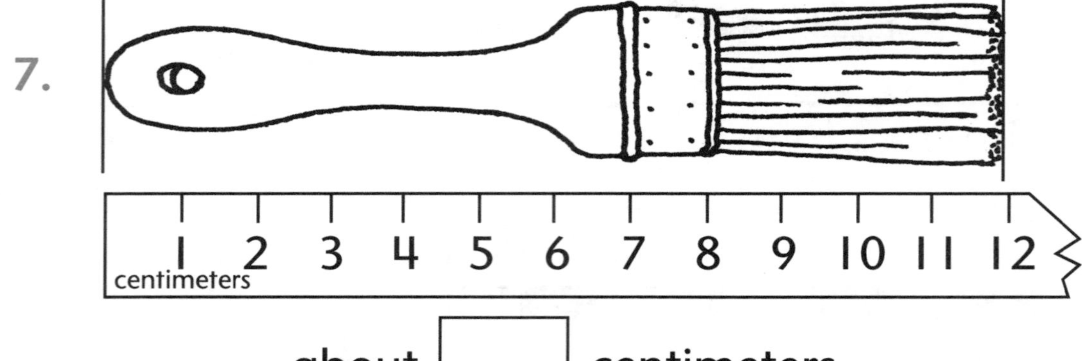

about ☐ centimeters

8.

9.

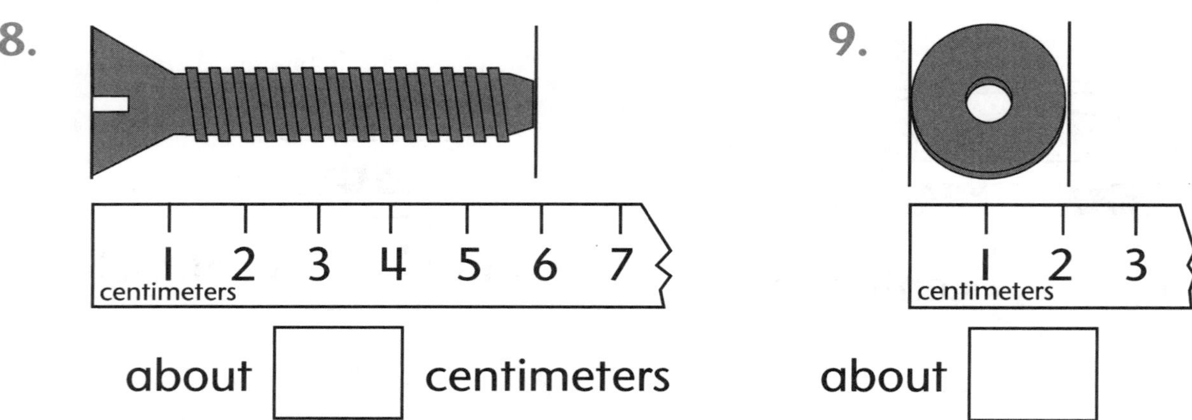

about ☐ centimeters

about ☐

★ Test Prep

About how many centimeters long is the screwdriver? Mark the space under your answer.

10

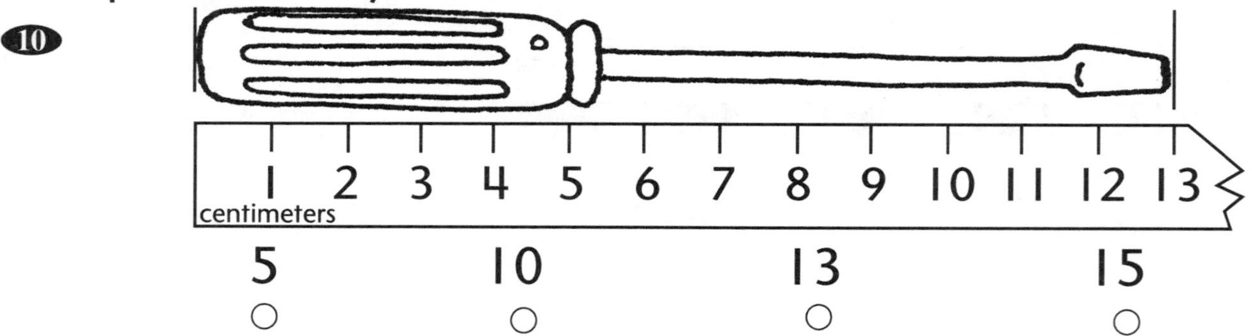

5	10	13	15
○	○	○	○

Name ______________________________

STANDARD

1 Understand

I need to find out how tall I am.

2 Decide

I will use a tape measure and chalk to measure myself.

3 Solve

I stand against a wall.
I use chalk to mark the wall to show where the top of my head ends. I measure from the floor to the chalk mark.

My height is about __________ centimeters.

4 Look back

I can look back at the tape measure to see if my answer makes sense.

Work with a partner. Act it out.
Complete the chart.

1.

	Partner 1	Partner 2
Height	about ______ centimeters	about ______ centimeters
Length of arm	about ______ centimeters	about ______ centimeters
Length of arm span	about ______ centimeters	about ______ centimeters

2. Who is taller? ____________________

3. Whose arm is longer? ____________________

4. Whose arm span is wider? ____________________

Name ______________________________

Lift each item.
The one that weighs more is **heavier.**

The one that weighs less is **lighter.**

The stapler is heavier than the pen.

Find objects like the ones shown. Lift each object. Ring the one that is heavier.

1.

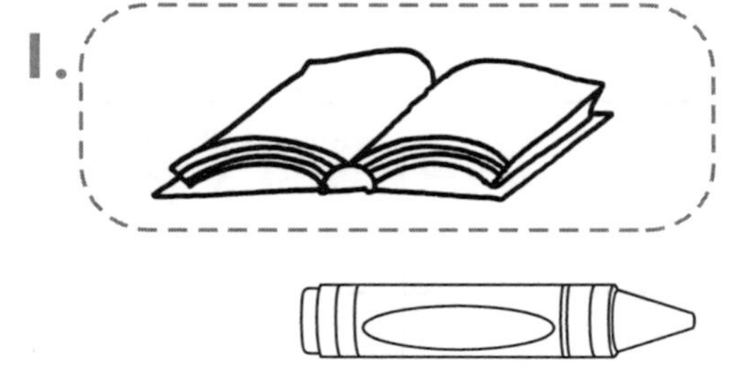

2.

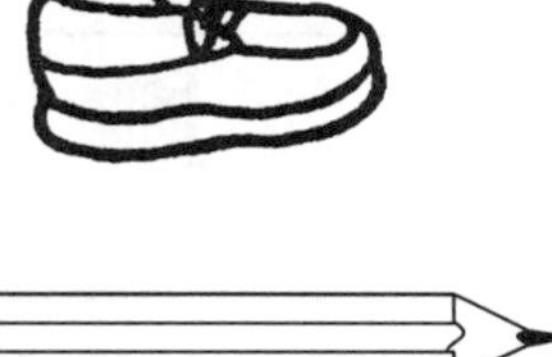

3.

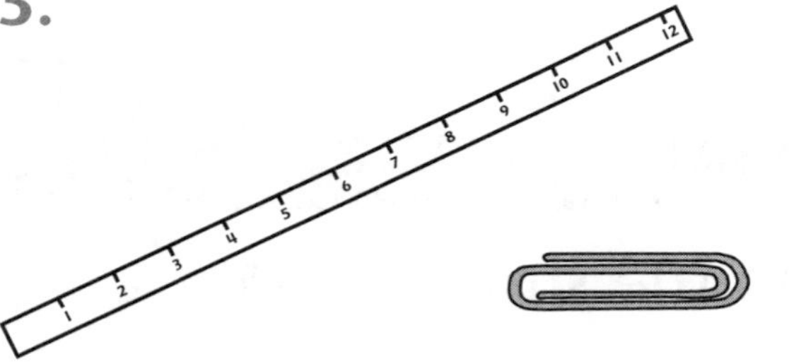

4.

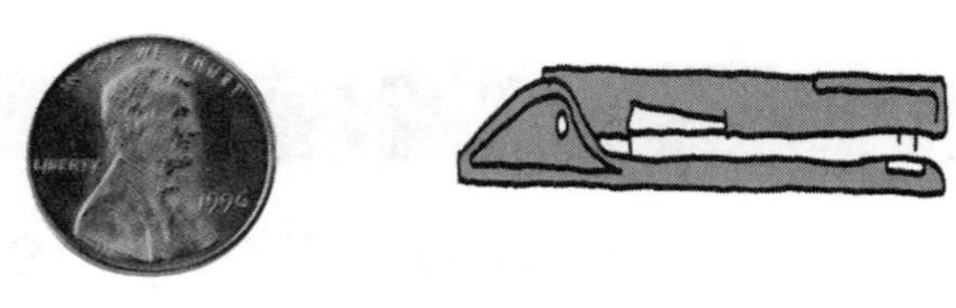

5.

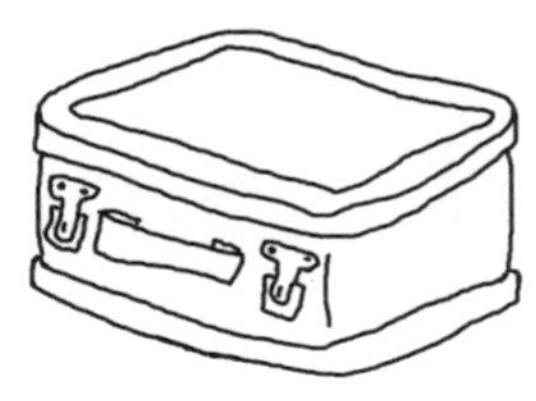

6.

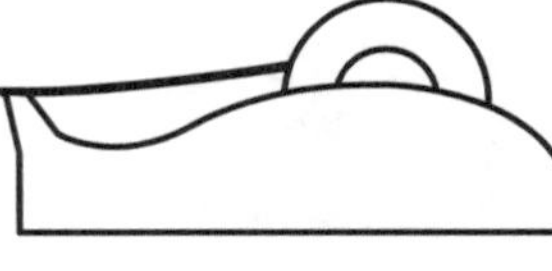

Use a balance.
Use cubes, paper clips, and pennies as units. Weigh each object using the different units.
Complete the chart.

	Object	Cubes	Paper clips	Pennies
7.				
8.				
9.				
10.	**Draw your own.**			

★ Test Prep

Which item is most likely heavier than the shoe? Mark the space under your answer.

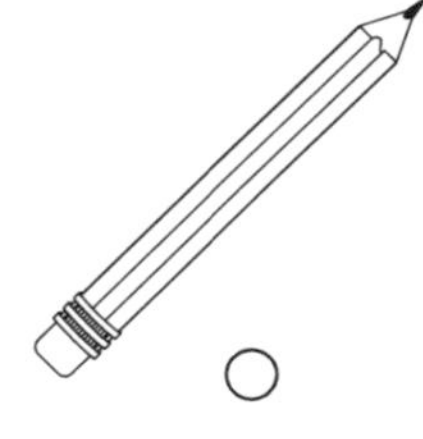 ○

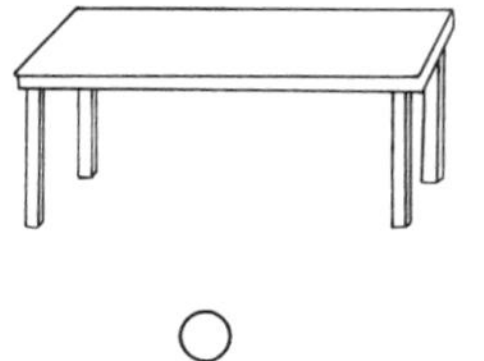 ○

 ○

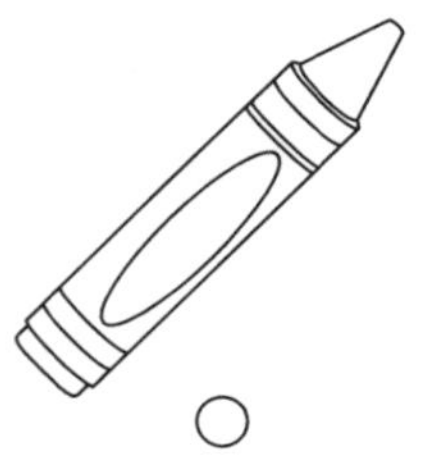 ○

STANDARD

Name ____________________

The pot **holds more** than the glass.

The glass **holds less** than the pot.

Ring which holds more.

1.

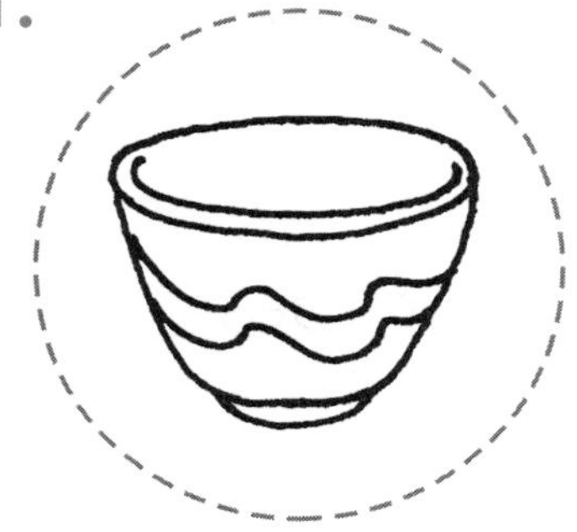

2.

Ring which holds less.

3.

4.

5.

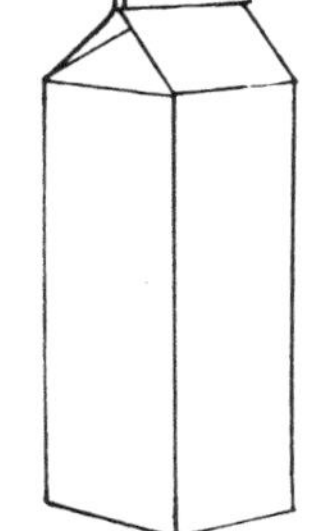

6.

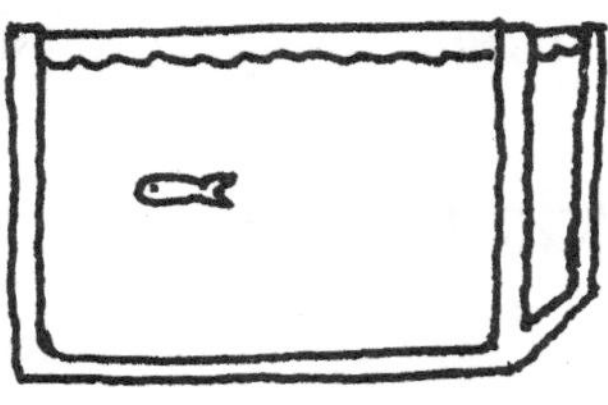

Ring which holds the most.
Cross out which holds the least.

7.   

8.  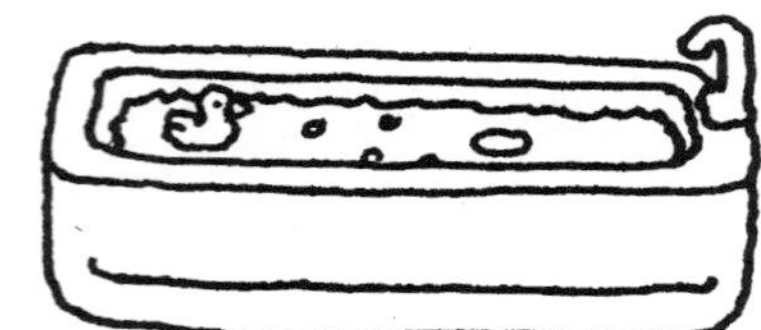 

Problem Solving Reasoning **You need a box and cubes. Solve.**

9. How many cubes filled your box? about ______ cubes

✓ Quick Check

Use a centimeter ruler.

How long is this line?

1. |———————————|

about _____ centimeters

Ring the object that is heavier.

2.  

Ring which holds more.

3.  

Name ______________________________

Ring the figure that shows equal parts.

1.

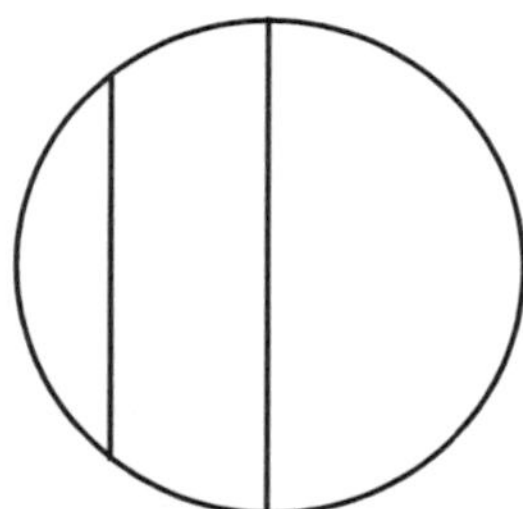

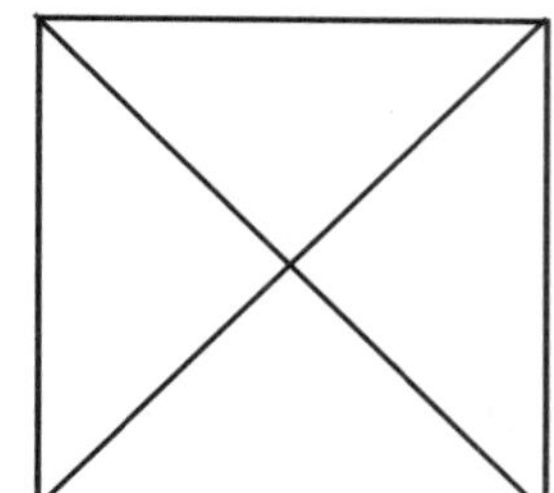

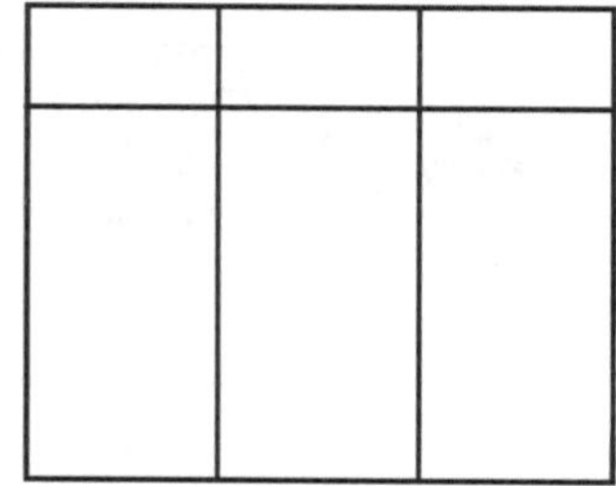

Ring the fraction shown.

2.

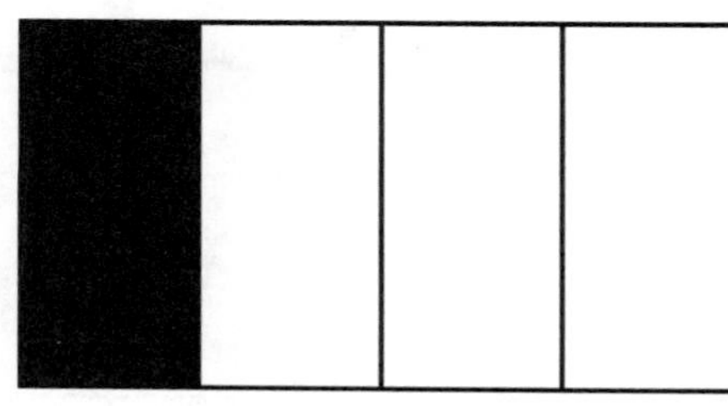

$\frac{1}{2}$ $\frac{1}{3}$ $\frac{1}{4}$

3.

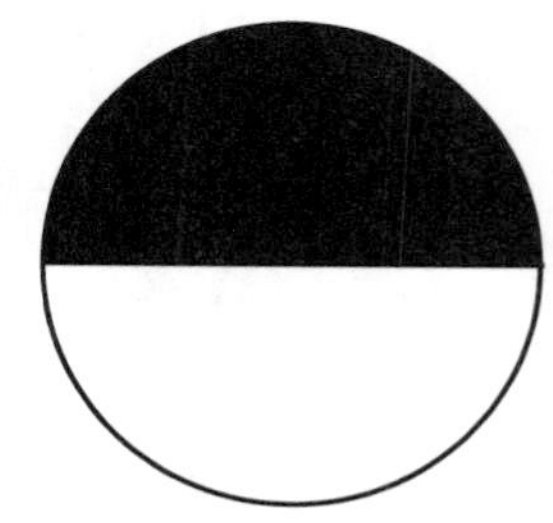

$\frac{1}{2}$ $\frac{1}{3}$ $\frac{1}{4}$

4.

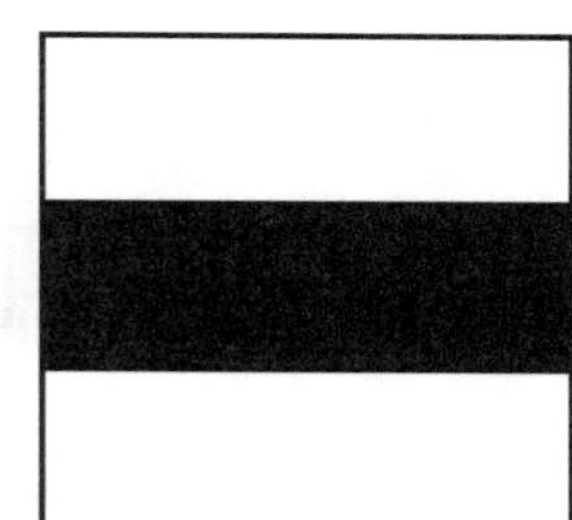

$\frac{1}{2}$ $\frac{1}{3}$ $\frac{1}{4}$

About how long?

5.

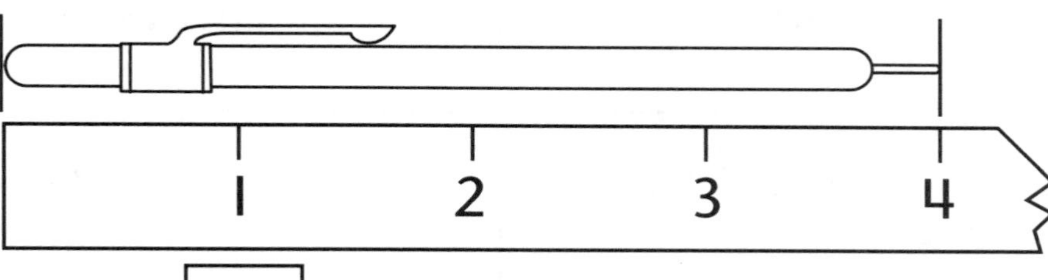

about ☐ inches

6.

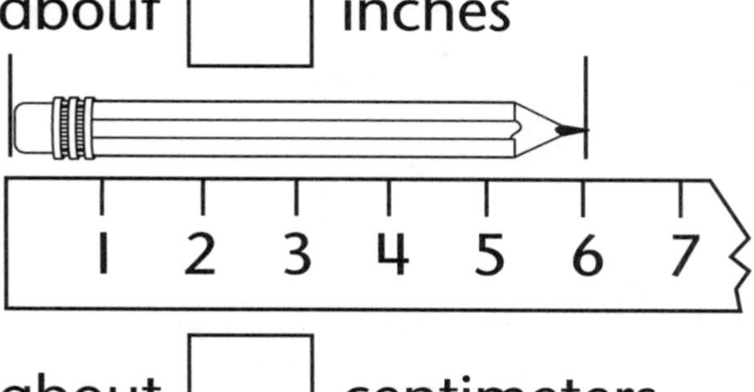

about ☐ centimeters

Ring the longer carrot.

7.

Ring the heavier object.

8.

Ring which holds less.

9.

Problem Solving
Reasoning

Use the chart to solve.

Object	Length in Inches	Length in Centimeters
paper clip	about 2	about 5
crayon	about 3	about 7
tape	about 4	about 9

10. Which is longer, the crayon or the tape?

____

11. How many centimeters long is the paper clip?
about _____ centimeters

Name ____________________

★ Test Prep

1

○ 6 + 3 = 9 ○ 9 + 0 = 9

○ 9 − 7 = 2 ○ 9 − 3 = 6

2

2 + 5 = 7

○ 5 + 2 = 7 ○ 7 − 2 = 5

○ 7 + 2 = 9 ○ 7 − 5 = 2

3

Tens	Ones
5	6

56 ○ 65 ○ 55 ○ 66 ○

4

40, ___, 60, 70, 80

42 ○ 50 ○ 30 ○ 55 ○

5

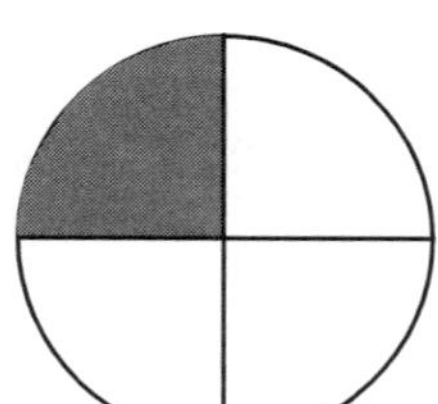

$\frac{1}{2}$ ○ $\frac{1}{3}$ ○ $\frac{1}{4}$ ○ 4 ○

6

 ○

 ○

 ○

7

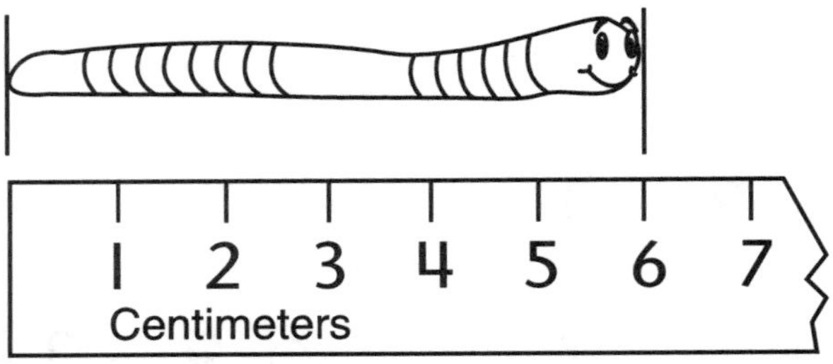

1 2 3 4 5 6 7
Centimeters

about 4 ○ about 6 ○ about 8 ○ about 7 ○

8

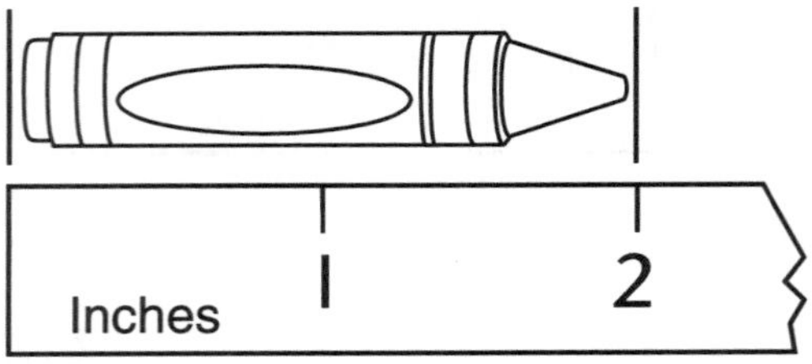

Inches 1 2

about 1 ○ about 2 ○ about 3 ○ about 4 ○

Decide on an answer. Mark the space for your answer.
If the answer is **not here**, mark the space for **NH**.

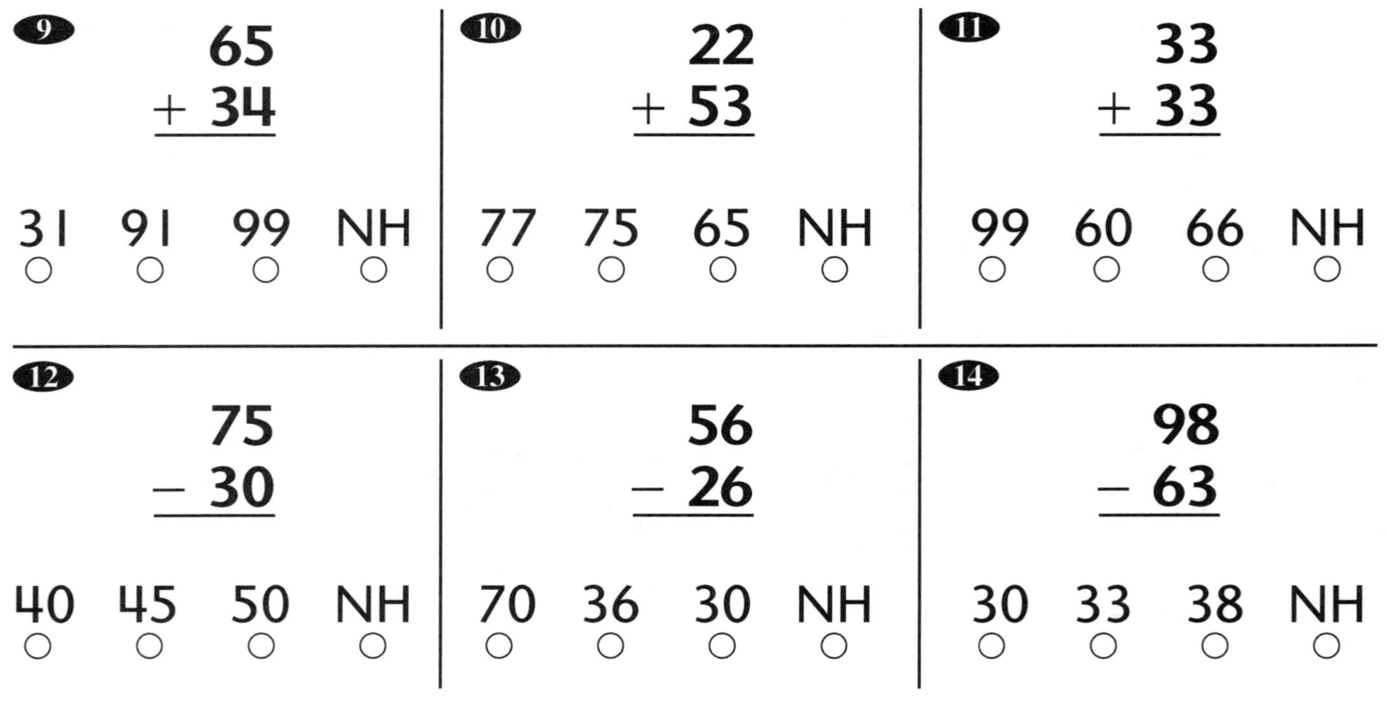

9

$$\begin{array}{r} 65 \\ +\ 34 \\ \hline \end{array}$$

31 ○ 91 ○ 99 ○ NH ○

10

$$\begin{array}{r} 22 \\ +\ 53 \\ \hline \end{array}$$

77 ○ 75 ○ 65 ○ NH ○

11

$$\begin{array}{r} 33 \\ +\ 33 \\ \hline \end{array}$$

99 ○ 60 ○ 66 ○ NH ○

12

$$\begin{array}{r} 75 \\ -\ 30 \\ \hline \end{array}$$

40 ○ 45 ○ 50 ○ NH ○

13

$$\begin{array}{r} 56 \\ -\ 26 \\ \hline \end{array}$$

70 ○ 36 ○ 30 ○ NH ○

14

$$\begin{array}{r} 98 \\ -\ 63 \\ \hline \end{array}$$

30 ○ 33 ○ 38 ○ NH ○

UNIT 11 • TABLE OF CONTENTS

Addition and Subtraction Facts through 20

UNIT 11 • TABLE OF CONTENTS

We will be using this vocabulary:

fact an addition or subtraction number sentence

fact family the related addition and subtraction facts

names for numbers the different expressions that are equivalent to the same number; for example: names for 12: 6 + 6; 7 + 5; 8 + 4; 9 + 3, etc.

Dear Family,

During the next few weeks our math class will be learning and practicing addition and subtraction facts through 20.

You can expect to see homework that provides practice with addition and subtraction facts.

As we learn about related facts and fact families you may wish to keep the following sample as a guide.

Related facts

$7 + 5 = 12$ $\quad$ $12 - 5 = 7$

Fact Family

$7 + 5 = 12$ $\quad$ $12 - 7 = 5$

$5 + 7 = 12$ $\quad$ $12 - 5 = 7$

Knowing addition facts can help children learn the related subtraction facts.

Sincerely,

Name ______________________________

Add or subtract.

1.  $9 + 2 = $ 11 $11 - 2 = $ 9

2.  $8 + 3 = $ ☐ $11 - 3 = $ ☐

3.  $7 + 4 = $ ☐ $11 - 4 = $ ☐

4.  $9 + 3 = $ ☐ $12 - 3 = $ ☐

5.  $8 + 4 = $ ☐ $12 - 4 = $ ☐

6.  $7 + 5 = $ ☐ $12 - 5 = $ ☐

Add or subtract.

7.

$$\begin{array}{r} 6 \\ +\ 5 \\ \hline 11 \end{array} \qquad \begin{array}{r} 11 \\ -\ 5 \\ \hline 6 \end{array}$$

8.

$$\begin{array}{r} 6 \\ +\ 6 \\ \hline \end{array} \qquad \begin{array}{r} 12 \\ -\ 6 \\ \hline \end{array}$$

9.

$$\begin{array}{r} 2 \\ +\ 9 \\ \hline \end{array} \qquad \begin{array}{r} 11 \\ -\ 9 \\ \hline \end{array}$$

10.

$$\begin{array}{r} 3 \\ +\ 9 \\ \hline \end{array} \qquad \begin{array}{r} 12 \\ -\ 9 \\ \hline \end{array}$$

11.

$$\begin{array}{r} 4 \\ +\ 7 \\ \hline \end{array} \qquad \begin{array}{r} 11 \\ -\ 7 \\ \hline \end{array}$$

12.

$$\begin{array}{r} 5 \\ +\ 7 \\ \hline \end{array} \qquad \begin{array}{r} 12 \\ -\ 7 \\ \hline \end{array}$$

13.

$$\begin{array}{r} 3 \\ +\ 8 \\ \hline \end{array} \qquad \begin{array}{r} 11 \\ -\ 8 \\ \hline \end{array}$$

14.

$$\begin{array}{r} 4 \\ +\ 8 \\ \hline \end{array} \qquad \begin{array}{r} 12 \\ -\ 8 \\ \hline \end{array}$$

Add or subtract.

15.

$8 + 4 = \square$ $12 - 4 = \square$ $2 + 9 = \square$

16.

$11 - 9 = \square$ $6 + 6 = \square$ $12 - 6 = \square$

17.

$\begin{array}{r} 11 \\ -\ 5 \\ \hline \end{array}$ $\begin{array}{r} 6 \\ +\ 5 \\ \hline \end{array}$ $\begin{array}{r} 12 \\ -\ 3 \\ \hline \end{array}$ $\begin{array}{r} 9 \\ +\ 3 \\ \hline \end{array}$ $\begin{array}{r} 7 \\ +\ 4 \\ \hline \end{array}$

18.

$\begin{array}{r} 11 \\ -\ 4 \\ \hline \end{array}$ $\begin{array}{r} 11 \\ -\ 3 \\ \hline \end{array}$ $\begin{array}{r} 8 \\ +\ 3 \\ \hline \end{array}$ $\begin{array}{r} 5 \\ +\ 6 \\ \hline \end{array}$ $\begin{array}{r} 11 \\ -\ 6 \\ \hline \end{array}$

Practice your facts.

19.

$\begin{array}{r} 7 \\ +\ 3 \\ \hline \end{array}$ $\begin{array}{r} 6 \\ +\ 4 \\ \hline \end{array}$ $\begin{array}{r} 6 \\ +\ 6 \\ \hline \end{array}$ $\begin{array}{r} 4 \\ +\ 5 \\ \hline \end{array}$ $\begin{array}{r} 3 \\ +\ 9 \\ \hline \end{array}$

20.

$\begin{array}{r} 3 \\ +\ 4 \\ \hline \end{array}$ $\begin{array}{r} 5 \\ +\ 4 \\ \hline \end{array}$ $\begin{array}{r} 3 \\ +\ 7 \\ \hline \end{array}$ $\begin{array}{r} 4 \\ +\ 8 \\ \hline \end{array}$ $\begin{array}{r} 1 \\ +\ 9 \\ \hline \end{array}$

Practice your facts.

21.

12	10	9	12	8
− 4	− 5	− 3	− 8	− 2

22.

12	10	11	7	12
− 6	− 4	− 9	− 6	− 9

23.

8	11	9	10	11
− 5	− 6	− 3	− 5	− 5

Problem Solving Reasoning

Solve.

24. Paul sees **9** flowers.
5 are blue.
The rest are not.
How many are not blue?.

_______ not blue

25. Hannah sees **12** ducks.
8 are flying.
The rest are not.
How many are not flying?

_______ not flying

★ Test Prep

Which is the related subtraction fact? Mark next to your answer.

26 **9 + 2 = 11**

- ○ 9 − 2 = 7
- ○ 11 − 2 = 9
- ○ 11 − 3 = 8
- ○ 12 − 3 = 9

STANDARD

Name ____________________

Complete the fact familiy.

1.
7 + 4 = [11]
4 + 7 = [11]
11 − 7 = [4]
11 − 4 = [7]

2.
6 + 5 = [11]
5 + 6 = [ ]
11 − 6 = [ ]
11 − 5 = [ ]

3.
7 + 5 = [ ]
5 + 7 = [ ]
12 − 7 = [ ]
12 − 5 = [ ]

4.
8 + 4 = [ ]
4 + 8 = [ ]
12 − 8 = [ ]
12 − 4 = [ ]

5.
9 + 2 = [ ]
2 + [ ] = [ ]

[ ] − [ ] = [ ]

[ ] − [ ] = [ ]

★ Test Prep

Which **3** numbers are in a fact family for **12**? Mark the space under your answer.

6

2, 9, 11	12, 10, 11	8, 4, 12	12, 8, 5
○	 ○	○	 ○

STANDARD

Name ____________________

Ring the names for the number.

1.  8 + 4   3 + 7   5 + 4 + 3   9 + 3

2.  7 + 1   12 − 4   4 + 5   10 − 0

3.  12 − 7   11 − 6   4 + 5   10 − 5

4.  11 − 0   3 + 4   2 + 4   9 − 2

Problem Solving
Reasoning

Use pennies, pictures, and number expressions to show names for 9. Tell whether or not your names for 9 match a friend's.

Quick Check

Complete.

1. 7 + 5 = ☐   12 − 5 = ☐

2. 8 + 3 = ☐   11 − 8 = ☐

3 + 8 = ☐   11 − 3 = ☐

Ring the names for **11**.

3. 11 − 9   9 + 2   6 + 2 + 3

STANDARD

Name ______________________

Add or subtract.

1. 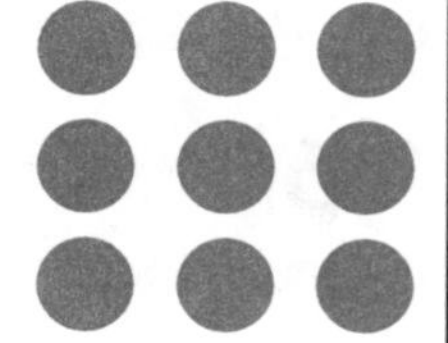

$9 + 4 =$ 13 $\quad 13 - 4 =$ 9

2. 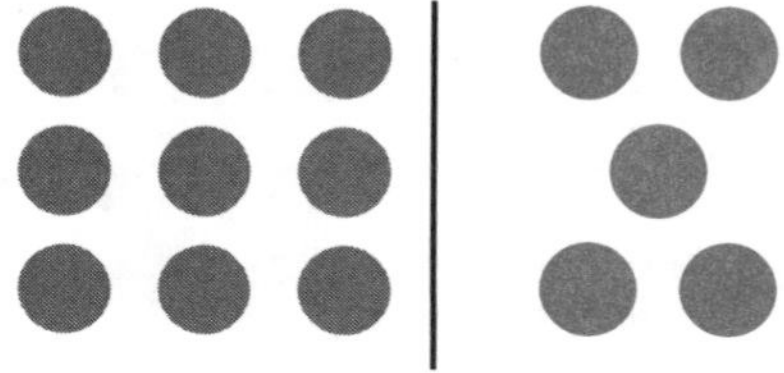

$9 + 5 =$ ☐ $\quad 14 - 5 =$ ☐

3. 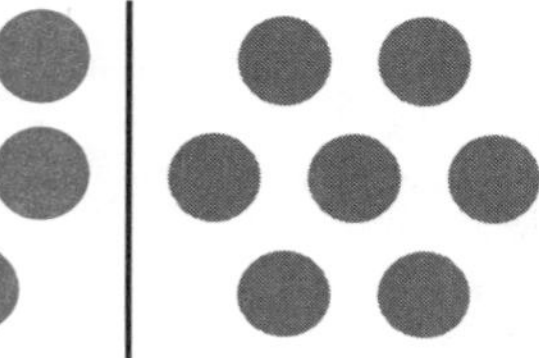

$8 + 7 =$ ☐ $\quad 15 - 7 =$ ☐

4. 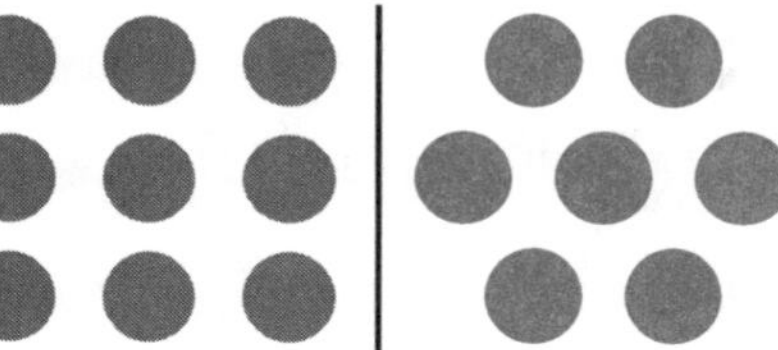

$9 + 7 =$ ☐ $\quad 16 - 7 =$ ☐

5. 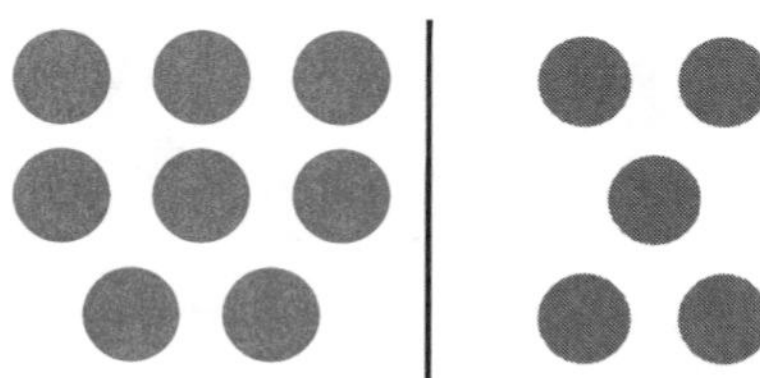

$8 + 5 =$ ☐ $\quad 13 - 5 =$ ☐

6. 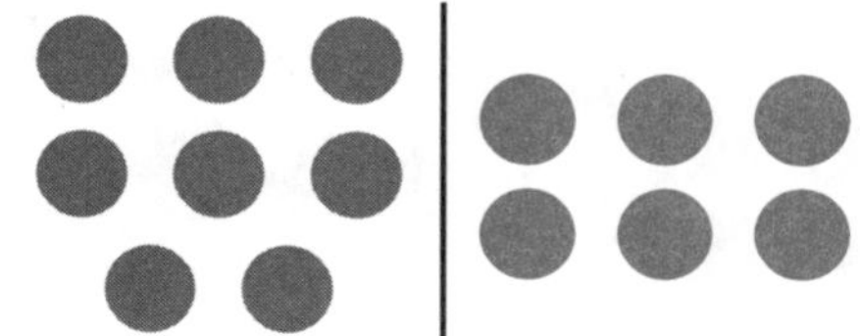

$8 + 6 =$ ☐ $\quad 14 - 6 =$ ☐

Add or subtract.

7.

$$\begin{array}{r} 6 \\ +\ 7 \\ \hline 13 \end{array} \qquad \begin{array}{r} 13 \\ -\ 7 \\ \hline 6 \end{array}$$

8.

$$\begin{array}{r} 6 \\ +\ 9 \\ \hline \end{array} \qquad \begin{array}{r} 15 \\ -\ 9 \\ \hline \end{array}$$

9.

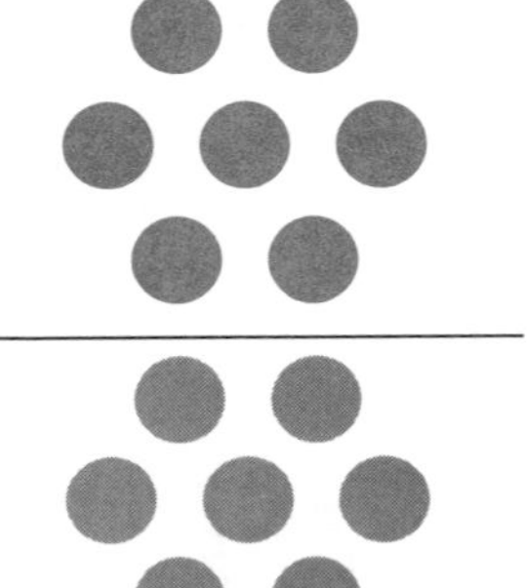

$$\begin{array}{r} 7 \\ +\ 7 \\ \hline \end{array} \qquad \begin{array}{r} 14 \\ -\ 7 \\ \hline \end{array}$$

10.

$$\begin{array}{r} 8 \\ +\ 8 \\ \hline \end{array} \qquad \begin{array}{r} 16 \\ -\ 8 \\ \hline \end{array}$$

11.

$$\begin{array}{r} 5 \\ +\ 8 \\ \hline \end{array} \qquad \begin{array}{r} 13 \\ -\ 8 \\ \hline \end{array}$$

12.

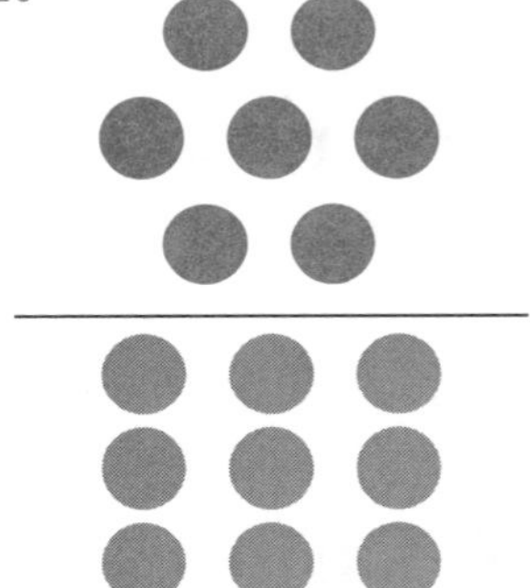

$$\begin{array}{r} 7 \\ +\ 9 \\ \hline \end{array} \qquad \begin{array}{r} 16 \\ -\ 9 \\ \hline \end{array}$$

13.

$$\begin{array}{r} 4 \\ +\ 9 \\ \hline \end{array} \qquad \begin{array}{r} 13 \\ -\ 9 \\ \hline \end{array}$$

14.

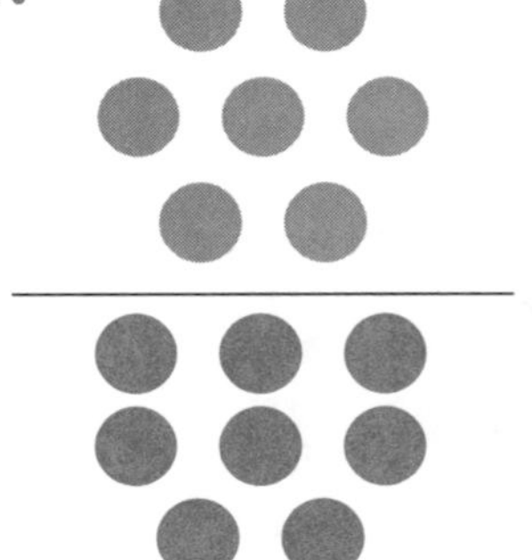

$$\begin{array}{r} 7 \\ +\ 8 \\ \hline \end{array} \qquad \begin{array}{r} 15 \\ -\ 8 \\ \hline \end{array}$$

Add or subtract.

15.

$5 + 9 = \square$ $14 - 9 = \square$ $8 + 8 = \square$

16.

$16 - 8 = \square$ $7 + 8 = \square$ $15 - 8 = \square$

17.

5	13	9	16	9
+ 8	− 8	+ 7	− 7	+ 6

18.

15	7	14	9	14
− 6	+ 7	− 7	+ 5	− 5

Practice your facts.

19.

6	3	6	8	7
+ 8	+ 9	+ 4	+ 3	+ 6

20.

7	4	5	7	8
+ 7	+ 8	+ 5	+ 4	+ 7

Practice your facts.

21. $\begin{array}{r} 15 \\ -\ 9 \\ \hline \end{array}$ $\begin{array}{r} 14 \\ -\ 6 \\ \hline \end{array}$ $\begin{array}{r} 15 \\ -\ 7 \\ \hline \end{array}$ $\begin{array}{r} 16 \\ -\ 9 \\ \hline \end{array}$ $\begin{array}{r} 10 \\ -\ 4 \\ \hline \end{array}$

22. $\begin{array}{r} 12 \\ -\ 4 \\ \hline \end{array}$ $\begin{array}{r} 10 \\ -\ 7 \\ \hline \end{array}$ $\begin{array}{r} 12 \\ -\ 5 \\ \hline \end{array}$ $\begin{array}{r} 14 \\ -\ 7 \\ \hline \end{array}$ $\begin{array}{r} 13 \\ -\ 4 \\ \hline \end{array}$

23. $\begin{array}{r} 13 \\ -\ 9 \\ \hline \end{array}$ $\begin{array}{r} 14 \\ -\ 5 \\ \hline \end{array}$ $\begin{array}{r} 16 \\ -\ 8 \\ \hline \end{array}$ $\begin{array}{r} 12 \\ -\ 6 \\ \hline \end{array}$ $\begin{array}{r} 11 \\ -\ 6 \\ \hline \end{array}$

Problem Solving
Reasoning

Solve.

24. Marina has **16** grapes.

She gives Pam **8** grapes.

Marina has ☐ grapes left.

25. Tony has **7** kites.

He gets **8** more.

Tony has ☐ kites.

★ Test Prep

26. Which is the related addition fact? Mark next to your answer.

14 − 6 = 8

○ 6 + 2 = 8
○ 9 + 5 = 14
○ 8 + 6 = 14
○ 8 + 4 = 12

Name ______________________

Complete the fact family.

1. $9 + 7 =$ [16]
$7 + 9 =$ [16]
$16 - 9 =$ [7]
$16 - 7 =$ [9]

2. $8 + 5 =$ ☐
$5 + 8 =$ ☐
$13 - 8 =$ ☐
$13 - 5 =$ ☐

3. $8 + 7 =$ ☐
$7 + 8 =$ ☐
$15 - 8 =$ ☐
$15 - 7 =$ ☐

4. $9 + 4 =$ ☐
$4 + 9 =$ ☐
$13 - 9 =$ ☐
$13 - 4 =$ ☐

5. $9 + 6 =$ ☐
$6 +$ ☐ $=$ ☐
☐ $-$ ☐ $=$ ☐
☐ $-$ ☐ $=$ ☐

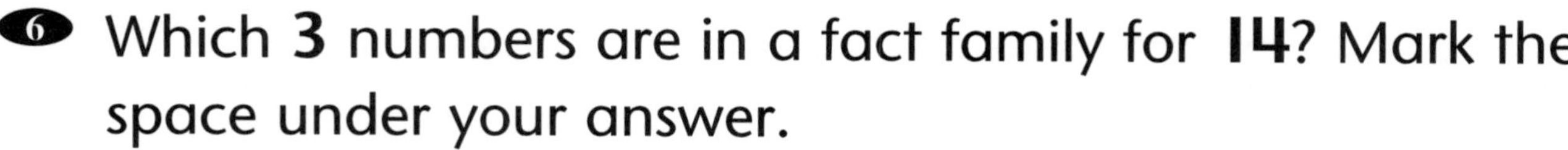

Which **3** numbers are in a fact family for **14**? Mark the space under your answer.

4, 9, 13	12, 13, 14	5, 9, 14	9, 13, 4
○	○	○	○

Ring the names for the number.

1.  9 + 4   8 + 7   3 + 7 + 3   6 + 5

2. 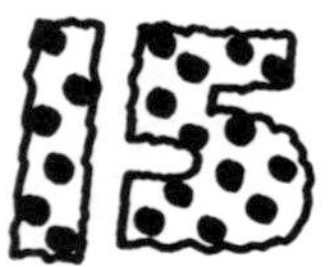 5 + 9   9 + 6   4 + 8   7 + 8

3. 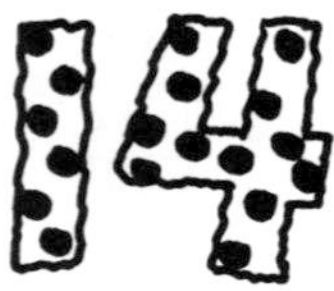 7 + 7   8 + 5   9 + 5   6 + 8

4.  8 + 8   7 + 7   6 + 6   7 + 9

Problem Solving Reasoning

Use pennies, pictures, and number expressions to show names for 12. Tell whether or not your names match a friend's.

Quick Check

Complete.

1. 8 + 6 = ☐   14 − 6 = ☐

2. 9 + 6 = ☐   15 − 6 = ☐

6 + 9 = ☐   15 − 9 = ☐

Ring the names for **13**.

3. 2 + 6 + 5   6 + 7   9 + 3

Name ______________________________

Add or subtract.

1. $8 + 9 =$ [17] $17 - 9 =$ [8]

2. $9 + 8 =$ [ ] $17 - 8 =$ [ ]

3. $9 + 9 =$ [ ] $18 - 9 =$ [ ]

4. 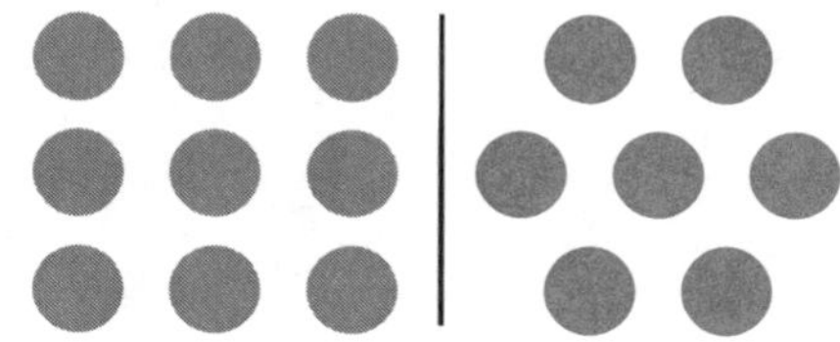

$9 + 7 =$ [ ] $16 - 7 =$ [ ]

5. 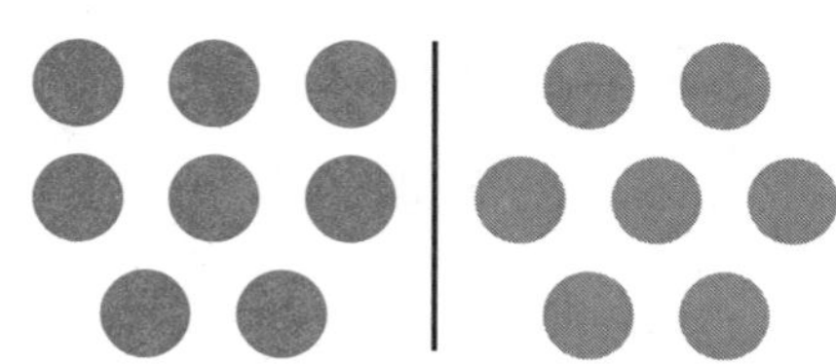

$8 + 7 =$ [ ] $15 - 7 =$ [ ]

6. 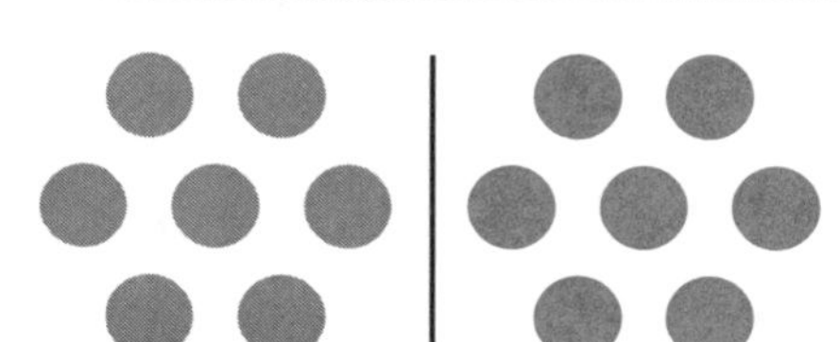

$7 + 7 =$ [ ] $14 - 7 =$ [ ]

Add or subtract.

7.

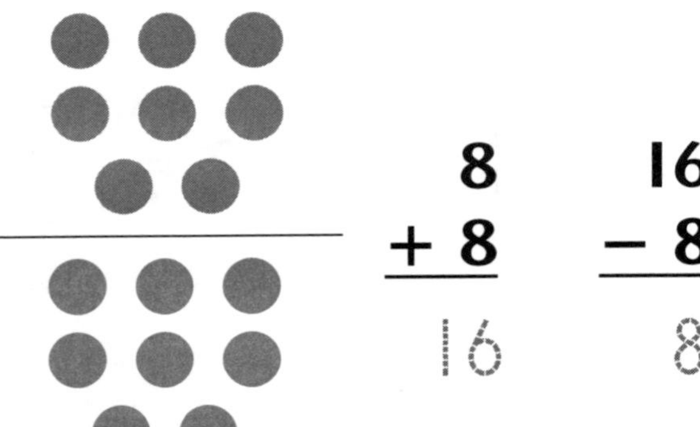

$$\begin{array}{r} 8 \\ +\ 8 \\ \hline 16 \end{array} \qquad \begin{array}{r} 16 \\ -\ 8 \\ \hline 8 \end{array}$$

8.

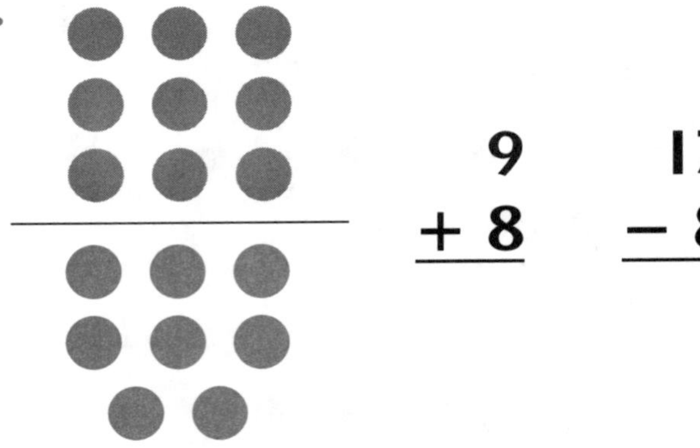

$$\begin{array}{r} 9 \\ +\ 8 \\ \hline \end{array} \qquad \begin{array}{r} 17 \\ -\ 8 \\ \hline \end{array}$$

9.

$$\begin{array}{r} 9 \\ +\ 9 \\ \hline \end{array} \qquad \begin{array}{r} 18 \\ -\ 9 \\ \hline \end{array}$$

10.

$$\begin{array}{r} 4 \\ +\ 8 \\ \hline \end{array} \qquad \begin{array}{r} 12 \\ -\ 8 \\ \hline \end{array}$$

11.

$$\begin{array}{r} 8 \\ +\ 9 \\ \hline \end{array} \qquad \begin{array}{r} 17 \\ -\ 9 \\ \hline \end{array}$$

12.

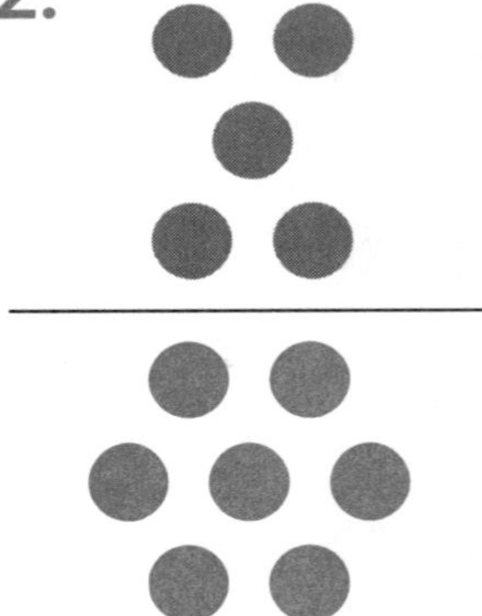

$$\begin{array}{r} 5 \\ +\ 7 \\ \hline \end{array} \qquad \begin{array}{r} 12 \\ -\ 7 \\ \hline \end{array}$$

13.

$$\begin{array}{r} 7 \\ +\ 9 \\ \hline \end{array} \qquad \begin{array}{r} 16 \\ -\ 9 \\ \hline \end{array}$$

14.

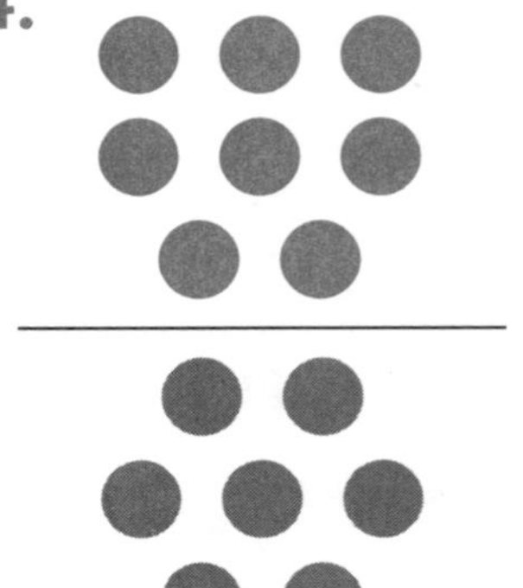

$$\begin{array}{r} 8 \\ +\ 7 \\ \hline \end{array} \qquad \begin{array}{r} 15 \\ -\ 7 \\ \hline \end{array}$$

Practice your facts.

15.

$9 + 7 = \square$ $8 + 9 = \square$ $18 - 9 = \square$

16.

$9 + 9 = \square$ $17 - 8 = \square$ $9 + 8 = \square$

17.

$8 + 6 = \square$ $13 - 8 = \square$ $7 + 6 = \square$

18.

$\begin{array}{r} 13 \\ -\ 4 \\ \hline \end{array}$ $\begin{array}{r} 8 \\ +\ 5 \\ \hline \end{array}$ $\begin{array}{r} 9 \\ +\ 6 \\ \hline \end{array}$ $\begin{array}{r} 12 \\ -\ 6 \\ \hline \end{array}$ $\begin{array}{r} 16 \\ -\ 7 \\ \hline \end{array}$

19.

$\begin{array}{r} 15 \\ -\ 9 \\ \hline \end{array}$ $\begin{array}{r} 6 \\ +\ 4 \\ \hline \end{array}$ $\begin{array}{r} 12 \\ -\ 3 \\ \hline \end{array}$ $\begin{array}{r} 9 \\ +\ 9 \\ \hline \end{array}$ $\begin{array}{r} 8 \\ +\ 7 \\ \hline \end{array}$

20.

$\begin{array}{r} 11 \\ -\ 9 \\ \hline \end{array}$ $\begin{array}{r} 12 \\ -\ 8 \\ \hline \end{array}$ $\begin{array}{r} 7 \\ +\ 8 \\ \hline \end{array}$ $\begin{array}{r} 14 \\ -\ 9 \\ \hline \end{array}$ $\begin{array}{r} 7 \\ +\ 9 \\ \hline \end{array}$

Practice your facts.

21.

18	17	8	16	7
-9	-9	$+8$	-7	$+7$

22.

6	13	16	5	9
$+9$	-9	-8	$+9$	$+8$

23.

8	17	14	9	7
$+5$	-8	-5	$+6$	$+9$

Problem Solving
Reasoning

24. Jean has **9** books. Jonah gives her **8** more books. Now Jean has ☐ books.

25. Tom has **18** tops. He loses **9** tops. Now Tom has ☐ tops.

Mark next to the related fact.

26 $9 + 9 = 18$

○ $9 - 9 = 0$

○ $17 - 9 = 8$

○ $18 - 9 = 9$

○ $18 - 10 = 8$

Name ____________________

Complete the fact family.

1. $9 + 8 = $ 17
$8 + 9 = $ 17
$17 - 9 = $ 8
$17 - 8 = $ 9

2. $9 + 9 = $ ☐
$18 - 9 = $ ☐

3. $6 + 5 = $ ☐
$5 + 6 = $ ☐
$11 - 6 = $ ☐
$11 - 5 = $ ☐

4. $9 + 4 = $ ☐
$4 + 9 = $ ☐
$13 - 9 = $ ☐
$13 - 4 = $ ☐

5. $8 + 4 = $ ☐
$4 + $ ☐ $ = $ ☐

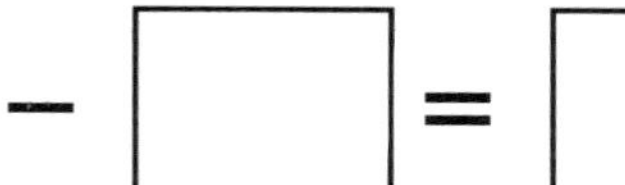

☐ − ☐ = ☐
☐ − ☐ = ☐

★ Test Prep

Which **3** numbers are in a fact family for **17**?
Mark the space under your answer.

6

8, 9, 17	16, 17, 18	7, 8, 15	8, 8, 16
○	○	○	○

STANDARD

Name ______________________________

Ring the names for the number.

1.  9 + 8   4 + 5 + 6 + 2   9 + 9

2.  8 + 8   4 + 5 + 9   9 + 9   7 + 9

Problem Solving Reasoning

Solve.

3. I read **4** pages on Monday, **3** pages on Tuesday, none on Wednesday, and **8** pages on Thursday. How many pages did I read so far this week? __________

Quick Check

Solve.

1. $\begin{array}{r} 9 \\ +\ 8 \\ \hline \end{array}$

2. $\begin{array}{r} 14 \\ -\ 6 \\ \hline \end{array}$

Complete the fact family.

3. 8 + 9 = ☐   17 − 9 = ☐

9 + 8 = ☐   17 − 8 = ☐

Ring the names for **17**.

4. 9 + 8   5 + 6   9 + 4 + 4

Name ______________________

STANDARD

Problem Solving Plan			
1. Understand	2. Decide	3. Solve	4. Look back

Solve.

1. Anna has some erasers in her desk. She puts **6** more in her desk. Now she has **13**. How many erasers does she have in her desk to start with?

   Think Do you need to add or subtract?

   subtract

   13 (−) 6 = 7

   Answer 7 erasers

2. Sam has **18** balloons. **9** of them float away. How many does he have left?

   Think Do you need to add or subtract?

   ____

   18 ◯ 9 = _____

   Answer _____ balloons

3. Nina has **15** seashells. That is **9** more than Tae has. How many seashells does Tae have?

   Think Do you need to add or subtract?

   ____

   15 ◯ 9 = _____

   Answer _____ seashells

4. Ann has **16¢**. That is **8¢** more than Rita. How much money does Rita have?

   Think Do you need to add or subtract?

   ____

   16¢ ◯ 8¢ = _____

   Answer _____¢

Solve.

5. Anthony catches **6** fish from the lake. Sue catches **8** fish. How many fish do they catch in all?

8 ◯ **6** = _____

Answer _____ fish

6. Jason gives **6** cards to Lauren and **6** cards to Angela. How many cards does Jason give in all?

6 ◯ **6** = _____

Answer _____ cards

7. Mike found **15** shells. That was **6** more than Ellen found. How many shells did Ellen find?

15 ◯ **6** = _____

Answer _____ shells

8. Jim pays **8¢** for a tart. He pays **9¢** for a piece of pie. How much money does he spend?

8¢ ◯ **9¢** = _____¢

Answer _____¢

Extend Your Thinking

Draw a picture to show problem 7.

9.

Name ______________________________

Solve.

1.	10 + 1 = 11	2.	11 − 1 = 10
	10 + 2 = ☐		12 − 2 = ☐
	10 + 3 = ☐		13 − 3 = ☐
	10 + 4 = ☐		14 − 4 = ☐
	10 + 5 = ☐		15 − 5 = ☐
	10 + 6 = ☐		16 − 6 = ☐
	10 + 7 = ☐		17 − 7 = ☐
	10 + 8 = ☐		18 − 8 = ☐
	10 + 9 = ☐		19 − 9 = ☐
	10 + 10 = ☐		20 − 10 = ☐

Problem Solving Reasoning Solve.

3. What pattern do you see in the addition facts? ______________

____

____

____

Add or subtract.

4. $\begin{array}{r} 9 \\ +\ 6 \\ \hline \end{array}$

5. $\begin{array}{r} 10 \\ +\ 3 \\ \hline \end{array}$

6. $\begin{array}{r} 12 \\ -\ 8 \\ \hline \end{array}$

7. $\begin{array}{r} 17 \\ -\ 7 \\ \hline \end{array}$

8. $\begin{array}{r} 18 \\ -\ 9 \\ \hline \end{array}$

9. $\begin{array}{r} 9 \\ +\ 8 \\ \hline \end{array}$

10. $\begin{array}{r} 6 \\ +\ 5 \\ \hline \end{array}$

11. $\begin{array}{r} 10 \\ +\ 9 \\ \hline \end{array}$

12. $\begin{array}{r} 4 \\ +\ 6 \\ \hline \end{array}$

13. $\begin{array}{r} 10 \\ -\ 5 \\ \hline \end{array}$

14. $\begin{array}{r} 7 \\ +\ 7 \\ \hline \end{array}$

15. $\begin{array}{r} 8 \\ -\ 7 \\ \hline \end{array}$

16. $\begin{array}{r} 9 \\ -\ 9 \\ \hline \end{array}$

17. $\begin{array}{r} 8 \\ +\ 8 \\ \hline \end{array}$

18. $\begin{array}{r} 6 \\ +\ 8 \\ \hline \end{array}$

19. $\begin{array}{r} 20 \\ -10 \\ \hline \end{array}$

★ Test Prep

20 Listen. Mark the space next to your answer.

○ $10 - 7 = 3$ ○ $10 + 7 = 17$

○ $17 - 7 = 10$ ○ $10 + 0 = 10$

Name ______________________________

Problem

José is third in line.
There are **8** more children behind him.
How many children are in the line?

1 **Understand**

I need to find out how many children are in the line.

2 **Decide**

I can draw a picture to find out.

3 **Solve**

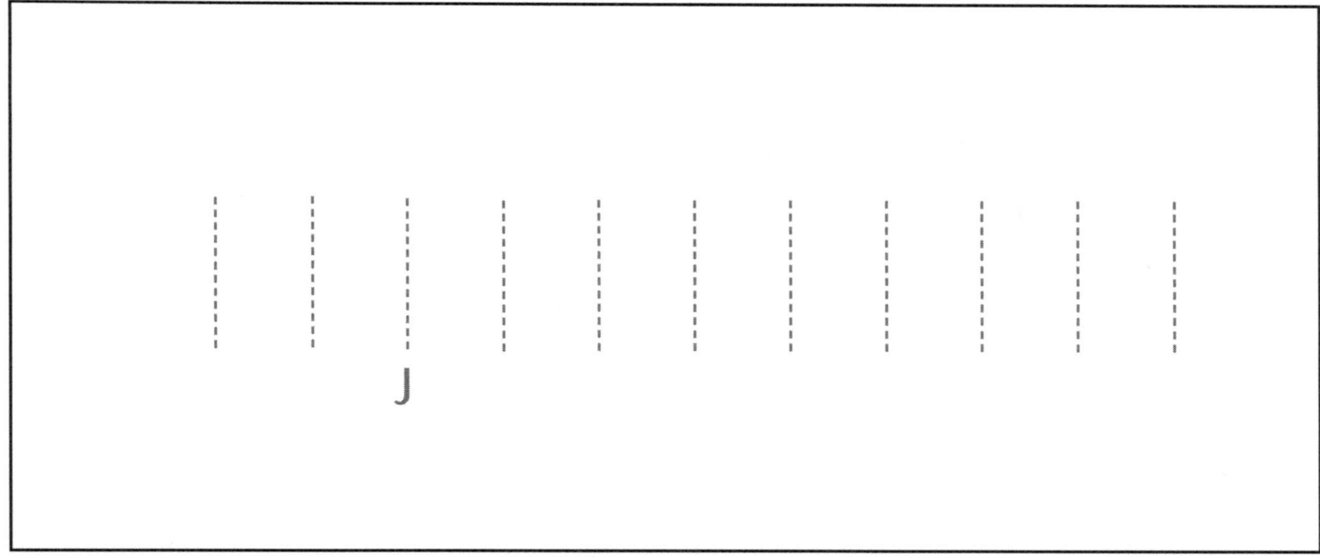

I can count ___11___ children in my picture.

There are ___11___ children in line.

4 **Look back**

I can check my answer by adding.

3 + 8 = 11

My answer makes sense.

Draw a picture to solve.

1. There are **16** children in the classroom. **9** of them are girls. The rest are boys. How many are boys?

   ______ are boys.

2. There are **12** eggs in a carton. **4** are broken. How many are not broken?

   ______ eggs

3. There are **17** cups of milk. **5** are large, **6** are small. The rest are medium. How many are medium?

   ______ cups

4. How can you check that your answer to problem **1** makes sense? ______________________________

   ____

   ____

   ____

Name ____________________

Add.

1. $8 + 7$
2. $8 + 8$
3. $9 + 6$
4. $6 + 7$
5. $9 + 7$
6. $5 + 8$
7. $10 + 8$
8. $9 + 9$
9. $7 + 7$
10. $5 + 9$

Subtract.

11. $14 - 7$
12. $16 - 8$
13. $15 - 8$
14. $13 - 6$
15. $15 - 9$
16. $13 - 4$
17. $17 - 9$
18. $19 - 9$
19. $13 - 8$
20. $16 - 9$

Complete the fact family.

21.

9 + 3 = ☐

3 + ☐ = ☐

☐ − ☐ = ☐

☐ − ☐ = ☐

22.

7 + 5 = ☐

5 + ☐ = ☐

☐ − ☐ = ☐

☐ − ☐ = ☐

Ring the names for the number.

23. 

9 + 8   8 + 7   6 + 2 + 4 + 5

24. 

9 + 6   3 + 5 + 7   4 + 5 + 4

25. 

10 + 2   5 + 5 + 4   6 + 6

Problem Solving Reasoning Solve.

26. There are **15** markers in a box. **6** are red. **7** are blue. The rest are green. How many are green?

_____ green

27. There are **7** white chicks and **9** black chicks. How many chicks in all?

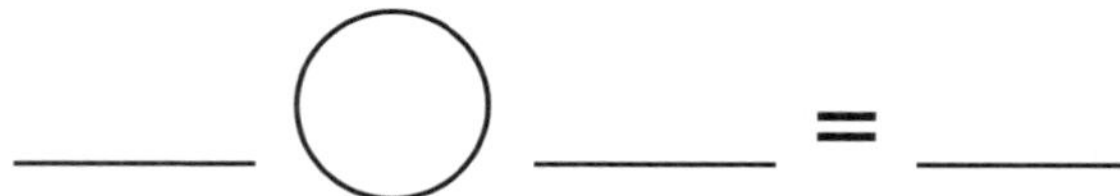

_____ chicks

28. There are **13** ducks. **5** fly away. How many are left?

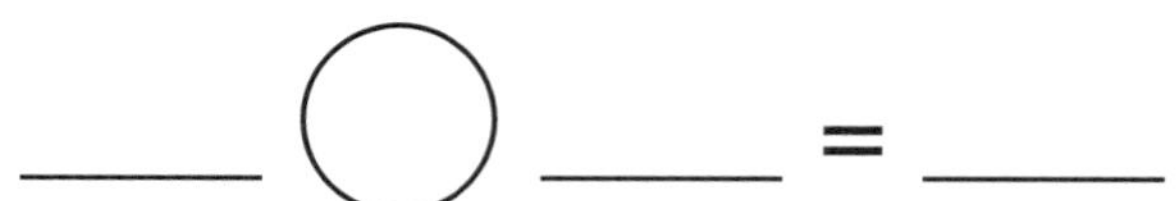

_____ ducks

Name ____________________

1

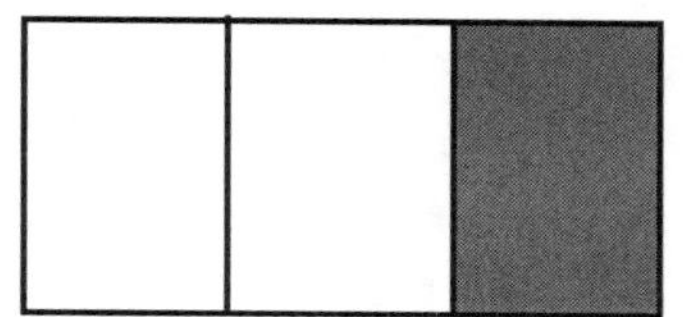

$\frac{1}{2}$	$\frac{1}{3}$	$\frac{1}{4}$	$\frac{2}{4}$
○	○	○	○

2

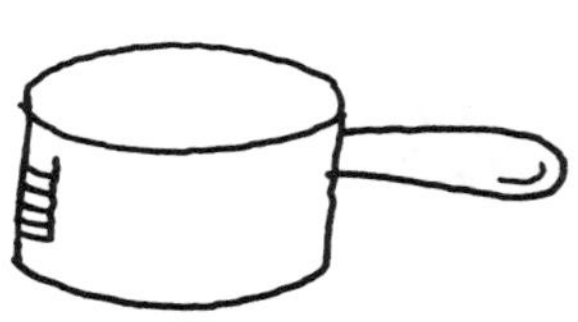

 ○  ○  ○  ○

3

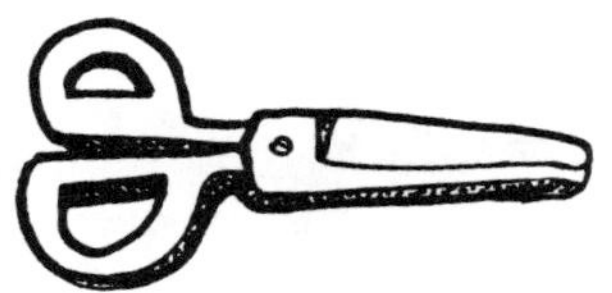

 ○  ○  ○ 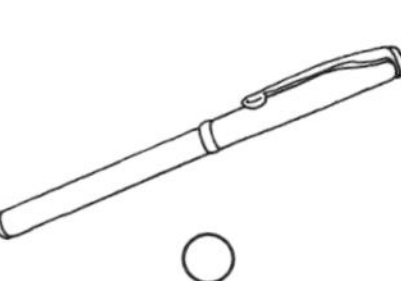 ○

4

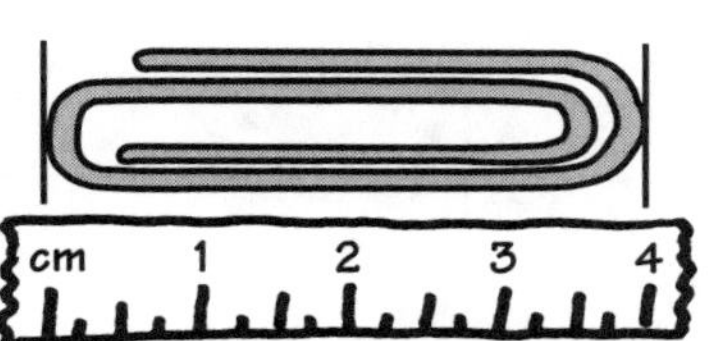

2	4	6	7
○	○	○	○

5

0	1	2	3
○	○	○	○

6

$7 + 6 = 13$

○ $10 + 3 = 13$ ○ $7 - 6 = 1$

○ $6 + 7 = 13$ ○ $7 + 7 = 14$

7

$8 + 8 = 16$	$15 - 8 = 7$	$15 - 9 = 6$	$15 + 8 = 23$
○	○	○	○

Decide on an answer. Mark the space for your answer. If the answer is **not here**, mark the space for **NH**.

8

$$\begin{array}{r} 54 \\ +24 \\ \hline \end{array}$$

30 ○ 70 ○ 78 ○ NH ○

9

$$\begin{array}{r} 71 \\ +18 \\ \hline \end{array}$$

67 ○ 89 ○ 99 ○ NH ○

10

$$\begin{array}{r} 63 \\ -40 \\ \hline \end{array}$$

20 ○ 23 ○ 30 ○ NH ○

11

$$\begin{array}{r} 98 \\ -28 \\ \hline \end{array}$$

60 ○ 78 ○ 76 ○ NH ○

12

$$\begin{array}{r} 9 \\ +4 \\ \hline \end{array}$$

14 ○ 13 ○ 12 ○ NH ○

13

$$\begin{array}{r} 16 \\ -7 \\ \hline \end{array}$$

9 ○ 8 ○ 6 ○ NH ○

14

$$\begin{array}{r} 10 \\ +8 \\ \hline \end{array}$$

10 ○ 8 ○ 2 ○ NH ○

15

$$\begin{array}{r} 6 \\ +8 \\ \hline \end{array}$$

12 ○ 13 ○ 14 ○ NH ○

add

3 + 4 = 7

addition sentence

3 + 5 = 8

after

9, 10

10 is after 9.

bar graph

Favorite Pets

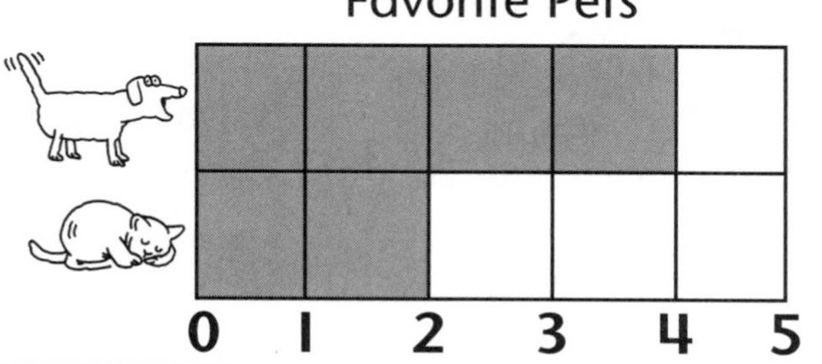

before

3, 4

3 is before 4.

between

1, 2, 3

2 is between 1 and 3.

calendar

November						
S	M	T	W	T	F	S
		1	2	3	4	5
6	7	8	9	10	11	12
13	14	15	16	17	18	19
20	21	22	23	24	25	26
27	28	27	30			

cent (¢)

= 1¢

centimeter

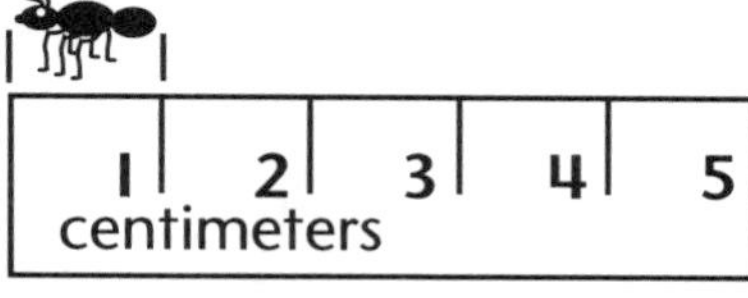

circle

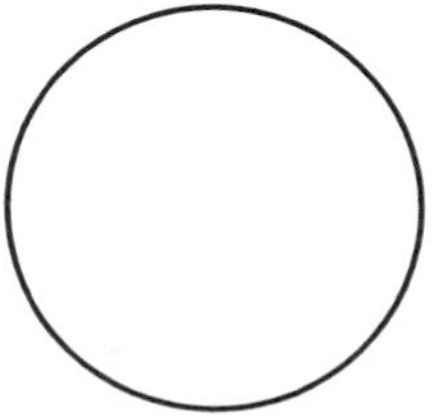

cone

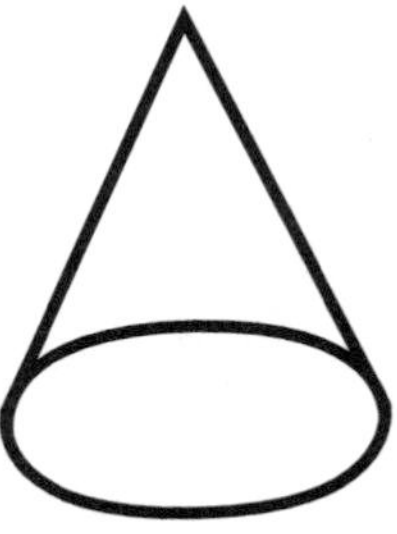

corner

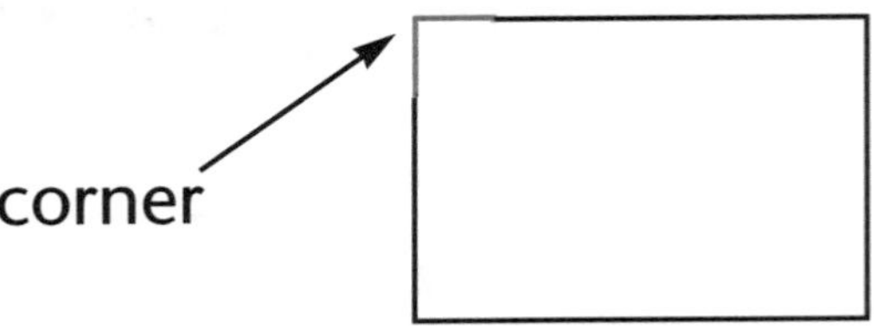

cube

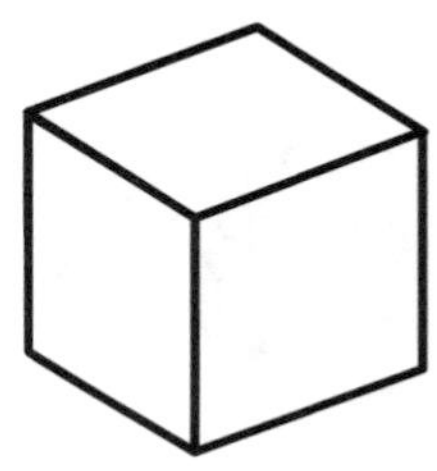

cylinder

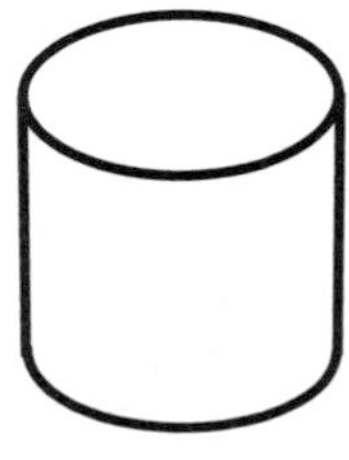

difference

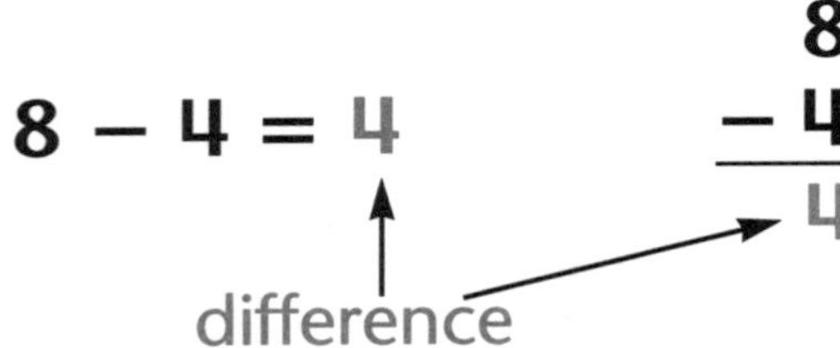

dime

10¢ **10** cents

equal parts

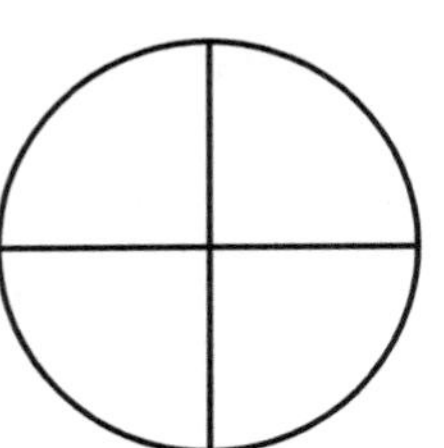

4 equal parts.

equals

2 + 6 = 8

2 plus **6** equals **8.**

is equal to

4 = 4

4 is equal to **4**.

face

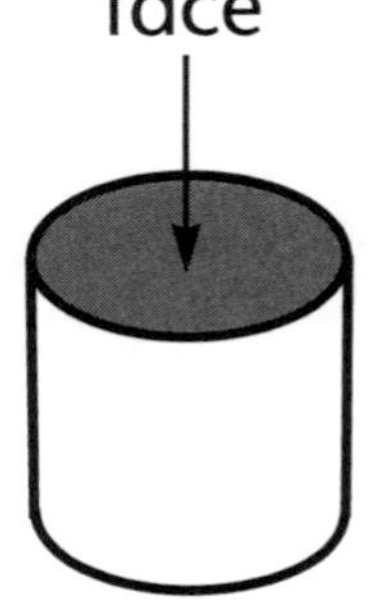

fact family

3 + 6 = 9 6 + 3 = 9

9 − 3 = 6 9 − 6 = 3

hour hand

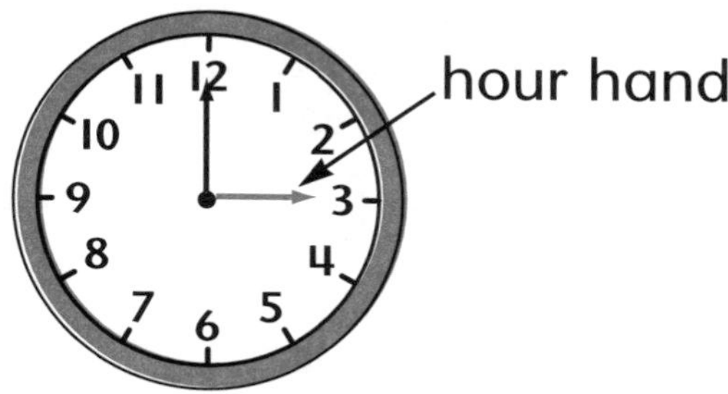

fewer

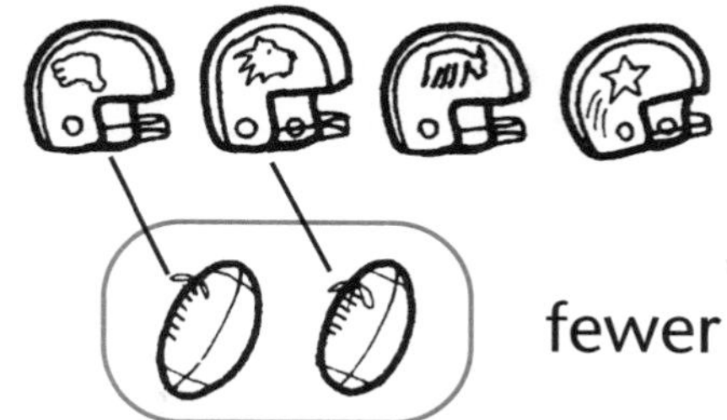

inch

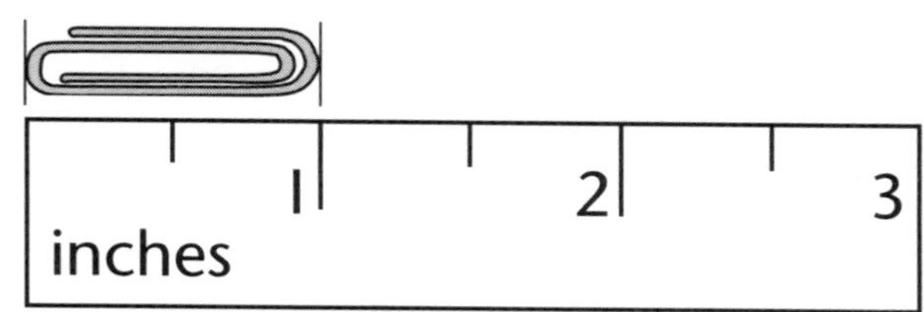

is greater than

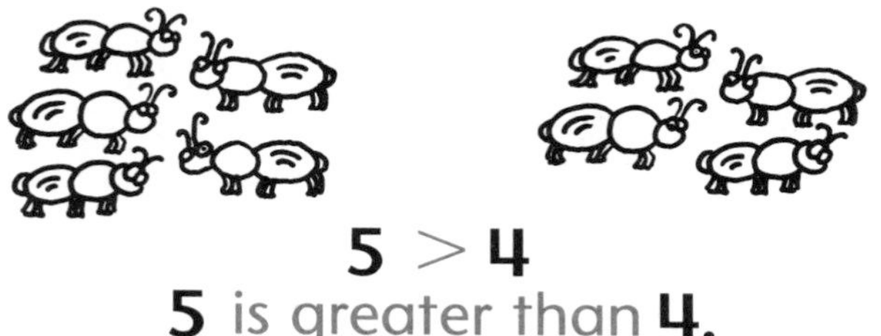

5 > 4

5 is greater than 4.

left

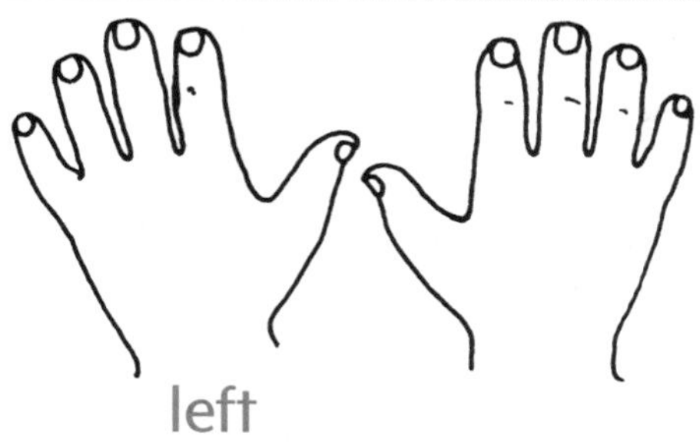

left

heavier

is less than

3 < 5

3 is less than 5.

hour

It takes about an hour to shop.

lighter

longer

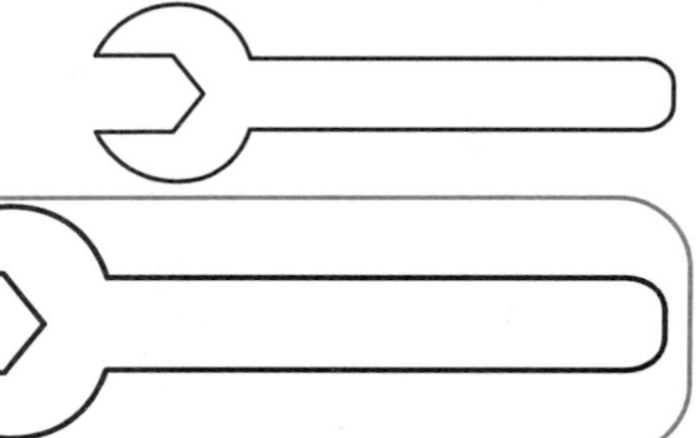

nickel

5¢

5 cents

minus

5 − 1 = 4

5 minus **1** equals **4.**

number line

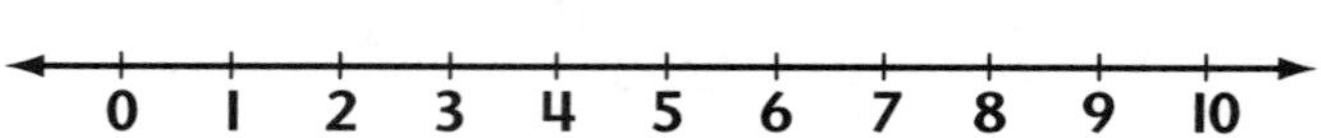

minute

It takes about a minute to set the table.

number sentence

8 + 2 = 10

6 − 4 = 2

minute hand

o'clock

4 o'clock **4:00**

more

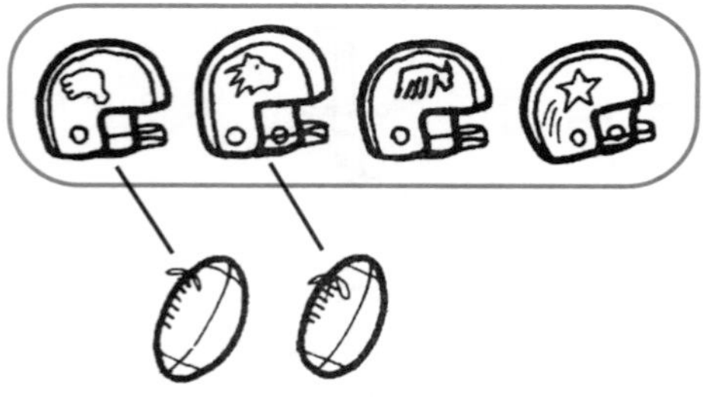

one fourth

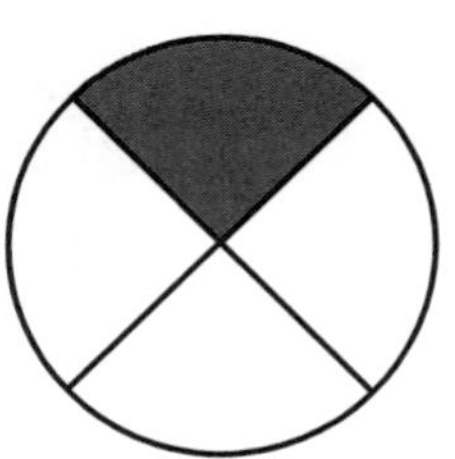

one half

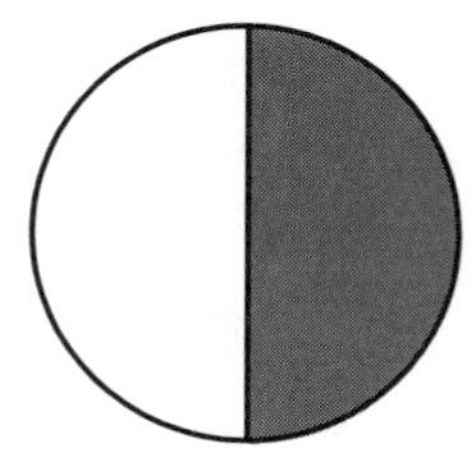

pattern

ones

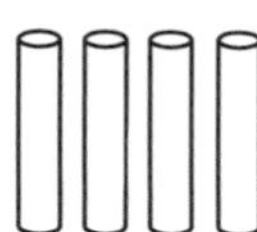

I ten and 4 ones
14

penny

1¢ 

one third

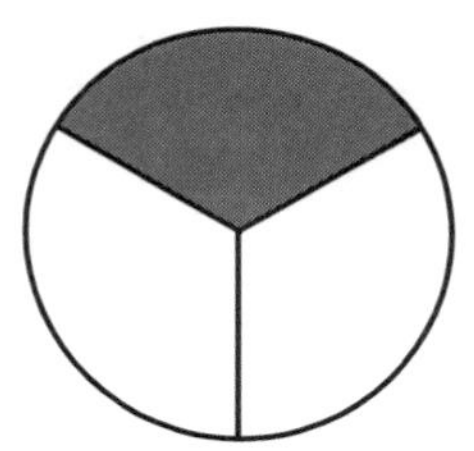

picture graph

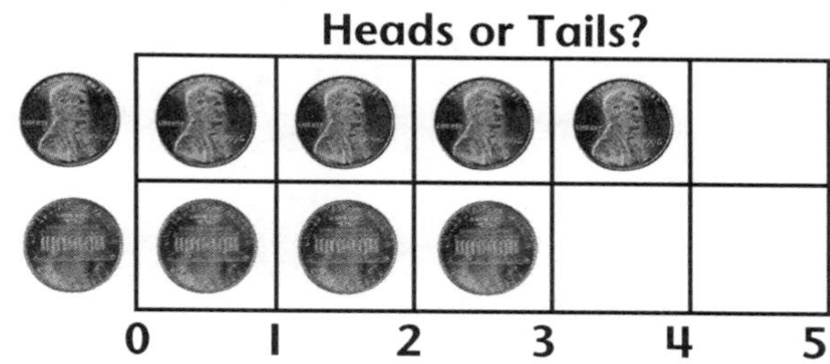

order

"0, 1, 2, 3, 4, 5, 6, 7, 8, 9, 10"

I count the numbers in order.

plus

4 + 1 = 5

4 plus 1 equals 5.

order property

4 + 3 = 7

3 + 4 = 7

pyramid

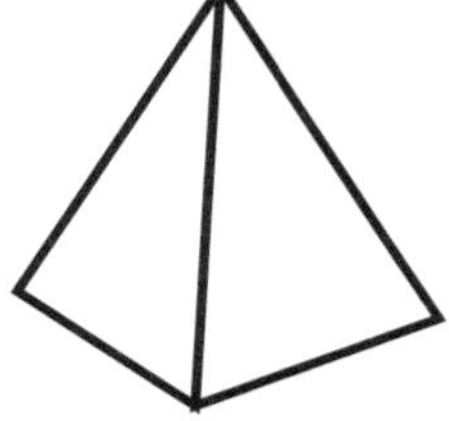

quarter

25¢

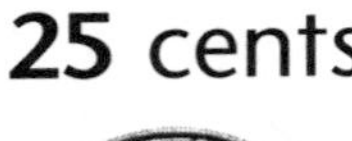

25 cents

shorter

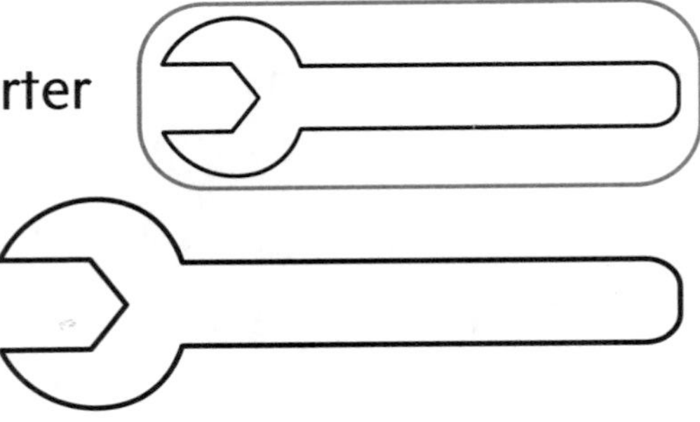

rectangle

side

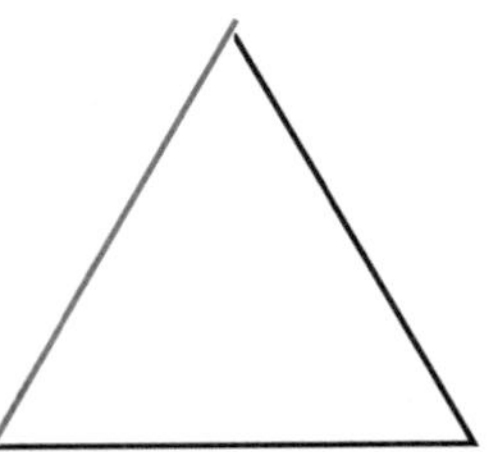

rectangular prism

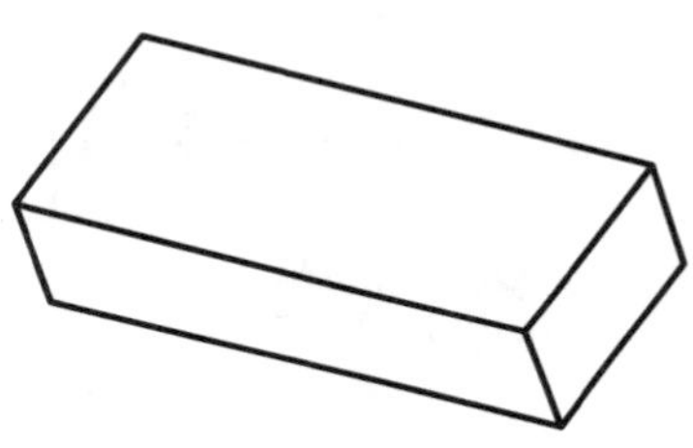

skip-count

2 4 6 8

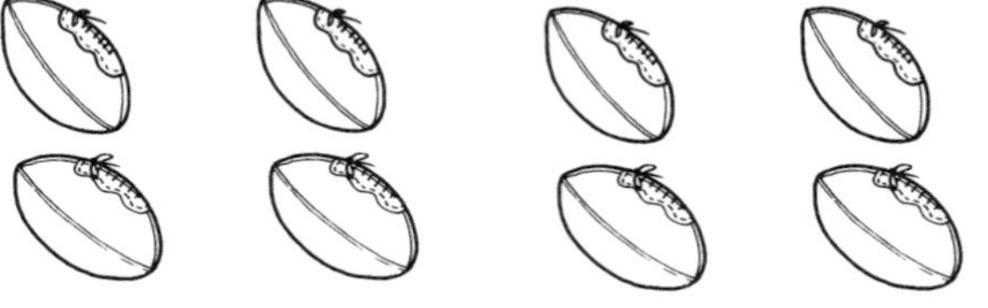

related facts

$9 + 1 = 10$

$10 - 1 = 9$

sphere

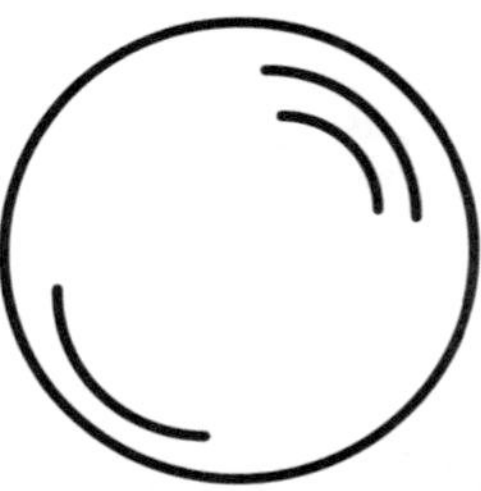

right

square

subtract

5 − 2 = 3

tally marks

subtraction sentence

8 − 2 = 6

telling time

4:00

hour

4:30

half hour

sum

3 + 4 = 7

$$\begin{array}{r} 3 \\ +\,4 \\ \hline 7 \end{array}$$

sum

tens

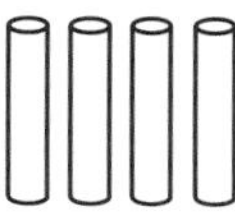

1 ten and 4 ones
14

symmetry

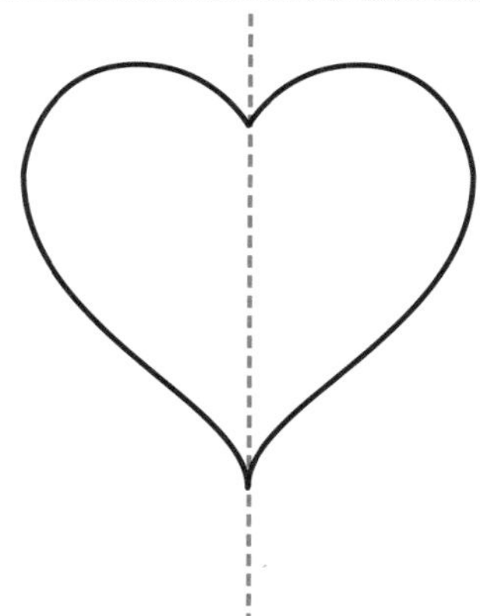

triangle

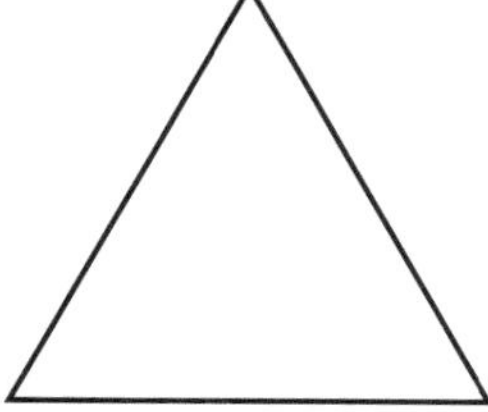